## COMPARISON IN ANTHROPOLOGY

Why and how do social and cultural anthropologists make comparisons? What problems do they encounter in doing so, and how might these be resolved? What, if anything, makes one comparison better than another? This book answers these questions by exploring the many ways in which, from the nineteenth century to the present day, comparative methods have been conceptualised and reinvented, praised and rejected, multiplied and unified. Anthropologists today use comparisons to describe and to explain, to generalise and to challenge generalisations, to critique and to create new concepts. In this multiplicity of often contradictory aims lie both the key challenge of anthropological comparison, and also its key strength. Matei Candea maps a path through that entangled conversation, providing a ground-up reassessment of the key conceptual issues at the heart of any form of anthropological comparison, whilst creating a bold charter for reconsidering the value of comparison in anthropology and beyond.

Matei Candea is a reader at the University of Cambridge and a former honorary editor of the *Journal of the Royal Anthropological Institute*. He is the author of *Corsican Fragments* (2010), and editor of *The Social after Gabriel Tarde: Debates and Assessments* (2010) and *Schools and Styles of Anthropological Theory* (2018).

## NEW DEPARTURES IN ANTHROPOLOGY

New Departures in Anthropology is a book series that focuses on emerging themes in social and cultural anthropology. With original perspectives and syntheses, authors introduce new areas of inquiry in anthropology, explore developments that cross disciplinary boundaries, and weigh in on current debates. Every book illustrates theoretical issues with ethnographic material drawn from current research or classic studies, as well as from literature, memoirs, and other genres of reportage. The aim of the series is to produce books that are accessible enough to be used by college students and instructors, but will also stimulate, provoke and inform anthropologists at all stages of their careers. Written clearly and concisely, books in the series are designed equally for advanced students and a broader range of readers, inside and outside academic anthropology, who want to be brought up to date on the most exciting developments in the discipline.

### Series Editorial Board

Jonathan Spencer, University of Edinburgh
Michael Lambek, University of Toronto

# Comparison in Anthropology

The Impossible Method

## MATEI CANDEA
*University of Cambridge*

# CAMBRIDGE
UNIVERSITY PRESS

University Printing House, Cambridge CB2 8BS, United Kingdom

One Liberty Plaza, 20th Floor, New York, NY 10006, USA

477 Williamstown Road, Port Melbourne, VIC 3207, Australia

314–321, 3rd Floor, Plot 3, Splendor Forum, Jasola District Centre,
New Delhi – 110025, India

79 Anson Road, #06-04/06, Singapore 079906

Cambridge University Press is part of the University of Cambridge.

It furthers the University's mission by disseminating knowledge in the pursuit of
education, learning, and research at the highest international levels of excellence.

www.cambridge.org
Information on this title: www.cambridge.org/9781108474603
DOI: 10.1017/9781108667609

First published 2019

Printed and bound in Great Britain by Clays Ltd, Elcograf S.p.A.

*A catalogue record for this publication is available from the British Library.*

*Library of Congress Cataloging-in-Publication Data*
Names: Candea, Matei, author.
Title: Comparison in anthropology : the impossible method / Matei Candea.
Description: Cambridge; New York, NY: Cambridge University Press, 2019. |
Series: New departures in anthropology |
Includes bibliographical references and index.
Identifiers: LCCN 2018038849 | ISBN 9781108474603 (hardback) |
ISBN 9781108465045 (paperback)
Subjects: LCSH: Anthropology – Comparative method. |
Anthropology – Methodology.
Classification: LCC GN34.3.C58C36 2019 | DDC 930.1–dc23
LC record available at https://lccn.loc.gov/2018038849

ISBN 978-1-108-47460-3 Hardback
ISBN 978-1-108-46504-5 Paperback

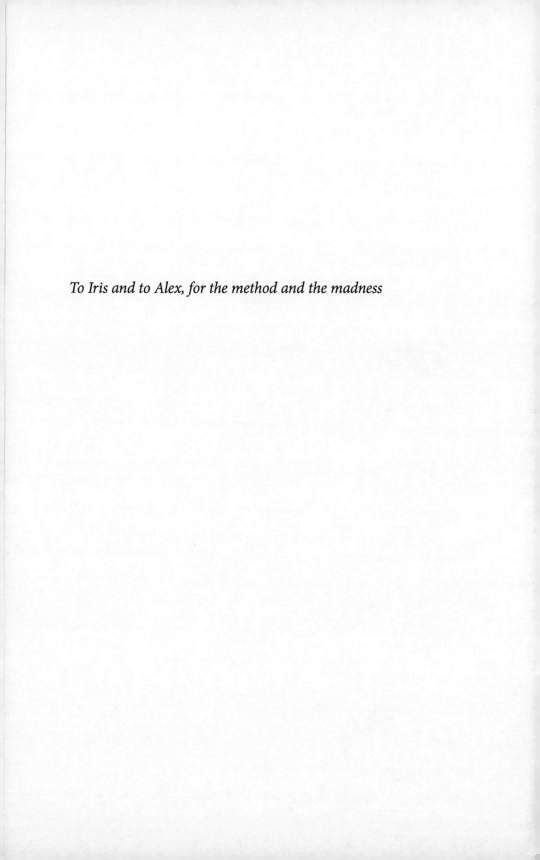

*To Iris and to Alex, for the method and the madness*

# Contents

# Contents

# Contents

# Figures

# Preface: What We Know in our Elbows

For 30 years at least, we have been able to fit together the pieces of a culture to make some sort of logical or psychological sense. But we still do not know how we do this, or what it means. Perhaps, as creatures that live in culture, we know in our elbows what sort of a thing a culture is, but have some fear of making this knowledge explicit. The problem is to make articulate and explicit the knowledge that we already possess in implicit form.

(Bateson 1967: 765)

This book started with a question: what is anthropological comparison today? This bears asking, because what Bateson writes about culture resonates also for comparison. We,[1] anthropologists, all live in comparison, and we all know in our elbows what it is, but an explicit account of our conventions remains strangely elusive, for reasons which this book seeks to examine, and in part, to remedy.

Having asked this question, I tried to trace the answer back through the enormous amount which anthropologists have written about comparison since the inception of the discipline. This ethnographic foray into anthropology's own analytics, which is retraced in Part I of this book, left me with the sense that trying to tease out our comparative conventions was an unexpectedly radical project. For, indeed, a key feature of anthropological discussions of comparison has precisely been a recurrent focus on invention.[2] Comparison is ever being reinvented, past visions abandoned, and new dawns glimpsed. The manifold problems and limitations of comparative methods are, time and again, blamed on the imperfections of our forebears, whilst our gaze is fixed on the horizon, on what comparison might become. In that context, to ask about convention, to ask what it is that, as a matter of fact, we do – and have been doing all these years – is less banal than it might seem. It is a way of 'staying with the trouble' of comparison, to borrow a phrase from Donna Haraway (2016). And in that trouble, in the imperfection, cross-cutting limitations and conflicting requirements is also, this book argues, where the value of comparison lies. What these pages seek to offer is not the promise of a new method, the dawn of yet another new comparatism – rather it is a refreshed vision of the potential of what we already do.

This book has been many years in the writing and I have in the process accumulated many debts. My most direct have been to the generosity of those who have read and commented on the entire manuscript – Catherine Candea, Harri Englund, Paolo Heywood, James Laidlaw, Victor I. Stoichita, Marilyn Strathern and Tom Yarrow. I have also benefited hugely from the reactions and advice of readers who have commented on parts of the manuscript, or on one of the many versions of an earlier paper (Candea 2016a),[3] the argument of which prefaces the one pursued in this book: Pierre Charbonnier, Alberto Corsín-Jiménez, Philippe Descola, Carlos Fausto, Simon Goldhill, Martin Holbraad, Caroline Humphrey, Geoffrey Lloyd, Morten Axel Pedersen, Gildas Salmon, Carlo Severi, Rupert Stasch, Pedro Stoichita and Victor A. Stoichita. Particular thanks go to the series editors, Michael Lambek and Jonathan Spencer, and to the anonymous reviewer for Cambridge University Press. The combination of generous advice, encouraging comments and bracing critiques from all of these readers has helped me avoid many pitfalls. For the remaining traps I have surely fallen into, they cannot be blamed.

For the more diffuse network of intellectual exchanges which have contributed to shape the arguments herein, it is impossible properly to account. However, I would like to thank colleagues at the Department of Social Anthropology in Cambridge and the Department of Anthropology in Durham, and audiences at seminars in Cambridge, Durham, Aberdeen, the New School of Social Research, Copenhagen University, the École des Hautes Études en Sciences Sociales, as well as the participants and organisers of the 2015 Sawyer Seminar (The History of Cross-Cultural Comparatism: Modern Doubts and New Beginnings) at the Centre for Research in the Arts, Humanities and Social Sciences.

This book would not have seen the light of day without the European Research Council. An important initial impetus for writing it was the elaboration of a proposal for an ERC grant in which the question of comparative method loomed large. The actual award of the grant 'Situating Free Speech: European Parrhesias in Comparative Perspective' (grant agreement 683033) provided both the necessity and the time to follow up on the promise of working out the fundamentals of comparative method.

I am grateful to all at Cambridge University Press, and in particular to Andrew Winnard who prompted me to embark upon a book of this kind in the first place and then, together with Stephanie Taylor, brilliantly shepherded the manuscript through production. The text was immeasurably improved by the outstanding copy-editing of Carol Fellingham-Webb.

I owe a very particular kind of debt also, for reasons which will become clear in the introduction, to researchers associated with the Kalahari Meerkat Project and the Large Animal Research Group in Cambridge, who, for nearly a decade, have allowed me to hang out ethnographically in the close yet distant field of behavioural biology. Even though this book is not about that, it would not have been possible without them. Particular thanks go to Tim Clutton-Brock, Andrew Bateman, Alecia Carter and Dieter Lukas.

Finally, I want to thank Kat for tolerating the 5 p.m. lows and the 5 a.m. highs, and for being, for ten years and still, that incomparable person who, as Marguerite Yourcenar somewhere described, 'leaves you divinely free, and yet requires you to be fully what you are'.

# Introduction

## Our Impossible Method

Why and how do anthropologists compare? What are the distinctive problems they encounter in doing so and how might these be resolved? What if anything makes one comparison better than another? When if at all can anthropologists build on one another's comparisons to cumulative effect? Outsiders to the discipline might be puzzled to find that until recently, such questions would tend to elicit a shrug of the shoulders amongst anthropologists at best, at worst a sort of despondency. Indeed, while anthropologists had developed an extensive critical arsenal for describing the reasons why comparison should by rights be impossible, constructive proposals for how such problems might be overcome were thin on the ground. The practice of comparison itself never went away, of course, but in the main, discussions of comparative method and epistemology had for some time been mothballed, relegated to the doldrums of a 'naive positivism'. The final word seemed to lie with Evans-Pritchard's famous dictum, according to which the comparative method, anthropology's only method, was impossible.

Now, anthropological comparison is back in the limelight and it is the 'crisis of representation' itself which is beginning to feel thoroughly *passé*. A new wind of epistemological confidence is blowing through the discipline, and comparison is explicitly reclaimed and brandished as the

1

distinctive anthropological method – indeed, as more than a method; as the epistemic, ethical and political heart and purpose of anthropology itself. Never since the 1950s has the discipline seen such an efflorescence of discussions of and proposals for comparison.[1] Most of these, however, are still scattered as contributions to debates within particular theoretical schools, or specific regional and thematic subfields. Furthermore, such discussions are often cast as unhelpfully stark dichotomies between the bright new comparatisms of tomorrow and the bad comparative method of old. The result of these new enthusiasms, superimposed on old concerns, themselves superimposed on older enthusiasms, is an impenetrable palimpsest – the anthropological conversation about comparison has descended into a cacophony. Some may claim that comparison is not impossible, but it is increasingly impossible to understand what that claim might mean.

This book is in two parts. The first maps the state of anthropological discussions of comparison and diagnoses the reasons for this double impossibility – the impossibility of doing comparison and the impossibility of keeping it clearly in view as a subject of methodological conversation. The second part seeks to reconstruct an archetypal account of anthropological comparison which can provide elements for resolving both kinds of impossibility.

This book is thus addressed, firstly, to social and cultural anthropologists. It outlines a solution to the impossibility of comparison which does not take the form of a methodological charter, or a path towards a unification of the discipline under the aegis of a single way of doing comparison. A fundamental feature of anthropology as presently constituted is the multiplicity of often incommensurable purposes to which we seek to put comparison: anthropologists use comparison to describe, to interpret, to categorise, to explain, to generalise, to critique descriptions, interpretations and typologies, to challenge explanations and unmake all generalisations, to evoke, to critique, to convince, to affect readers, to reflect and to create new concepts. Many of us define our vision of anthropology as fundamentally wedded to some of the aims above, and fundamentally opposed to some of the other aims above. That multiplicity is productive and characteristic of the discipline. But it follows that no single method, narrowly defined, can serve as a means to so many ends. And yet, in building our comparisons, we draw from a shared repertoire of moves and techniques which we combine and recombine in different ways and to different effect. At that methodological level, our comparisons remain shareable even when our aims are not. In that intersection of devices lies the key to the possibility of anthropological comparison, and the distinctive sense in which we are, still and despite our differences, a discipline. This book proposes a systematic account of that shared space of anthropological comparison.

In so doing, the book is addressed also to readers beyond the discipline, in the social sciences and humanities, and more broadly still. Whereas in a fairly obvious sense comparison is everywhere in other disciplines also, inherent in any kind of description, analysis or explanation, anthropology is distinctive in having made comparison its key defining feature. Elsewhere 'comparison' or 'comparative method' is often more narrowly defined, appearing as a particular rather than a constitutive concern (see, for instance, Detienne 2008; Yengoyan 2006a for the case of history). This difference in focus is the key to the potential value of this book for non-anthropologists. For while I will argue below that anthropologists have at times been insufficiently explicit in talking about the implications, entailments and limitations of their comparative moves, they have still been, in the main, more explicit than most. The fact that anthropology has built itself around comparison has led the discipline to produce, over the years, more versions and visions of the comparative method than any other discipline; anthropologists have borrowed, transformed and reimagined comparative devices from nearly everyone else, from the systematics of biology, to the concept creation of continental philosophy, from the quantitative persuasions of sociology or economics, to the interpretive visions of comparative history and literature or the various formalisms of linguistics. Just as often, anthropologists have imagined their own comparisons in explicit contrast to these and other external alternatives. If this wild profusion has made it difficult to obtain a clear view of what if anything anthropological comparison is, it simultaneously provides a kind of concentrated experiment in the multiplication of method. The discipline of anthropology has been a natural experiment of comparatism. Readers from other disciplines may find something of value in a systematic account of that profusion – both where their own familiar concerns are reflected in perhaps unusual forms, and where these are combined with strange ones drawn from elsewhere.

## Too General, Too Specific

In fairness, the difficulty of keeping comparison in view as an object is not particular to anthropology. There is something inherently elusive to the notion itself. For what is comparison? The question initially seems to evoke two objects: one is general and the other specific. Upon closer examination, however, the two seem to blur irremediably and confusingly into one another.

I have stopped counting the books dedicated to anthropological comparison which open with the commonplace that comparison is a basic and universal human (or even animal) cognitive strategy, such that 'thinking without comparison is unthinkable' (Swanson 1971: 145).[2] A strikingly elegant definition of comparison in this general sense, by philosopher Condillac, is quite simply 'double attention': comparison is little more at heart than the act of giving one's attention to two objects at once (Condillac 1795: 1.7; Goyet 2014: 162). In this sense, anthropologists compare all the time, as indeed does everyone else. There initially seems to be little more that one can usefully say about such a broad topic.

Secondly, however, anthropologists writing about comparison soon point to a particular method or set of methods, central to and distinctively employed in the discipline of anthropology. Here, on the other hand, there seems to be rather too much to say. For as soon as one looks for 'the comparative method' in anthropology, this dissolves through both internal pressures and external ones. External pressures: the ways of comparing which anthropologists claim as their own, also exist beyond the discipline (in sociology, history, biology, linguistics, literature, etc.), and in most cases long pre-dated the identification of anthropology as a distinct discipline. Internal pressures: the fact that whereas anthropologists do tend to agree in the abstract that their discipline is comparative, they have rarely reached agreement on any finite set of comparative methods, let alone any single comparative method, which might be characteristic or even mutually acceptable.[3] Anthropological comparison splinters according to schools, periods, paradigms which seem irreconcilable in their purposes and assumptions.

However elaborate anthropological methods and discussions of comparison become, the lurking sense of a general cognitive operation underlying comparison keeps luring us into thinking that these distinctions are perhaps after all mere froth. Is not anthropological comparison ultimately just an elaboration of 'double attention'? The very simplicity of this formula acts as a sort of acid, dissolving carefully elaborated distinctions between types and modes of comparison. We are led back towards broader understandings of comparison as a cognitive operation.

To an anthropologist, however, the generality of comparison remains after all quite specific. However 'general' one might seek to be about something like comparison, a moment's examination brings us back to the fact that these generalities are themselves historically and culturally situated. Francis Goyet (2014), in his brilliantly concise genealogy of comparison, evokes the widespread rhetorical exercise of *comparatio*, at which cultivated Europeans sharpened their wits and tongues from Antiquity until at least the eighteenth century: putting $x$ and $y$ in parallel in order to draw out, carefully and usually at some length, their differences and similarities. We shall return to *comparatio* at some length in Chapter 4, but for now, I raise its spectre only to make clear that 'comparison' comes to us with a particular conceptual history, a gendered, classed, culturally marked history of European academic exercises and scholastic references, replete with ontological assumptions, metaphorical loads and evaluative connotations.

Not to put too fine a point on it, anthropologists might argue that comparison in this 'general' sense is quite specific not just in where it comes from, but consequently also in what it takes for granted and entails. Comparison, at its most 'general', already comes with implications of a world of things which are different and specific, from which cognitive operations elicit similarities and generalities. It sits neatly with assumptions of cognitive mastery, of a conceptual judge standing above and outside a world of things. In other words, the 'general' image of comparison fits quite neatly with a bundle of assumptions anthropologists have occasionally picked out as specifically 'western' (Strathern 2004) – although there is no reason to assume that they are exclusively so. A comparative account of non-western comparativisms is beyond the scope of this book, but forays into that topic (e.g. Humphrey 2016; Lloyd 1966, 2015) suggest that it would be self-regarding indeed to imagine that Euroamericans somehow have a monopoly on elaborate, explicit and formally grounded comparativism.

At the same time, an account of *anthropological* comparison cannot evade the shadow cast on our disciplinary visions of comparison by imperial western projects of the nineteenth and twentieth centuries. The early nineteenth century saw an efflorescence of comparative disciplines – comparative anatomy, comparative physiology, comparative grammar, geography or law. The thought that this move might be extended to a comparative science of human groups was underpinned in obvious ways by a colonial order of things in which human populations became available, both conceptually and practically, as objects of study (Asad 1973b). Comparison's methodological problematics were entwined, from the start, with the political problematics of empire, as Ann Laura Stoler (2001) has shown. Once this 'specific' context of the 'general' meaning of comparison is seen, it cannot be unseen. Any attempt to shed historical specificities and cultural equivocations in view of a more abstract, formal definition can bracket but not erase these specificities.

This is why, for many anthropologists writing over the past forty years or so, comparison is not just equivocal but also deeply suspicious. And yet, it is unavoidable. After all, the very device through which anthropologists reveal comparison as particular (as western, for instance) is itself comparative. What is 'western' here but a comparative term? Thus, in the very move which reveals it as particular, comparison seems to become general again. And in turn, those generalities point to other particulars. In 'provincialising' (Chakrabarty 2007) western generalities, anthropologists find themselves part of a long genealogy of comparison as critical self-questioning, reaching at least as far back as Montaigne. In this vein, the discipline's attachment to comparison can mark it out, not as the handmaiden of colonialism, but rather as a permanent thorn in the side of western pretensions (Geertz 1988). For some, such as Lloyd, comparison as self-critique indeed names a general 'valence' of comparatism *tout court* (Lloyd 2015: 30–31). And thus we are back with generality.

We seem to have reached an impasse. The specific meaning of comparison haunts attempts to generalise it. The general meaning shadows attempts to specify it.

## The Pinch of Salt

To this general slipperiness is added a further difficulty: the engrained mental habit, and scholarly convention, of taking things 'with a pinch of salt'. This is another key to the paradoxical way in which comparison seems to be simultaneously impossibly complicated and wholly self-evident. Most anthropologists are more or less acutely aware of the heap of objections raised at some point or other against almost every aspect of anthropological comparison – from the problem of identifying units of comparison, to the possibility of commensuration, to the politics of comparative representation ... And yet – there's the paradox – we go on.

Thus we invoke cultural units, social groups or patterns of behaviour, while all the time implying that we are well aware these are just convenient fictions and that reality is far more complex. We analogise entities while mentioning in passing that of course they are also, in other ways, profoundly different, or contrast them while gesturing to the fact that in many other ways they fade into one another. Some of us appeal to philosophically abstruse techniques for challenging the very grounds of what counts as an object or a relation, all the while appealing to ethnographic particulars grounded in descriptions and generalisations of the most conventional kind. At every turn, an implicit or explicit appeal to taking things 'with a pinch of salt' keeps these contradictions out of view.

In one sense this is fine – such bracketing is unavoidable and productive. One core argument of this book is precisely in praise of bracketing. It is in part an argument for seeing comparisons as bundles of heuristics which get jobs done, an argument for recognising the value of our humble and unassuming comparative techniques, which churn away below the level of grand epistemological debates. These comparative moves, tricks and fixes bracket extensively, they make no guarantees to absolute truth or exhaustiveness, and yet they keep the discipline going, keep it together, and produce exciting new work. It would be impossible to do any kind of intellectual work – or to live any kind of life – without bracketing. The vision of complete explicitness is a mirage.

There is a world of difference, however, between bracketing something and just forgetting about it. Heuristics are valuable primarily because we know when they fail (Wimsatt 2007). Or to put the point otherwise, in the language of politics rather than engineering, it is fine to exclude, black-box and simplify *as long as we have a path back to and remain responsible for what is being left out* (Barad 2007). An analogous point has been made about habit (Latour 2012: 266): habit relies on *omitting* certain things, and in so doing, it makes the world inhabitable. Here would be no living, and no doing, without habit. But habit becomes a problem when it softly slides from omitting something to *forgetting* it. This closes off the possibility of living or doing otherwise.

Mostly, the approach in this book seeks to be constructive rather than critical, even at the risk of occasionally seeming rose-tinted. My aim is not to point to failings, but to open up possibilities. But if there is a critical argument at the heart of this book, it is that anthropologists have too often taken the impossibility of comparison for granted and just 'got on with the job', spraying caveats along the way, like a squid sprays ink – to ward off attackers. The resulting landscape is one in which we seem to be forever saying things we don't quite mean, to others who don't quite mean them either, but often in different ways or for different reasons. It is this habit of 'taking things with a pinch of salt' as much as anything else, which contributes to the sense that if we really thought about it, comparison would be impossible – so best not think about it too much.

A comparison comes to mind with the work of the behavioural ecologists I have studied over the past decade (see, for instance, Candea 2010b, 2013a, 2013b, 2018a). Behavioural ecologists tend to refer to the animals they study as individuals animated by particular purposes and strategies, by analogy to rational economic actors. Thus they might say that dominant female meerkats 'choose' whether to 'invest resources' in their children or in their grandchildren. A number of anthropologists have criticised this mapping of natural relations on economics, and the resultant naturalisation of economic assumptions (Sahlins 1976). When asked about this way of speaking, senior behavioural ecologists will patiently explain to the anthropologist outsider that this language is an 'as if', a way of translating in simple terms the theoretical hypotheses of sociobiology, and that they are not of course naive enough to believe that meerkats might actually be making such calculations. If anyone is naive, they archly point out, it is the anthropologists who could believe that serious scientists might be so taken in by their own metaphors – sociobiologists even coined a term, 'the Sahlins fallacy', to characterise such naive critiques (Segerstråle 2000). Of course, they point out, while speaking amongst themselves, they don't need to qualify this short-hand – everybody knows what they mean.

And yet, some more junior researchers I spoke to were not so clear about where the 'as if' began and the putative description of actual animal perspectives ended. They had, of course, all learned the theor-etical principles of sociobiology as undergraduates – clearly none of them believed that meerkats might be sitting around calculating gen-etic coefficients of relatedness. And yet, they felt that there might be a grain of literal truth to that way of speaking – after all, some of them pointed out, these meerkats really do seem pretty clearly selfish and cal-culating about their relationships with others. The point is not that these more junior scholars were naive or unscientific. The point is that the individualist economic language of sociobiology is not an outlandish and isolated heuristic. It chimes in neatly with many other assumptions Euroamericans might make about the behaviour of other beings. Not to mention the fact that sociobiological visions of animal life were popularised through animal documentaries from the 1980s onwards, feeding the obviousness of the metaphor back into an authoritative depiction of animal experience. In that context, keeping the heuristic of animals as rational maximisers sharply in view *as a heuristic* takes sustained and constant work, and the general assumption that 'we know what we mean when we say …' is not conducive to that sort of work.

The situation is analogous in anthropology with respect to a number of aspects of comparative method. Take, for instance, the units of com-parison we invoke – cultures, say, societies, groups, or indeed, as in my example here, disciplines such as anthropology and behavioural ecology. We too learn as undergraduates that such entities are convenient short-hands and fictions, and come to feel that when speaking amongst ourselves we hardly need to labour that point. Note that this is a point about comparison twice over: these 'units' serve as the building blocks of our comparisons, but they are themselves, more often than not, crafted by more or less implicit analogy to other domains. The vision of a social or cultural world divided into units gained some of its conviction by analogy to the organic realm, in which one might more readily imagine distinct objects of that sort. It persists as a useful fiction, despite the numerous objections which have been raised against that analogy – just as behavioural ecologists analogise animals as rational economic actors, while knowing (mostly) that there are limits to that analogy. Like them, we are (usually) able to highlight the limits of these analogies – where they break down, where key disanalogies come in which limit them. We might occasionally unfold these quick analogies into fuller comparisons, attentive both to differences and to similarities, for the benefit of naive outsiders ('well, yes, you could think of a discipline like behavioural ecology as a unit, but also not, because ...'), but amongst ourselves, we too tend to speak to each other of these entities in an off-hand way, black-boxing our implicit comparisons, with their trailing edges, on the tacit assumption that we all know what we mean when we refer to 'a discipline'. But do we?·I tacitly assumed, in writing the previous paragraph, that my reader would give me the benefit of assuming I knew that, of course, behavioural ecology is not a singular undifferentiated unit whose individuals all view the world in the same way. But maybe you didn't – maybe you do think that behavioural ecology is a clearly defined and bounded unit; or maybe you don't, but deduced from the above that I think that. The vision of human life as actually made up of cultural and social units is so pervasive and common-sensical that reminding ourselves we are invoking it heuristically takes some explicit work.

This matters because, occasionally, making those fictions explicit raises embarrassing problems. This happens when some aspect of the coherence of what we had just been saying required the fiction of certain devices to remain out of sight. Does my own comparison between anthropology and behavioural ecology still make sense once the fictional nature of both units is brought centre stage? It probably does for some purposes – for instance, for the purpose of a quick and dirty analogy of the kind I have drawn here – but probably not if my purpose was to give a thoroughgoing ethnographic comparison between the two disciplines. Then I might have to consider, for instance, that they are not constituted as disciplines in the same way as each other.

Of course, agreeing – broadly – not to think about these issues is a solution of sorts. We could forget about the epistemology and focus on the effects – conceptual, interpretive or political – of our comparisons. A collective agreement to take things with a pinch of salt might be sufficient to keep anthropological comparison ticking along. But one runs the risk of thinking we are speaking about the same things, or bracketing the same things, when in fact we are not. This is clearly a contributing factor to the disjointed nature of our conceptual conversations about comparison – just as that cacophony makes it difficult to draw from it much comfort about the possibility of comparison. The two problems feed off one another.

As much of a shame is another risk: if our heuristics remain implicit and under the radar, we will be less likely to find new ways to combine and recombine them. This is why in being an argument for heuristics, this book is also an argument against 'the pinch of salt'.

## A Roadmap to the Book

### Part I. Impossibilities: Making Sense of an Entangled Conversation

A first requirement, then, is systematically to identify in what ways comparison has been deemed to be impossible. Once we have stared that impossibility squarely in the face, we will have a better sense of quite what we omit when we do compare, and what the costs or entailments of such omissions are. This is the aim of the first part of this book, which focuses on anthropological writing about comparison. This first part takes an ethnographic, rather than a critical stance, on our own concerns and practices. The key question that drives it is, quite simply, how can one make sense of the sheer multiplicity of ways in which anthropologists have written about comparison?

The discipline of anthropology was born in the midst of an ongoing conversation between philosophers, linguists, biologists, lawyers and others about questions of comparative method. In embracing comparison as its defining method, the discipline internalised that conversation and made it into the beating heart of its epistemological and methodological agenda. The number of reflections on the topic of comparison by anthropologists, be it in full-length articles or books, or in the margins of specific arguments, is quite simply overwhelming. Comparison is a subject that is in some way or other entailed by almost every other methodological or epistemological discussion in the discipline. Pull at any thread, and you will soon be unravelling some argument about anthropological comparison. Talk about anthropological comparison for long enough and you will have talked about most of anthropology.

The sheer multiplication of these reflections on comparison has created its own difficulty: it has become very hard to pin down quite what this conversation is about – or indeed to what extent it is still a conversation at all. It is thus often hard to decide whether anthropologists writing about comparison are speaking about the same thing, locked in an argument that has lasted more than 150 years, or at cross-purposes, talking past each other about very different things in incommensurable theoretical languages.

Indeed, we are by now faced with a second-order problem: many anthropologists writing on comparison have already tried to put some order into this conversation. Since they found it impossible to attempt to review all of these different works, their approach has often been itself typological: a bevy of contrasts have been drawn between different kinds of comparison, different methods and paradigms. Many are those, in sum, who have already sought to compare approaches to comparison. But these devices for reducing complexity themselves don't line up. They cut across each other, producing new entanglements. In scanning the anthropological literature on comparison today, we have not only different visions of comparison, but different visions of how one might compare these visions. The conversation – if it ever was that – has become a cacophony.

In the first half of this book, I will not try to adjudicate between these different ordering devices – to decide which is the proper nomenclature of anthropological comparisons – let alone which is the proper way of comparing. The aim of this first part is not to interrupt that conversation, but rather to listen as closely as possible and try to pick out as many of the different voices, tones and arguments as are still discernible. If we attend closely enough, we might find ways of triangulating anthropological comparison by drawing on the very multiplicity of perspectives which anthropologists themselves have brought to the issue. My aim in doing so will be to look for regularities and patterns, recurrent themes and contrasts in that conversation itself. Others have begun by drawing up a typology of comparisons. By contrast I will try to describe the principles whereby such typologies themselves were drawn up. The first part of the book, in sum, compares the ways in which anthropologists have compared comparisons.

Each of the three chapters in the first part of the book maps a distinct vision of the comparative method which emerges from the literature. The first vision (Chapter 1) imagines one, shared comparative method for anthropology. Evans-Pritchard's seminal account of anthropological method (1950) will stand as an exemplar of this imaginary. This vision of a single method provides a foil against which to reprise all of the many objections that have been raised against aspects of anthropological comparison. We have seen 'the comparative method', and it is impossible. A second recurrent vision (Chapter 2) imagines a contrast between two comparative methods – usually a bad older one versus a better, newer alternative. Here, the seeming impossibility of comparison emerges as a feature of past errors – another comparatism is possible! The difficulty is that none of these binaries lasts for very long, and new contrasts open up over and again in the history of the discipline. There always seem to be two ways of comparing, but these are never quite the same. The 150-year-long anthropological discussion of comparatism – of which this very long chapter gives a rather quixotic and non-exhaustive overview – turns into a labyrinth of forking paths. Comparison may seem to be possible at any given point, but such hopes are always temporary. More profoundly, the grounds of what the discussion is even about keep shifting – comparison emerges as not only impossible, but impossible to characterise.

In Chapter 3 we examine the recurrent realisation that there is no single comparative method, nor merely two, but many. This multiplicity itself has been understood in two ways, however. Some see comparatisms succeeding one another in the history of anthropology through a series of radical paradigmatic breaks or *caesuras* – following Pina-Cabral (2010:168) I will call this a 'caesurist' vision. Others envision comparison as a bundle of heuristics – techniques or methods which can be borrowed, repurposed and recombined by practitioners with different theoretical assumptions and purposes. Each vision in its own way makes sense of the entangled conversation described in Chapter 2. Each, however, leaves something important out. Each vision comes with its own implicit normativity, and these are at cross purposes. Chapter 3, which acts as a conclusion to Part I, argues that the combination of a heuristic and a caesurist view is required to make sense of the historical multiplicity of anthropological comparison.

## Part II. An Archetype: An Argument for Comparisons that Resist

If the first part seeks to diagnose impossibilities, the second part seeks to articulate the possibilities, but also the limits of anthropological comparison at the present juncture. We will thus take a second pass over a number of the same problems, topics and examples first evoked in Part I, but in a different key. Rather than merely trace the rhythms and disjunctures of our existing debates, Part II seeks to articulate the elements of a clearer conversation. If Part I was the 'ethnography', Part II is the 'argument'. This argument could be boiled down to the following three propositions: *anthropological comparison is possible*; *it comes in a multiplicity of forms which give a procedural common ground to the discipline, shared means for our often irreconcilable purposes*; and *the relative strength and value of anthropological comparisons lies in their ability to resist the ends to which we seek to put them.*

What is promised here, as noted in the preface, is not a(nother) new comparatism. Rather the purpose of the second part, as it fleshes out these propositions, is to foreground the potential of what we already do, while defusing some of the ways in which we needlessly talk – or shout – past each other. The device adopted for these purposes is that of drawing up an *archetype* of comparison by teasing out the main polarities and contrasts which structure the phenomenal variety of anthropological comparisons. As outlined in Chapter 4, an archetype is not a blueprint or single set of methodological injunctions for how to compare. Rather it maps, simultaneously, the different ends to which comparison can be put, and the common ground of methodological techniques and fixes commonly used to pursue these divergent purposes.

The argument develops that presented in an earlier paper in which I contrasted two forms of anthropological comparison (Candea 2016a). On the one hand, 'frontal comparisons'[4] in which an ethnographic 'other' is contrasted with a presumed 'us'; on the other, 'lateral comparisons' between cases laid side by side, from which the analyst is absent.[5] I argued in that piece that while these two modes of comparison are often contrasted as global approaches (a positivist lateralism versus an interpretivist or postmodern frontalism, for instance), they are better viewed as two complementary heuristics, intertwined at the heart of any anthropological argument. Each of these heuristics has specific affordances, and specific limits and blind-spots. Anthropological enthusiasms seem recently to have run towards frontal comparison, identifying the critical potential of us/them comparisons as the fundamental ground of anthropological know-ledge, and relegating the comparison of 'this' and 'that' to the role of a mere adjunct of this important purpose. It is time, I argued there, to rebalance our attention and take seriously the potential of lateral comparison.

The present book takes a wider view. It analyses the distinction between frontal and lateral comparison into a set of three more funda-mental contrasts: between the elucidation of sameness and the pursuit of difference (Chapter 5), between pinpointing things and tracing relations (Chapter 6), and between the pursuit of objectivity and of reflexivity (whose intersection with the former two pairs of contrasts will occupy us in chapters 7 and 8, respectively). In one view, each of these pairs maps a radical alternative, a pair of incommensurable purposes to which comparisons could be put. In another view, each pair describes a heur-istic contrast, the combination and recombination of which animates anthropologists' shared comparative devices. Taken together, the entanglement of these cross-cutting ends and interlocking means entails a particular kind of rigour, constitutive of anthropology as a discipline and of its place in the world (Chapter 9).

You may have gathered by now that this book is a slightly strange prop-osition. It is neither a methodology manual nor a history of anthropo-logical comparison, although readers in search of the one or the other may find some elements of both in here. As for methodology, while this is not a purpose-built manual of heuristics – in the manner, for instance, of Andrew Abbott's excellent *Methods of Discovery* (2004) – readers will nevertheless encounter in this book all manner of comparative tips, tricks and devices, of varying complexity, which may hopefully inspire them in articulating their own heuristics. As for a history of anthropological comparison, such a thing would need to be a history of anthropology, and that enterprise is far beyond the scope of a book such as this. In particular, readers will not find much material here pertaining to the properly historical questions of institutional and political-economic context in which the many historical varieties of anthropological comparatism developed. This is rather a conceptual addendum or appendix to the history of anthropological comparison proper, which remains to be written (although see Handler 2009; Salmon 2013a, 2013b; Stoler 2001; and more generally, Kuklick 1991; Kuper 1973, 1999, 2005; Stocking 1991a, 1991b, 1998).

This book, most properly, is an essay in the sense of an attempt, but a proper sense of quite what it is attempting can only come gradually, as the argument proceeds. The boiled down summary above will give a sense of why that might be. This is not simply an argument about comparison, or an argument for comparison – although it is certainly that – but it is also an argument made *through* comparison. And since the substance of the argument is that comparisons ought to be thick (cf. Scheffer and Niewöhner 2010), intricate and take time, that they ought to oppose resistances to our desire to get to a pre-defined point (Yarrow forthcoming), I will try to practise what I preach. I have sketched a horizon; now begins the process of getting there. What may make this book worth reading is what you don't yet know, namely, what is going to happen along the way.

## A Negative-Space Ethnography

In claiming that this argument is comparative, I do not mean that it will proceed through a comparison of ethnographic cases, as is most usual in anthropological discussions, nor even through a comparison between anthropological comparisons and the comparative devices of other, non-Euroamerican epistemic traditions – although that is a fascinating project also (see Humphrey 2016; Lloyd 1966, 2015;). In the main, this will be a comparison of anthropological approaches to comparison.

There is thus a recursive (cf. Holbraad 2012) dynamic throughout this book. In order to introduce and delineate different kinds of comparative devices – radical contrasts, recursivity, typologies, decompositions of binaries into a series, caveated generalisations, structural transformations, and others for which, as yet, we have no name – we shall simultaneously be deploying these very devices and applying them to the texts and practices in which we discern them. When we come to 'the point', finally, in the conclusion, the book itself will stand (or fall) as an instantiation of what it has been arguing for.

There is another sense in which this book is grounded in comparison. To make this explicit is to move from the broad theoretical concerns outlined so far, to one very specific source of this project in my own earlier ethnographic work. Indeed, there is the ghost of an ethnographic object here. As mentioned above, I have for the past decade been studying the practices, ethics and equipment (both material and epistemic) of a nearby yet distant discipline, namely behavioural biology. In the process, like all anthropologists, I have frequently been made to reflect on the light shed on my own – our own – practices by a consideration of those of the people I worked with.[6] The contrast between behavioural biology and social anthropology could thus be deployed as what I have just called a 'frontal comparison', one of those partly fictional us/them pairs that anthropologists are so fond of (cf. chapters 7 and 8). Let's run with that fiction for a moment. It has particular potential in relation to our topic, since anthropological discussions of comparison have so often gazed upon biology as an intimate other – be it in admiration and envy or fear and loathing.

In studying behavioural biologists, ethnographic reflexivity was often forced upon me by very direct challenges about the comparative value of what I was proposing. Occasionally uncomfortable, facile yet obviously false analogies ('So we're *your* meerkats?') alternated with direct challenges which called me out to articulate explicitly the principles of anthropological method, and the value of anthropological analysis, in terms understandable to my informants, and commensurate to the terms in which they had been articulating themselves.

There was no straightforward way for me to do so. Commensuration was a less anodyne requirement than it might first appear. The kind of social and cultural anthropology which I had been trained in was fundamentally premised on its incommensurability with the biological sciences. This sort of difficulty has been encountered by other anthropologists. In a comment on Susan Harding's ethnography of fundamentalist Christians (e.g. Harding 1991), Robbins notes that 'empathetic understanding of kinds of Christianity forged in opposition to modernist scientific outlooks presents an affront to disciplinary self-understanding such that for anthropologists to say that those Christians make sense in their own terms is to question whether anthropologists make sense in theirs' (Robbins 2007: 9). To this one might add that much of social anthropology itself has been forged in opposition to modernist scientific outlooks. Consequently, a social anthropologist studying behavioural biology is faced with a different kind of intimate other, but one whose disciplinary way of making sense on their own terms similarly questions the way in which we make sense in ours. More precisely, in order for my disciplinary devices to make sense, they had to resist being made commensurable with theirs. 'Interdisciplinarity' is a free and easy shibboleth in the biological sciences. Addressed as a requirement to social anthropologists, it often becomes an injunction to stop being such a pesky trouble-maker, and to give an account of oneself on the terms set by the 'proper' sciences.

That problem focused my attention on the limits of the commensurability of purposes between and within disciplines. Partly, my sense of the incommensurability between anthropology and behavioural ecology – my unwillingness to agree to redescribe my discipline on their terms – derived from the extent to which I value anthropology's own commitment to sustaining a set of incommensurable theories, purposes and possibilities within itself. The meaning and value of behavioural ecology was underpinned in an important sense by a shared commitment to a very general evolutionary theoretical framework. As my primatologist colleague Jo Setchell once brilliantly put it, evolutionary anthropologists – one might substitute behavioural biologists here – have many species and one theory, whereas social anthropologists have one species and many theories (Candea 2012). What makes us and them incommensurable is in part the fact that we have different stances on what commensurability should look like.

There was something else going on. As fieldwork progressed – and again this is a classic phenomenon many anthropologists have experienced – I started to judge myself as I imagined they might judge me. The behavioural ecologists I spoke to – partly because on one scale, they shared 'just one theory' – came to seem refreshingly pragmatic and explicit about their research strategies and devices. Their seminars were full of constructive criticism and cross-cutting advice about fixes, techniques, bits of methods. Have you considered this? Did you try that? What if you redefined this variable, or tweaked this measuring device? They tinkered, collectively and individually, with experiments and the set-up of comparative observations, until the right sort of outcome could be repeated (Knorr-Cetina 1999). By contrast, my own discipline – seen through my imagination of their perspective – came to seem mired in destructive and dismissive criticism, and a stultifying inexplicitness about what it was our various devices were even trying to do.

In a word – *horresco referens!* – I had science envy. This was not, however, the kind of science envy which drove earlier generations of anthropologists to try to find natural laws of society or to ennoble the discipline through new demarcations and stringent eliminativist programmes. What I found myself envying was precisely the lack of grand gestures, the unconcern for philosophical foundations and epistemological niceties, which opened up the way to a mucky, hands-on, collective tinkering. This is the spirit of the scientist as 'backwoods mechanic' which philosopher of science William Wimsatt has so nicely captured (Wimsatt 2007: 9–10). No behavioural biologist, it seemed to me, would have wasted time wondering whether comparison was impossible.

Like many self-critical idealisations of 'the other' born out of ethnographic immersion, this was of course a partial vision at best. Ask any practising biologist: 'real science' is not always that pragmatic, or supportive, or unbothered by trends and schools. Indeed, the view that science might be all those things emerges as much from rose-tinted ethnographic glasses, as from a relentless and paradoxical kind of idealisation of scientific practice in the Actor–Network Theory tradition of science studies which has shaped my own perspective. This is a paradoxical idealisation, insofar as it consists in claiming precisely that science is not idealist – that its essence lies in an immanent and pragmatic tinkering, a kind of joyful permanent re-engineering of the world. Critical science studies scholars have long pointed out all that is omitted from this view. Actor–Network Theorists and their allies might retort that they are proposing a normative redescription, trying to nudge practising scientists towards abandoning the remainder of their epistemico-ethical generalities (Despret 1996; Latour 2004; Stengers 2009).

But even if science were or could become as Latour or Stengers redescribe it, or as Wimsatt wishes it, it would still not constitute a straightforward model for anthropology. I wouldn't for a moment consider paying the price of theoretical unification to purchase the right to relaxed immanent tinkering. This is why nothing in this book is to be taken as a suggestion that social anthropologists ought to change their practices in order to become, or to try to mimic, 'proper' scientists – even if we imagine the latter as backwoods mechanics. Their problems are not our problems, their solutions not our solutions. But the double experience of ethnographic engagement with and detachment from behavioural biologists left me with an interest in the ways in which we already have our own analogues of the sorts of things I found admirable about them. This is a book about our existing forms of tinkering, our distinctive way of valuing heuristics, our hands-on recombination of devices. But it is also a book about our difference, the ways in which we keep finding new directions in which to point away from and talk past each other while still, in some important senses, remaining a discipline in and through that very process.

This concern with what constitutes us as a discipline in part explains one rhetorical strategy of this work, which is to spend significant energy on excavating the temporal depth of our current comparative problems and our comparative devices. Aside from 'the pinch of salt', another classic move in anthropological discussions of comparison which this book sets itself against might be called 'the sideswipe'. This is the recurrent way in which anthropologists writing about comparison breezily wave away everything that happened up to a certain point as being characteristic of some naive and now irrelevant set of assumptions. 'Positivist' comparison is a usual suspect, but the sideswipe has also been aimed at 'pluralist' comparison, or at 'generalising' comparison, or earlier at 'functionalist' comparison. The thought that these 'internal others' of the discipline all map on to each other is just one of the problems with this convenient rhetorical device. Another is that it minimises the amount that is carried over from these older forms of comparison each time the slate is purportedly wiped clean. The sideswipe is the complement of the pinch of salt – we grandly declare, for instance, that we have now dismissed the assumptions of those earlier naive generalisers, and proceed to generalise nevertheless, under cover of 'taking things with a pinch of salt'.

Just as the pinch of salt finds a more rigorous and valuable counterpart in the figure of the heuristic, the sideswipe too has a positive counterpart in this story, in the figure of the *caesura* (Chapter 3), the self-conscious break which articulates a new end, a new difference. But there is a world of difference between articulating a new purpose and simply refusing to take one's own disciplinary history into account. The point in dwelling, as much of this book does, in that older history – in the problems and possibilities of comparison as envisaged by Tylor, Durkheim, Malinowski, Radcliffe-Brown, Benedict or Lévi-Strauss – is not to repeat the cynical or world-weary point that everything has been said before. Partly this archival sensibility is informed by the sense that amongst the rubble of old paradigms, one might find radical solutions to new problems (cf. McLean 2013: 71n16). But most fundamentally, I dwell with those older texts because they directly interrogate why it had seemed so natural, when addressing behavioural ecologists, to say 'we' in speaking of anthropologists. As Chua and Mathur (2018) have shown, that disciplinary 'we' is informed both by the changing political economies of the academic world system and by enduring structural forms of anthropological argument. While the two strands are profoundly interwoven, the precise modalities of their articulation are often more complex than might at first appear. Fully tracing both of these strands and providing a sophisticated account of their interrelations, in order to rethink who 'we' are and want to be, can only be a collective project. This book's contribution to that project lies primarily in its detailed examination of the latter strand: 'classic' debates about comparison are a key site in which one can observe some of the conceptual regularities which give that anthropological 'we' its sense of conviction. At the heart of what is too easily glossed – reverentially or critically – as 'the canon' lies something more evanescent: 'that sense of *déjà vu* [which] is also a sense of habitation within a cultural matrix' (Strathern 2004: xxv). Tracing some of the concrete regularities and repetitions which inform this *déjà vu* – this sense that comparison is obvious, that 'we all know what it is' – is a preliminary to thinking further about what 'we' – the increasingly, productively, critically diverse 'we' of contemporary anthropology – might do with, within and beyond that matrix.

Clifford Geertz described Ruth Benedict's anthropological accounts of, variously, the Kwakiutl, the Zuni, or the Japanese as a kind of 'negative-space writing' about the West (Geertz 1988: 113). The present book is in a sense the opposite. It is ostensibly and substantially about anthropology, but it is also a kind of negative-space ethnography of one of its mirrors and opposites – biology, that intimate other of anthropological discussions of comparison, that tempting and frustrating other world in which comparison was never impossible.

# Part I

Impossibilities

# Part I

Impossibilities

ONE

❧

# The Impossible Method

There's only one method in social anthropology, the comparative method –
and that's impossible.

(Evans-Pritchard, quoted in Needham 1975: 364)

## Introduction: On Seeing One Comparative Method

For long stretches of the history of anthropology, authors who wrote about
comparison imagined there to be a single Comparative Method. They had
different visions of what this might consist in, and argued bitterly over how
it might be done, or whether indeed it ought to be abandoned in favour of
something else. But they felt they were broadly talking about the same thing,
for better or for worse. This ideal of a single comparative method has mostly
faded, as we shall see in the subsequent chapters, in favour of a view of multiple methods. I will recall it here, however, as a convenient device through
which to take a first look at the problem of the purported impossibility of
anthropological comparison. Let us imagine a single comparative method,
and then carefully examine – no pinch of salt allowed! – all of the objections
which have been lined up against it.

Evans-Pritchard himself provides a very convenient springboard
for this imagination. What was comparison for Evans-Pritchard when
he characterised it as anthropology's only method? We may never
know: Evans-Pritchard's famous dictum, which gave the title to this

book, and the exergue to this chapter, is nowhere in print – save in a recollection by Rodney Needham. It cannot therefore be replaced in its context. However, one might look for an answer to the clear outline of his vision of anthropological method which Evans-Pritchard articulated in the famous Marett Lecture (1950), and later expanded upon in his book *Social Anthropology* (1951). By contrast to what was then commonly invoked as the Comparative Method, Evans-Pritchard terms his an 'experimental method'. I will examine the dynamic whereby comparative methods multiply, and some moves are at times defined as comparison and at others not, in the next chapter. For now, I will broadly treat the entire account as about comparison in various forms.

Evans-Pritchard described the anthropologists' craft as consisting of a number of sequential and logically distinct operations. In the first 'phase',

[h]e goes to live for some months or years among a primitive people. He lives among them as intimately as he can, he learns to speak their language, to think in their concepts and to feel in their values. He then lives his experiences over again critically and interpretively in the conceptual categories and values of his own culture and in terms of the general body of knowledge of his discipline. In other words, he translates from one culture to another.

(Evans-Pritchard 1950: 121)

This first phase is what I would term a frontal comparison. In the second phase, the anthropologist 'seeks by analysis to disclose the latent underlying form of a society or culture':

This structure cannot be seen. It is a set of abstractions, each of which, though derived, it is true, from analysis of observed behaviour, is fundamentally an imaginative construct of the anthropologist himself. By relating these abstractions to one another logically so that they present a pattern he can see the society in its essentials and as a single whole.

(Evans-Pritchard 1950: 122)

Finally, in the third phase, the anthropologist 'compares the structures his analysis has revealed in a wide range of societies' (Evans-Pritchard

1950: 122). What Evans-Pritchard has in mind here is not the type of grand armchair exercise which was then commonly called 'the Comparative Method', but rather a slow piecemeal procedure adapted to a discipline the practitioners of which were each first and foremost fieldworkers themselves. As Evans-Pritchard outlines in greater detail in his book, the vision is one in which one anthropologist conducts a study and reaches some conclusions (say, about the role of religious cults in social life):

If he formulates these clearly and in terms which allow them to be broken down into problems of research it is then possible for the same, or another, anthropologist to make in a second society observations which will show whether these conclusions have wider validity. He will probably find that some of them hold, that some of them do not hold, and that some hold with modifications. Starting from the point reached by the first study, the second is likely to drive the investigation deeper and to add some new formulations to the confirmed conclusions of the first ... A third study is now made, and then a fourth and a fifth. The process can be continued indefinitely.

(Evans-Pritchard 1951: 89–90)

This third phase is what I would term lateral comparison. Evans-Pritchard's account is particularly valuable for the clear way it lays out how much is required for anthropological comparisons to operate. This will enable us to note, systematically and point by point, how each of these steps has at one moment or another been found to involve requirements which were unfulfillable or assumptions which were unacceptable.

The stepwise clarity of his account is such, in fact, that one can attempt a diagrammatic representation (see Figure 1.1). This figure is broadly self-explanatory, but a few implications are worth spelling out. Firstly, while the arrows denote the three subsequent moves described by Evans-Pritchard (translation, abstraction and comparison) against the grain of Evans-Pritchard's own terminology, I will treat all three (and not simply the third move) as part of a general account of comparative method. Secondly, the diagram highlights the crucial difference

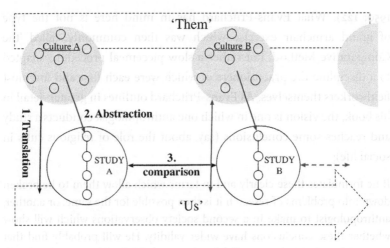

Figure 1.1 Evans-Pritchard's 'experimental method'

in Evans-Pritchard's account, between 'cultures' – what ethnographers encounter and experience – and 'studies', the abstractions which anthropologists generate based on those experiences, and then compare amongst themselves. Finally, the figures at the top and bottom of the picture make explicit an assumption of Evans-Pritchard's model, namely that this anthropological method operates at the interface between 'our' culture and those of 'primitive peoples'. Perhaps more tenuously or unfairly, the arrow on the lower rectangle suggests that, by implication in Evans-Pritchard's model, the path of anthropological knowledge is progressive, moving 'our' conceptual categories and our cultural self-understanding forward and 'driving the investigation deeper' with each case. On the 'them' side of the encounter feature, by contrast, a set of static cases, providing empirical material for our knowledge practices.

That final slightly barbed comment notwithstanding, I should say that I am not picking on Evans-Pritchard here either as characteristic of his period, or as a straw man against which to deploy 'our' greater sophistication. As to the former, as the next chapter will make clear, Evans-Pritchard is interesting precisely because he is anything but characteristic. His account cuts across some of the main attempts to categorise twentieth-century anthropology into separate paradigms. It was written at a time when Evans-Pritchard's thinking idiosyncratically bridged aspects of functionalist, structuralist and interpretive approaches.

Indeed, I am interested in his account of comparison precisely because in its generality it can be adapted or twisted to fit profoundly different visions of comparison. As we shall see in a moment, almost every element of this picture has been challenged at one point or another, and few if any contemporary anthropologists would accept this as an account of anthropological comparison today. Nevertheless, while the terms and assumptions have nearly all fallen away – including, most obviously, the characterisation of anthropology as a study of 'primitive peoples' – in its structure, Evans-Pritchard's account remains as close as we have in the history of anthropological discussions of comparison to a 'general', comprehensive vision of the various dimensions of anthropological comparison. Almost all other visions of comparison examined in this book can be constructed by bracketing or excising some parts of this picture, expanding others or redirecting the arrows. But precious little would need to be *added*, structurally speaking. As a result Evans-Pritchard's experimental method provides something approaching what I will describe in the second part of this book as an 'archetype' of comparison. As we shall see in the intervening pages, however, it remains both too specific and too mired in particular commitments and assumptions to serve as such an archetype for our purposes today. This initial vision will require some deconstruction and reconstruction – but I anticipate.

Having splayed out Evans-Pritchard's account of method as a general canvas, we can now consider three broad families of objections to anthropological comparison as imagined above. Let us name these objections in terms of *mapping* (the difficulty of specifying the objects and relations of comparison), of *communication* (the problematic relations comparison assumes between anthropologists and people studied), and of *purpose* (the fundamental question of what comparison is for). To these, one might initially be tempted to add political or ethical problems, but in fact, these hardly form a separate category: the political and the epistemological are interwoven throughout this section.

Many of these problems have been stated over and over again in the history of anthropology, in slightly different forms. It is by design that I tend to evoke here some of the earliest instances of these issues being raised. As I will point out in the next chapter, recent anthropological discussions of comparison have tended to take as their starting point a sense that until a relatively recent intellectual period – postmodernism, the crisis of representation or 'the 80s' – comparison was just business as usual. There is something to that view, in that the period marked an intensification of critique, and it became easier simply to dismiss comparative attempts, rather than merely critique (aspects of) them. But comparison has been problematised from the very start of anthropology itself. As I will argue in the next chapter, anthropological comparison was born impossible.

Which is to say that, if I now turn to listing the many problems with a vision of comparison articulated by Evans-Pritchard in the mid-twentieth century, it is not in order to present Evans-Pritchard's vision as a simplistic foil for our own more sophisticated ones. Many of the challenges and problems I list below had been clearly identified long before Evans-Pritchard's calmly confident account. The point is that the shadow of impossibility hovers over comparison as soon as it is articulated somewhat clearly and systematically.

## Problems of Mapping

One family of objections is commonly envisaged as relating to *mapping* (Salmond 1982; cf. Strathern 2004: xvii). These focus on the difficulties of identifying (in time, as well as space) the objects, properties and relations invoked in comparison. One can imagine problems of mapping in different styles or genres, depending on the way the objects and relations of comparison themselves are imagined. Thus, one simple vision of mapping is literally that of cartography (Salmond 2014: 170): what objects in the world correspond to the shapes in Figure 1.1? What are the *units* of comparison? Where, when are they, and what are their boundaries or limits? As Handler noted, this 'problem of units' (Handler 2009: 631) attaches, firstly, to the set of objects which act as contexts or 'cases' for comparison – Evans-Pritchard invokes cultures or societies – and secondly, to the traits, properties or parts of these objects, upon which the comparison actually bears – for instance, 'religious cults' in Evans-Pritchard's example.

Let us begin with cases. Mapping problems are particularly acute in relation to two specific contextual units invoked by Evans-Pritchard, at the top and bottom of Figure 1.1. The characterisations of some societies as 'primitive' has rightly been excoriated and abandoned by contemporary anthropologists, even though accusations of (crypto-) 'primitivism' against contemporary anthropological positions are still common (Kuper 2005). Conversely, the purported unit constituted by 'our own culture' has, similarly, been deconstructed: as anthropologists have pointed out over and over, the ways in which the 'self' features in anthropological accounts is often little more than as a straw man. And the assumption that all anthropologists hail from the same cultural background was already a politically naive oversimplification in Evans-Pritchard's day, let alone today (Chua and Mathur 2018). The 'us' is a fiction (Pina-Cabral 2006: 667). And yet, the contrast between 'them' and 'us' plays a more than incidental role in Evans-Pritchard's account – it acts as a fundamental epistemological device of the entire operation, enabling the first move of 'translation'.

Aside from the problems with these two particular units, the very image of societies or cultures as units, cases or objects has long been identified as troublesome. The contemporary reader might be tempted to dismiss the image of societies, peoples or cultures as stable units neatly lined up for consecutive analysis as a typical mid-twentieth-century fantasy, pre-dating the critical examination of global connections, leaky boundaries and transnational systems of power (Wolf 1983: 3; cf. Gingrich and Fox 2002b: 2;). There is a measure of truth to this view, insofar as the assumption that anthropological comparison was concerned with 'primitive', 'simple' or 'small-scale societies', without recorded history, was one classic response to 'unit problems' for nineteenth- and early twentieth-century anthropologists (as I will discuss in the next chapter). And this in turn posed particular difficulties for anthropologists who later self-consciously engaged in comparative study of 'civilisations' – large complex entities with well-documented histories. One could think here of attempts to build a comparative anthropology of Islam by anthropologists such as Geertz (1971) or Gellner (1983; see Asad 2009a for a critique of both projects), or of Dumont's work on India (1966). The fiction of 'small-scale societies without history' had left anthropologists free rein to imagine themselves as sole experts, whereas a focus on 'civilisations' raised the added difficulties of engaging with the extensive scholarship of historians and sociologists on the latter's own turf.

However, the scalar difference is to some extent a mirage – the unit problem doesn't really shrink with scale, nor was it discovered in the second half of the twentieth century. The problem – as we shall see in the next chapter – is as old as anthropology itself. Here is Radcliffe-Brown, the usual suspect of sociological realism, writing about 'societies':

At the present moment of history, the network of social relations spreads over the whole world, without any absolute solution of continuity anywhere. This gives rise to a difficulty which I do not think that sociologists have really faced, the difficulty of defining what is meant by the term 'a society.' They do commonly talk of societies as if they were distinguishable, discrete entities, as, for example, when we are told that a society is an organism. Is the British Empire a society, or a collection of societies? Is a Chinese village a society, or is it merely a fragment of the Republic of China? If we say that our subject is the study and comparison of human societies, we ought to be able to say what are the unit entities with which we are concerned.

(Radcliffe-Brown 1940: 4–5)

As for 'cultures', Eggan notes that, by the 1920s, many anthropologists writing in the Boasian tradition had already come to view culture as 'a mere aggregation of traits brought together by the accidents of diffusion' (Eggan 1954: 750). Note that I am extending the rubric of 'mapping' here to point to problems not simply of spatial but also of temporal extension: the simple point that an identification of units requires a historically dubious freeze-framing (Van der Veer 2014: 2) is hard to square with Evans-Pritchard's own insistence in this very paper on anthropological work as essentially historical – a point which Edmund Leach gleefully picked up (Leach 1964: 283; cf. Abbott 2004: 151). In sum, in invoking societies and cultures as cases in 1950, Evans-Pritchard was thus already invoking fraught and fictional realities.

A similar set of problems attaches to the identification of those second kinds of units – the traits, institutions or more generally, the properties of the first kind of objects. Comparison as described above does not in fact bear on cultures or societies directly, but on another kind of units, attributes or particulars of these contextual ensembles. In Evans-Pritchard's discussion these are a series of abstractions derived from the observation of standardised behaviours – comparative categories (e.g. 'religious cults') which simply require clear formulation in order to serve as a support for cumulative enquiry. Rodney Needham (1975; see below, Chapter 2) famously unpicked that hope when he made the Wittgensteinian observation that most of the terms invoked in comparative studies by anthropologists (be they specific ones like descent group, or general ones like kinship or belief) pointed to 'polythetic sets' – collections of things which shared some, but not all features. Such terms were useless for any kind of systematic comparison, since ultimately it was possible to imagine two elements of a polythetic set (say two instances of the set 'religious cults') which shared nothing at all. Furthermore social phenomena properly examined were polythetic sets of polythetic sets, 'all the way down': in social life there were no actual elements or particles (Needham 1975: 364). In sum – just as villages are no less complex than empires, particulars such as cultural traits or social institutions are no less elusive, in terms of mapping, than cases.

Problems of mapping go beyond the basic cartographic question of identifying the relevant units. For the model of comparison articulated above to make sense, there need to be not only cases and particulars, but also some systematic relations between those two kinds of entities. In some accounts this is envisioned as a 'mereographic' (Strathern 2004: xxix) or 'part–whole' relation – cultures are *made up of* cultural traits or expressive behaviours; societies *made up of* social institutions or social roles. However, as soon as they posited mereographic wholes with parts whose relations were systematic, anthropologists opened them-selves up to the charge that comparing particulars across cases led to an unacceptable loss of context (Gingrich and Fox 2002b: 12). A double bind is here written into the very structure of anthropological comparison from the start. Added to which, as Evans-Pritchard himself noted, 'It is no more than an assumption that human societies are systems of the kind they are alleged to be' (Evans-Pritchard 1950: 120).

Mapping could be imagined outwith mereography, of course. A classic alternative, partly instantiated in Evans-Pritchard's own focus on abstraction, is the structuralist reimagination of mapping not in terms of parts and wholes, but in terms of the specific branch of geometry known as topology (Leach 1966: 7–8). This involves imagining social and cultural life in terms not of objects but of systems of relations. This in turn opens up the question of how these forms and systems are to be related to observable ethnographic particulars. Evans-Pritchard's own vision suggests a relation of substance to form: a culture/society as an empirical substance with a 'latent underlying form', which the anthro-pologist derives by abstraction. This form is a particular – the particular form of *this* society – an attribute (although not in any sense a 'part') of the culture or society in question. This alternative between seeing cases as mereographic (part–whole) systems and seeing them as forms-with-structures does not, however, resolve problems of mapping – one is still left with the problem of identifying structures. The structuralist comparison of forms relies on the fairly sizeable gambit that abstraction can reliably reveal an orderly form 'underneath' messy real-life societies or cultures. Was this form really there, critics soon came to wonder, or was this just 'a somewhat arbitrary extraction of polar patterns at the whim of the individual structuralist virtuosos' (Gellner 1987: 157; Douglas 1970)?

Many have gone further and rejected the very notion that comparison might bear on objects or structures of any kind. The very notion of 'structures' underlying or floating over messy reality has been ruptured by a slew of, firstly, historical and then postmodern critiques. Systems and structures are no longer the order of the day. If reality in fact consists of differences, relations, flows, transformations and intensities, then all of the above problems and solutions are misconceived. But this vision in turn brings new problems – for how might one then identify those relations, flows and intensities? The problems of mereography regarding parts and wholes return as problems regarding entities and relations.[1]

In sum, the problems of mapping focus on the way objects, properties and relations can all be troublesome. One classic way of articulating these questions of mapping is through the notion of commensurability. Comparison as envisaged by Evans-Pritchard requires that the cases and particulars are in some way commensurable: critiques which strike at the delineation of units, contexts and attributes, and at their relations, strike at the commensurability of entities both within and between cases. It is important to note that these problems are interlinked. The difficulty is not specifically with the notion of culture, or society, for instance. It is not sufficient to substitute a more specific or restrictive case (let's say a discipline, or an event, or a village, or a professional category in a particular town) and leave everything else unchanged. Aside from the fact that mapping difficulties will attach to any unit however circumscribed, the more profound problem lies in the broader structure of the operation, which seems to require a very particular set-up: two or more commensurable cases which speak to some real unit, with commensurable sorts of relations to a set of commensurable particulars. On the face of it, that seems like quite a lot to ask for in a social and cultural world which so much of contemporary anthropology agrees is overwhelmingly and irreducibly 'complex' (Dan-Cohen 2017).

One radical solution to these problems – examined at length in Chapter 5 below – has been to challenge the very notion of commensuration, and to articulate anthropological comparison as essentially about something else: the drawing out and accentuating of differences between incommensurable cases, for instance (Viveiros de Castro 2004; or, less radically, Handler 2009; Lazar 2012). But while these reconfigurations transform the problems of mapping, they do not dissolve them. For these alternative 'non-commensurating comparisons' still rely – often extensively – upon a reference to units, contexts, cases and particulars. Sometimes, along with these new proposals, radically new ways of defining and articulating some of these entities are found. But mostly, as I will argue, these are still produced and shored up by (often unexamined) work of commensuration on other scales.

## Problems of Communication

To these mapping problems is added another broad family of problems which bear on the relation between the anthropologist and her or his 'object'. The life-span of anthropology as a discipline has broadly speaking accompanied that of what John Durham Peters has termed 'the problem of communication' (Peters 2001): how can one (and ought one to?) bridge the distance between self and other? This is so often evoked as a specifically anthropological problem – and indeed, it so often seems to need to be reinvented from scratch as if newly discovered – that I will dwell a moment on Peters's broader genealogy of 'the problem', which provides a refreshing step back.

Like comparison itself, the problem of communication – which is obviously much more than a question of speech or language – has a long and diverse genealogy. Indeed, again like comparison, one might be tempted to think of it as universal or foundational of human experience. Nevertheless, Peters shows that 'the problem', as we today tend to think of it, coalesces in a precise and recognisable form in Europe in the late nineteenth century. As Peters helpfully points out, the current parameters of the problem of communication were set by

[t]wo words coined in the late 19th century ...: 'solipsism' in 1874 and 'telepathy' in 1882 ... Both reflect an individualist culture in which the walls surrounding the mind were a problem, whether blissfully thin (telepathy) or terrifyingly impermeable (solipsism). Since then, 'communication' has simultaneously called up the dream of instantaneous access and the nightmare of the labyrinth of solitude.

(Peters 2001: 5)

The 'problem of communication', Peters argues, still today tacks back and forth between the poles of solipsism and telepathy. Peters identifies five broad philosophical possibilities, already evident in the 1920s, which continue to orient and inhabit discussions of the relations between self and other between those two poles:

Communication as the management of mass opinion; the elimination of semantic fog; vain sallies from the citadel of the self; the disclosure of otherness; and the orchestration of action ... Heidegger wants uncanny poetry in the woods, Ogden and Richards want universal clarity of meaning, Dewey wants practical participation and aesthetic release, Kafka narrates personal nightmares of interpersonal asymptotes, and Bernays wants to manufacture goodwill as Hitler wants to manufacture bad will. Heidegger's celebration of language's uncanniness lives on in deconstruction's repeated exposé of the impossibility of communication; Ogden and Richards' project survives in semantics and in the culture of scientific research more generally and informs what is probably still the dominant view of communication, the successful replication of intentions; and Dewey's vision anticipates language pragmatics and speech act theory's interest in language's seemingly modest, but astounding ability to bind people in action.

(Peters 2001: 19–20)

It is no coincidence that anthropological comparison in its modern form is usually imagined to emerge at roughly the same period as Peters's problem of communication. From the very start, anthropological comparison was entangled with the equally impossible horizons of solipsism and telepathy. The last three philosophical options outlined by Peters (the impossibility of ever reaching the other, the dream of eliminating semantic fog, and the recognition of the successful coordination of action) have framed disciplinary debates about comparison in anthropology in various guises. They emerge and recombine most obviously in anthropological discussions of translation and incommensurability (Handler 2009; Lezaun 2010; Povinelli 2001), but also more broadly of themes such as intersubjectivity, cultural critique, othering, orientalism, fieldwork methodology and the like.

From this 'communicational' vantage point, a range of further problems assail our model of the comparative method, attaching particularly to the various arrows in Figure 1.1. 'Translation' is an obvious one. The breezy confidence with which Evans-Pritchard suggests that some time spent in a place makes their values 'culturally intelligible' for a foreigner as they would be for an insider (Evans-Pritchard 1950: 121) has been much shaken, both by those who feel that cultural worlds are not so easily penetrable, and by those who would reject the assumption that such distinct worlds ever existed to begin with. These two objections, taken together, mark the reason why cultural relativism always seems to come either too early or too late (Laidlaw 2014: 27, with reference to Williams 2005: 69). The problem might be not simply an inability to understand – a constant process of 'mutual mistranslations, emended, painstakingly' (Handler 2009: 637); it could take the opposite form, that of believing we understand, that we have identified common terms, when in fact we overlook a fundamental difference (Viveiros de Castro 2004). Entwined with these epistemological objections comes the observation that translation, be it linguistic or conceptual, is inherently power-laden from the start (Asad 1986; Povinelli 2001). To the problem of expressing the coherence of lives lived and thoughts thought in one language through the frames of another, is added the problem that different languages themselves tend to be accorded unequal access to the production of universalisable knowledge (Van der Veer 2013: 19; see also McDonald 1989).

The difficulties are not simply structural. More pointedly, authors such as Geoffrey Lloyd have made the observation that comparisons between 'us' and 'them' are always driven by an implicit or explicit agenda of relative valuation and imply a particular moral relationship. Lloyd claims that there are five valences of such (in my terms, frontal) comparatisms: establishing the superiority of the self, the superiority of the other, the similarity of self and other, the incomprehensibility of the other, or the potential to learn from the other (Lloyd 2015: 30–31; see also Handler 2009; Laidlaw 2014: 213–225). Whether or not one accepts this particular list of options as comprehensive, it certainly foregrounds the point that the political and ethical effects of solutions to the 'problem of communication' directly raise the question of 'who controls the comparison and with what end in view' (Lloyd 2015: 31). And of course, the thought that *anyone* controls the comparison, or that it obeys its stated 'end', is still a reassuring one: once one opens up the possibility that our comparisons travel beyond the purposes we had in mind, the difficulties multiply rather than decrease.

Additionally, the problem of communication adds a further twist to the mapping issues raised above: *whose* are the units and terms of comparison? Most salient for contemporary anthropologists are the culturalist, feminist and postcolonial critiques which led to a realisation that the domains and categories of anthropological analysis involved an unacknowledged extension of western assumptions and interests to contexts where there was no reason to suppose they would apply.[2] The epistemological concern about the comparative extension of 'our' categories had already been prefigured, of course, long before Evans-Pritchard's account. Franz Boas, for instance, had famously noted that a term such as 'murder' cannot serve as a comparative term since, in different cultural contexts, it can designate fundamentally different things:

The person who slays an enemy in revenge for wrongs done, a youth who kills his father before he gets decrepit in order to enable him to continue a vigorous life in the world to come, a father who kills his child as a sacrifice for the welfare of his people, act from such entirely different motives, that psychologically a comparison of their actions does not seem permissible.

(Boas 1911: 173)

However, at the intersection of the multiple strands of feminism and postcolonial scholarship, this basic epistemic worry was reconfigured as a thorny political double bind, which has remained front and centre of anthropological consciousness. For, once the 'problem of communication' is seen in a political and not merely epistemic light, it becomes clear that neither simply extending western concepts and commitments (for instance by automatically applying western feminist political visions to non-western women) nor giving up on them (for instance by refusing to consider gender inequality as a cross-cultural concern) will do (Mohanty 1984; Strathern 1987a; Ong 1988; Abu-Lughod 1990; Mahmood 2005; Nzegwu 2006; see Johnson 2018).

With the problem of communication, abstraction, too, takes a blow from a different direction. If Evans-Pritchard's confidence about translation is striking, what then of his even breezier confidence that his 'abstractions' make society sociologically intelligible in ways that 'no native can explain [and] no layman, however conversant with the culture, can perceive' (Evans-Pritchard 1950: 121–122)? The confidence in the superior explanatory power of anthropological abstractions has been thoroughly shaken by the epistemic crisis of the 1980s, as well as the appetite for accounts which seek to upstage in this way informants' own sense of what they are up to. The politically unsavoury implications of such accounts – in which concreteness lies with informants and abstraction with the anthropologist – have come to seem obvious. An important strand of contemporary anthropological sensibilities rests on inverting this dynamic, and seeking humbly to recover the sophistication and complexity of informants' own abstractions, rather than trump those with our own. The anthropologist's privilege in knowing better than (some of) his or her informants has sometimes been reinvented in the guise of 'critique', but this is more often imagined as a matter of an alternative standpoint (cf. Harding 2005), than in the vein of Evans-Pritchard's appeal to a superior, professionally grounded, capacity for abstraction.

More broadly, in Evans-Pritchard's model, as I noted above, anthropology's knowledge and its objects are treated asymmetrically in a temporal sense. One term is imagined historically – the progression of anthropological knowledge – while the other is imagined spatially – a world of peoples/cultures/societies awaiting cultural analysis and comparison. Anthropologists have (since and indeed before Evans-Pritchard's time) objected not only that the world too is in time, but also that this dynamic itself is a distancing device with important political implications (Chakrabarty 2007; Fabian 1983).

'Communication' raises difficulties not only in the relations between anthropologists and their subjects – Evans-Pritchard's first move – but also in relations between anthropologists themselves – Evans-Pritchard's third move. The thought that successive anthropologists can deploy each other's accounts as scientists deploy each other's studies had always required heavy qualification. Anthropologists of the nineteenth and twentieth centuries were often critical of their contemporaries' and predecessors' reliance on doubtful 'people–person reports' (Handler

2009: 631) produced by missionaries and other amateur ethnographers (see, for instance, Tylor 1871: 219 on Tongan numerals). Part of the answer then seemed to lie in the professionalisation of the discipline – the creation of shared standards of enquiry and reporting (Lewis 1955). Evans-Pritchard was well aware that differences between ethnographers still made each ethnographic study a personal as much as an objective record. This was the key to the value of ethnography and of people–person reports as a tool for enquiry – like Malinowski before him, Evans-Pritchard (e.g. 1951: 88) conceptualised field-based knowledge as a 'personal equation' (Kuklick 2011). But for him, these personal elements could be assumed to roughly 'even out' as the number of studies increased, and could in any case be considered separately from the work's objective content (Evans-Pritchard 1951: 89–90). The so-called 'crisis of representation' of the 1980s took these problems of calibration and made them fundamental: ethnographies had to be understood as fictional through and through (Clifford and Marcus 1986; Geertz 1988).

Proponents of this shift in perspective reassured readers that they meant 'fictional', in the sense of 'made', literary constructs, rather than in the sense of being 'false' (Clifford and Marcus 1986: 6–7). But there is something slightly disingenuous about that caveat, since it is hard to imagine what remains of an older sense of factual truth and accuracy – let alone 'calibration' or 'triangulation' – once this point has been thoroughly integrated. The aesthetic form of the ethnographer's one-to-one relation with 'a culture' had ceased to convince (Strathern 2004). In its wake, anthropologists still invoke people–person reports, but these emerge now as complex literary constructions, and ones deeply embedded in the political and conceptual contexts of their writing. These accounts' internal coherence and external reliance on context make them as hard to compare as 'cultures' themselves were in a relativist's imagination (cf. Herzfeld 2001: 262). In other words, the same double bind arises in relation to monographic texts as arises in relation to societies imagined as units: the very reason studies are valuable for comparative purposes, on Evans-Pritchard's account – because they are contextualised wholes made up of systematically arranged parts (see also Thornton 1988) – is also what makes their comparison difficult and their cumulation impossible. The implied arrow in the bottom right of Figure 1.1 – the arrow envisioning the progressive cumulative development of anthropological knowledge – has faded away.

## Problems of Purpose

The essential point to remember is that the anthropologist is working within a body of theoretical knowledge and that he makes his observations to solve problems which derive from it … We tell our anthropological students to study problems and not peoples.

(Evans-Pritchard 1951: 87)

This brings us to the final – and in a sense the thorniest – problem of anthropological comparison: what is it for? This is not simply an existential question for the individual practitioner – although it can be that. For comparison as outlined above to work, its purpose needs to be shared across a collective of practitioners. But such an agreement on purpose is not simply lacking in contemporary anthropology. The multiplicity of divergent purposes which animate our devices is constitutive of the discipline as it stands – as it was already, I would argue, in Evans-Pritchard's day.

Consider the paradox of Evans-Pritchard's own position. He excoriated the naive realism of evolutionists or diffusionists who imagined they were comparing things themselves, bits of society or culture – 'peoples', rather than 'problems'. But a shared disciplinary set of assumptions was required to make that leap out of empiricism. When one was comparing bits of reality, the world itself could act as the unifying force. When one started comparing problems, there had to be a disciplinary agreement on shared problems and categories. In sum, for Evans-Pritchard, anthropological comparison required that anthropologists work in what one might retrospectively characterise as a shared paradigm.

And yet, on the other hand, Evans-Pritchard's article was itself articulated around a major shift in purpose, to which we will return in the next chapter: the move from comparison aimed at producing scientific generalisation, to comparison imagined as a means to an interpretive understanding of human experience. Evans-Pritchard's proposal is in a sense self-defeating: it simultaneously proposes a vision of anthropology as a cumulative comparative enterprise *and* articulates this vision in terms of a radical break with the past – in the figure of his erstwhile mentor Radcliffe-Brown (Radcliffe-Brown 1951). Even if all of the methodological and epistemological problems raised in the previous two sections could be resolved, the basic and profound divergence between the interpretive aims proposed by Evans-Pritchard and the positivist aims proposed by Radcliffe-Brown puts paid to the vision – which both, ironically, shared – of comparison as a cumulative, collaborative enterprise.

These two anthropologists, colleagues in the same institution, one of whom had been a mentor to the other, and who both envisioned their discipline as a cumulative enterprise, were not after all in the same comparative business. What hope is there, then, for the contemporary assemblage of anthropologists of a myriad national, conceptual and empirical traditions, writing and working in a time when the metaphor of scientific cumulation has, to so many of us, lost its appeal? Is it any wonder that, as a few anthropologists occasionally lament (Graeber 2015: 1; Toren and de Pina-Cabral 2009), there seems to be little agreement within anthropology today even over what we should be disagreeing about, let alone a paradigmatic integration or shared sense of purpose? Particular schools and research foci emerge around core concepts (affect, infrastructure, detachment), topics (labour, Christianity, expertise) or approaches (the anthropology of ethics, the ontological turn), but even these seem brittle and driven by an internal logic of fissiparity. Between them, the ground is increasingly so broad that there seems to be little in the way of productive engagement. Evans-Pritchard's language of hypothesis-testing and his image of anthropology as an experimental 'field science', a collective of practitioners with shared problems and a shared purpose, seem very distant indeed.

In some respects and in some quarters, politics has come to stand for that figure of shared comparative purpose. Embracing the observation that anthropological comparison is inherently political can provide an alternative ground for articulation. Compared with this shift, differences of purpose such as those between Radcliffe-Brown's and Evans-Pritchard's come to seem mild. Some might dream of restoring the arrow at the bottom right-hand side of Figure 1.1, to point now not to epistemological but to social progress, one 'good' comparison at a time. However, there is no reason to assume that 'good politics' as a criterion for comparative work is a more robust and less brittle medium of articulation than that of scientific cumulation proved to be. For, to some, the political task of comparison rests in challenging western knowledge practices, as in a permanent conceptual revolution which constantly draws the rug from under the feet of our own episteme (Holbraad et al. 2014), while for others the task is that of standing firmly on our critical epistemic ground, to train an anthropological, comparative view on objects like human rights (Hastrup 2002), jihad (Nader 2017) or fascism (Holmes 2016), or to trace and reveal responsibilities, inequalities and suffering (cf. Robbins 2013). These two kinds of 'good politics' have little to say to each other. At their intersection lies the thorny problem of the political-epistemic authority of anthropology's comparative activity itself. The discipline's voice and authority remains grounded precisely in the ability to make claims which, while political, are also something other or something more than political (scholarly, empirical, conceptual, etc.; Jean-Klein and Riles 2005): our distinctive use of comparison is usually what is pointed to here. Comparative activity in those discussions is both a resource and a problem, as Fox and Gingrich point out:

The need to clarify responsibly the power-related preconditions for comparative activities ... is merely one side of the coin. The other side to negotiating unequal power relations concerns how we convey the topics and the results of these comparative activities to the public – and to its hierarchies of power.

(Gingrich and Fox 2002b: 9)

Visions of unity persist, of course, in other quarters. While Evans-Pritchard's rejection of the project of a scientific anthropology is now probably shared by the majority of contemporary practitioners, some lament the loss of an earlier vision of shared scientific purpose (Bloch 2005; Bloch and Sperber 2002). Others go further and imagine the possibility of unifying anthropology under the banner of a 'science of culture', and call for anthropologists to band together to work towards a shared set of 'etic' terms (see Goodenough 1970), a mutually agreed, institutionally managed 'empirical observation language' akin to that developed by various natural sciences (Hunt 2007: 73). Hunt argues that the natural sciences have managed pretty well, by disciplining themselves into communities of practitioners, to build conventional shared languages which could capture and measure the most complex and fluid phenomena. This, however, requires that 'the entire aggregate of observers ... reach consensus on what procedures are to be used and what names are to be used' (Hunt 2007: 55). Quite possibly, if all anthropologists were to suddenly drop their current pursuits to unite behind that project, many of the problems of mapping outlined above could be resolved. Judging by what happened in analogous processes of 'making science' in other disciplines, those problems that could not be resolved in this way would probably just be neatly set aside as not pertaining to a properly scientific anthropology.

The difficulty relates to purpose. I suspect many contemporary anthropologists simply don't share Hunt's founding assumption, namely 'the assumption that a scientific cultural anthropology is worth doing if it can be done' (Hunt 2007: 155). The difficulty lies not in persuading them that it is possible to pile stable generalisations about social and cultural phenomena upon one another, if we all agree to use words in the same way: they just won't be convinced that that would be an interesting thing to do. And of course, the point cuts both ways. Anthropologists bent on using comparison to unpick generalisations and shatter typological visions can win many battles. But they are unlikely to win the war, if that consists in convincing proponents of a scientific anthropology that this unpicking constitutes a valid horizon for anthropological practice.

In this sense Hunt may well be right in claiming that 'the problems with developing further a science of culture are to be found in us rather than in nature' (Hunt 2007: 163). But if indeed 'we have met the enemy and he is us' (Hunt 2007: 163), that enemy is insuperable by definition. Anthropology as presently constituted is defined by its multiplicity of divergent purposes and ends, of which that of developing 'a science of culture' is only a very minor – and embattled – one.

If a unitary vision of anthropology were to defeat 'the enemy', it would be a pyrrhic victory indeed. The cost would be extinguishing the plurality of anthropology as it has been constituted at least since the time of Evans-Pritchard. The dominion of anthropology as a 'science of culture' would be the unmaking of anthropology as it presently exists. Once again, the converse is also true – an anthropology from which Hunt's and others' visions of scientific purpose were expunged would also be significantly poorer than the current dispensation. Our disagreements make us who 'we' are (cf. Chua and Mathur 2018).

Like Hunt, I believe that anthropological comparison is possible. But the challenge, taken up in the second part of this book, lies in articulating an account of this possibility which doesn't require us to give up on our differences – incommensurabilities, even – of purpose. We are some way off envisioning that possibility just yet.

## Conclusion: From Problems to Impossibility

Indeed, as outlined above, the situation seems pretty desperate. Their accumulation alone makes these various problems with comparison seem insuperable. But what turns a pile of problems into an impossibility is the fact that they are not independent of each other. Rather, these problems are linked together into a complex network of double binds. Each problem, taken separately, might be resolvable, but the solution itself throws us up against further problems.

Take, for instance, the communication problem of translating concepts across cultures – Boas's 'murder' problem. One classic response is to jettison our own analytical repertoire and ground the analysis in 'indigenous concepts'. But this in turn opens up a mapping problem: are these cultural repertoires really so distinct from one another and internally coherent? Perhaps we could counter then that this coherence is intended topologically, not mereographically. But if so, are such mapping decisions not, in the end, another instance of us deploying 'our own analytical repertoire'? We might then focus on turning comparison inwards, contextualising anthropological knowledge practices themselves as inherently western. But doesn't this return us to a binary and potentially imperialist vision of a modern 'us' and a pre-modern 'them'? And so on it goes. The aspirant comparatist is propelled into a field of problems, bouncing from one to the other like a pinball. The various elements, moments and moves of Evans-Pritchard's comparative method are not individually impossible, perhaps, but they are *incompossible*, to use philosophical jargon – not all of them are possible together (Leibniz 2012: 661–662; cf. Messina and Rutherford 2009). As in Bateson's canonical description of double binds, when one is right, one is forever finding oneself to be right for the wrong reasons (Bateson 1972: 245; Candea 2018a).

We seem to have reached an impasse. No wonder anthropologists have been tempted to reach for the pinch of salt. But let's defer that move for a moment longer, and take a second pass over the problem of the impossibility of comparison.

TWO

# The Garden of Forking Paths

It is part of the thesis of this paper that there is no distinctive 'comparative method' in anthropology, and that the persistence of this expression has led to unnecessary confusion and artificial dichotomies in much of the theoretical writing on this subject.

(Lewis 1955: 259)

Almost instantly, I saw it – the garden of forking paths was the chaotic novel ... In all fictions, each time a man meets diverse alternatives, he chooses one and eliminates the others ... In Ts'ui Pen's novel, all the outcomes in fact occur; each is the starting point for further bifurcations.

(Borges 2000: 286)

## Introduction: On Seeing Two Comparative Methods

There is a straightforward way to unlock the double binds outlined in the previous chapter: decide that the problems listed there do not, after all, apply to one single method. Periodically, this point was made explicitly by anthropologists writing on comparison: there is no single comparative method, but rather many methods for comparing, each with its characteristic aims, strengths and weaknesses (Lewis 1955). Once we see not one but many comparative methods, we simultaneously see that some of the problems listed in the previous chapter apply here, others there. The paralysing sense that *all* of the requirements of comparison are impossible *at the same time* falls away. Indeed, things identified as problems in relation to one kind of comparison emerge as solutions in relation to other kinds of comparison. Every time it is rediscovered, this vision of a multiplicity of comparative methods seems empowering. Thus, for Gingrich and Fox, to 'make a fresh start in considering comparison, it is essential to emphasize the heterogeneity of dominant and subaltern traditions in anthropology's comparative legacy' (2002b: 5; for other similar 'fresh starts', see Holy 1987; Scheffer and Niewöhner 2010).

This vision of a multiplicity of comparative methods in turn lends itself to a comparative procedure. Pretty soon, anthropologists started to compare comparisons. Sifting through the abundant primary and secondary anthropological literature which has dealt explicitly with comparison as a theoretical and methodological problem, I will examine some key ways in which anthropologists have made sense of the multiplicity of comparison. Despite Lewis's warning about false dichotomies, the observation that comparison is multiple is often resolved back into a binary contrast.[1] With striking regularity, when anthropologists explicitly reflect on comparison as a methodological or conceptual problem, they find not one method, or many, but – in essence – two: a fork in the road. Thus, anthropologists have sought to mark out a 'radical' kind of comparison as opposed to an empiricist kind (Dumont 1986), to contrast positivist and interpretive comparisons (Holy 1987), or to split comparison into dominant and subaltern (Gingrich and Fox 2002b), pluralist and post-plural (Holbraad and Pedersen 2009), representative and disjunctive varieties (Lazar 2012). Others went further and sought to leave 'comparison' behind altogether in view of something else: equivocation (Viveiros de Castro 2004) or multi-sitedness (Marcus 1995), or alternatively, to see comparison as the counterpoint of another method, such as fieldwork, translation or reflexivity (Herzfeld 2001). Yet as we saw above, subdividing comparison internally or seeking external alternatives to it comes back in the end to much the same thing. A looser, more encompassing version of the idea of comparison can be invoked to reveal these alternatives to comparison as, in fact, alternative forms of it.

All of these binaries do not build up to a total branching picture, a coherent typology of comparisons. Rather, each anthropologist seems to want to begin again, to 'make a fresh start', a clean break. With each of these distinctions, previous or alternative distinctions are forgotten, encompassed or reformulated, often without much attention to what is being retained and what is being added. And so, at any given moment, there seem to be 'two ways' of doing comparison. While these binaries sometimes point to a complementarity, more often the relationship is imagined as antagonistic and historical: one must be relegated for the other to fully emerge. We glimpse a bright, possibly utopian future in which comparison might no longer be impossible. This has been characterised as a 'caesurist' vision, which is to say, one that casts the history of theory in terms of radical epochal breaks (Pina-Cabral 2010: 168; after Martins 1974). Normally, this is a term of theoretical abuse, but, as I will argue in the next chapter, caesurism also has its virtues.

By tracing some of these recurrent 'new beginnings', these repeated forks in the road, the present chapter takes a second pass at the longstanding anthropological conversation over comparatism.[2] Despite its broadly chronological structure, this chapter makes no claims to being a proper historical account of the development of anthropological comparison. It is an overview of a set of intellectual positions staked over 150 years in the discipline, which seeks to draw out some of the key conceptual regularities of an extended and extremely intricate debate. It makes no claims to exhaustiveness, or even to representativity – no such account could. Neither does it have space, as a proper history of anthropological comparison surely would, to relate the diverse positions outlined below, and the epochal shifts between them, to their broader institutional, economic and sociopolitical contexts. Rather than seek to do so in necessarily caricatured and abbreviated terms, I would rather leave readers with an explicit sense of this gap and enjoin them to read the following discussion as a theoretical complement to, rather than a substitute for, a properly historical account of anthropological comparison and its many contexts (on which, see, for instance, Asad 1973a, Goody 1995; Kuklick 1991; Kuper 1973, 1999, 2005; Stocking 1991a, 1991b, 1998; Stoler 2001).

## Fork 1. The Comparative Method vs Naive Comparisons: The Birth of an Impossible Method

Up to now sociologists have scarcely occupied themselves with the task of characterizing and defining the method that they apply to the study of social facts.

(Durkheim 1964: 48)

### *An Impossible Charter: John Stuart Mill's Methods of Induction*

Where to begin the sequence of anthropological comparatisms? Histories of the discipline conventionally begin in the nineteenth century, although in terms of comparison as in so much else, the roots of anthropology lie far deeper. Any beginning will thus be arbitrary, in *medias res*, and mine may seem more so than most, for I will begin with J. S. Mill. Mill was not an anthropologist nor particularly concerned with anthropology, but he provides a convenient starting point for two reasons. The first reason is that Mill's discussions of induction[3] – and the crucial place of comparative method in those discussions – loomed large in some of the earliest anthropological attempts to formalise a Comparative Method for the discipline. Mill forms one conceptual juncture, between the long genealogy of comparison briefly hinted at in the introduction and the first explicitly anthropological attempts to formulate a comparative method. The second reason was that – ironically – Mill had also presaged the impossibility of the Comparative Method, for a discipline such as anthropology at least, in terms which seem surprisingly to echo contemporary concerns.

As Lloyd (see, for instance, 2015) has documented, western epistemology at least since Aristotle has viewed comparisons and analogies in particular with suspicion, and sought to build knowledge on firmer ground. As we shall consider again below, in his writings on rhetorics and in his biology, Aristotle is more sanguine about the potential of analogies, and can be recuperated 'as explorer rather than as censor-in-chief' (Lloyd 2015: 120). In Aristotle's formal accounts of demonstrations, however, the only way in which a universal may properly be secured by the examination of similar cases – rather than merely suggested, as in a rhetorical argument (Aristotle 1997: I.18) – is when the induction can be said to be complete. But for practical purposes the vision of a complete induction is rather obviously problematic (Lloyd 2015: 54).

In this context, Mill is one of a number of epistemologists who imagines new inductive uses for comparison. Mill followed Bacon in noting that induction by enumeration, in which similarities between known cases were listed as a ground for generalisation, was a rough and imperfect method (Mill 1856: 340–344). Some seeming invariances were mere surface phenomena, which a single contrary example might at any point unpick; others pointed to truly decisive causal relations. However many instances one accumulated, simply showing similarities between them could never provide the solid ground for a broader generalisation. The problem of a properly scientific induction was, therefore, to distinguish in any given case what actual links obtained between particular causes and particular effects, by 'varying the circumstances'. To this end, one needed to attend to both similarities and differences in a series of carefully selected cases. Mill formulated a number of inductive methods, which rested on different kinds of comparison (Mill 1856: 417–441).

In the 'method of difference', one compared otherwise similar instances in which the phenomenon under investigation occurred with others in which it did not. If, all other things being the same, one single change produced the phenomenon in question, one had isolated the cause. This was the jewel in Mill's inductive crown – the experimental method *par excellence*, ideally instantiated in laboratory experiments under controlled conditions, in which instances could be replicated at will, and their circumstances carefully varied until one could eliminate all similarities but one, and thus find, by elimination, the cause which led to the effect.

In cases in which such direct experimental control was impossible, or as a preliminary means of generating hypotheses to be tested by the method of difference, Mill recommended the 'method of agreement', in which one compared otherwise different instances in which the phenomenon occurred. This method was available to sciences which proceeded by observing situations in the world, but could not replicate them in the laboratory: if in different instances that had only one particular in common one found the same phenomenon, one had an inkling that this phenomenon was linked to that particular. Note that, as with the method of difference, the requirement was extremely stringent: one had to eliminate *all* similarities between these different cases *but one*.

Yet even so, for Mill the method of agreement was weaker than the method of difference because it could not control for the crucial fact that the same effect might be produced contextually by different causes – Mill's doctrine of the multiplicity of causes, to which we shall return below.

The final inductive method proposed by Mill – which came to play a particularly influential role in early anthropological accounts of the Comparative Method – did not require the elimination of phenomena, either through experimental intervention or by finding in the world instances which presented just the right kind of similarities and differences. This was the 'method of concomitant variation', to which I return below.

Mill's discussion of induction provided one extremely powerful argument to later anthropological comparativists. This was contained in the claim that,

For the purpose of varying the circumstances, we may have recourse (according to a distinction commonly made) either to observation or to experiment; we may either find an instance in nature, suited to our purposes, or, by an artificial arrangement of circumstances, make one ... There is, in short, no difference in kind, no real logical distinction, between the two processes of investigation.

(Mill 1856: 411)

With or without explicit reference to Mill, the thought that, by selecting the right cases, an observational science might, through careful comparative procedures, come to approximate the rigour of the experimental sciences became a foundational trope for many anthropologists of the nineteenth and early twentieth century (Durkheim 1964; Evans-Pritchard 1951; Nadel 1951; Radcliffe-Brown 1951). Many of the earliest explicit pronouncements on Comparative Method in anthropology imagined it, in the shadow of Mill's discussion, as a method for scientific induction, which broke with the loose drawing of analogies characteristic of earlier unsystematic comparisons. The Comparative Method – as Nadel put it in a discussion which explicitly starts from Mill – was born as a method for discovering universal propositions of the form 'if A, then B' (1951: 223).

And yet there is a profound irony here. Mill himself, having unwittingly written the charter, as it were, for anthropology's Comparative Method, left with it a fairly forceful caveat to the effect that it would prove to be impossible. Indeed Mill – who had illustrated his discussion of induction with examples taken from physics, chemistry, geology and the like – was adamant that the complexity of *social* phenomena was such as to make direct induction from a comparison of cases illusory. He pointed in particular to the fact that the same effect could be produced contextually by different causes. In 'the phenomena of politics and history',

Plurality of Causes exists in almost boundless excess, and the effects are, for the most part, inextricably interwoven with one another. To add to the embarrassment, most of the inquiries in political science relate to the production of effects of a most comprehensive description, such as the public wealth, public security, public morality, and the like: results liable to be affected directly or indirectly either in *plus* or in *minus* by nearly every fact which exists, or event which occurs, in human society ... So little could be concluded, in such a case, from any possible collation of individual instances, that even the impossibility, in social phenomena, of making artificial experiments, a circumstance otherwise so prejudicial to directly inductive inquiry, hardly affords, in this case, additional reason of regret.

(Mill 1856: 462–463)

For Mill, the study of complex phenomena could not proceed through direct induction from complex cases. A science of complex phenomena, in which Mill included not only the study of society, politics and history, but also psychology and even physiology, had to start from established laws induced from the examination of simpler phenomena; it would then deduce the complex relations between them; finally, it would test these deductions through a comparison of complex cases. Mill named this three-part method the 'deductive method'. The application of the deductive method to social phenomena – whose simpler laws would have to be derived from the study of the human mind and those in turn from those of physiology – seemed a distant prospect at best.

Mill thus left anthropologists both with a hope – the hope of an inductive science grounded in the comparison of situations encountered in the world – and with good reasons to despair – the complexity of those phenomena and the doctrine of the plurality of causes. The suspicion that the comparative method was impossible for societies, at least, provided the context for the earliest self-conscious attempts to outline such a method in anthropology. The Comparative Method was born impossible.

## Comparing Nevertheless: Typology and Concomitant Variation

When the contemporary anthropologist, having trawled through pages of Mill's confident scientism, suddenly stumbles upon his warnings about the impossibility of comparative induction due to the complexity of social phenomena, the effect is that of a powerful shock of recognition. Mill's often acerbic comments – 'Whoever makes use of an argument of this kind, not intending to deceive, should be sent back to learn the elements of some one of the more easy physical sciences' (Mill 1856: 463) – would not be out of place in the mouth of recent critics of the scientific pretensions of the social sciences (Latour 2005; Stengers 2011). The vision of social life as 'too complex' for generalisation is one of the most widespread koans of contemporary anthropology (Dan-Cohen 2017). And here we find it articulated in the mid-nineteenth century! The mystery then seems to be, what anthropologists – or at least those anthropologists who had sought to draw inductive generalisations from comparisons – thought they were doing in the interim.

One answer is that the Comparative Method in anthropology was born as an attempt to defer its own impossibility, to grasp tentative and carefully caveated scientific victories from the jaws of complexity. It was born also – following the pattern of Mill's own critique of previous naive inductions – through a self-conscious break with previous 'naive' attempts at comparing societies and peoples. The Comparative Method was born as a fork in the road, one of a pair – its shadow was naive comparison. From the start, as it were, anthropologists could hope that the 'other' kind of comparison was the impossible one. In the face of these impossibilities and naiveties, anthropologists of the nineteenth century sought to make a new start.

One set of solutions focused on a redefinition of simplicity. Mill's warnings about simple and complex phenomena named an enduring concern for anthropological comparatists. But, for a period, anthropologists felt they had envisioned a solution. Instead of seeking simple laws in phenomena of a different order (those of the human mind), as Mill had suggested, anthropologists thought they might find simplicity within social and cultural phenomena themselves. Many drew on contemporary imaginations of a scale of complexity in human societies and cultures, which made 'simple societies' an effective starting point for the study of basic sociological regularities, which could then be recombined for the study of more 'complex' cases (Durkheim 1915, 1964; Benedict 1934), as Talia Dan-Cohen (2017) showed in a perceptive genealogy of the concern with complexity in anthropology. One might say that anthropologists, in effect, translated Mill's 'deductive method' on to a different plane: they sought to move, not up a scale of phenomena (from biology through psychology to sociology), but rather along a scale of social forms, from simple to complex.

This move, central to the comparative visions of Spencer, Tylor or Durkheim, endured long after the demise of explicitly 'evolutionist' approaches, in part explaining the otherwise puzzling persistence of the notion of 'primitive' societies in accounts of the discipline, such as Evans-Pritchard's, which were otherwise so resolutely opposed to nineteenth-century evolutionism. In reference to my discussion of mapping in Chapter 1, this move sought simplicity in terms of the 'cases' or objects of anthropological comparison. A complementary move was to seek simplicity in terms of the particulars, or attributes, of those objects. The appeal to 'customs' (Tylor 1889) or 'institutions' (Durkheim 1964) as definite elementary units of social life provided seemingly more tractable objects of study than the vague generalities which previous comparatists had sought to identify – 'the public wealth, public security, public morality, and the like' (Mill 1856: 462). Comparatists such as Durkheim thought that one might build back up to those more complex objects, from these simpler elements, rather than need to delve down into the simpler laws of the human mind.

The twin practices of categorising societies along a scale from simplicity to complexity and of identifying simple units of social and cultural

# Fork 1. The Comparative Method vs Naive Comparisons

life meant that these early comparatisms were much concerned with the drawing up of typologies. The basic principle of typologising was abstraction, as described by Mill, namely a procedure of building classes by identifying similarities in empirical phenomena:

[t]he mental operation which extracts from a number of detached observations certain general characters in which the observed phenomena resemble one another, or resemble other known facts, is what Bacon, Locke, and most subsequent metaphysicians, have understood by the word Abstraction.

(Mill 1856: 337)

An assemblage of similarities into nested classes was the main device of traditional typology. Retrospectively, evolutionist comparative methods would come to be identified by later authors as essentially *about* typology (e.g. Salmon 2013a). However, I would argue that typology, for nineteenth-century authors such as Tylor or Durkheim, was a preliminary to the actual business of induction. The Comparative Method, in other words, was already a compound of methods – a compound of typological abstraction and inductive generalisation. We might today identify the former as the key feature and failing of these early comparatisms, but for these authors themselves, the focus, emphasis and hope lay – rhetorically at least – with the latter: not with the mere building of typologies of societies and their particulars, but with the next step, namely the inductive search for general laws based on comparisons across these various units.

This is where one particular comparative device offered a complementary solution to the problem of complexity. Mill's method of concomitant variation followed the principle that '[w]hatever phenomenon varies in any manner whenever another phenomenon varies in some particular manner, is either a cause or an effect of that phenomenon, or is connected with it through some fact of causation' (Mill 1856: 434). For Mill, the method of concomitant variation, which in effect pointed to quantitative correlations between phenomena, was in some senses

63

the weakest, since it could only suggest 'some fact of causation'. It was, however, the most easily suited to the messiness of the objects of study available to the observational (rather than experimental) sciences, since it did not require the elimination of all differences or all similarities between the different cases compared.

With or without reference to Mill, the study of concomitant variations became a core device of a number of early anthropological comparatisms. By cutting through the requirement that an object be completely known, this device sidestepped an obviously impossible standard when the object was a culture or a society. More positively, it spoke to a basic evolutionary-functionalist intuition: the thought that societies were ordered in such a way that a transformation in one aspect would correspond to transformations in other aspects.[4] This intuition, and with it the study of concomitant variation, became central to nineteenth- and early twentieth-century anthropological comparatisms.

I will now compare two classic nineteenth-century attempts to articulate a self-definedly scientific comparative method for anthropology, each of which recombined typology and concomitant variation to different effect.

### E. B. Tylor's Adhesions

While E. B. Tylor had read Mill's *Principles* (see, for instance, Tylor 1871: 218–219), he did not explicitly refer to concomitant variation in his own classic proposal for a comparative method (1889).[5] Nevertheless, the correlation of variations is central to the vision of comparison as articulated in his piece. Tylor started from a tabulation of the customs of hundreds of peoples, to seek higher than average 'adhesions' or correlations between seemingly unrelated customs in different societies. For instance, Tylor notes of the three customs of teknonymy (the parent is named after the child), the husband's residence in the wife's family and ceremonial mother-in-law avoidance, that 'their concurrence might be expected to happen between once and twice in the list of peoples of the world. In fact it is found eleven times. Thus, we have their common causation vouched for by the heavy odds of six to one' (Tylor 1889: 249).

Later commentators have focused primarily on the evolutionist logic of Tylor's comparatism – the fact that the 'common causation' which he has in mind here was to be sought in 'the working of the uniform laws governing the human mind' (Boas 1896: 901). And it is true that Tylor's main aim in this article and elsewhere was to reconstruct what he imagined to be a single sequence of development of humanity, from primitive to modern. In Tylor's vision, a comparative set of cases in space was also simultaneously a set of cases in time: the peoples he compared represented, to him, different historical, and not merely geographical, social forms. It has become a commonplace in anthropology to contrast such evolutionist comparisons aimed at historical reconstruction and the later comparative visions of structural-functionalists, focused on the typological categorisation of social structures (see below).

This classic contrast tends to overshadow the important sense in which Tylor's arguments, like those of other classic evolutionists such as Spencer (Candea 2018b; Perrin 1976; Spencer 1896), were already functionalist. This functionalist logic was directly related to Tylor's interest in co-variation. Indeed, I would go further and argue that, once it is applied against the background assumption of the organic analogy – the vision popularised in anthropology by Comte and Spencer of societies as akin to biological organisms – the method of concomitant variation, or 'co-variation' as Nadel has it, becomes implicitly or explicitly the core device of functionalist comparison (Eggan 1954: 748; Nadel 1951). For, indeed, once one envisions societies on the model of organisms, the identification of pairs of phenomena which vary together across different societies can be taken to point to the functional interrelation of analogous parts in each case. Thus the primary effect of Tylor's identification of co-variation was to show that different customs were not randomly assembled, but rather, precisely, that they were functionally interrelated: as the customs of residence shifted from requiring the married couple to live with the wife's parents to requiring them to live with the husband's parents, thus the customs of politeness shifted from rules of polite distance between husband and in-laws towards rules of polite distance between wife and in-laws. The vision of society here is the distinctively functionalist one of a complex whole whose interrelated parts form an integrated system – although, as we shall see, it is precisely the seeming 'glitches' in this system which are of interest to Tylor.

This is not yet a system which works by itself, following solely the inherent laws of social function – as in the purified vision outlined by Durkheim and later Radcliffe-Brown. For Tylor, functional interrelations, such as those between these two variations above, were still ultimately rooted in the universal workings of the human mind. Surely we could see, he argued, that anyone, whether 'savage' or 'civilised', would find it awkward to have to live with their in-laws (Tylor 1889: 247–248)! Is it any wonder that rules of polite distance apply where this cohabitation takes place? I will return to the peculiar dynamic of this demonstration when I discuss 'ejection' in Chapter 7. Suffice it to say for now that Tylor carefully separated this hypothetical dive into the mind of 'Primitive Man' from his quantitative correlations. Not unlike Mill's 'deductive method' (see above), Tylor's method involved three steps: the identification of correlations; the hypothetical identification of causes for these correlations; and the testing of such hypotheses through further comparison of cases.

Tylor's ultimate goal was to induce from these shifts broader conclusions about the direction of travel of social change, imagined as a unitary process through which all societies passed at different rates. This is why he was particularly interested in what seemed on the face of it like anomalies, exceptions to functional coherence: these were clues to the direction of historical change. Thus the fact that, amongst the peoples in his sample, avoidance rules between husbands and in-laws also existed in cases in which the couple did not reside with the wife's parents – where they could serve no functional purpose – was used as evidence to suggest that these rules were a 'survival' from an earlier stage in which the couple would have resided with the wife's parents. The fact that, in his sample, no rules of avoidance between the wife and her in-laws existed in cases where the couple lived with the wife's parents, confirmed this induction about the historical direction of travel of these social forms: here such rules of politeness had had no cause to develop *yet* (for a more detailed discussion of this case, see Candea 2018b).

## Emile Durkheim's Series

Another classic nineteenth-century proponent of the Comparative Method, Emile Durkheim, was by contrast quite explicit in equating anthropology's Comparative Method with Mill's method of concomitant variation (Durkheim 1964: chapter VI). Durkheim concurred with Mill that any attempt to generalise from a mere consideration of similarities between different cases was naive – all the more so in the intricate cases provided by human societies in which one could never hope to exclude (or indeed even be fully aware of) all the possible variables. In Durkheim's view, earlier authors' appeals to quantity were a futile gesture which had led previous comparatists to accumulate swathes of examples, and thus driven them to the indiscriminate use of materials of unequal quality. This was, incidentally, an early identification of the 'people–person report' (see Chapter 1) as causing systematic difficulties for comparison.[6] It was also echoing and transposing into anthropology Mill's Baconian critique of induction by enumeration.

The method of concomitant variation, Durkheim pointed out, enabled a different deployment of quantity. This rested not on the accumulation of examples, but rather on the demonstration of a quantitative correlation – a proportionality – between variables in a number of well-chosen and carefully contextualised cases. If one could show that two phenomena varied together, even in a small

67

number of cases, the demonstration of a causal connection was surer than that provided by the accumulation of countless examples. Comparatists would thus be free to rely on a few well-grounded sources and do away with the need for countless ethnographic tidbits. In specifying the choice of cases, Durkheim made much of the need to identify different social 'species', in order to know whether one was comparing within or between kinds of society. Establishing a proper typology was thus a crucial first step (Durkheim 1964: chapter IV). Once such typologies had been drawn up, however, the search for concomitant variation took over.

Mill had introduced the method of concomitant variation with considerable caveats, as pointing only to often indistinct causal relations, and retained the method of difference as the ultimate arbiter of causation. Durkheim, by contrast, elevated the method of concomitant variation to a philosophically exalted status: it alone, of the methods of induction, could show causality 'from the inside' (Durkheim 1964: 151). Durkheim in this way prefigures Nadel's later claim that co-variation points to 'the invariant relations between facts upon which all scientific explanations must rest' (Nadel 1951: 222). Of course, Durkheim agreed that the causation pointed to by concomitant variation might be indirect, but the answer to this was simply – much as for Tylor – to decompose the method into three steps: the identification of correlations, an interpretation of these correlations, and a test of these correlations through further comparisons.

The key to the value of concomitant variation, for Durkheim, was to use the right series of cases. In the *Rules*, Durkheim considers the study of variations within a single society (such as variations in the rate of suicide, correlated with differences in, say, age or marital status), and within societies of the same 'species' – a notion which he defined in a very particular way, as we shall see below. But these emerge as lesser options. Indeed, somewhat mind-bogglingly, Durkheim claims that 'one cannot explain a social fact of any complexity save on condition that one follows its entire development throughout all social species' (Durkheim 1964: 157), along a scale of forms imagined to range from simple to complex. As Jenkins notes, Durkheim later moved from his rather summary attempt to build a scale of forms in terms of complexity, to a more sophisticated scale of forms constructed around concomitant variation (proportionality) itself: the degree of condensation or separation of component institutions (Jenkins 2010: 105). This is the key to the grand applications of his method of concomitant variations in his work with Mauss on primitive classification, which works through 'a sequence of Australian, Middle and North American and Chinese examples, focused around the variation in degree of identity or detachment between social structure and social thought in each case' (Jenkins 2010: 106). Similarly, in *The elementary forms of religious life* (1915), as in Mauss's *The gift* (1970), social examples are arranged around an axis running from concentration to dispersal.[7] Durkheim's imagination of a single 'variable' running through a series of societies, however inconsistent, enabled a particular vision of comparison which was distinct from the historical reconstructions of Tylor, or the later functionalist presentism of Radcliffe-Brown. In particular, as Durkheim and Mauss followed where their serial comparative method led them, the initial aims of comparison as inductive explanation and identification of causal relations were progressively displaced. Durkheim's own characterisation of the method was prescient in this regard:

This method, which might be termed 'genetic', would yield at one stroke the analysis and the synthesis of the phenomenon. For, on the one hand, it would show us in dissociated state its component elements by the mere fact that it would reveal to us how one was successively added to the other. At the same time, thanks to the wide field of comparison, we would be much better placed to determine the conditions upon which their formation and association depend.

(Durkheim 1964: 157)

Once analysis and synthesis are simultaneous, the careful distinction which Mill, following Bacon, had introduced between description (the recapitulation of the known) and induction (generalisation from the known to the unknown) begins to fade as the method is applied. There are, certainly, general propositions outlined in each of the above-mentioned classics by Durkheim and Mauss (about the social function of religion, about reciprocity, or about the social construction of knowledge). But the strict inductive project of linking up causes and effects fades into the background as analysis and synthesis blur into each other. The search for laws and generalisations increasingly plays second fiddle to the identification of variation. This is perhaps why these works have remained classics despite the falling away of the explicit rationale which underpinned them. Once concomitant variation – proportionality – is unshackled from a strict appeal to quantity, it can shade into an ingenious method for arranging the known such as to produce new contrasts and ideas, and new insights into both human history and the present, rather than laws or a generalisable 'take-home point'. Just as Tylor's compound methods moved back and forth between the arrangement of cases and hypothetical plunges into the mind of 'primitive man', Durkheim's (and Mauss's) series transcended the aim of inductive generalisation which had initially served to justify them. These are classic instances of a point which will recur throughout this book, namely that methods can have a tendency to subvert the aims for which they were articulated – which is why we manage to get more out of them than we put in (Strathern 2002: xxvii).

Be that as it may, the *explicit* rationale for Durkheim's and Tylor's accounts of comparative method was generalising and inductive: they sought to discover laws from the comparison of particulars in a selection of cases. The ontological ground of these laws was conceived differently – the universal workings of the human mind for Tylor, the inherent effects of social form for Durkheim. In both cases, what is presented as a single method is actually decomposable: both Tylor's and Durkheim's methods are compounds or collections of different comparative moves, each with its own assumptions, logics and ends. The study of concomitant variation forms an important aspect, but this is combined, in Tylor's case, with a projection into 'the Mind of Primitive Man' and with an attempt at historical reconstruction, and, in Durkheim's case, with a distinctive approach to categorising societies along a scale of simplicity to complexity. Beyond these two cases, the identification of concomitant variation was the core move of a range of comparative enterprises which combined an evolutionist concern with the reconstruction of the path of human progress, with a functionalist attention to the interaction of different aspects in each society. Spencer's explanation of social progress through the correlated differentiation and coordination of the parts of social organisms (1899) is one instance. Engels's (1972) and Marx's (1973) tracing of the concomitant transformation of economic and political arrangements is another.

Tylor's and Durkheim's discussions shared a number of other features: the claim to a radical epistemological break from earlier naive comparison; an attempt to seek simplicity in social phenomena (both in the cases invoked and in their particulars); and most crucially perhaps, a side-stepping of Mill's caveat about the plurality of causes. Tylor and other evolutionist comparatists did so implicitly, by seeking, as the final cause of all the phenomena of social evolution, the universal workings of the human mind. Durkheim, by contrast, attacked Mill head-on. Only philosophers, he claimed, would be muddle-headed enough to imagine that the same effect might be produced by different causes. Scientists knew better. If suicide, for instance, can be shown to depend on more than one cause, then it is simply because there is more than one type of suicide (Durkheim 1964: 149). For Durkheim the case was simple:

If ... we wish to use the comparative method scientifically, i.e., in conformity with the principle of causality as it arises in science itself, we shall have to take as the basis of the comparisons established the following proposition: *To the same effect there always corresponds the same cause.*

(Durkheim 1964: 150)

### Fork 2. The Historical Method vs the Comparative Method: A Boasian Crisis

Up to this time we have too much reveled in more or less ingenious vagaries. The solid work is still all before us.

· (Boas 1896: 908)

## *Boasian Challenges*

Confident though it was, Durkheim's claim would prove hard to sustain. Francis Galton, speaking from the audience in response to Tylor's above-mentioned paper, had famously raised the rejoinder that correlations – concomitant variations – between customs might be caused quite simply by one people borrowing another people's customs (Galton in Tylor 1889: 270–271). The mapping challenge was devastating: the comparative method as Tylor had conceived it assumed that cases were independent of each other, and that their particulars formed a broadly coherent, functionally interrelated set. Deviations from this functional coherence could then be explained as survivals of an earlier, itself functional, situation. But if the particulars of one case could simply travel to another case, that meant that nothing at all could be induced, either from a semblance of functional interrelation or from exceptions to that interrelation.

Franz Boas later developed this point into a devastating critique of the Comparative Method, which, without explicit mention of Mill, invoked in effect the principle of the plurality of causes. As we saw, a fundamental tenet of the evolutionary uses of comparison such as Tylor's was that human societies developed in a certain direction, which could be reconstructed by comparing societies currently at different points along this developmental arc. This comparison could be used to reconstruct the steps or stages along the way, such as, in our example above, the move from residence with the wife's family to residence with the husband's family. This in turn was one of the many such micro-changes that, interwoven in that paper, led Tylor to suggest a broader direction of movement from matriarchal towards patriarchal forms of social organisation (Tylor 1871: 252).

As Boas pointed out, the entire structure of such evolutionist arguments relied on the denial of the plurality of causes. Evolutionists, he argued, were naive to assume that the existence of the same phenomenon in different societies necessarily pointed to the parallel workings of the human mind faced with similar problems. For '[e]ven the most cursory review shows that the same phenomena may develop in a multitude of ways' (Boas 1896: 903). Boas did not simply have in mind Galton's objection – that the co-occurrence of two 'traits' might signify that they had been borrowed together. More broadly, careful historical reconstructions of particular practices, such as those surrounding the wearing of masks, for instance, could show them to have been derived, independently, through a whole range of different processes from a whole range of different sources. The objection hit at the heart of the assumption that different societies might be used as proxies for different points on the same timescale.

Note that Boas's challenge here follows the same structure as Mill's critique of naive induction by enumeration – one cannot generalise merely from similarities between cases. If the same phenomena can have developed in historically different ways, then there is no reason to assume that different peoples can be used as proxies for a set of temporal cases. Boas's critique in effect attacked the foundational move which had enabled the study of concomitant variation, namely the drawing up of typologies of cultures and their parts (Salmon 2013a).

While – to return to the distinction made in Chapter 1 – I have presented the above critiques in an essentially 'mapping' form, there was another, 'communicational' aspect to Boas's insistence on the plurality of causes. This was evident, for instance, in Boas's critique of comparative categories such as 'murder', examined in the previous chapter. Before we even get to asking whether the *correlation* between two particulars might derive from different causes – from coincidence, shared borrowing or independent functional arrangement – the very identification of the same particular in different cases could become undecidable. For what seemed like the same phenomenon might derive from different psychological motives. In other words, it might not be the same phenomenon at all. This move forms the precise counterpart and debunking of, for instance, Tylor's attempt to plunge into the mind of 'Primitive Man' to recognise there a universal embarrassment at living with in-laws (see Chapter 7). For some commentators (Salmon 2013a: 195), this communicational problem is the essential aspect of Boas's critique: not his attack on evolutionism, or more broadly on the search for laws in social phenomena, but rather his challenge to the cross-cultural application of anthropological categories. Certainly this attack on 'the sovereignty of similarity', as Salmon nicely puts it (Salmon 2013a: 194), is what is most likely to speak directly to the concerns of contemporary anthropologists, and is part of what has led to the rediscovery in Boas of a precursor to contemporary concerns.

Boas's return to a caveat about the multiplicity of causes thus provided a bundle of different challenges to the Comparative Method, which bore on some of the different aspects we have seen in the previous section. The thought that the same phenomenon in different societies might be independently derived made a nonsense of the evolutionist attempt to read a collection of contemporary societies as proxies for different points along the same history. The thought that concomitant variations between two sets of particulars may have been caused by the borrowing of both particulars (Galton's point) worked directly against the functional logic which sought in concomitant variations the proof of functional interdependence. Finally and most devastatingly, the point about the different psychological causes of superficially similar phenomena struck at the basic anthropological ability to identify particulars for cross-cultural comparison at all. No wonder, then, that Boas's interventions have been described as leading to a profound epistemic crisis in anthropology (Salmon 2013b: 5), one which prefigured the more famous crisis of the 1980s.

## Boasian Proposals

While there is general agreement amongst later commentators on the fact that Boas provided a set of profound challenges to existing visions of anthropological comparison, and also on the identification of Boas as the 'father' of American cultural anthropology, there are a number of different reconstructions concerning what Boas in fact proposed as an alternative to the Comparative Method. Boas's own account of his alternative 'Historical Method' was primarily articulated, in a rather modest vein, around the problem of control (cf. Eggan 1954) – the building of 'safe' regional comparisons of related societies as an antidote to the ungrounded flights of fancy of the evolutionists' distant comparisons of unrelated cases. Like Mill, one might say, Boas focused on selecting appropriate cases for comparison. One needed to first ascertain which causes phenomena derive from, before one could safely compare them:

We must demand that the causes from which it developed be investigated and that comparisons be restricted to those phenomena which have been proved to be effects of the same causes. We must insist that this investigation be made a preliminary to all extended comparative studies ... In short, before extended comparisons are made, the comparability of the material must be proved.

(Boas 1896: 904)

In practice a careful and controlled historical method would take the form of 'a detailed study of customs in their bearings to the total culture of the tribe practicing them, and in connection with an investigation of their geographical distribution among neighboring tribes' (Boas 1896: 905). Boas insisted, however, that alongside this careful and painstaking task of reconstructing local historical variations, the historical method would also return to the problem of establishing laws governing the growth and transformation of cultures.

One later line of commentators noted that Boas's second aim had not really been taken up either by himself or by his students (Eggan 1954). A commonplace retrospective view of Boas's historical method therefore came to be that it represented just that: a demand for good, careful history, an essentially descriptive project grounded in a scepticism about generalisation. Radcliffe-Brown played a role in the elaboration of this version of Boas, as we shall see below.

Boas's project was also remembered as straddling a different and equally troublesome rift: that between a holist vision of cultures as coherent meaningful totalities, and a diffusionist view of cultures as a mere contingent assemblages of traits. In this view (Eggan 1954: 749–750; Handler 2009: 631–633; Stocking 1989), Boas performed an admirable but unstable balancing act. His insistence on the simultaneous study of diffusion and integration within culture areas is in some ways analogous, structurally speaking, to Durkheim's 'genetic method' of seeking both the analysis and the synthesis of phenomena simultaneously. But – in this account – Boas's balancing act could not be sustained by his students and followers. For some of them, 'Culture came to be viewed as a mere aggregation of traits brought together by the accidents of diffusion' (Eggan 1954: 750), whereas for others[8] a consideration of the 'distinct psychological causes' of seemingly similar phenomena eventually led to the sense of cultural integration and cultural relativism of the culture and personality school.

In other words, on this view, Boas gave shape to the mapping problem which would continue to haunt comparatists on both sides of the Atlantic, what Handler and others have called 'the unit problem' (Handler 2009: 629; see also Kuper 2002), or rather the problem of the interrelation of units and traits. This is in essence the fundamental difficulty with any mereographic (part–whole) comparison, which we encountered in the previous chapter and which has been identified again and again in the history of the discipline: mereographic comparison is meaningless without the core assumption that phenomena within cultures or societies are linked together in some systematic way, even while its key technique is, precisely, to decontextualise these phenomena in order to compare them.

Reconstructions of a core ambivalence at the heart of Boas's project encourage us to see it retrospectively, and anachronistically, as the synthesis of two subsequent positions: diffusionism and holistic relativism. An alternative account, by Gildas Salmon (2013a), characterises Boas's vision of comparison as a translation into anthropology of a particular set of principles drawn from comparative grammar and evolutionary biology. Drawing on Foucault (1970),[9] Salmon characterises the comparative approach of both of those disciplines in the nineteenth century as a move away from typology – the organisation of particulars into broader categories. By contrast, biological or grammatical comparisons operate on families of variants. Their units are not abstracted classes of beings but rather congeries of particular individuals, related to each other through specific historical transformations. Thus, for instance, Darwinian evolutionism happens ultimately, not to 'species' – which are little more than a convenient typological heuristic for designating groupings of animals – but to concrete populations of individuals (Salmon 2013a: 201). Indeed this opposition between 'typological thinking' and 'population thinking' has become a classic way in which historians of science mark the break between creationist and Darwinian biologies (Mayr 1959; cf. Amundson 1998). The Darwinian revolution, goes the usual story,[10] involved a move from species as eternal abstract types, Platonic *eidos*, ideas in the mind of God, to the tracing of constant variation amongst concrete populations of individuals in environments. Similarly, it is not social types (as in Tylor's or Durkheim's cases), but actual cultures, which form the object of Boas's comparatism.

These cultures are historically related to each other, like the 'populations' of evolutionary biology, through multiple, complex and contingent paths. Thus, one could reformulate a large proportion of

Boas's caveat about the plurality of causes in the vocabulary of evolutionary phylogenetics. That discipline, when it encounters traits shared between organisms, seeks to distinguish homologies (traits inherited from a common ancestor) from homoplasies (traits evolved independently in two separate lineages), and when it encounters different traits in related organisms seeks to distinguish which is 'ancestral' (present in their most recently shared ancestor) and which 'derived' (produced by mutation in one branch of the tree; see Sober 2000: 177). To these genealogical questions inherited analogically from evolutionary thinking, Boas added the importance of lateral transmission, specific to cultural and linguistic variation (Salmon 2013a: 209).

By starkly opposing his reconstruction of Boas's method to the 'typological' comparatisms of Tylor and Durkheim, Salmon is perhaps a tad uncharitable to the latter. There was more going on there, as we saw above, than the mere identification of similarities in view of organising particulars into broader categories. Nevertheless, Salmon's account has the benefit of giving a coherent vision of Boasian comparatism as a concrete alternative to the Comparative Method which Boas's critical writing excoriated. This reconstruction makes sense of Boas's claim that his method could simultaneously take on the account of particulars and the search for laws, and it echoes the visions of a recent generation of scholars who have sought in the original sophistication of Boas's views of culture some solutions to contemporary anthropological problems (Bashkow 2004; Bashkow et al. 2004; Bunzl 2004; Orta 2004).

## Fork 3. Comparison vs Description: Varieties of Functionalist Hope

### The Rise of Single-Case Comparison

Why is a single instance, in some cases, sufficient for a complete induction, while in others, myriads of concurring instances, without a single exception known or presumed, go such a very little way towards establishing an universal proposition? Whoever can answer this question knows more of the philosophy of logic than the wisest of the ancients, and has solved the problem of induction.

(Mill 1856: 344)

[Malinowski] never thought strictly in comparative terms. His generalizations jump straight from the Trobrianders to Humanity, as undoubtedly he saw the Trobrianders as a particularly instructive species of Humanity.

(Nadel 1957a: 190)

By the early twentieth century, a new contrast emerged which in some quarters eclipsed the one outlined in the previous section. This derived from the focus on the careful delineation of single case studies, spearheaded by Bronislaw Malinowski's functionalism, in opposition to broader historical questioning. From this perspective, the alternative opened up by Boas came to seem less than radical. As Evans-Pritchard later noted, 'the functionalist anthropologists ... regarded the fight between evolutionists and diffusionists as a family quarrel between ethnologists and none of their affair' (1951: 47).

On the face of it, the Malinowskian position might evoke the deeply entrenched contrast recurrently drawn, throughout the history of anthropology, between particularising descriptions and generalising comparisons. Thus it seemed obvious to later commentators such as Radcliffe–Brown, to whose position we return below, that the rise of carefully contextualised, holistic field-studies in the Malinowskian mould had drawn attention away from 'comparative studies' (see also Nadel 1957a: 190; Radcliffe-Brown 1951: 15; cf. Strathern 1981: 666). Indeed, Malinowski himself, in *Argonauts of the Western Pacific*, frequently evokes the distinction between single case studies and comparative generalisation, distinguishing his own 'pure ethnographical description' of the Trobriand case from sociological or comparative research (Malinowski 1922: 100; see also 169, 516).

And yet I will suggest that this is not quite the whole story. The previous section has argued that Boas's challenge to the Comparative Method was itself comparative. In the opposition between comparative and historical methods we found, not an argument about whether or not anthropologists should compare, but rather – again – two visions of *how* they should compare. The same is importantly true of the Malinowskian position. This too, properly considered, proposed an alternative comparatism, rather than an alternative *to* comparatism. This is what I want to capture through the seemingly paradoxical notion of a 'single-case comparison'.

For indeed, if we look in detail at *Argonauts*, we will find that a number of comparative moves underpin Malinowski's descriptions. If we follow Malinowski's explicit invocations of comparison in *Argonauts*, we find three different kinds of comparative moves, each with its own logic. The first two look 'inside' the case under consideration, while the third looks 'outside' it. The first kind of comparison operates on observed 'particulars'. As a methodological treatise for ethnography, *Argonauts* represents one of the first – and indeed, in the history of anthropology, one of surprisingly few – careful statements of the practice whereby ethnographic knowledge is built up from the ethnographic observation of particulars (for another, see Descola 2005a). As Malinowski makes clear, this operates through a careful comparison of particular instances, events and 'cases' – 'Each phenomenon ought to be studied through the broadest range possible of its concrete manifestations; each studied by an exhaustive survey of detailed examples' (Malinowski 1922: 17) – sorting out the unusual from the representative, the sincere from the mechanical and so forth (Malinowski 1922: 13, 426). Malinowski formulates this principle of exhaustive comparison of detailed examples, and their organisation, where possible, into a synoptic chart, as 'the method of statistic documentation by concrete evidence' (1922: 17). This lies somewhere in between Evans-Pritchard's moves of 'translation' and 'abstraction'; through it, Malinowski describes the process whereby the ethnographer comes *simultaneously* to understand and to produce a systematic account of his or her object by comparing particular fieldwork experiences. He also suggests a point we shall return to in Chapter 5, namely the quantitative implications of qualitative accounts.

Here, on a smaller scale, we have the same vision of a careful generalisation by induction that we have already encountered earlier in this chapter on the scale of grand comparisons between cultures or social types: from fourteen observed instances of the Kula (Malinowski 1922: 16), whose particulars were compared and tabulated and re-tabulated 'at least half a dozen times' (Malinowski 1922: 13), emerges finally the broader description of the Kula as an institution. This is a limited generalisation, which aims at the level of the phenomenon itself (the Kula, for instance, Magic, or 'Trobriand Man'), but not necessarily beyond.

A second type of comparison operates also 'within the case': this works, however, not across instances of the same phenomenon, but specifically across different domains or aspects of culture. Malinowski singles out these particular comparisons as theoretically promising. For instance:

There is one aspect of the Kula, however, to which attention must be drawn from the point of view of its theoretical importance. We have seen that this institution presents several aspects closely intertwined and influencing one another ... [I]t seems to me that a deeper analysis and comparison of the manner in which two aspects of culture functionally depend on one another might afford some interesting material for theoretical reflection. Indeed, it seems to me that there is room for a new type of theory.

(Malinowski 1922: 515)

And thus we return, on the scale of differences within a single case, to the functionalist concern with concomitant variation, already in evidence in Tylor's grand evolutionist comparisons. There is thus something of a sleight of hand, as has been often noted, in Malinowski's claim to have originated a 'new' functionalist theory. The shift in this vision – what is 'new' about the theory Malinowski proposes – is the strict detachment of functional questions from evolutionary ones. Tylor's comparisons used the evidence of both function and lapses in function to reconstruct a series of stages and survivals. Malinowski's attention to concomitant variation foregrounds functional relations in order to produce an account of one case as a coherent totality.

The third kind of comparison will seem the most obvious to modern readers of Malinowski, given how central this move has become in understandings of what anthropology is all about. These are what I described in the introduction as 'frontal comparisons' between aspects of Trobriand reality and that which Malinowski then thought of as 'our own' (see also discussion in Chua and Mathur 2018). Malinowski invokes this move explicitly as 'comparison' in two passages which repay closer reading. In one, he famously compares Kula valuables to crown jewels. The purpose of the comparison is partly to clarify his description of the Kula, but it also contains an implicit response to the Boasian challenges concerning the identification of the same phenomenon in different societies:

The comparison with the European heirlooms or Crown jewels was given in order to show that this type of ownership is not entirely a fantastic South Sea custom, untranslatable into our ideas. For – and this is a point I want to stress – the comparison I have made is not based on purely external, superficial similarity. The psychological and sociological forces at work are the same, it is really the same mental attitude which makes us value our heirlooms, and makes the natives in New Guinea value their vaygu'a.

(Malinowski 1922: 91)

The other instance is instructive because it makes the more general point that the identification of order or structure in 'primitive societies' is the preliminary to making them comparable:

It is a very far cry from the famous answer given long ago by a representative authority who, asked, what are the manners and customs of the natives, answered, 'Customs none, manners beastly,' to the position of the modem

Ethnographer! This latter, with his tables of kinship terms, genealogies, maps, plans and diagrams, proves the existence of an extensive and big organisation, shows the constitution of the tribe, of the clan, of the family; and he gives us a picture of the natives subjected to a strict code of behaviour and good manners, *to which in comparison the life at the Court of Versailles or Escurial was free and easy.*

(Malinowski 1922: 11, emphasis added)

In sum, Malinowski's frontal comparisons between 'us and them' could be carried, both by an interpretive observation about shared psychological causes, and by an appeal to the existence of similar structures. In both cases these frontal comparisons are explicitly geared to establishing the continuity between Trobriand culture and 'our own'. The impetus was universalising, and the device recalls Mill's Method of Agreement – it consisted in suggesting a general point by pointing to a similarity between otherwise radically different instances.

One could read this move in two ways, however. The first was as a sort of methodological prolegomenon to description, a way of establishing intelligibility, for the purpose of one specific account. In this view, the proper role of comparisons between 'us' and them' – as of the other two kinds of comparisons 'within the case' described above – was to enable the description of particular cases. This description in turn would be methodologically subservient to (large-scale) comparison 'proper'. Evans-Pritchard was articulating that very attitude when he placed frontal comparison (his 'translation') at the beginning of the process of anthropological knowledge production, noting: '[the anthropologist] translates from one culture to another. At this level social anthropology remains a literary and impressionistic art' (Evans-Pritchard 1950: 121). On this view, one might say that for the Malinowski of *Argonauts*, as for later proponents of a more fully frontal anthropology, 'comparison is in the service of translation and not the opposite' (Viveiros de Castro 2004: 5).

But Malinowski's polite disinterest (in *Argonauts* at least) in those further lateral comparative moves invites a more radical reading of this reversal of polarities. Frontal comparisons between 'us' and 'them' could be read not simply as a device for pinpointing the particular, but also as a device for scaling phenomena straight up from one case to humanity in general. What most discomfited later partisans of the Comparative Method such as Radcliffe-Brown or Nadel – as Strathern has noted (Strathern 1981: 666) – was Malinowski's tendency to bypass the Comparative Method entirely and move to the general straight from the particular. Malinowski's informants in the Trobriands came to stand for 'Primitive Man' in a frontal encounter with 'us' – and where the two coincided, Malinowski induced 'Man' *tout court*. To critics such as Radcliffe-Brown or Nadel, there was a sleight of hand there, a refusal to submit to proper lateral comparative methods of generalisation. As Fortes regretfully noted, 'It has taken twenty years for the Trobrianders to be placed in a proper comparative perspective in British social anthropology' (Fortes 1953: 19).

Before we turn to how 'a proper comparative perspective' came to be envisioned, let us pause to draw one key conclusion from Malinowski's case. Even if one agrees to name as 'Comparative Method' a particular procedure operating upon social systems on a global scale, and as 'description' the production of case studies which are to be fed into that method, Malinowski's case reminds us that this 'description' itself rests on comparisons, on a smaller scale or in a different direction. This is a well-worn point – the ubiquity of comparison as a basic cognitive technique for encountering the world – which we encountered in the introduction. But its radical implication must not be underestimated: taken seriously, the fact that descriptions rest on comparisons, just as comparisons rest on descriptions, troubles the distinction between the two, and suggests that attempts to articulate them into a stable hierarchy are likely to prove unstable. This will become a key point of the argument of the second part of this book.

## Typology Reborn: Radcliffe-Brown and the 'Art of Subsuming'

Without systematic comparative studies, anthropology will become only historiography and ethnography.

(Radcliffe-Brown 1951: 16)

... anthropology was the art of subsuming

(Salmon 2013a: 195)

In one of the most famous contributions to anthropological debates about comparison, Alfred Reginald Radcliffe-Brown (1951) entered the lists in defence of the method, in its classic, generalising and rule-seeking inductive form – the method of those he himself called the 'arm-chair anthropologists' (Radcliffe-Brown 1951: 15). Radcliffe-Brown had both Malinowski and Boas in his sights – and also, more proximally, Evans-Pritchard, whose Marett Lecture lambasting Radcliffe-Brown's scientific pretensions for anthropology, and assimilating anthropology and history, was delivered the previous year.

But the gauntlet picked up by Radcliffe-Brown was subtly different to the one that Boas had thrown down. In effect, Radcliffe-Brown subverted Boas's own claims about the Historical Method's ability to take on both particulars and the search for laws. Radcliffe-Brown revoked also the contrast opened by Malinowski between 'pure ethnographical description' and various forms of historical speculation. For Radcliffe-Brown (1952: 1–3), historiography and ethnography – Boas and Malinowski, one might say – lay on one side of a newly sharpened divide: both were merely *idiographic* pursuits of particular descriptions, while social anthropology (a branch of 'comparative sociology') represented the *nomothetic* search for general propositions.

Thus recast and, as it were, 'de-fanged', Boas becomes less an enemy than an ally in Radcliffe-Brown's search for the distinctiveness of 'comparative sociology'. Anthropology is characterised by two methods, Radcliffe-Brown claimed:

One is the 'historical' method, by which the existence of a particular feature in a particular society is 'explained' as the result of a particular sequence of events. The other is the comparative method by which we seek, not to 'explain,' but to understand a particular feature of a particular society by *first* seeing it as a particular instance of a general kind or class of social phenomena, *and then* by relating it to a certain general, or preferably a universal, tendency in human societies. Such a tendency is what is called in certain instances a law.

(Radcliffe-Brown 1951: 22, emphasis added)

We can see how far this formulation has moved from Boas's position as characterised in the previous fork. But what is also of interest is the subtle game Radcliffe-Brown is playing with the notions of explanation and understanding. Indeed, the use of these notions in the passage might strike the unwary reader as strange. After all, we expect Radcliffe-Brown to claim explanatory power for his own, comparative sociology, and leave only the crumbs of description and 'understanding' to the historian. It is precisely in terms of such a distinction between positivism and interpretation that Evans-Pritchard had, the previous year, savaged Radcliffe-Brown's narrowly 'explanatory' ambitions (Evans-Pritchard 1950). In implicit response, Radcliffe-Brown plays a clever game with two terms which, *de facto*, are sometimes used interchangeably in the epistemological literature: explaining and understanding. He defuses Evans-Pritchard's charge by evoking, and allowing to subsist side by side, three competing accounts of explanation (cf. Godfrey-Smith 2003: chapter 13). One – causal explanation – he reserves for history. Another, as expected, he retains as the special prerogative of social anthropology, under the rubric of 'understanding': this is the 'Deductive-Nomological' theory of explanation favoured, precisely, by the logical positivists of the Vienna Circle. On this view, to explain (or understand) a phenomenon is to be able to derive it in a logical argument which includes a law of nature (Godfrey-Smith 2003: chapter 13).

Note that the notion of law here is much more heavily caveated than Radcliffe-Brown is usually given credit for. Like Mill (1856:455) before him, Radcliffe-Brown made explicit that 'laws' were to be understood merely as 'tendencies', quite far from the simpleminded determinism with which the idea of functional 'social laws' is often associated. Mill's discussion makes the logic of this caveat explicit: the common observation that every law has exceptions would by itself make a nonsense of the very idea of a law. The point can, however, be reformulated by stating that effects are usually the confluence of multiple causes, and thus the point of application of multiple 'laws', each in itself absolute. This vision of compound effects reintroduces space for a large measure of variation and complexity, particularly in social phenomena.

This might be part of the explanation for the often noted fact that Radcliffe-Brown's purported search for functional 'social laws' yielded meagre and disappointing results (Evans-Pritchard 1950). In this paper, for all its bombastic reference to laws of social statics and social dynamics, the only actual 'law' suggested is a pretty tautological affair, namely the 'law' that wherever there exist moieties in society, these are thought of as being in what Radcliffe-Brown terms a relation of 'opposition' – a union of opposites (Radcliffe-Brown 1951: 18). Since the notion of 'opposition' has been derived from the example of moieties, this is a faint 'law' indeed – little more, in fact, than a broader reformulation of one aspect of the very notion of moiety itself. In sum, Radcliffe-Brown's much trumpeted search for laws is actually envisaged as a rather distant and caveated goal, a pious wish.

Crucially, however, the search for laws is only half of what 'understanding' is for Radcliffe-Brown. The first, prior step is typological generalisation itself. Comparative understanding, he suggests, requires one *first* to classify and *then* to search for laws. This stepwise approach is not new – we saw it in the comparative methods of Tylor and Durkheim. What is new, however, is a distinct shift in emphasis. It is with classification, I would argue, rather than with nomological explanation that, in practice, Radcliffe-Brown's comparative enthusiasms and attentions really lie.

Typological 'understanding' operates through the progressive move upwards in generality from particulars – Mill's 'abstraction'. Small things are shown to be instances of bigger ones. Thus the exemplification of comparative method given in Radcliffe-Brown's paper takes us from the dual organisation of tribes in New South Wales, via the observation of a more general tendency to invoke birds as emblems for social groups, to the broader category of totemism, to a general, and perhaps universal, cognitive and social principle of 'opposition'. To understand here is, indeed, to subsume – to comprehend.

Despite claims to be recovering the Comparative Method, then, there is a distinct shift in emphasis from the method articulated by nineteenth-century comparatists. While he recuses their interest in historical matters, Radcliffe-Brown shares with the nineteenth-century comparatists an interest in typology, and a functionalist vision of societies as organisms made up of interrelated parts, discoverable through concomitant variation. But the relation between these two elements – typology and functionalism – is transformed. For Tylor or Durkheim, typology – the organisation of societies into simple and complex, the identification of the same 'customs' in different cases – was a preliminary to the study of concomitant variations, which revealed the historical transformation of functional interdependencies. Durkheim did have quite a lot to say about the proper drawing up of typologies, on which more below. However, this was emphatically a preliminary. With Radcliffe-Brown, typology comes to occupy the centre stage, partly because of the intervening critiques of the Comparative Method, by Boas and others, which had made the drawing up of typologies seem so problematic. What Radcliffe-Brown is really bent on demonstrating, in this paper, is not the power of the Comparative Method for discovering (implicitly functionalist) 'laws' – of that, as we have seen, this paper gives little serious evidence – but rather the possibility of typologising, which implicitly becomes a means of understanding in its own right, not so much a preliminary for comparison, as its key outcome. What Salmon wrote of Tylor is fully the case with Radcliffe-Brown: here anthropology truly becomes the 'art of subsuming' (Salmon 2013a: 195).[11]

## Regional and Distant Comparisons: Radcliffe-Brown's Zig-Zag

Key to Radcliffe-Brown's ability to reclaim the ground of the Comparative Method after Boas's critique is a particular device which turns on a successive and alternating deployment of comparisons between distant and closely related societies – comparisons of the near and the far. As we saw above, Boas had set up an opposition between the uncontrolled comparisons of evolutionists who picked and chose cultures without regard to their actual historical relations, and the carefully controlled regional comparison of related cultures in a local area. This opposition tied control to the local, and made generalisation seem inherently dubious. Malinowski had shown, by contrast, that close and distant comparisons could be played off one another to productive effect. As we saw above, in a monograph such as *Argonauts*, tiny comparisons of ethnographic particulars within a particular case were combined with distant comparisons between 'them' and 'us', to shape the coherence of a case study, an 'example' which simultaneously spoke to something more than itself alone (cf. Højer and Bandak 2015). Here again, however, it was the use of distant comparisons to generalise that had come under fire.

Radcliffe-Brown articulated the near and the far to a different effect again, namely to defeat Boasian strictures against the possibility of meaningful generalisation. In a cursory view, the example of comparative analysis which Radcliffe-Brown presents in the paper we have been discussing relies on moving 'up' from one particular case (the dual organisation of tribes in New South Wales) to a universal one (the putatively universal principle or law of 'opposition'). But on a closer examination, the path this subsumption takes is actually an intricate zig-zag. The discussion begins with 'a few tribes in new South Wales' which share a very particular feature: they are organised in matrilineal exogamous moieties characterised by reference to birds. It then moves continents, to the Haida of north-west America, to find, there too, this very specific feature – matrilineal exogamous moieties characterised by birds. The tightness of the analogy – even the *species* of birds evoked by the Haida (eagle and raven) 'correspond very closely indeed to the eaglehawk and crow of Australia' – combined with a huge geographic distance, is a device for defeating the Galton/Boas problem of the diffusion of shared traits. To a diffusionist, Radcliffe-Brown notes, this similarity would have been evidence of a historical connection between the two peoples. He leaves this observation hanging. The comment could be read as sarcasm – a demonstration of the inanity of diffusionism. More profoundly, however, it suggests that the whole question of derivation is in effect epiphenomenal, has no bearing on what is so clearly of interest here, namely the structural similarity between the two instances. Any historical link would have to have been deep indeed, and there could be no *contemporary* relation between these two instances. In sum, a combination of tight categorisation and great geographic distance contributes to cementing the solidity of the form Radcliffe-Brown identifies. To all intents and purposes, comparisons across wide expanses of space and/or time involve variables which are 'independent' from the point of view of conceptual or structural coherence. Whether they are historically related through diffusion, or effects of independent developments – whether they are, to reprise an earlier distinction, 'homologies' or 'homoplasies' – becomes an interesting but separate question.

In the next move, Radcliffe-Brown does the converse: he returns to Australia, and loosens the conceptual framework, to take in other kinds of dual, moiety-like organisations – patrilineal moieties, divisions of the society by sex and by age-set – all of them associated with species. The comparative device here is the opposite of the previous one, which established the reality of a very specific form through a distant comparison. Here a comparison of putatively related societies within a 'region' seeks to map different local variants of this form, which are then compared to pull out the core principles they all share. In this way, Radcliffe-Brown broadens his initial definition, producing a more general and more abstract 'problem'. Matrilineal exogamous moieties characterised by reference to birds turn out to have been a subset of a more general and more abstract set: social divisions characterised by reference to birds.

These two complementary moves, distant and regional comparisons, continue to alternate throughout the paper, which travels back and forth – with frequent returns to Australian particulars – to the Andaman Islands, Cambridge and Oxford, ancient Greece and pre-World War II China.

This is no quasi-evolutionist progression through increasing stages of complexity, as in Durkheim and Mauss, nor is there any attempt to reconstruct a sequence as in Tylor. In fact, Radcliffe-Brown occasionally pauses to consider possible historical connections – did the ancient Greek concern with binary oppositions come from China via the Pythagoreans? Could it have related to the social structure of ancient societies in the Yellow River area? – and in each case again, these problems emerge as interwoven with but ultimately separate from the increasingly clear and simple conceptual feature which Radcliffe-Brown is slowly elaborating: the principle of the union of opposites. Through this principle, geographic and historical distance are finally eliminated: 'This Yin–Yang philosophy of ancient China is the systematic elaboration of the principle that can be used to define the social structure of moieties in Australian tribes' (Radcliffe-Brown 1951: 21). The route to this typological achievement, however, doesn't simply follow a path of generalisation by increasing the distance across which comparisons are mapped. Rather Radcliffe-Brown's Comparative Method zig-zags through space and time in a sequence of alternations between regional and distant comparison, each with its particular, complementary, effects. Showing the same feature in distant and putatively unrelated societies establishes the reality of a typological form. Teasing out the deeper commonality between different forms in a local area allows a move up the scale of abstraction and generality.

One might say, then, that in response to the Boasian challenge, Radcliffe-Brown took what was formerly a mere preliminary step of the Comparative Method – typology – and, I would argue, allowed it to take over from functionalist 'explanation' as comparison's key aim.[12] Typology also assumed a new technical shape through the device of alternating regional and distant comparisons. This device subverted Boas's own distinction between safe regional comparisons and hazardous comparisons of unrelated cases. Here, both kinds of comparisons were combined to achieve the aim of a solid typology.

## Varieties of Generalisation at Mid-century

This distinction between regional and distant comparison, and more broadly the interweaving of control and generalisation, became a central theme of often impassioned debates around comparative method in the mid-twentieth century (Eggan 1954; Lewis 1955). In this contrast the potentially radical 'historical method' proposed by Boas was tamed as, in effect, just a call for careful 'control'.

A telling node in these mid-century debates concerns George P. Murdock's grand attempt in *Social structure* to ground comparative generalisations about human kinship in a statistical treatment of 250 different societies worldwide. Although not claiming to have achieved this in his book, Murdock's vision was that of basing comparison on 'a statistically representative sample of all known cultures, primitive, historical, and contemporary' (Murdock et al. 1950: xii). This work drew upon and showcased the growing Cross-Cultural Survey database which Murdock had established at Yale University's Institute of Human Relations. Later renamed the Human Relations Area Files, this collection of indexed ethnographic materials on – currently – around

400 societies in the world (History and Development of the HRAF Collections 2013) continues to be used by scholars seeking comparative answers to questions about human universals (Jankowiak et al. 2015). As articulated by its proponents, the method pioneered by Murdock aimed at 'a worldwide survey of … all known primitive cultures, seeking to test by means of mathematical statistics theoretical generalizations about human society or cultures' (Naroll 1970: 1227).

Murdock's reintroduction of a statistical imaginary broadly dormant since Tylor, reframed in the context of the discussions above, represented the furthest stretch of the polarity between global and regional comparison. Some mid-century authors such as Eggan, whose own preference lay in regionally grounded comparatism, nevertheless felt that accommodation between Murdock's visions of global statistical correlation and regional controlled comparison was conceivable (Eggan 1954: 756, 759).

Other partisans of regional comparison, such as Isaac Schapera, soon pointed out that Murdock's book suffered not only from a failure to adhere to its own methodological and sampling principles (Schapera and Singer 1953: 357–359), but also, and more profoundly, from a fundamental inability to address the 'unit' problem. The difficulty of defining statistically independent units struck again, as it had for the previous grand statistical visions of Tylor. Schapera's objection was, however, more profound than Galton's and Boas's points about the borrowing of cultural traits – which Murdock had in any case sought to disarm through a 'historical' appendix (1949: ix–x, 323–352). Rather, Schapera went for the nub of the question: for what, after all, is to count as 'a society' or 'a culture' in the first place? Murdock, argued Schapera, was thoroughly confused about this – admittedly irresolvable – question (Schapera and Singer 1953: 357–359). Schapera's proposed alternative was to return to regional comparisons, within which a fairly complete survey could be undertaken and meaningful generalisations about types of institutions could actually be generated, albeit only ever relative to a particular problem. The point was – following Radcliffe-Brown's lead – to compare not individual societies, but rather shared structural forms (see also Fortes 1953).

A radically different set of possibilities were opened up at the intersection of comparison and description, by Manchester School anthropologists' experiments with 'extended-case' studies (Englund 2018; Van Velsen 1967). The starting point was Gluckman's pioneering *Analysis of a social situation in modern Zululand* (Gluckman 1958 [1949]), a single case focused on the closely described interactions and tensions between people from different social groups: Zulu, Swedish missionaries and South African officials. As in Malinowski's case above, this was a description to which comparison was internal, but in a radically different way and to a radically different effect. By moving the frame towards the intersection of groups, comparisons pointed not to holistic coherence ('their culture', which could be scaled up through a contrast with 'ours'), but rather to tensions which spoke directly to global questions of colonialism, racism, political economy and the spread of Christianity. Here again, as in Malinowski's example – but through a very different dynamic – a single, particular case could speak directly to 'general' questions, without the need for an elaborate comparative zig-zag. The shift from situational analysis towards an 'extended case methodology', in which specific actors were followed through time and through structural changes, brought history back into the picture, rearticulating forms of explanation which Radcliffe-Brown had sought to keep apart (Englund 2018).

In sum, the master contrast between comparing and describing in mid-century anthropology proliferated into a number of sub-contrasts. On the one hand, those seeking to build comparative generalisations out of descriptive cases disagreed over the scale at which such generalisation could prove meaningful, and the respective role of comparisons bearing on the near and on the far. On the other, those who focused on the drawing up of cases diverged in the role played by comparison within cases themselves. History could be put to different uses in each of these positions, which could in turn be recombined in multiple ways. Comparative visions proliferated – this was the period in which Lewis, seeking to overview the field, found he had to discuss twenty-eight separate works which sought explicitly to theorise anthropological comparison, published within the space of only four years (Lewis 1955: 262–263).

And yet, these very different visions shared a language: they invoked and reconfigured broadly shared contrasts between culture and society, the particular and the general, history and structure. While often at odds about the ways in which social facts ought to be classified and compared and on what scale, these very different positions were grounded in a broad agreement that classification and comparison of empirical material to reach broader theoretical conclusions was in principle possible. They shared also an essentially mereographic aesthetic, in which the key problem of comparison was the tension between contextualising and decontextualising parts taken from broader wholes. While particular positions were crafted in fierce opposition to each other, the vision of a basically productive coexistence of different comparative techniques and different explanatory projects was accessible.

Evans-Pritchard's account of comparison, outlined in the previous chapter, was one such vision. It can be read as an intervention into these arguments about the relative place of description and comparison, where it offered a compromise of sorts, while also striking out in a new direction. It reminded readers of the inherently comparative nature of the act of building case studies – even though his own language, in which such comparisons between us and them are translations, and his labelling of his own method as 'experimental' rather than comparative, still registers the prevailing association of comparison with the grand nomothetic enterprise of Radcliffe-Brown. In Evans-Pritchard's account, however, the tension between the field and the armchair becomes an internal tension within a single process and a single person. Collaboration amongst anthropologists becomes the work of equals: fieldworker/analysts building on each other's ethnographies. The grand armchair generalisations of the past are left behind, as are what he elsewhere dismissed as 'lengthy monographs' full of haphazard observations (Evans-Pritchard 1940: 261). On the horizon lies a systematic collaborative enterprise of fieldworkers driven by and constantly reconfiguring shared theoretical frameworks and questions. The sense of confidence exuding from Evans-Pritchard's account is partly an effect of the combination of early twentieth-century responses to Boas's challenges. Malinowski had dramatised the possibility of cultural translation, Radcliffe-Brown and others had driven home the importance of structural regularities in society – even though they fiercely disagreed over the scale at which these were located. Anthropological comparison was going strong.

## Fork 4. Topology vs Typology: Structuralist Alternatives

My purpose is to distinguish between two rather similar varieties of comparative generalization, both of which turn up from time to time in contemporary British social anthropology. One of these, which I dislike, derives from the work of Radcliffe-Brown; the other, which I admire, derives from the work of Lévi-Strauss.

(Leach 1966: 2)

In its insistence on abstraction, however, Evans-Pritchard's account also bears the mark of a different faultline which emerged at mid-century and produced another profound alternative in visions of comparison – a vision which would soon eclipse the relevance of the functionalist and evolutionist distinction between case studies and comparative generalisation (Salmon 2013b: 7). This was the emergence of a distinctively structuralist comparison, most famously associated with the work of Claude Lévi-Strauss. Lévi-Strauss (1958, 1966) and other structuralist authors, such as Leach (1966), Needham (1975), and in a slightly different vein,

Dumont (1986), who articulated their programme through a frontal opposition to many of the comparatisms we have detailed in the previous section, now subsumed under one general and dismissive heading, namely that of empiricist typologising. In the structuralist view, the cardinal sin of all anthropological attempts to compare to date – and most egregiously amongst these, of the comparative work of British functionalists – had been to seek to build theoretical systems out of the collation of resemblances between empirical particulars. This bespoke a misplaced and naive realism about cultural traits and social institutions, as if these could be picked up and laid side by side like so many seashells on the shore – to use Radcliffe-Brown's memorable image (Leach 1966: 2). The critique was more far-reaching, as we shall see, than Boas's caveat about the multiplicity of causes. It bore on the very possibility of abstracting comparative terms from empirical observations. As Leach notes, generalisation remained the aim of comparison for structuralists, but its meaning had to be radically reconfigured.

The structuralists were ready to make a fresh start. At the heart of their alternative comparative method lay a radical critique of existing procedures of abstraction, a shift from mereography (the question of the relation between parts and wholes) to topology (the study of the transformation of wholes), and a redefinition of the source of regularities in social and cultural life. The next sections take these three points in turn.

## A Problem of Definitions

Recall again Mill's definition of abstraction '[t]he mental operation which extracts from a number of detached observations certain general characters in which the observed phenomena resemble one another' (Mill 1856: 337). A classic approach to typology and classification combines this procedure of abstraction by generalisation, with a mereographic vision of organisms, societies or cultures as wholes with parts. Typology builds up from observed similarities between the parts of organisms or societies, and generalises from these certain 'characters' which can then be used to construct classes, such as 'vertebrates' or 'matrilineal societies'. There is a particular economy of similarity and difference here: individuals, be they organisms or societies, are different, but they can be classified and compared because their parts are similar and can therefore be seen as instances of the same character (Holy 1987: 2).

As I noted above, this particular kind of mereographic typological abstraction was commonly associated with the comparative method, even though it played a different role for different authors: a starting point for Tylor, an end in itself for Radcliffe-Brown. We saw also that this procedure was not uncontested: Boas challenged the anthropological identification of similarities across cultural and historical contexts by noting that these might be mere surface similarities produced by different causes, rather than true instances of the same phenomenon.

There was, however, a more fundamental problem raised by the complexity of the phenomena anthropologists sought to compare, even in the societies they imagined as 'simple'. An early intimation of the difficulty of applying the typological procedure above to social realities – and also, as we shall see below, the first intimations of a 'structuralist' solution for social science – can in fact be found in Durkheim. As we saw above, Durkheim's comparative method required, as a preliminary step, a typological arrangement of societies in a series from the simple to the complex. And yet attempts to classify societies based on differences and similarities between their particular 'characters' are futile. Durkheim noted:

To attempt an inventory of all the characteristics [caractères] peculiar to an individual is an insoluble problem. Every individual is an infinity, and infinity cannot be exhausted. Should we therefore stick to the most essential properties? If so, on what principle will we then make a selection?

(Durkheim 1964: 110)

This observation bears primarily on the problem of typologising whole societies. But the difficulty of classificatory abstraction would soon be stated more comprehensively. The classic statement comes from Wittgenstein, and its most rigorous theoretical exposition in anthropology was articulated much later by Rodney Needham. Needham's critique is distinctively articulated, but it dovetails with other structuralist critiques of functionalist typological comparison. Needham starts from Wittgenstein's observation that verbal concepts are usually formed, not in the systematic way outlined in Mill's account of abstraction, but in fact by *serial* analogies, assembling together particulars which share some similarities and then accreting further particulars which share other similarities, to constitute classes united not by a single shared property, but by a set of *family resemblances* (Needham 1975: 350; Wittgenstein 1973). Needham notes that an analogous vision of classes as effectively loose and open-ended, rather than logically constituted, emerged in biology under the term of 'polythetic sets'. This emerged as a reaction to the move away from pre-Darwinian taxonomies – the move we encountered in the discussion of Boas above. Once species are viewed not as separate created units but as a messy profusion of entities related by descent, it becomes necessary to loosen the principles of one's taxonomies, in such a way as to include, precisely, family resemblances between species (Mayr 1959; Needham 1975: 353).

This polythetic method of constituting classes is, Needham notes, the one which anthropologists have in practice used to define their comparative concepts, such as different 'descent systems'. One can see a detailed example of it in action in Radcliffe-Brown's zig-zagging comparisons of the near and the far, examined above: 'totemism' and, even more obviously, 'opposition' are classes constituted by serial analogies: despite appearances of yielding one simple shared feature, they are actually constituted by picking out not one single respect in which practices resemble each other, but a number of related respects. Indeed, Needham suggests that any attempt to constitute classes in the social sciences can only ever proceed in this way, since 'in social life ... there are no established phenomena, in the form of isolable social facts for instance, which correspond to the elements and particles in nature' (Needham 1975: 364).

This method of constituting classes is practical for the description of messy reality, but it cannot translate into the categories of *substitutable* particulars assumed by formal logic – monothetic, as opposed to poly-thetic sets. Ultimately, through the play of serial resemblances, a poly-thetic set might include particulars which shared no properties at all.

Needham drives the point home by applying it to Murdock's grand taxonomical endeavours in *Social structure* (1949): 'When, therefore, the descent systems under comparison are analysed by polythetic criteria, instead of being typed by a few monothetic features ... the presumed resemblances are reduced or abolished; the comparison is vitiated, and the attempt to work out evolutionary interconnexions is thereby doomed to failure' (Needham 1975: 360). Schapera had critiqued Murdock for believing that societies can count as units, and instead proposed a regional comparison based on the form of social institutions. Needham holds Murdock up as an exemplar of the naive belief in *any* kind of stable typology of isolable social facts. The abstraction had to become *more abstract.*

Polythetic sets, Needham noted, are a convenient device for describing ethnographic and historical reality – as such, anthropologists cannot do without them, any more than anyone else can. But the theoretical work of anthropological comparison cannot be built out of them. At that level, a 'formal theoretical terminology' needs to be built, not up from particulars, but rather from logical contrasts and oppositions – sym-metry, alternation, transitivity, complementarity (Needham 1975: 365).

To borrow a later distinction from Alfred Gell (1999: 52), one might say that the split highlighted by Needham – in line with other structur-alist thinkers – points to a distinction between two orders of relations. The 'formal theoretical terminologies' devised by anthropologists are made up of 'internal' relations – relations between terms which are defined only by their place in a system. Paradigmatic systems of 'internal' relations are mathematics, formal logic, or language in a structuralist view. In each of these, a term is strictly defined – exhausted – by its relations to other terms. The relations are 'internal' here, in the sense that they belong within a theoretical system. Such systems, be they the system of logic, mathematics or semiotics, are simply in this sense *collections of differences*: this is this insofar as it is not that.

While a philosophical idealist might seek to withdraw completely within such a closed system, realists of various stripes usually conceive of another kind of relationality, which is not contained within a theoretical system. Outside or beyond the system, on this view, lies a 'real world': the empirical experiential reality which anthropologists and other people encounter and seek to make sense of is not a system, but a messy and contingent assemblage of elements whose relations to one another are of various kinds – historical, causal and so forth. By contrast to the 'internal relations' which constitute terms within a system, Gell characterises these as 'external relations' – 'relations between objects which are theoretically independent of one another' (Gell 1999: 33). These relations can be similarities or differences and there is no a priori reason to assume they form a system of any kind.[13]

The problem of abstraction, in this view, could be recast as the problem of passing from the realm of external relations to the realm of internal relations. The classic Millian procedure of abstracting from the former to the latter is what Needham and the structuralists sought to disallow. This kind of abstraction relies on what we could call *caveated generalisations*. For instance, on the face of it, Radcliffe-Brown's zig-zagging procedure might seem to yield a formal concept of precisely the kind Needham has in mind: the logical notion of opposition. But the method of its production is what Needham takes issue with. In his move towards abstraction, Radcliffe-Brown had made the basic empiricist move of abstracting categories upwards from observed similarities. He had simply controlled for Boas's caveats about multiple causes, by tracking similarities across related and distant examples. Through this procedure, Radcliffe-Brown felt he could move 'up', through successive abstractions, from specific practices described in Australia, to 'the principle of opposition', through a set of intervening and increasingly abstract abstractions (matrilineal exogamous moieties, totemism, etc.). The multiple attempts to 'control' comparisons, the endless methodological musings at mid-century about proper ways of working up from case studies, were all worrying away at this problem of how one might articulate a description of particulars with a comparative generalisation.

On Needham's view, however, this was all more or less wasted time. *Any* procedure seeking to bridge the gap between the messy world of family resemblances and the clear-cut world of logical categories will necessarily require a series of fudges. At every step, it will be taking things with a pinch of salt. This is roughly what biologists do when they invoke polythetic sets. This is also what anthropologists do when they claim that social facts, customs, traits, societies themselves and the broader categories to which these societies belong can be defined 'well enough' as long as one takes these definitions with a pinch of salt and controls them in various ways. Needham relentlessly hunts down such fudges between empirical particulars and abstract concepts in the work of biologists and anthropologists alike. The singlemindedness of Needham's attack on the pinch of salt deserves quoting at length:

In Beckner's formulation, as he points out, 'the vague term "large number" occurs twice in the definition' (24), and there is no rule of method for deciding in general, or for any given context, what is to count as a large number. The same kind of uncertainty attaches to the phrases 'over-all similarity', 'balances of resemblances', and a 'majority' of characters. No matter how the definition of a polythetic class is expressed, the difficulty is to know where to draw the line. This problem is not resolved by the admission that 'there will always be the possibility of borderline cases' (Beckner 1959: 24), for the location of the border is itself a function of the degree of numerical preponderance that is thought sufficient, and this in principle is always contestable. In any event, the consequence is that 'it is never certain, but only more or less probable, that a member [of a polythetic group] possesses any given feature' (Sokal and Sneath 1963: 171). A numerical taxonomy, therefore, leaves the social anthropologist in much the same definitional quandary as when he is faced with the question what is to count as an instance of a given institution.

(Needham 1975: 362)

What Needham's critique disallows is not caveated generalisation per se – this is fine for the purposes of description – but rather the move from such generalisations into the articulation of a theoretical system. When it comes to the articulation of theoretical arguments, structuralist abstraction had to take a different path. Instead of moving up from observed similarities through increasingly abstract classes to purported universals, the structuralist move seeks to detect within or below the empirical particulars themselves the traces of a closed system of differences. This shift involved a move away from a vision of societies and cultures in terms of parts and wholes, characteristic of functionalism, and towards a concern with the formal properties of whole structures.

## A Structuralist Solution

The *locus classicus* of this revision of the comparative method is in Lévi-Strauss's discussion of totemism (Lévi-Strauss 1963, 1966). Functionalist authors had sought to explain totemism as a set of relations between particular social groups and particular natural species in their environment. These relations were simultaneously symbolic (totems represented the group) and practical (totemic species were chosen because they were of particular pragmatic or aesthetic relevance to the group in question). In both respects, totemism played a functional role – integrating members of the group around their shared symbol, and integrating the social group with its natural environment. Lévi -Strauss unpicked this explanation by noting that no amount of ad hoc explanation could make sense of the particular species chosen. It was only once one let go of the question of a direct link between a particular group and a particular animal – and therefore of the functionalist explanations these links enabled – that one could see totemism for what it was: a relation between, on the one hand, a set of animals, and on the other, a set of human groups. In terms of Gell's distinction above, this means moving attention away from the external relations between objects in the world (particular groups and particular species), each of which would require a particular explanation, and looking instead at the internal relations within, respectively, a system of animals and a system of groups.

Thus redefined, 'totemism' is no longer the name of a class made up of (roughly) similar kinds of social practices across different societies. It becomes the name of a particular arrangement of differential internal relations with its own distinctive structure. Totemism is the name of a structural arrangement made up of a set of natural terms mapped on to a set of social terms. This redefinition of the phenomenon opens up a new path for comparison. It provides a non-polythetic criterion for identifying empirical instances of the phenomenon in the world. More profoundly, it allows totemism to be compared to other versions of the same structural form – the mapping of a system of natural differences on to a system of social differences – on different scales. Thus language itself was seen as the paradigmatic example of this type of structural arrangement – it selected particular sounds from the human vocal spectrum, arranged them into a system, and mapped this system on to a system of meanings. At the highest level of abstraction, totemism is an instance of a particular kind of symbolic thinking which Lévi-Strauss called 'the science of the concrete' (Lévi-Strauss 1966).

The rupture is stark in respect of what I have termed in the previous chapter questions of 'mapping'. Most of the problems and possibilities of anthropological comparison up to this point had been mapped in essentially mereographic terms: they had engaged with social and cultural realities as parts with wholes – societies and institutions, cultures and traits. In one way or another, debates bore on the problems of identifying these parts, wholes and their relations, on the possibility of comparing parts across wholes, or within them, on the dangers of contextualising and decontextualising. With structuralist comparison, this mereographic vision was overtaken by a set of essentially *topological* problems and possibilities which rearticulated proportionality in a different register (Leach 1966: 7). Topology is the branch of mathematics concerned with the properties of space which are preserved through deformation: it looks at the way one structure or form can transform into another.

The fundamental variable in topology is the degree of connectedness. Any closed curve is 'the same as' any other regardless of its shape; the arc of a circle is 'the same as' a straight line because each is open ended. Contrariwise, a closed curve has a greater degree of connectedness than an arc. If we apply these ideas to sociology we cease to be interested in particular relationships and concern ourselves instead with the regularities of pattern among neighbouring relationships.

(Leach 1966: 7)

In a topological vision, one can compare 'regularities of pattern' across different wholes without first reducing them to their constituent parts. As Leach puts it, '[c]onsidered mathematically society is not an assemblage of things but an assemblage of variables' (Leach 1966: 7). Which is another way of saying that structuralists found evidence in social reality itself of the closed systems of internal relations which others had sought to derive by typological abstraction from concrete particulars.

Stated like this, it might be hard to distinguish structuralists from empiricists who had also sought to find patterns in social behaviour. From the current (post-)postmodern vantage point, the structuralists' faith in the existence of deep regularities beneath the messy phenomena of social and cultural life might seem naive. The structuralists' own accusations of naivety against the empiricists who sought to compare social phenomena themselves (like seashells on the shore ...) might thus seem somewhat ironic. But the important point to bear in mind is that the structuralist move shifted the location of regularity in a profound way. It sought the locus of the regularity, and the generative rules forming the observable patterns of social life, not in some natural law acting upon social phenomena directly, but in the ordering properties of the human mind. As Gildas Salmon has argued, in one of the most sophisticated expositions of this logic, the objects of structuralist comparisons were truly 'the structures of the mind' (Salmon 2013b).

Structuralists agreed that systems of internal relations were, of course, a conceptual figment, a human contrivance. Empiricists who sought to build them out of messy particulars of observed social behaviour were naive to think otherwise. But the structuralists' point was that the people anthropologists studied themselves produced such contrivances. There was a system of internal relations to be discovered in empirical social reality because other minds had already put it there:

If we consider that formal terms such as 'symmetry' or 'transitivity' are not peculiar to a particular linguistic and intellectual tradition, but denote properties which must be discriminable (either conceptually or in social practice) by any cultural system of thought, then it follows that the terms are intrinsically appropriate to the study of exotic collective representations. Alternatively, a more speculative notion is that the formal terms denote mental proclivities and constraints which are universal to mankind in the fabrication (deliberate or not) of categories and articulatory relationships. According to either of these conjectures, the kind of theoretical terminology to which I have referred would thus naturally qualify as basic predicates.

(Needham 1975: 366)

Structuralist comparison bore, therefore, not on social facts themselves, but on the generative rules and conceptual ordering principles which had produced them. The structures structuralists discovered in society were indeed things of the mind, logical conceptual relations. But the analyst's mind could discover them because it was of fundamentally the same kind as the mind of the people whose social and cultural lives these were. Thus, while the move to structuralist comparison can be described, on one scale, as a shift from a focus on similarity to a focus on difference – from typological abstraction to the identification of systems of difference – it is grounded, on another scale, on a profound assumption of similarity, indeed of human cognitive universality. This faith in the universal ordering devices of the human mind ultimately underwrote structuralist comparison. It explains, amongst other things, the lighthearted way in which structuralists sometimes waved away the question of whether their identifications of pattern were accurate or mere fictions, and the ease with which they seemed to subordinate empirical reality to formal contrivance. Consider, for instance, Lévi-Strauss's neat summary of the structuralist method:

> The method we adopt ... consists in the following operations: (1) define the phenomenon under study as a relation between two or more terms, *real or supposed*; (2) construct a table of possible permutations between these terms; (3) take this table as the general object of analysis which, at this level only, can yield necessary connections, the empirical phenomenon considered at the beginning being only one possible combination among others, the complete system of which must be reconstructed beforehand.
>
> (Lévi-Strauss 1963: 16, emphasis added)

The aesthetics of this statement is enough to make any empiricist's blood boil: empirical phenomena are reduced to a secondary, subordinate role, merely one outcome of a possible system which the analyst has constructed, based on terms which are described in an offhanded fashion as 'real or supposed'! It is unsurprising that some hard-headed British commentators dismissed structuralism as a mere playful idealism (Douglas 1970; Gellner 1987). But, as long as one believed in the unity of the human mind, structuralism was no such thing. It simply assumed that the same forms of abstraction existed both in the anthropologist's mind and in that of his or her subjects (Needham 1975: 366). Under cover of that assumption, a rigorous enough conceptual analysis by the former should echo the actual principles through which the latter had produced those regularities in the first place (Salmon 2013b: 11–14).

Individual structuralists differed in the way they characterised this universality, however, and later commentators have interpreted them in different ways also. Thus, for instance, Needham's talk of universal cognitive operations is the sort of observation which led some critics to dismiss structuralism as a naive form of cognitive universalism, a theory too beguiled by the metaphor of the mind as binary computer. But one can read a much greater set of subtleties there (e.g. Boon 2009). Salmon, for instance, outlines in Lévi-Strauss's elucidation of the science of the concrete an extremely sophisticated account of the symbolic operations of transformation. It is at the level of this extremely complex symbolic logic – and not in some basic propensity to cognitive binarism, say – that one finds the correspondence between anthropological analytics (the 'transformational analysis' of Lévi-Strauss's study of myths) and the procedures through which myths themselves were produced, through transformational borrowing between cultures (Salmon 2013b, esp. chapter VII).

However that may be, the articulation of similarity and difference is recast: empiricist comparison classified different societies by pointing out that they shared similar parts. Structuralist comparison operates upon systems of differences whose comparability is grounded in the similar cross-cultural operation of the human mind. To return to the terms introduced in the previous chapter, the structuralist revolution in respect of 'mapping' – revolutionising the mereographic vision of cultures as things in the world – was enabled by a profound assumption of similarity in terms of 'communication' – a telepathy of sorts between the mind of the analyst and the mind of the subject.

## A Genealogy of Topology: Structuralism in Biology and Anthropology

Having drawn the contrast quite starkly between structuralism and its alternatives, I will pause in this section to consider a few entanglements which make the distinction less clear-cut. In particular, structuralism is often opposed to functionalism as a vision of anthropology mapped on to linguistics by contrast to one mapped on to biology – and as is well known, the structural linguistics of Saussure and Jakobson was a key conceptual influence on Lévi-Strauss's work. Concomitantly, it has become conventional to distinguish sharply the invocation of 'structure' in the work of British 'structural-functionalist' anthropologists such as Radcliffe-Brown and (the early) Evans-Pritchard – in which structure is taken to refer to an empirical property of actual social systems – and the use of the same term by Lévi-Strauss and later structuralists in France and Britain – in which it is taken to refer, as we saw above, to a conceptual arrangement. This neat contrast is pedagogically useful for avoiding confusions amongst undergraduates, and it does point to important conceptual shifts, as outlined above. But it obscures some profound continuities also between these various invocations of structure. A serious genealogical retracing of the many roots of Lévi-Straussian thinking such as that provided by Salmon (2013b) is beyond the scope of the present account. I will focus merely on one strand of that story, namely the relation between structuralist anthropology and structuralist biology. Recalling that thread of the genealogy gives us a more sophisticated vision of typology, and contributes also to a better understanding of the partial echoes between the structural-functionalism of Radcliffe-Brown and the structuralism of Lévi-Strauss.

To trace this rather more entangled genealogy, let us rewind the tape back to Durkheim's articulation of the problem of typology (Durkheim 1964: 110; see above): since one cannot simply typologise from the 'characters' of a society, how can we identify social species and arrange them into a scale from simple to complex? I noted above that Durkheim's own solution foreshadowed structuralism. It consisted in effect in basing typology on the overall form of societies. It was not the empirical particulars – the actual 'characteristics' – of society that would form the basis of a typology, but an abstract feature of their form. Starting from the abstract possibility of a social unit with no internal subdivision, and working upwards from there, one could distinguish societies into 'species' of increasing complexity: societies made up of simple aggregates of undivided units formed one species, those made up of aggregates of such aggregates formed another, and so on up the great chain of history and complexity which would lead to modern societies (Durkheim 1964: 112–116).

In sum, Durkheim proceeds from an abstract logical operation to define a scale of species as a recursive mathematical progression. The result is a scale of forms, marked by an abstract and arbitrary – but logically consistent – criterion. Durkheim's move is specific to the problem of identifying social species. On other scales – such as when it comes to describing social institutions or social facts – his approach is the classic one of abstraction from empirical particulars, shared with Tylor or Radcliffe-Brown. But on this particular scale, Durkheim – the foremost proponent of the organic analogy – has devised a solution which is distinctive and, as it were, proto-structuralist.

The move echoes and was interwoven with an ongoing tension in nineteenth-century biology, which has been described as, precisely, a tension between continental structuralist biology and British functionalist biology (Amundson 1998; Gould 2002: 251–341). Indeed what Amundson writes of nineteenth-century biology could come straight from the pages of a discussion of mid-twentieth-century anthropology:

The continental biologists favored structural explanations, the British favored functional explanations. Functional facts seemed concrete and empirical to the British, and in comparison the continental structuralist theories (positing hypothetically-inferred unities) seemed transcendental.

(Amundson 1998: 171)

So what exactly was at stake in this biological distinction? Let us follow for a moment Amundson's exposition. The contrast between biological functionalism and biological structuralism cuts across the more famous distinction between creationist and Darwinian biology, but is barely less significant. As Stephen Jay Gould argues in his monumental *The structure of evolutionary theory*, the 'designation of [function or structure] as the causal foundation of biology virtually defines the position of any scientist towards the organic world' (Gould 2002: 252). Amundson focuses on the debates between functionalists and structuralist biologists to recast our understanding of the role played by typology in the nineteenth century. As noted earlier, a classic way of parsing nineteenth-century biology has become to contrast, on the one hand, creationism, associated with a typological vision of species as Platonic ideals – timeless, essential, divinely created – and on the other, Darwinian evolutionism, which ushered in a focus on populations of individuals in particular living conditions, related to each other by descent with modification. This is the story told most prominently by proponents of neo-Darwinism such as Mayr (1959), and it is a loaded one, piling up on the 'losing' side of the shift to Darwinism the conceptual sins of essentialism, idealism, typologism, metaphysics and blind faith in scripture.

Amundson's alternative historiography draws attention to a different and no less acrimonious divide running through pre-Darwinian biology – that between a teleological focus on function and a morphological focus on structure. For most[14] British biologists, the neat adaptation of each species to its particular conditions of existence was an empirically observable fact, and one from which functional conclusions could be drawn without undue speculation. These conclusions were inherently teleological: they explained the form of organisms in relation to their purpose – form was a means to an end. By contrast, the mainly[15] continental biologists whom Amundson calls 'transcendental anatomists' (Amundson 1998: 156) studied embryological development and comparative anatomy for structural patterns, shared elements of form between different species. Backgrounding the question of function, they sought geometrical laws to explain the formal properties of types which cut across the empirical diversity of organisms and species. Many of these highly speculative laws were 'generative' – they showed how, from a shared archetype, a diversity of related forms might be produced through geometrical transformation.

The distinction between teleologists and morphologists does not map neatly on to that between creationists and evolutionists. In both teleological and morphological camps there were wide varieties of philosophical, metaphysical and religious commitments. Thus while functionalism became a mainstay of Darwinian evolutionism – the changing functions of organs being one key point of his demonstrations of the effects of natural selection – it had also been a core feature of the doctrine of British natural theologians, who sought in the exquisite functional adaptation of organisms to their environment the evidence of divine design. The latter were the most fervent critics of the study of formal relations and typologies – these empty categorical abstractions which drew attention away from particularity of species in environments. Conversely, while some transcendental anatomists saw in types an explanation for the origin of species – seeing species in effect as ideas in the mind of God – many treated such theological and historical questions as moot. And through their belief in the empirical reality of types, the morphologists ushered in the vision of a world of gradually related forms which was to play such an important role in Darwin's work. As Amundson puts it:

It is a great irony that 'typology' should have been identified as the philosophical grounding of special creationism. In transcendentalist vocabulary, species are not Types, but at best members or representatives of Types. True special creationists, like the Natural Theologians, denied the reality of Types. The transcendentalist principle of Unity of Type asserts the objective relatedness of some species with other species, and some kinds with other kinds. Without a belief in such a reality there would have been no grounds to hypothesize common ancestors for particular groups of species. Typology, or belief in the objective reality of organic Types, was a step away from creationism and towards evolution.

(Amundson 1998: 173)

The transcendental vision of archetypal forms fed directly into Darwin's interest in ancestors, and provided a template for the Darwinian vision of organisms as families of variants. Structure and function could be recombined in a range of ways, both in Darwinian biology and by post-Darwinian biologists who twisted Darwinism in more 'structuralist' directions, such as D'Arcy Wentworth Thompson, whose influence on Lévi-Straussian structuralism is well documented (Leach 1974: 64, 142; Salmon 2013b: 97–108).

Amongst non-biologists, D'Arcy Thompson is often remembered for his distinctive diagrams of 'transformations', through which the shape of one species of animal – a fish, for instance – could be distorted, flattened in one dimension, elongated in another, to yield the pattern for other, related species. The theoretical underpinning of these diagrams was a critique of what Thompson saw as an excessively teleological and atomist turn in Darwinian evolutionism. In the Darwinian vision, the focus on natural selection brought with it an obsession with the evolutionary characters of organisms (things like eyes, wings, spines), imagined as quasi-autonomous modules, shaped through time in relation to particular purposes. Organisms in turn came to seem like mere aggregates of these parts. And yet, there were limits to what natural selection could produce, Thompson pointed out – limits which derived from the physical properties of particular structural arrangements (e.g. Thompson 1961: 15–48). The length of a spine, the thinness of a bone, could not be increased indefinitely, without reaching a point of structural fragility. An animal's size could not increase or decrease indefinitely without becoming unsustainable. This was why, in practice, Thompson pointed out, the structuralists had had a point: the variety of biological forms fell within certain basic geometrical and mathematical ratios (of surface to mass, for instance), and one could learn quite a lot about the evolutionary constraints upon organisms by looking at the structural problems and efficiencies of architectural designs (Thompson 1961: 241–258).

Once one paid attention to organisms as whole structures, Thompson noted, one also came to see that related organisms often differed from each other not simply in the possession of distinct characters, but in terms of certain specific proportional alterations to their overarching form. Thompson believed that these proportional alterations could be stated in mathematical and geometrical terms: draw a grid over the image of one particular species, subject this grid to certain definite mathematical alterations (expand the distance between lines vertically or horizontally, apply a radial distortion to one part of the grid so the lines fan out, etc.), and you will find yourself with the shape of another related species (Thompson 1961: 268–325).[16]

This vision of the production of variation by overall 'trans-formation' provided a radically different conception of the process of evolutionary change from that of the selective 'tweaking' of particular organs to fit them to new functions. Concomitantly, this provided a radically different possibility, also, for comparison. Insofar as comparison of this kind bore on forms, not characters, it quite simply sidestepped the problem raised by Durkheim, namely that of identifying the given 'characters' of each species (Candea 2018c). This vision was no longer mereographic: as D'Arcy Thompson noted of his proposed approach, one could in this way compare wholes without ever having to define their parts: 'our essential task lies in the comparison of related forms, rather than in the precise definition of each; and the *deformation* of a complicated figure may be a phenomenon easy of comprehension, though the figure itself have to be left unanalysed and undefined' (Thompson 1961: 271).

Lévi-Strauss quoted the above in his own *Anthropologie structurale* (Lévi-Strauss 1958: 358; see Salmon 2013b: 100) and we can see why: Thompson's vision of organisms is clearly a key conceptual forebear of the structuralist shift in the vision of societies. This is the same shift as that described by Edmund Leach when he wrote that '[c]onsidered mathematically, society is not an assemblage of things but an assemblage of variables' (Leach 1966: 7). Once again, a revolutionary solution had older roots. Indeed, Durkheim's solution to the problem of typology had, in effect, said precisely the same thing: the problem could not be solved by moving upwards from particular characters of society, but only by looking at the variables of its overarching form – its proportional degree of complexity. More profoundly, at the heart of this vision lies – again – the venerable Aristotelian figure of proportional analogy, which we have previously encountered in the guise of the method of concomitant variation which thus, quietly, survived the shift from functionalism to structuralism.

We can pause to draw two conclusions. The first concerns structuralism's identification of the unity of the human mind. The partial genealogy of structuralism in biology highlights the importance of this move, by linking it to the basic metaphysical problem of any kind of structuralist account: how can one explain the regularities of form – the peculiar way in which different entities come to share topological characteristics – once functional adaptation is discounted or backgrounded? In pre-Darwinian biology, structuralists appealed to ideas in the mind of God, or simply left the question unresolved (Amundson 1998: 172). Darwin found in genealogy an answer to the same problem: biological forms could be seen as topological variants of each other insofar as they were related by descent. As Needham also noted, this premise partly justified biological typologising, but no similar appeal could be made in the case of social facts. The particular structuralist version of the unity of the human mind (Salmon 2013b) steps in to fill that gap.

The second point concerns the enduring entanglement and constant recombination of structural and functional concerns in anthropology and biology. In particular, we should not rush to assume that we know what nineteenth-century and early twentieth-century anthropologists had in mind when they drew analogies between anthropology and biology. It takes historical work to excavate what nineteenth-century biology looked like to contemporary anthropologists, and therefore what conclusions the famous organic analogy might suggest. Based only on the brief outline above, we can see that tensions in biology between a study of function and a study of structure, and the complex relation of both questions to the study of history, provided a rich matrix for analogical thinking for anthropologists. Thus, for instance, when Evans-Pritchard criticised 'the functionalist theory' of Radcliffe-Brown, he was mapping it on to teleological biological explanations. In a more generous view, Radcliffe-Brown (following Durkheim) had effectively spearheaded a subsumption of the question of function into the question of structure, since the function of a social fact was to be explained in effect by its role in maintaining the structure (Radcliffe-Brown 1940).[17] In his later work, Radcliffe-Brown was turning to a study of formal structural patterns in which functionalist teleology played a rather ancillary role. Indeed, the characteristic feature of Radcliffe-Brown's comparatism as I described it above, namely his foregrounding of typology and backgrounding of inductive 'explanation', could be seen precisely as part of this move. Radcliffe-Brown even explicitly articulated his 'principle of opposition' as a cognitive universal, in a way which prefigured the structuralist moves examined above. This fundamental change in perspective could be achieved without abandoning the organic analogy: a tension between structure and function was built into biology itself.

On that reading, Evans-Pritchard's call for 'abstraction' (see previous chapter) can be seen as a mid-point between the structural-functionalism of Radcliffe-Brown and the structuralism of Lévi-Strauss. Evans-Pritchard had made much of the fact that evolutionists and diffusionists were naive cultural realists (Evans-Pritchard 1951: 92). They imagined cultures or peoples on the one hand, traits or customs on the other, as bits of reality which one might compare to each other directly. Once students are enjoined to study problems, not peoples, he noted, and once comparison bears not on societies themselves but on formal structures derived by abstraction, many of the old difficulties of cultural taxonomy fall away. But Evans-Pritchard's invocation of abstraction still bore the mark of his earlier structural-functionalist assumptions: it envisaged a process of deriving particular abstractions from observed behaviour and *then* relating these into a system.

In sum, the conventional typological distinction between the 'structure' of structural-functionalism and the 'structure' of structuralism overwrites a more profound kinship between these approaches – in another view they, too, belong to a family of variants.

## *The Structuralist Revolution*

We saw above that while 'functionalist' comparisons shared a basic mereographic vision of societies as organisms, they formed a family of variants rather than a single method – ranging from the evolutionist-functionalisms of Tylor or Durkheim, through the single-case comparisons of Malinowski, to the structural-functionalisms of Radcliffe-Brown or Nadel. At the latter end of that scale, functionalisms begin to shade into structuralisms. Structuralist thinking itself flowered in many forms, not only within the work of Lévi-Strauss, but also in the partial recombinations of structuralist and functional concerns in the work of Mary Douglas (1966), in the engineering-inspired 'generalisations' of Leach (1966), in the recombination of structuralism and Marxism (e.g. Godelier 1980), in the distinctively frontal structuralist comparisons of Louis Dumont (1966), or most recently in the neo-structuralisms of Philippe Descola (2005b) or Viveiros de Castro (1998). We shall return to some of these later in this book, but for now suffice it to say that there were profound differences between these authors' approaches to comparison.

Conversely, the structuralist revolution was only ever a partial one. Under the topological comparatisms of the structuralists, on a lower level of abstraction, the older descriptive ethnographic work continued through caveated generalisations. Thus, for all his methodological puritanism, Needham nevertheless admitted, as we saw above, that the fudges inherent in polythetic classification remained the only available procedure for describing ethnographic particulars. Any statement about a state of affairs in the world can be seen on some scale as a matter of caveated generalisation – it characterises a situation, leaving out some of its aspects. This rejoins the point about the comparative infrastructure of ethnographic description which we saw explicitly outlined by Malinowski above. Whatever professions of conceptual purity anthropologists might make about their higher-order theoretical statements (and here I have in mind not simply structuralists, but also post-structuralists, ontological turners or what have you), insofar as they rely on ethnography, they will be appealing to those tiny more or less caveated micro-generalisations produced out of the banal everyday comparison between instances, events, things different people said, etc. In the shadow of grand theoretical revolutions, the basic Malinowskian work of caveated comparative micro-generalisation keeps ticking along.

Nevertheless, with all these caveats, the structuralist alternative articulated at mid-century came to mark one of the most famous and enduring splits in the history of anthropological comparatism. This new approach to comparison provided a handle through which the multiplicity of comparative methods we have examined above could be reduced to one shared, and now unsatisfactory, assumption – an empiricist belief in the comparison of actual 'things' on the ground, societies and cultures as assemblages of parts. In sum, what had seemed to be very different approaches to comparison became, in this view, one term of a new contrast.

Furthermore, this new contrast made a nonsense of the major alternative which had occupied authors, namely the contrast between description and comparison (Salmon 2013b: 7). A new vision of abstraction, worked through most thoroughly by Lévi-Strauss, made it impossible to dissociate descriptions from comparisons, since comparisons bore not on the descriptions themselves, but on abstracted systems.

Once again, comparison seemed to come in two forms. On the one hand, an empiricist, mereographic form which was broadly shared amongst evolutionists, functionalists and diffusionists, both in their classic versions and in the later attempts to map cultures and traits in the Human Relations Area Files, or the neo-evolutionism of Sahlins and Service (1960; Gingrich and Fox 2002b: 3); on the other hand, a bevy of new topological structuralist solutions. Much was lost by this neat reduction, and yet it focused attention on a key enduring contrast in anthropological discussions: the contrast between comparisons which work from similarity and comparisons which work from difference. This contrast – which, as we shall see again below in relation to Weber, was hardly new – was a simplification of the actual procedures of structuralist and empiricist comparatism. Both, as we have seen, deployed an attention to similarities and to differences. But it pointed to the profound rearticulation of the role played by difference and similarity respectively, concomitant to the shift in perspective between mereographic abstraction (categorising wholes by noting the similarities between their parts) and topological abstraction (comparing systems of differences which are all instances of the same human cognitive principles). This contrast between comparisons based on similarity and comparisons based on difference – usually to imply the superior conceptual sophistication of the latter – would run and run. Even after post-structuralism had had its way with structuralism and its closed systems of internal relations, the contrast would be constantly reinvented as a tool with which to bludgeon conceptual opponents (cf. Chapter 5).

## Fork 5. The Frontal vs the Lateral: Interpretivism and its Heirs

Comparison is used here by the anthropologist in order to demystify the monolithic, monological, essentialising rhetoric of modern science. This is a completely different use of comparison from one that seeks to subsume the entities compared in an encompassing, privileged, and supposedly superior theoretical framework.

(Lambek 1991: 44)

## The 'Two Traditions'

The radical alternative between structuralist and empiricist comparatisms outlined above would eventually come to be eclipsed, or at least relativised, by the rising prominence of a different distinction: the contrast between positivist and interpretive varieties of comparison (Holy 1987). For proponents of this shift in perspective, in the 1970s and early 1980s, comparison had to become 'an enterprise embedded in the conceptualization of anthropology as an interpretive humanity concerned with cultural specificity and diversity rather than as a generalizing science concerned with cultural and social universals' (Holy 1987: 11).

The contrast between positivism and interpretation was hardly new, of course: it could be traced back throughout the history of the social sciences, and we have encountered it already in Evans-Pritchard's critique of Radcliffe-Brown (1950). Proponents of an interpretivist critique of positivist comparison in the late twentieth century often saw themselves as the defenders of one of two great 'traditions' in social science. One of the clearest instances of a retrospective parsing of the history of comparison into positivist and interpretive modes comes from Richard Handler in a passage which deserves quoting at length:

Comparison in anthropology differs depending on which of two grand epistemological traditions, the positivist and the interpretive (corresponding to Durkheim's emphasis on social facts as things, and on collective representations, respectively), it engages. In traditions we can loosely call positivist, it is thought possible to identify phenomena (from material items like tools to social institutions like 'the family' to cultural assemblages like 'ancestor worship') that exist in different cultural settings; in other words, classes of things that are in some important sense 'the same' no matter the particularities of their historical and cultural context. Typically, in this tradition, analysis of similarity and difference leads to generalizations about causality linked, often, to ideas about human nature or about the nature of culture and society. In traditions we can loosely call interpretive, objects of study are not considered to be given in advance; rather, they are thought to be constructed in semiotically mediated exchanges between 'observer and observed,' outsider and insider, anthropologist and 'native.' In this tradition, the anthropologist starts with concepts or models (like the family or ancestor worship) that orient research, but that cannot be assumed as apt analogues for realities that exist elsewhere. Anthropological research and writing leads to revised understandings of one's initial terms (and the familiar worlds to which they belong) as well as to an emergent understanding of other peoples' worlds. This kind of anthropology aims not for causal analysis, but for comparative reinterpretation of both insiders' and outsiders' cultural worlds.

(Handler 2009: 628)

Often, the positivist/interpretivist reading grid has been used to distinguish authors from each other (canonically, 'Durkheim the positivist' versus 'Weber the interpretivist'). In more sophisticated accounts such as Handler's, however, the contrast between positivism and interpretivism can be seen as a tension internal to the work of particular authors, such as Durkheim or Benedict (Handler 2009: 633–635). As elsewhere in the social sciences (Abbott 2001), the contrast between positivism and interpretivism operates as a deictic distinction which replicates at different scales, yet it can also be used to characterise epochal or paradigmatic breaks. This is what happened in the late twentieth century, when a new dawn of interpretivist comparison was seen by some to have marked the end of positivist comparison. For Holy, indeed, one of the problems which needed to be explained is why, in 1987, there were *still* some positivists around (Holy 1987: 9).

Yet something new is at stake with each recurrence of the contrast. Handler's description provides an illuminating guide to one important accretion of the interpretivist/positivist distinction as it informed discussions of comparison in late twentieth-century anthropology. It highlights the way in which this contrast came to be aligned with a contrast between lateral comparison – laying cases side by side – and frontal comparison – comparison between observer and observed, 'us' and 'them'. The association was powerful: on the one hand, a distanced, 'third-person' positivist gaze, taking in objects from above, in order to generalise; on the other, an engaged, interpretive, 'second-person', reading, keen to challenge our own concepts and 'expand our horizons' by engaging with the other (Lambek 1991).

Seen like this, the positivist/interpretivist distinction could seem to sum up everything that anthropological debates about comparison had ever been about: it emerged as a master contrast, encompassing earlier contrasts between a focus on difference and a focus on similarity, between explanation and description, between generalisation and particularity, between science and humanities (see also Keane 2005). In this late-twentieth-century recapitulation, the interpretivist position was driven increasingly away from the problematics of what Evans-Pritchard had called 'comparison' and towards those of what he termed 'translation'. As we shall see below, on the horizon of this vision lay an unsettling sense that interpretivism might make lateral comparison *tout court* impossible, since 'our' categories could never stand the test of lateral extension. The 'third-person' project of lining up 'cases' was first merely upstaged, and then, with the turn to postmodernism, politically and epistemically undercut, by the face-off between 'the observer and the observed'. While for its critics this equated to abandoning comparison, proponents argued forcefully that the hermeneutic, second-person encounter of us and them is not just comparative, but indeed represents a, if not the, fundamental form of anthropological comparison (Lambek 1991).

## Whither Weber? On Not Losing Sight of Interpretive Lateral Comparison

It is worth pausing to note that – like so many others – these 'two traditions' were in an important sense being invented anew. In what is now becoming visible as a recurrent pattern, we find that with this new binary reading grid, a number of formerly important distinctions were eclipsed. In some quarters, functionalists, evolutionists and structuralists were all recast as, in essence, scientistic generalisers (Holy 1987: 3; Gingrich and Fox 2002b), to be contrasted with those more open-minded anthropologists who sought to find in the interpretation of culture a challenge to their own modes of thinking.[18] Implicitly, these critiques extended also to the various Marxist, neo-Marxist or transactionalist approaches which had emerged in counterpoint to functionalism and structuralism (Humphrey 2018; Sneath 2018). As ever, much is reinvented, and much is also lost in the articulation of radical epochal shifts.

The strangest elision, perhaps, if interpretivism is read as a challenge to lateral comparison, is that of Max Weber's own interpretive comparatism. Indeed, Weber's classic *Economy and society* shows that this seminal 'outline of interpretive sociology' was nothing if not a call for large-scale historical and sociological comparison, of the lateral kind. Even though, as Roth points out in his monumental introduction, 'Weber rendered no systematic account of his strategy of comparative study' (Roth 1978: xxxix), some key themes can be reconstructed from his writings, and they cut across the distinctions drawn by Handler above. Certainly, Weber rejects the conceit that 'subsumption of historical events under … abstractions [is] the purpose of scholarly work' (Roth 1978: xliv; Weber 1924: 517). But neither is the main purpose quite captured by the concern with the 'comparative reinterpretation of both insiders' and outsiders' cultural worlds' (Handler 2009: 628). True, Weber subordinates the search for analogies, that mainstay of evolutionist and functionalist comparatisms, to the elicitation of differences. But the description of particularity or the challenge to 'our own concepts' is not the end-point – rather, 'the purpose of the comparison must be the *causal explanation* of the difference' (Roth 1978: xxxviii, my emphasis; Weber 1924: 257, 288).

Most fundamentally – despite their shared critique of the 'arts of subsuming' (Salmon 2013a: 195) – for Weber, unlike for Boas, comparability per se is not truly in doubt. Yes, Weber excoriates the naive empiricism which confuses heuristic categories and real 'entities in the manner of biological organisms' (Roth 1978: xliv; Weber 1924: 517). But the process whereby the concerns of the observed might challenge the categories of the observer doesn't interrupt the orderly deployment of heuristic comparative devices, concepts and ideal types, which forms the mainstay of *Economy and society*.

Weber's interpretive comparatism lived on of course, notably in the work of the most famous avatar of anthropological interpretivism: Clifford Geertz. Here is Geertz on the value of comparison in relation to religion in *Islam observed*:

Is the comparative study of religion condemned to mindless descriptivism and an equally mindless celebration of the unique? I think not. The hope for general conclusions in this field lies not in some transcending similarity in the content of religious experience or in the form of religious behaviour from one people to another, or one person to another … The central task is to discover, or invent, the appropriate terms of comparison, the appropriate frameworks within which to view material phenomenally disparate in such a way that its very disparateness leads us into a deeper understanding of it.

(Geertz 1971: 54–55)

The sense in which this vision of comparison builds on Weber's is immediately obvious – the concern is with foregrounding and starting from difference, yet without coming to rest there. Interpretation and lateral comparison go hand in hand.

Nor is *Islam observed* some strange or epiphenomenal deviation from the norm of Geertz's writing. Lateral comparison beats the tempo of his career, from grand comparative theorisation of 'the integrative revolution' (Geertz 1963) through to his famous exploration of personhood in Java and Bali (Geertz 1974), to some of his later forays into global comparison in essays such as 'The world in pieces' (Geertz 1998).[19] All of this belies the classic vision of Geertz as a mere purveyor of 'cultural portraits' (Yengoyan 2006a: 5).

It shows more broadly that there is no necessary conceptual tension between interpretivism per se and lateral comparison as has been convincingly argued, for instance, by Keane (2005). Indeed, and well beyond Geertz, the Weberian project of a historically grounded, interpretively attuned comparatism is alive and well in anthropology, most notably perhaps in the journal *Comparative Studies in Society and History* (see for instance Yengoyan 2006b), or in the work of authors such as Van der Veer (2016) or Detienne (2008).

And yet, for all this, the late twentieth-century recension of the interpretivism/positivism divide did play an important role in the set-up of the current situation in which, as Yengoyan wistfully observes, 'Social scientists ... normally conceive of culture as the source of difference in which comparisons either fail or are not fully realized' (Yengoyan 2006a: 5). Geertz's own work, despite his recurrent interest in lateral comparison, remains frequently invoked as an exemplar of particularism or observer-observed dynamics – as the epitome, in fact, of the kind of us/not-us narrative structure which Geertz himself attributed to Benedict (see below, Chapter 7). One strand amongst many, in the formation of late twentieth-century anthropological interpretivism is a tense recombination between two ghosts: the memory of Weber's confidence in ideal types battling with the phantom of Boas's concerns about the translatability of concepts.

## *From Mapping to Communication, from the Lateral to the Frontal*

In sum, remapping the alternative between positivism and interpretivism on to an alternative between scientistic lateral comparison versus interpretive frontal comparisons is in an important sense an act of selection and erasure. In its original Weberian formulation interpretive comparison was not primarily concerned with the power of the particular, or with a Levinasian dialogue between the other and 'our' assumptions, nor did it imagine eschewing explanation. This reconfiguration of the contrast does, however, point to a real and profound reorientation in anthropological discussions of comparison in the 1970s and '80s. This was a shift towards a foregrounding of the relationship between observer and observed in the process of anthropological comparison – or to put it more technically, in relation to the distinction introduced in Chapter 1, a shift in emphasis from epistemic concerns about 'mapping' to epistemic (and, increasingly, political) concerns about 'communication'.

In Holy's account, this difference is cast in terms of a contrast between description and comparison. The tension between describing particular cases and generalising beyond them, which, as we saw above, structuralism had eclipsed, was thus once again reinstated as the key problem of the discipline. The 'positivists', Holy argues, had expended much energy on worrying about questions of comparison and generalisation, but little on the problem of description (Holy 1987: 4). Now, clearly, those whom Holy calls positivists had engaged the problem of the selection and definition of their units of comparison. As we saw above, this was a key point of discussion. But the mode in which they considered these questions did indeed cast these units as 'objective forms' (Holy 1987: 4). Identifying such forms was far from unproblematic, but the problems were understood as problems of mapping – what goes where – rather than as problems of communication – questions of the relationship between the observer and the observed. This is not to say that late twentieth-century interpretivism eschewed the possibility of going beyond an ever repeated self–other binarism. It simply marked that frontal move as the core one, from which multiplicity would eventually follow.[20]

This was primarily a shift in purposes rather than practices, however – or rather a shift in which practices are explicitly valued and reflected upon. It was a shift in what anthropology as a discipline came to foreground as important forms of rigour (see Chapter 9). Thus, questions of communication had not been absent from the work of those Holy characterises as positivists. They did in fact concern themselves with issues of evidence, the quality of ethnographic reports, problems of interpretation, the translation of indigenous concepts and the cortège of issues associated with this (Evans-Pritchard 1951: 82–84; e.g. Lewis 1955: 268). It is simply that, in the main, they treated these as issues of individual technique and skill, workmanlike things which good anthropologists ought to learn to do well (e.g. Evans-Pritchard 1951: 90). Malinowski, with his detailed methodological charter for ethnographic fieldwork, was the key exception to this pattern. But once this original charter had been laid out, these skills and techniques of ethnography became a subject to be discussed in pedagogical situations, advice passed on from supervisors to students and so forth. They no longer seemed to require extensive explicit discussion in published academic fora, in the way that the more elaborate 'conceptual' problems of comparative generalisation did. While problems of 'mapping' were assumed to require a shared set of operational rules which invited much explicit discussion and debate, questions of 'communication' were in the main left to the individual initiative and possibly genius of practitioners, under the assumption that a set of tacit standards were in place.

The profound shift introduced by the late twentieth-century interpretivist alternative was a reversal of these assumptions and priorities – a reversal which in many respects echoes to this day. In the main, the situation in the past three to four decades (long after the demise of self-conscious 'interpretivism' per se) has been the opposite of the one described in the previous paragraph. Questions of communication – of the relationship between observer and observed – have taken centre stage. In some way or other, explicit anthropological discussions of method tend to circle around the epistemic, ethical and political implications of 'communication', laying down principles and making explicit arguments about whether and how it should be done. Questions of mapping – questions concerning the units of comparison, of what constitutes a proper 'case', category or topic – have taken something of a back seat. Theoretically speaking, such questions have tended to be subsumed into questions of communication: identifying units for comparison is now mostly thought of as, precisely, a relational issue – one that happens in the encounter between observer and observed, albeit still, as we shall see below, mostly at the behest of the former. Boasian (and Levinasian) worries have taken the place of Weberian confidence.

As a result, the anthropological craft of selecting units for comparison, naming bits and bobs of reality, referring to groups of people or kinds of activity, continues apace as a workaday practice, much of it under the epistemological radar. In discussions and in print, anthropologists are constantly drawing comparisons between different subsets of their field experience, between different sites they have worked in, between different published cases within their broad geographic or thematic area of specialisation, or beyond: caveated generalisation is ineradicable. But this is rarely assumed to require any broader elaboration of shared standards on what is 'comparable' and how. In sum, rather like questions of communication in the 1940s and '50s, questions of mapping today have mainly become a space of individual endeavour, regulated by tacit knowledge and mostly implicit skill-sets. Part of being a 'good' anthropologist involves exhibiting initiative and genius through clever and unexpected juxtapositions of inventively delineated cases, while good intellectual workmanship includes the ability to pitch surveys of 'the relevant literature' in such a way as to make a neat space in which one's own case can have a transformative effect (and not just 'fill a gap').

But we have little in the way of theoretical discussion of – let alone a sense that there should be a disciplinary consensus on – how this might be done. The thought that anthropologists might need to reach collective agreement on questions of mapping, independently of each anthropologist's encounter with their own interlocutors, would have seemed obvious to Evans-Pritchard; stated like this, it would seem impossible and perhaps undesirable to most practising anthropologists since the 1980s. I turn to these questions again in Chapter 9.

## Similar Within, Different Without

This reversal in concerns was correlative to a shift in aims. On Holy's account, this might seem again a simple reversal of an earlier polarity. Where 'positivist' comparison saw the description of the particular as a first step towards the aim of comparative generalisation, for Holy's 'interpretivists', the description of an unfamiliar case (and its correlative challenge to 'us') is itself the aim: 'the main objective of the comparative method is no longer that of testing hypotheses but rather that of identifying or highlighting cultural specificity' (Holy 1987: 15). There was, again, a marked shift here from Weber's own critique of generalisation, whose point was not simply to identify difference, or deploy it reflexively, but to *explain* it.

By contrast, grafting the critique of generalisation on to an anthropological concern with rich, holistic description led in a different direction. We saw in the case of Malinowski that the drawing up of holistic descriptions of particular cultures relies both on internal comparisons between different aspects of the same culture, and on external comparisons between 'us' and 'them'. Late twentieth-century interpretivism inherits this device of alternating the near and the far comparisons, but it does so through the Boasian stream rather than a strictly Malinowskian one. In that formulation, as Handler showed for Ruth Benedict, the internal comparisons within cultures played much the same role as for Malinowski – showing the internal coherence across different aspects of domains of culture – while external comparisons, by contrast, were more sharply oriented towards the elicitation of difference, if not incommensurability (Handler 2009: 632). Malinowski had used comparisons between the Kula and crown jewels to refine his description of the former through the consideration of both similarities and difference. But his theoretical take-home point had been to highlight – contra Boas – the common psychological causes between the two phenomena. By contrast Benedict's comparisons (2005) between the USA and Japan, for instance, while they also used the consideration of similarities and differences in order to specify the picture of Japan, came to rest rhetorically on difference: the aesthetic schema, as Geertz had noted, was 'Us/not-Us' (Geertz 1988). Interpretivism inherited this dynamic alternation between internal and external comparisons: comparison across different realms within the same cultural context draws out similar properties, or similar generative rules; comparisons between them and us point to differences (Holy 1987: 12–13).

To make one's aim the identification of cultural specificity might on the face of it seem like a mere reversal of the Radcliffe-Brownian order of priority between comparison and description. More accurately, it reverses the order of priority established by Evans-Pritchard between comparison and translation. For the aim is not simply that of drawing up a case, but rather of drawing up a case *in relation to us*. This reversal of priority – comparison in the service of translation and not the opposite – has been claimed over and over again as a radical move (Asad 1986; Viveiros de Castro 2004), because it names a classic critical potential of anthropology honed and foregrounded to great effect by late twentieth-century interpretive anthropology. In the same move, 'their' reality is brought into view, and 'our' assumptions are challenged or relativised. The flipside of an understanding of the other is a conceptual self-critique: 'The importance attached to comprehending the actors' meanings, experiences, and views of reality brings into question all a priori definitions and hypotheses' (Holy 1987: 8).

Schneider's critiques of the study of kinship (1984) are a case in point of the critical potential of interpretivist anthropology. Comparing and contrasting the logic of his argument with that of critiques of kinship in the above-mentioned work of Needham (1975) or Leach (1966) is a good way of pinning down the different logics at stake. Both sets of critiques unpicked the procedure of generating kinship typologies from the study of empirical particulars. Both did so by examining the conceptual logic of anthropologists' categorising practices. And both were inspired in some measure by structuralist thinking. But Leach and Needham proposed a general conceptual critique of typology as applied to society, whereas Schneider grounded his critique in the observation that there was a specifically *western* cultural logic to the way the problem of kinship had been articulated (see also Holbraad and Pedersen 2017: 74–76). Generalising about kinship was illusory because the very notion of kinship as articulated by anthropologists was a cultural particular. Thus, while Leach and Needham could come to rest in a different vision of structural abstraction, Schneider's critiques bore on structuralist kinship theory as much as that of the functionalists. Where Schneider came to rest was precisely in the relational elicitation of cultural difference, a difference which could not be subject to a higher-order systematisation.

One might thus say that, from the point of view of comparative method, there was little that was 'new' to mark out an interpretive turn – all of its elements have been encountered before. And it is striking that much of what Holy writes about 'interpretivism' can be applied also to rather different contemporary strands of anthropology, such as the interest in social constructionism, or Dumont's characteristic version of structuralism, which like Schneider's ultimately eschewed broader systematisation (Dumont 1986; Iteanu and Moya 2015: 7; see Chapter 8). In these various forms, the vision of an interpretivist 'turn' in the late twentieth century names a particular moment when, more than before, both the problems and possibilities of anthropology seemed to rest in the comparisons we drew, not laterally across different cases, but frontally between a 'them' and an 'us' (Candea 2016a; see chapters 7 and 8 below).

## A Postmodern Involution

On this account – as on many others (e.g. Laidlaw 2018) – the much-discussed 'epistemic crisis' of the 1980s, marked most famously by *Writing culture* (Clifford and Marcus 1986), represented an intensification rather than a break from interpretivism.

By foregrounding the relational nature of the process of identifying cultural difference, interpretivism had introduced a radical undecidability: was this difference between us and them an empirical one, or an effect of the comparison itself? Was the holism imputed to the other essential or relational? The postmodern focus on anthropology as writing and fiction, the relentless tracking of the rhetorical tricks and devices through which anthropologists had sought to constitute a vision of cultural wholes, and their own textual authority in describing them – this was essentially the mark of a change of mood, rather than a profound conceptual rupture. It brought home the point that if 'all a priori ... hypotheses' had to be brought into question, then the ones surrounding cultural holism – which had underpinned interpretivism itself – ought to be pretty high on that list too. The effort to objectify anthropological writing itself cast a pall over the cheery, 'pinch of salt' confidence of Geertzian interpretivism, which envisaged interpretation as imperfect, but broadly doable (Geertz 1973c). Rather than assume translation could be done and just get on with the job, postmodernists focused on *how* it had been and could be done, both well and badly.

Where postmodernism introduced something more radical than a mere change of mood, was in the profound way the goodness and badness of writing came to be redefined. Under the influence of Foucault (e.g. 1979), of feminist and postcolonial critiques (Asad 1973a; Haraway 1989; Said 2003; Spivak 1988), questions of communication came to be recast as not merely conceptual but also indistinguishably political ones. The conceptual critique of 'our categories' collided with problems of voice, silencing and othering of the people anthropologists worked with. More profoundly the very alternative between treating questions of comparison as issues of mapping and treating them as issues of communication became in itself a political alternative. Mapping – the identification of contexts, structures, elements, traits and relations – came in some quarters to be seen as politically suspicious as much as epistemologically dubious – an attempt to reach for an external, god's eye view.

In sum, from the perspective of a discussion of anthropological comparison, the crisis of representation was not so much a rejection of interpretivism as an intensification, a purification, a limit case or vanishing point of late twentieth-century interpretivism itself. By focusing inwards on the devices of anthropological writing, it made writing itself into an object; it expanded self-critique from the merely epistemic into the political. But its core theme, the core alternative it articulated for comparatists, remained that sketched by late twentieth-century interpretivism – the alternative between comparisons which leave the observer out of the frame and comparisons which include the observer.

## Fork 6. Old Worries, New Hopes: Anthropological Comparatisms Today

Certainly, let us compare.

(Detienne 2008: 37)

### *Naivety and Nihilism*

In identifying the five 'forks in the road' outlined above, I have been commenting on distinctions drawn by others. Some of these are so well-known as to be banal to most anthropologists. Others have been somewhat obscured by the passing of time or have come to be understood in various ways. While I have made selections and emphasised some aspects of these distinctions over others, I have been working at second-hand, from what commentators on comparison explicitly cast as stark epochal alternatives.

In this section, I will hazard an epochal characterisation of my own. In the past three decades or so, there has been a flowering of very different 'returns' to the problem of comparison. These are profoundly different – as we shall see below – in their tone, in their philosophical assumptions and in their aims. But one thing these various developments share, above and beyond their obvious and often embittered differences, is a sense that a confidence in anthropological comparison has been lost and must be recovered. From this vantage, the history of anthropological comparatism is read as one of early excessive naivety, followed by concentrated and equally excessive scepticism. Anthropologists today frequently invoke a hopeful yet somewhat naïve period (roughly speaking up to the 1960s), in which their forebears practised comparison without sufficient self-examination, followed by 'various waves of criticism during the late twentieth century [which] cast serious doubt on what previously had seemed a self-evident cornerstone of anthropology' (Gingrich and Fox 2002b: 2). This sense of a 'before and after' comes with the implicit or explicit message that we are now entering a third phase: one of reconstruction, in which the radical and ultimately disabling 'nihilism' (Buchanan 1996: 485) associated with the 'crisis of representation' can be left behind, and comparison can be imagined anew, shorn of the sins of 'positivism' (Jensen et al. 2011), generalisation and essentialism (Scheffer and Niewöhner 2010; Van der Veer 2016).

The previous sections show how much is, once again, lost by the parsing of the history of anthropological comparatism in this way. Comparison was never self-evident – indeed, as I argued above, it was born impossible – and many of the critiques articulated in the late twentieth century had been prefigured as early as the nineteenth. 'Positivism' tends to figure as an increasingly straw-mannish and shadowy enemy (Roscoe 1995), and stern disapproval of 'generalising' can be expressed forcefully even as one retains, in practice, the device of caveated generalisation (Candea 2017; Van der Veer 2016). As for the purported nihilism of the postmodernists, it overlooks the fact that the crisis of representation did not abandon comparison, so much as focus on its devices and effects, often with a clear set of political commitments in view. But, as with the previous forks, this simplified parsing of the history of comparison as naivety followed by nihilism nevertheless reveals something about the current moment, namely the ubiquity of a perceived need to just get on with, and get 'back to' the business of comparison.

It is important to note, before I begin to describe some of these new hopes, that I am not trying to characterise here all of the ways in which comparison is invoked or deployed in anthropology today. Some strands of anthropology have been pretty stable and consistent in their deployment of comparison, and weathered through the crisis of representation with relatively minor readjustments. In some cases, such as cognitive (Irvine 2018) or linguistic (Stasch 2014) anthropology, the existence of a subfield with well-defined and shared problems, means and ends has had an insulating effect – comparison has proceeded because one broadly knew what it was for. There are also quarters of the discipline in which broadly structuralist, or interpretivist, or even functionalist comparatisms are deployed, without much soul-searching. In these quarters, however, there tend to be fewer explicit discussions of comparison, or calls to return to, recover or reinvent it – precisely because, broadly speaking, it works. Elsewhere, comparison has, on the contrary, been the focus of continuous reflection and attention. The journal *Comparative Studies in Society and History*, founded in 1958, deserves special mention in this context, because it has managed not only to keep alive, but constantly to reignite – generation after generation – the flame of an interdisciplinary, historically grounded comparatism which has given anthropology some all-time classic essays (Ortner 1995; Sahlins 1963; Stoler 1989; more broadly, see the essays and discussions collected in Yengoyan 2006b).

In other words, there are many contexts within anthropology in which a narrative of loss and recovery of comparison would strike one as odd. The discipline at large, however, has seen a flowering of discussions of comparison in the past two decades or so, articulated around the triptych of naivety, nihilism and new hope. From radically different theoretical perspectives, many articulate the feeling that a confidence in comparison has been lost and needs to be recovered.

## Some New Hopes

This desire to return to, recapture or reinvent comparison has been articulated in a number of distinctive ways, all of which inform also, in more or less obvious ways, my own account in the second half of this book. In one important strand of the recent literature on comparatism – a strand one might think of as a 'pragmatic comparatism' – the key ingredient of a return to comparison is that old favourite, the pinch of salt. Having waved away the excesses of positivism, and established that one is not aiming to discover universal laws, or imagining that anthropology could be a scientific endeavour, one can safely return to comparison as the elicitation of important insights by contrasting empirical similarities and differences between cases, without jettisoning our hard-won reflexive and critical perspective (Gingrich and Fox 2002b; Pina-Cabral 2010; Van der Veer 2016). The time has come for a 'constructive comparatism' (Detienne 2008: 23), a 'post-deconstructionist manifesto against the dangers of incommensurability' (Detienne 2008: back cover). What is proposed is typically a self-consciously modest comparison, made of 'fuzzy units' and 'medium scale theory' (Gingrich and Fox 2002b: 19–20), built of categories that are 'neither too strong nor too weak' (Detienne 2008: 25). Its 'purpose is not to come to some general truth but to highlight something that is not general, something specific without any pretense to general truth, but definitely of broader significance' (Van der Veer 2016: 26). Authors writing in this vein (see also Herzfeld 2001) tend to demonstrate the value of comparison through examples of concrete instances and arguments. These works make a virtue of not proposing a grand methodological charter, a new epistemological schema – surely there has been too much of that already!

There is an echo, in these rediscoveries of the virtues of modest, caveated comparison, of the mid-century reasonableness of authors such as Lewis or Eggan, who, with one eye on Boas and another on Radcliffe-Brown, stayed away from grand generalisations and saw value in the drawing of different sorts of similarities and contrasts between related and distant societies. But there is an important shift. The objectivist, scientific horizon and rhetoric which framed those earlier comparatisms have been replaced with reflexive, humanistic ones. Self-critique and understanding are the key aims here.

Viewed from a purely disciplinary perspective, the insistence on the evils of positivism, scientism and generalisation which characterises this pragmatic strand of writing on comparison might seem merely rhetorical, flogging a dead horse (cf. Keane 2005). But this writing is not merely addressed to anthropologists. It arises from an institutional moment in which anthropology has increasingly been forced to make itself accountable to broader interdisciplinary standards, be it in the struggle for research funding or in the strengthening of audit and efficiency regimes in universities. In an increasing number of contexts, anthropology needs to give an account of itself, of its distinctiveness and value. In that broader interdisciplinary context, the scientifically framed search for laws and generalisations is a very live horse indeed and sorely, these authors feel, in need of flogging. At the same time, no one will fund a discipline in crisis (of representation or otherwise).

It is in this context that the alternative between an earlier naive positivism and a nihilist crisis of representation seems to loom over the discipline. The reasonable, middle-of-the road tone of some recent returns to comparison are an effect of seeking to chart a route between the Scylla of positivism – aligning anthropology on a broader vision of the scientific social sciences – and the Charybdis of postmodern involution – which ends up speaking only to the converted. It addresses one message to anthropologists – get over your self-doubt and get back to business! – and another outside the discipline – look, we have a good thing going here, and it doesn't need to look like science. This is not simply a self-interested matter of access to research funds or of convincing university administrators. The above calls for a renewed commitment to comparison are also often motivated by an explicit set of concerns with political engagement and critique. For authors in this strand of hopeful and pragmatic writing on anthropological comparison, the technique remains our best tool for tracking down power and inequality, and for having a say on the issues of the day (see also Astuti 2007).[21]

Another contemporary attempt to recapture comparison from the jaws of the crisis of representation takes an entirely different route. Its roots lie in Roy Wagner's and Marilyn Strathern's systematic working out of the point that the nature/culture distinction itself is an element of a western conceptual scheme (Strathern 1980; Wagner 1981; cf. Holbraad and Pedersen 2017: chapters 2 and 3). In one sense, this observation was clearly 'just' a further turn of the Schneiderian screw, and belonged in some respects squarely within the self-regarding problematics of the crisis of representation. But since the critique bore on the very terms through which that critique itself could be articulated (is the nature/culture distinction … 'cultural'?), the observation required a more profound reconfiguration of the anthropological enterprise. By relativising the nature/culture distinction itself, this move in effect recast the grand paradigm shift from positivism to interpretivism as, after all, just another internal squabble. Whether one imagined anthropology as a natural science of society, or on the contrary as a humanistic hermeneutics elucidating the meanings of culture, one was still, after all, working with a western nature/culture distinction which itself required examination. Like *Writing culture*, then, this move challenged 'culture' and thus put in doubt the key engine of anthropological comparison. But it did so precisely *through* comparison. What it demonstrated, in other words, was that comparison could survive the demise of culture.

One outcome of this trajectory is the recently much discussed ontological turn (Holbraad and Pedersen 2017; Heywood 2018c) which, in its various forms, has picked up and reconfigured a number of the techniques and contrasts examined in the sections above – from the self-othering of the interpretivists, to the distinctive abstraction of the structuralists – to distinctive effect. Comparison here becomes 'controlled equivocation' (Viveiros de Castro 2004) – a commitment to recognising the way anthropologists' usual concepts can make a nonsense of the worlds of the people they work with, which leads to the crafting of new conceptual devices drawn recursively from an ethnographic encounter with alterity. While this ontological turn envisions comparison as a permanent repetition of the same frontal move of conceptual invention (cf. Chapter 8), other invocations of ontology have gone intensely lateral, crafting grand comparative edifices on the ashes of the erstwhile distinction between nature and culture (Descola 2005b; Latour 2012; Salmon and Charbonnier 2014).

Yet another – more diffuse – family of comparative moves focus not on a reinvention of the frontal contrast between 'us' and 'them', but on a recuperation of another figure which has woven in and out of our account above, namely genealogy. Boasian diffusionism, 'relexicalised' (Brightman 1995) in a postmodern vein, provides a way into examining concrete variety and transformation of culture which is more than a literary fiction and yet stops short of imagining some essentialist closure. Beyond the most explicit proponents of a neo-Boasian anthropology (Bashkow 2004; Bashkow et al. 2004), one can sense a broader return to the aesthetics and problematics of diffusionism. Multi-sited methodology and cognate approaches, in which anthropology travels to follow a concept, people or practice through multiple locations literal or metaphorical, is one echo of this (Falzon 2009; Marcus 1995). Another instance of a similar imaginary can be found in the vision of anthropology as engaged in a flow of 'lateral theory' (Howe and Boyer 2015): concepts move sideways across cases, but also in and out of anthropology, coming from, passing through and returning to various other fields of activism, politics or expertise. Howe and Boyer's description gives an accurate portrayal of a widespread contemporary way with concepts of the discipline: anthropologists pick up a term from others (be it affect, financialisation or infrastructure), make it travel some way along different cases, shifting and changing as it goes, and hand it back to pick or trace another. When the procedure is successful, the cases themselves have been redescribed along the way. This neo-diffusionist vision of studies speaking to other studies subverts the contrast between description and generalisation: it provides a third, 'transparticular' (Howe and Boyer 2015) way of doing more than a case study and less than a generalisation (see also Højer and Bandak 2015).

While the aesthetics of the ontological turn and of the broad family of moves one might think of as neo-diffusionist are in many respects inverses of each other (stark binary contrasts on the one hand, travelling transformations on the other), there is also a deep kinship between the two positions. This stems from their shared attempts to subvert the sort of dualist framework articulated in my discussion of Needham and Gell above. Neither of these reinventions of anthropological comparison has much truck with the distinction between, on the one hand, a messy world of empirical realities, and on the other, a logical system of concepts. Thus, a key device of the ontological turn was to collapse the distinction between concepts and things (Henare et al. 2007). This means not only viewing concepts as ethnographically derived, but also insisting on the fact that such ethnographically derived concepts cannot be detached from their source or location (Holbraad 2017; Holbraad and Pedersen 2009). Neo-diffusionism operates a similar collapse by bringing concepts into the world and making them travel. As much as Boas, there are echoes here of the 'material semiotics' of Actor–Network Theory (Latour 2005).

Indeed, if we sacrifice detail to neatness, we might say that the onto-logical turn and neo-diffusionism are mirror images of each other. The former collapses the messy world of external relations into the neat uni-verse of concepts. Everywhere, it finds coherently ordered philosoph-ical systems, ontologies galore: its one watchword is that there can be no *nonsense* in the world, unless it be in 'our own' conceptual schemes, which thus need to be perpetually challenged and improved. The latter by contrast collapses concepts into the rough and tumble of the empir-ical world and its contingent external relations. Anthropologists are on the ground cheek by jowl with other experts, tracing and manipulating concepts as they twist and transform in moving from place to place. For the neo-diffusionists then, as for the Wittgenstein of the *Blue Book* and the Foucault of the genealogical period (Bunzl 2004; Gross 2001), serial analogies and family resemblances are not the problem but the solu-tion – a key mode of thought whose inherent indiscipline, its constant subversion of stable systematic categorisations, is its key virtue.

At the intersection of the various strands above lies the observation that, however much anthropologists may be dubious about their own comparative devices, comparison is already in the world – the people anthropologists study are themselves constantly comparing. This vision builds on earlier concerns with authorship and authority but taking these in a different direction, recognising that anthropologists are always-already enmeshed in collaborative ways of making know-ledge with informants who are themselves recognised as experts. The point has been made most forcefully by anthropologists in communi-cation with Science and Technology studies, who came to take seriously their subjects' practices of commensuration, be they those of scientists (Candea 2012; Helmreich 2009; Latour 2005; Rabinow 2012; Walford 2015), surgeons (Mol 2002b), lawyers (Latour 2009; Riles 2011), NGO workers (Riles 2000), bankers (Holmes 2013; Maurer 2005) or fisheries inspectors (Gad 2012; Gad and Bruun Jensen 2016). These engagements with 'other comparatisms' highlight the comparative expertise of the subjects of anthropology, reimagined as themselves para-ethnographers (Holmes and Marcus 2005). It opens the door to a reimagination of anthropological comparison as a matter of conceptual collaboration, accompaniment (Rabinow 2011) or inspiration (Gad and Bruun Jensen 2016; Scheffer and Niewöhner 2010). Like the ontological turn, these moves defer conceptual authority to the ethnography. But, like the pragmatic comparatists with whom I opened the section, they tend to envision not a single, well-honed technique for conceptual invention, but rather a negative injunction to defer our own devices, so as to open the door to an uncharted multiplicity of comparative possibilities (Gad and Bruun Jensen 2016: 2). Anthropological comparison, in this view, is only one contributor to the lateral travel of concepts, which it feeds off and feeds into, but does not monopolise or control.

### An Immanent Turn?

The diversity of contemporary returns to comparison, breathlessly mapped above, is both exciting and daunting. And yet, for all their deep epistemological differences, these different moves can be said to share two key features. One, as we noted above, is a sense that a more positive vision of comparison must be recovered from the ashes of the 1980s epistemological bonfire. The other is a very explicit concern with the fact that anthropological comparison is irremediably *in* the world and not (or not only) *about* it. Anthropologists reinventing comparison today may look to Boas or Lévi-Strauss for inspiration (or indeed Frazer; Willerslev 2011). But one element of the landscape has irremediably changed. Comparison in its various contemporary forms is imagined as inescapably *immanent*. As we saw above, this point comes in a more or less theoretically convoluted form – from a pragmatic approach to political engagement, to a (neo-)pragmatist vision of thought as action.

Of course, the vision of anthropologists standing outside or beyond objects of study had always been troublesome. After all, anthropologists have always been, self-consciously, people studying people. A tension between anthropology in the world and anthropology about it has been with the discipline in some form, therefore, since its inception. The interpretive critique of positivism (which in its general sense goes back to the late nineteenth century) was, after all, an exemplification of this point in an epistemological sense, since anthropology is the study of humans by humans. But positivists themselves had imagined a continuity between rules in the social world and rules in their own minds and methods (see below, Chapter 7). Calls for a specifically *critical* recognition of our immanence also have nineteenth-century roots (consider Karl Marx), long before the point was taken up in the mid- to late twentieth century, by neo-Marxist, feminist and postcolonial theorists (Bayly 2018; Humphrey 2018; Johnson 2018).

Nevertheless, most of these recognitions of the immanence of anthropological knowledge had come with 'fixes' to get a vantage point on one's object of study, to transcend and stand outside it at least for the duration of an account. What is today remembered as the crisis of representation is the moment when, in various quarters, such fixes themselves were declared unacceptable. It made little difference whether a transcendent outside was imagined in the form of scientific omniscience, of structuralist abstraction, of a place behind and above informants, reading their culture over their shoulders (Crapanzano 1986: 74), or the critical sophistication which reveals our subjects' delusions and self-delusions. The desire to stand outside *at all* is what came in some quarters to seem suspect.

If the various returns to comparison of the past twenty years are distinctive, it is in their shared (albeit somewhat unfair) sense that earlier

recognitions of the immanence of anthropology had led to a kind of with-
drawal, a shrinking away from comparison, into mere epistemological
self-examination. For these various approaches, by (partly imagined)
contrast, the recognition of the immanence of anthropology must lead
to some kind of action, which will in some way or other be simultaneously conceptual and political. The alternatives they propose combine
these requirements in various ways. A middle-of-the-road realism with
caveats allows anthropologists to have a say on important contemporary
problems. A pugnaciously critical engagement with the world spotlights
suffering and injustice. A turn to ethics or to ontology enables, in very
different ways, a reformulation of the age-old concern of 'taking seriously' the worlds, aims or purposes of others. These alternatives might
seem irreconcilable, but they share the sense that comparison is a
requirement precisely because it is immanent: anthropologists owe it to
the world. The limits of past approaches duly acknowledged, we need to
get on with it. It is time – once again? always? – to 'make a fresh start
with comparison' (Gingrich and Fox 2002b: 5).

## Conclusion: The Shadow of Two Forms

Let us pause to look back over the road travelled in this chapter. Unlike
the previous chapter, which presented one general model of comparison and listed all its impossibilities together, in this sequential view
we find comparison moving ever forward, through a series of solutions
to previous problems. With each 'fresh start', the impossibility of comparison is identified as the effect of the failings of a previous vision of
comparative method. An alternative method is proposed which solves
this impossibility. Comparison becomes possible at last – until the next
fresh start. This view of comparison as a series of solutions reassembles
the objections accumulated in the previous chapter in some semblance
of historical order, and gives a sense of how we got where we are. But
it is ultimately no more useful for the practical purpose of getting on

with comparison, because these solutions are not in any straightforward sense cumulative. Each new solution relies on negating or disregarding the premises of previous ones. With each fresh start, the purpose of comparison shifts, subtly or radically. In the end, these solutions have little to say to each other. Viewing their sequence together invites once again the disheartening suggestion that comparison is still after all impossible by essence, rather than accidentally.

For one thing, there is something faintly comic about the multiplication of methods in such a short space of time – the method of concomitant variation, the historical method, the comparative method, the genetic method, the experimental method, the method of statistic documentation by concrete evidence ... One is brought to mind of Poincaré's sarcastic comment that '[n]early every sociological thesis proposes a new method which, however, its author is careful not to apply, so that sociology is the science with the greatest number of methods and the least results' (Poincaré 1914: 19–20; quoted in Nadel 1951: 1). To those less inclined to mirth, there is something depressing about the regularity with which the same or similar problems and solutions seem to be rediscovered. There is a sobering effect of finding that much of what we thought was new is old. And yet the aim of the chapter is not to recapitulate the cheap wisdom that everything has been said before. For repetition can also be the mark of rootedness, the mark of the paradoxical resilience of anthropology as a discipline (Strathern 2004: xxv).

The problem which this chapter has tried to bring attention to is not repetition, then, but a particular kind of not-quite-repetition. It is this accumulation of people saying *nearly but not quite* the same thing, which produces an overwhelming effect. Through a succession of radical contrasts which don't straightforwardly build or map on to each other, the anthropological discussion of comparison seems to descend into a cacophony, an indistinguishable shouting match of different claims to method, or, to shift the metaphor, into a Borgesian methodological labyrinth of branching and recombining paths. As in the vision given in the previous chapter, comparison once again seems impossible, but this time for a different reason. The impossibility of comparison is no longer the effect of an accumulation of problems heaped upon one single method; it is, rather, the impossibility of finding one's way through this multiplicity of partly overlapping, partly divergent methodological proposals.

And yet, from this mess, from this sequential enumeration of particulars – particular authors, particular works, particular methods – we have seen two regularities progressively beginning to emerge. The first has been, loosely, the organising device of this chapter: namely the formal argumentative device of opposing, at any given time, two kinds of comparison to each other: naive and scientific, nomothetic and idiographic, comparative and historical, empiricist and structuralist, positivist and interpretive. This binary device, ever repeated, cleans up the record and stills the cacophony, by gathering together all there is to say about comparison into two 'kinds'. On the one hand – vaguely gestured to – lies the varied collection of mess and nonsense which 'they' have been calling comparison; on the other – clearly and precisely outlined – 'our' or 'my' proposal for an alternative. This device echoes in the realms of epistemology – while reversing its dynamic – anthropologists' classic move of opposing a brief sketch of all of 'our' misconceptions, to a clear account of 'their' alternative world. Let us call this form – the categorisation of comparison into two kinds –a *caesura*.

A second form which recurs, cross-cutting the previous one, is that of identifying particular moves, tips, tricks and devices, which travel across these different breaks. Some belong to families which bear grand, famous names in the history of epistemology – translation, induction, abstraction; others have no particular name, such as Radcliffe-Brown's alternation of regional and distant comparisons, or Boas's translations from typological into substantive visions of units. These moves can be borrowed surreptitiously, or reformulated explicitly, or they can just silently endure through paradigm shifts, accommodating changes in scale and changes in purpose. They form families of variants, rather like Boas's cultural traits. Let us call these forms *heuristics*.

*Caesurae* and *heuristics* are, themselves, comparative devices. More specifically, they have been deployed by anthropologists for the purpose of comparing different kinds of comparisons. They articulate alternative perspectives on the multiplicity of comparative methods. In the next chapter, which acts as a conclusion to this first part of the book, we take a step back to consider and compare these two comparative devices, their respective powers and limits, and to sketch the beginning of a way out of the impossibility of comparison.

# THREE

# Caesurism and Heuristics

### Introduction: On Seeing Many Comparative Methods

Let us survey the argument so far. As a first pass over the problem of the impossibility of anthropological comparison, Chapter 1 started from one particular, mid-century attempt to articulate a general picture of anthropological comparison, and used this as a canvas against which the variety of problems, objections and difficulties which have been raised against comparison can be mapped and categorised. In this view, the impossibility of anthropological comparison is the effect of these interlocking objections. Each is resolvable in isolation, but taken together they form an impenetrable skein.

In Chapter 2 we took a different, sequential optic, in which the comparative method is multiplied into a series of subsequent forks in the road. Over and again, the figure of identifying 'two ways of doing comparison' organised anthropological discussions. But these subsequent distinctions do not line up. With each subsequent fork in the road, anthropologists identify a different set of problems and remap the landscape in a way which does not so much resolve the problems identified at the previous turning point, as it brackets or turns away from them. That vision provides a different account of the impossibility of comparison.

If Chapter 2 took a leisurely stroll through this Borgesian 'garden of forking paths', trying to remain attentive to what is retained and what is lost at each turn, the present chapter takes a second look at the garden, from a more elevated position. As one passes through it, there are only ever two paths. Seen from above, however, this recurrent binarism maps a multiplicity, a plurality of forms of comparison. But pluralities, as Strathern noted, 'have their own configurations' (2004: 21). The chapter looks to the work of anthropologists, epistemologists and philosophers of science, for two distinct visions of how the plurality of anthropological comparatisms might be configured. One of these configurations relies on elucidating fractal patterns produced by a repetitive caesurism; another seeks to identify enduring tricks, tips and devices which crosscut the ostensible breaks and branchings – humble heuristic cogs constantly recombined into new conceptual engines. These two visions of multiplicity are importantly at odds with each other. Together, they give us a double grip on the slippery way comparison can be simultaneously one, two and many.

## Making a Break from Caesurism

Yet, to the methodologist, as opposed to the historian, this diversity of opinions poses less difficulty than might appear, for much of it can itself be accounted for by the persistent compulsion of one side to reject all of the recommendations of the other.

(Runciman 1983: 2)

The first of the two 'forms' identified in the conclusion to Chapter 2 – caesurism – has frequently been decried as a historiographic sin within anthropology and cognate disciplines:[1]

The procedure involved is the following: firstly, to postulate a break in understanding at a certain moment in history, corresponding to some sort of new theoretical insight marked by a master – be he Marx, Lévi-Strauss, Lacan, Foucault, Schneider, or Deleuze – and then, secondly, to cast into irrelevance all that came before. This procedure typifies and catalogues, in a linear process of overcoming, the various modes of carrying out anthropology as if they were unitary and indivisible, as if they were 'prototypes' or *episthèmes*. Thus, it produces ahistorical critical objects that, much as they may be useful for the teaching of undergraduates, are difficult to identify with any intellectual honesty: 'structural-functionalism', 1980s relativism, 'classical kinship theory', and so on ... The pretension that such breaks can exist is often self-interested and derives from a type of academic anxiety of influence mixed with a desire not to consider the arguments of 'old timers'.

(Pina-Cabral 2010: 168)

Pina-Cabral's critique of caesurism echoes, in the realm of epistemology, his own and others' critiques of anthropological binarisms more generally (Carrier 1992; Pina-Cabral 2006). The tendency to divide the world into 'us and them' is a classic comparative device (see below chapters 7 and 8) – little wonder perhaps that it recurs in anthropologists' comparisons of comparison. Applied to the history of theory, however, Pina-Cabral charges that this othering takes on particular chronological properties. It becomes historicist, if not outright evolutionist. Thus Pina-Cabral notes that caesurism is linked with a certain historical sensibility which he characterises as a futuristic expectation (Pina-Cabral 2010: 153) that can lead to utopian or dystopian postures.

To the critic, the way in which anthropologists have made sense of the history of comparison through binary contrasts certainly seems to validate these observations. At each juncture, old errors are pointed out and a bright new future is announced. This recurrent binarism leads to a paradox: on the one hand, it produces a pervasive sense of having left behind what came before, the destabilising or exhilarating feeling of a great flight forwards; on the other, it drags behind it the niggling sense that the same problems keep recurring. Comparison seems to be impossible not *de jure* but simply because previous approaches have got it wrong. If only we could fully exorcise those old demons, we might be left alone with the good, proper, version of comparison which we have now, finally, identified! We seem to be forever in the position of having '[t]o make a fresh start with comparison' (Gingrich and Fox 2002b: 5).

The literature on comparison occasionally reveals, however, an alternative to the caesurist view. Pina-Cabral's suggestion that we '[give] up on radical breaks and [search] for humbler solutions' (Pina-Cabral 2010: 154) echoes a different vision of anthropological comparison, in which comparison is multiple – a bundle of decomposable techniques and possibilities. Ironically, these identifications of 'humble techniques' themselves tend to be cast as a radical break from past practice. This is the move proposed by Gingrich and Fox (2002b): they too see two versions of comparison, one of which is an enemy, a litany of past errors which need to be left behind: this is 'comparison in the narrow, if well-established, sense of a "hard-science" methodology employed to support some universal theory or meta-narrative', upon which they propose to wage 'a concerted analytical attack' (Gingrich and Fox 2002b: 1–2). The crucial faultline lies, for them, between these grand or dominant imaginaries of comparison – each of which is thought to define *the* Comparative Method – and the multiplicity of 'subaltern' comparatisms which historically flourished in their shadows, at their margins and in their wake. The image is still double, but it contrasts, on the one hand, a vision of a unitary method and, on the other, a vision of comparison as constituted of bundles of heuristics of which some at least can be recuperated and re-engineered (cf. Wimsatt 2007) for new contexts and problems.

For all the sense of novelty, however, the move is old. Alongside the identification of a radical paradigmatic break between positivist and interpretive versions of comparison, Holy (1987) had also noted that comparisons come in different forms and work to different effects. Like Gingrich and Fox, Holy linked his binary vision with his multiple one: he accused the positivists of believing that there could be only one kind of comparison, and saw multiplicity emerging from the new possibilities offered by the paradigm shift to interpretivism (Holy 1987: 2). And yet, turning even further back, to Lewis, who was a positivist by Holy's standards, reveals once again the same move. Lewis (1955) similarly took anthropologists to task for imagining a unitary comparative method – the guilty party for him was Boas with his distinction between historical and comparative methods – and sought to trace instead a multiplicity of techniques which worked in different ways and to different ends. Already, the Comparative Method had unravelled into a panoply of options and techniques.

The figure of the heuristic is in some senses the opposite of the figure of the caesura. Where the latter sees epochal breaks, divisions and incommensurable paradigms, the former tracks particular conceptual devices which travel from one paradigm to the next, humble practical solutions to recurrent problems. It is ironic, as noted above, that when a vision of anthropological comparison in terms of heuristics appears in the literature, it is often precisely in the form of a caesura. I will argue below that this facile irony hides a rather more interesting theoretical point, namely that whatever the merits of a heuristic view, caesurism also has its uses. For now, let us try to specify what is at stake in the heuristic alternative to the caesurist vision of comparison outlined in the previous chapter.

## A Heuristic View

What we really need to avoid is not errors, but significant ones from which we can't recover. Even significant errors are okay as long as they are easy to find.

(Wimsatt 2007: 24)

As Andrew Abbott notes in his manual of sociological heuristics, the notion comes from the Greek root *heuriskein*, 'to find' – heuristics are methods of discovery (Abbott 2004: 80–81). 'Finding' here could mean inventing new concepts or discovering clues to the shape of objects in the world, or some recombination of the two if one doesn't believe in that distinction. Either way, the notion of heuristics indexes a focus on getting things done, rather than providing perfect accuracy. This is a particularly liberating move in relation to comparison, which can so easily become locked into longstanding philosophical debates about accuracy.

Analogy in particular, as Lloyd (2015) has shown, has been suspected as potentially misleading at least since Aristotle. Recuperating analogy as a heuristic (Lloyd 2015: 58–88; see also Abbott 2004) allows one to see value in the device even in the absence of systematic rules for getting it right. The same is true for the many other comparative devices explored in the previous chapter.

This – extremely widespread – heuristic attitude to comparatism can come with a range of philosophical commitments, from the reductionist's acceptance that things are always more complex, but you have to say *something*, through a vision of a 'multidimensional reality' which affords a plurality of accounts (Lloyd 2015), to a philosophical post-representationalism in which 'getting things done' is, in effect, all there is – whether one likes that point couched in a pragmatist (Quine 1951), performative (Austin 1975), Rortyan (1983) or Deleuzian (Deleuze and Guattari 1994) language.

There are many important reasons why one ought to care about those deep philosophical differences, and the fact that an appeal to heuristics can be used to fudge them is in some ways problematic. However, in another view, the ability of heuristics to cut across or fly under the radar of these grand philosophical distinctions is precisely their key value. Heuristics can cut across grand philosophical battle lines, and the smaller battle lines of caesurist distinctions in comparative method. In the previous chapter, we have encountered heuristics in both function-alist and Weberian attempts to categorise social facts or track concomi-tant variation despite the complexity of the world, heuristics also in the ontological turn of anthropology as a perpetual creation of concepts, and heuristics in the neo-diffusionist vision of travelling lateral theory.

Consider for instance the method of concomitant variation described above (Chapter 2). This Millian inductive method was a cornerstone of evolutionist and functionalist comparatisms: it enabled generalisations on the basis of identified co-variations between empirical cases. The structuralist approach to comparison attacked the very foundations of those various empiricist approaches. And yet we find the method of concomitant variation translated into a structuralist technique by Leach – one of the classic critics of functionalist comparatism. Thus, in his famous contrast between erstwhile typological comparatisms and his own – broadly structuralist – proposal for 'generalisation', Leach exemplified the latter in the following way:

Any *two* points can be joined by a straight line and you can represent this straight line mathematically by a simple *first* order algebraic equation. Any *three* points can be joined by a circle and you can represent this circle by a quadratic or *second* order algebraic equation. It would be a *generalization* to go straight on from there and say: any *n* points in a plane can be joined by a curve which can be represented by an equation of order *n-1*. This would be just a guess, but it would be true, and it is a kind of truth which no amount of comparison can ever reveal.

(Leach 1966: 2)

Leach's procedure of (comparative) generalisation as stated in this example is a direct application of the method of concomitant variation. It is an inductive generalisation from the observation that, in two cases, the order of the equation varies concomitantly with the number of points. Leach's 'generalisation' can be seen as a restatement, on a more abstract plane, of the basic functionalist method of concomitant variation: instead of identifying concomitant variations between empirical particulars (institutions and the like), it identifies co-variations between structural forms.

Or to take another, more general example, which we have already alluded to in the previous section, consider the key move of pinpointing difference where previously others had seen similarity. This was central to the structuralist reconfiguration of abstraction (Chapter 2). It was also important for interpretivist recuperations of Malinowski. It plays a central role in Viveiros de Castro's (2004) proposal for a 'controlled equivocation' as the opposite of 'translation'. As this example suggests, heuristics are often articulated around binaries – moves from one alternative to another, and back again. This point is crucial to Abbott's (2004) account, and I will return to it below.

In sum, a heuristic view doesn't simply envision multiple methods, it also sees multiplicity within what had been envisioned as single methods. In a heuristic view, the various comparative methods examined in the previous chapter are in each case a concatenation or combination of smaller methods, tools, devices and tricks.

## The Normativity of Heuristics

By itself, however, the recurrent vision of comparison as a bundle of 'methods of discovery' might not seem to take us very far. It appears as a primarily negative, 'anything goes', sort of view. There is a vagueness of a different order also: when anthropologists and others refer to particular claims or moves they make as 'merely heuristic', this is often just exculpatory hand-waving – a way of saying we don't quite mean it, shouldn't be taken literally and so forth, in some unspecified way. This is what I described in the introduction as an appeal to 'the pinch of salt'. Of course, a core feature of an appeal to heuristics as noted above is that they need not be true, just useful. But there is a world of difference between an appeal to heuristics which specifies their aims and their conditions of failure, and one that doesn't. The latter is merely a way, in sum, to divert attention from the failings and limitations of particular arguments, rather than to confront such points of failure.

A thinker who has very usefully examined the question of where and how heuristics fail is philosopher of science William Wimsatt. Heuristics, according to Wimsatt, are devices – be they conceptual tools, technical apparatuses or indeed biological adaptations – which share six main characteristics (Wimsatt 2007: 346). They

1 make no guarantees,
2 are cost-effective,

3 are systematically biased,
4 transform a problem into a non-equivalent but intuitively related problem,
5 are purpose-relative, and
6 are descended from other heuristics.

The usual off-hand exculpatory reference to heuristics only takes in points 1 and 2. Point 4 captures the idea that heuristics are tools for transforming problems, for generating or discovering new ideas. But I am particularly interested here in point 3: *heuristics are systematically biased.*

Too often in caesurist visions of comparison, as in Wimsatt's account of classic scientific training, 'errors are ok only if they are someone else's or belong to prior generations' (Wimsatt 2007: 3). By contrast, a heuristic view makes errors, failings and limitations into an important and useful aspect of practice. The emphasis here is on 'systematically'. That is to say, the point is not simply that heuristics always fail, but rather that they fail in regular and predictable ways. Thus attempts to identify cultural units systematically under-represent internal diversity and blurred boundaries. Attempts to trace the extension of phenomena or the movement of 'traits' across contexts systematically have a problem theorising the way these different traits might come to hang together in a more than random jumble. Appeals to ethnography to challenge existing theoretical assumptions systematically tend to under-represent the caveats these assumptions came with. And so on.

Wimsatt describes this distinctive pattern of error as a heuristic's 'footprint' (2007: 80). Having a consistent footprint is one of the main keys to the value of heuristics. It allows one to decide for which purposes a heuristic is useful – for which ends it is a good means – and for which it will be systematically misleading (cf. point 5). This explicit focus on footprints distinguishes an appeal to heuristics from a gesture towards the pinch of salt, or an 'anything goes' position. Heuristics are means to ends – they need to earn their keep. This is another way of saying that Wimsatt's appeal to heuristics is normative – and not only in an epistemological sense. There are two main normative strands implied in a heuristic view. The first, particularly prominent in Wimsatt's version of heuristics, concerns the quality of 'robustness'. The second is an attention to the distinction between omitting something and forgetting it, which recasts the classic anthropological concern with 'reflexivity'.

## *Robust, Not Brittle*

Robust knowledge practices are internally heterogeneous, they approach a problem from multiple directions at once, they deploy different heuristics with distinct footprints. Wimsatt deploys an analogy used also by Wittgenstein to characterise family resemblances: robust knowledge practices are like a many-stranded rope, in which a few strands can break but the rope still holds. The opposite of robust is 'brittle'. Brittle arguments are like a chain which breaks if any of its links proves weak. What Wimsatt terms 'robustness analysis' is the concern with matching up different heuristics which can support each other in useful ways (2007: 44). Conversely, it seeks to detect collections of heuristics which have significantly overlapping footprints – which systematically fail in the same way – thereby tending to produce, when used together, a false sense of robustness (2007: 82–84).

We can exemplify this last point in relation to the opposition between empiricists and structuralists. Mid-century comparatists who sought to recombine Radcliffe-Brown and Boas, the near and the far, control and generalisation, envisioned themselves as deploying a range of very different comparative heuristics: one could compare distant or close cases, related or unrelated societies; one could compare within cultures or seek by comparison to elucidate cultural wholes; one investigator or different investigators could restudy the same context at different points in time; comparisons could draw on fieldwork in one or more locations, on library data, and so forth. Different, also, were the aims: generalising, testing hypotheses, challenging western assumptions, documenting variation, etc. These different heuristics all functioned as controls for each other, and could thus provide a robust picture of sociocultural reality. But from a structuralist vantage point, this rich diversity of comparative heuristics all shared the same empiricist footprint: in one way or other, they all sought to work 'up' from differences and similarities identified in empirical cases. As a result, they systematically treated polythetic sets of features as if they were monothetic ones (Needham 1975). They could not serve as controls for one another since they all, ultimately, failed in the same way. The vision of robustness was illusory. The result was still after all just 'tabulated nonsense' (Leach, cited in Holy 1987: 3).

In sum, for Wimsatt,

A theory in which most components are multiply connected is a theory whose faults are relatively precisely localizable. Not only do errors not propagate far, but we can find their source quickly and evaluate the damage and what is required for an adequate replacement. If this sounds like a design policy for an automobile, I can say only that there is no reason why our scientific theories should be less well designed than our other artifacts.

(Wimsatt 2007: 53)

Wimsatt's identification of heuristics with tools is not metaphorical. He characteristically approaches epistemology and ontology as continuous – robustness is a feature not simply of arguments, but also of biological adaptations (many animals have different senses which triangulate each other's grasp on the world), and of well-built technological devices. Few anthropological commentators on comparison are thoroughgoing evolutionary epistemologists of Wimsatt's stripe. But this vision of a quasi-Darwinian proliferation of methods is not without echoes in discussions of anthropological comparison:

Today, it is possible to move beyond the ruins of a monopolistic claim to one kind of comparison and beyond the stifling of intellectual competition it visited upon anthropology. Now, a rich plurality of qualitative comparative methodologies has emerged – none claiming exclusive rights, each offering its insights and evidence.

(Gingrich and Fox 2002b: 12)

There is a particular normativity to the thought that a healthy discipline is one in which many methods compete without an overarching framework.

I will return below to the important epistemological and political issues raised by the technophilic-Darwinian echoes of the notion of heuristics. Certainly, a number of its entailments should give us pause, as we shall see. But one valuable effect of the view is that it shares with contemporary science studies an attention to the materiality of knowledge practices. Wimsatt's relentless invocation of engineering as a model for epistemology pushes through metaphor and into a truly immanentist view of knowledge as one amongst the practical activities of humans in the world. Whereas the caesurist distinctions above were concerned with concepts, arguments and theoretical positions, a heuristic view pushes us to think of conceptual tools as part of a broader panoply of techniques and fixes.

Looking at anthropological comparison from this perspective, we would be asking about the material devices which scaffold, enable or subvert particular kinds of comparative work. Some of these, such as monographs, or the distinction between 'home' and 'fieldwork', have been extensively examined as heuristic forms in their own right. Others, such as the use of diagrams (Gell 1999: 31–32; Lynteris 2017) or the creation of large databases in mid-century anthropology (L'Estoile 2005), are beginning to attract the attention of anthropologists and historians. But there are many other material devices for anthropological comparison which – perhaps because they are so banal – have not received such sustained attention: edited volumes and their introductions, seminars, peer review and the distinctive ecology of 'generalist' and 'thematic' journal publishing, alongside newer developments such as blogging or the changing ways in which referencing databases and word processors transform what can be kept in view at one time. Rather than imagine these in terms of a 'social context' for the intellectual work of comparison, Wimsatt's heuristic view chimes in with the material-semiotic point that these are in effect a concatenation of apparatuses. A heuristic view which treats these 'technical' and 'conceptual' fixes in a truly symmetric fashion would bring to anthropologists' considerations of their own practices the kind of approach which many have long enjoined in the study of other knowledge practices (e.g. Knorr-Cetina 1999; Latour and Woolgar 1979).

In line with this attention to the humdrum, daily practical aspects of comparative work, the heuristic view's normative focus on robustness also enjoins a suspicion of the often 'brittle' claims to theoretical revolution – the claim that, through some clever reconfiguration of elementary terms and relations, everything is transformed, and everything is explained (Wimsatt 2007: 341). We have seen many of these 'brittle' claims in the history of comparatism. Indeed, most caesuras are articulated around them: change these few elements of your repertoire, and you have made a nonsense of all that came before. Stop thinking you can abstract from empirical particulars, or stop trying to generalise based on Euroamerican categories, and a new world of methodological possibility opens up. Comparison becomes possible at last. What a heuristic view entails is some attention to all that is, of necessity, conserved across these radical breaks. Some heuristic devices are explicitly taken and rearticulated, certainly. But others just persist silently, under the radar of epistemological revolutionaries themselves.

Thus, from the early twentieth century onwards, anthropologists have continued to gather together edited volumes, to publish in a mix of 'regional' and 'generalist' journals, and to expect to hear, in a 'good' presentation by a colleague, a 'proper' balance of ethnography and theory. Each of these practices, which rumble along broadly undisturbed as brittle conceptual revolutions come and go, carry their own epistemological undertow. For instance, in all of these contexts and others, anthropologists keep one eye on describing the particulars of their 'material' in ways which colleagues who know the area and the literature will find broadly convincing. Whatever epistemological somersaults they might be achieving on other scales of their accounts, on this basic level, anthropologists are still in the main deploying classic realist techniques of caveated generalisation (cf. below, Chapter 5). These modest, enduring practices through which we convince and cross-check each other make anthropology, in the main, a fairly robust discipline. But this robustness entails an epistemological and methodological multiplicity, which relativises claims to radical rupture.

## *Omitting, Not Forgetting*

We shall give a technical meaning to the difference between 'forgetting' and 'omitting'.

(Latour 2012: 266, my translation)

The other normative strand in heuristically minded accounts – beyond Wimsatt specifically – concerns the alternative between forgetting and omitting. All heuristics have footprints, and therefore omit things; the question is whether one is remaining aware of or forgetting what has been omitted. A heuristic goes bad when it forgets it is a heuristic – when it forgets the things it had initially omitted. In this sense, heuristics are (like) habits in Bruno Latour's characterisation:[2] without their systematic omissions there can be no sustained activity, but they go bad when their omissions lead us to forget the possibility of alternatives (Latour 2012: 261–284). The point can be made in an exclusively epistemological vein, as a warning against the ossification of paradigms; or it can be made in a simultaneously political vein, as a reminder that no omission can ever be politically or ethically 'innocent' (Barad 2007; Haraway 1989). Indeed we shall see in a moment that this point can be turned back on to the heuristic view itself, which occasionally forgets that it is itself just that, namely a heuristic, with important omissions.

This concern with keeping heuristics live by remembering their omissions has a distinguished pedigree within anthropology. In its most basic form it is another word for reflexivity – the commitment, as Benedict puts it, to being 'conscious of the eyes through which one looks' (Benedict 2005: 22). In a more precise sense of an attention to the entailments of one's theoretical devices, one finds this commitment, for instance, in the epistemological work of Siegfried Nadel (1951, 1957b). There is one of the most consistent and thoroughgoing attempts to make explicit the footprint of functionalist heuristics, to clearly and honestly map out where they fail and how far they can be made to travel. In a very different genre, Marilyn Strathern's work to make our own analytical strategies evident (e.g. Strathern 2004) partakes in one key respect of the same sensibility. The aims, language and hopes for anthropology are of course radically different, as we shall see again below. But these two authors share the commitment to keeping the limits of our knowledge practices in view.[3]

The general point about the need for reflexivity is now so widespread in anthropology as to be little more than a banal methodological truism. But what is characteristic of heuristic approaches like Nadel's or Strathern's is the sustained intellectual effort to keep in view, not just the generally limited nature of all strategies, but *the particular limits of specific strategies one nevertheless chooses – or has – to deploy*. Part of the reason why Strathern's writing is so famously 'difficult' is because of this constantly and relentlessly heuristic view, in which everything is written with one eye on the practice and effect of writing it. The point is not, as some critics have suggested (Iteanu and Moya 2015), to deploy tools merely in order to subvert them, as in a classic deconstructionist mode. Rather the point is to stop omissions from silently slipping into forgetfulness.

The distinction between forgetting and omitting relates directly to the point that heuristics are necessarily flawed. The normative force of this point is unambiguous, be it epistemologically or politically: a heuristic view enjoins you to own your errors, and not to dismiss others too quickly because of theirs.

## Caesurism as a Heuristic: Seeing Fractal Patterns in Theoretical Debates

When you come to a fork in the road, take it.

Yogi Berra

The heuristic view thus seems to give us a counterpoint to caesurism, and introduces a rather different tone into discussions of comparison. Thinking in these terms shifts the ways in which disciplinary debates are carried out. To the image of the past as a junkyard of broken theories and methods, a heuristic view counterposes the image of the past as a treasure-trove of ingenious possibilities and unexpected 'fixes'. Conceptual opponents and predecessors become potential allies rather than simply useful exemplars of failure. Treating our own and each other's concepts, techniques and methods as a bundle of perfectible heuristics has two valuable effects. One is to keep sharp the sense that our knowledge practices are *at most* heuristic – thereby avoiding the somewhat tiresome debates produced by and around grandstanding proposals for any particular approach as the only, or the most valuable, or the most moral, way to do anthropology. The other valuable effect is to remind us that particular concepts, approaches and so forth, even if flawed or limited, might be *at least* heuristic. That is to say that they can do useful work despite and even because of their points of failure. Diagnosing such points of failure becomes, not a destructive 'ruination' (Navaro-Yashin 2009) of other approaches or paradigms, an 'all-or-nothing critique' (Pina-Cabral 2009), but rather a critical recognition of temporary vantages and unstable achievements (Anderson 2001: 32).

But this vision of heuristics as an alternative to caesurism brings us straight back to the irony identified above. When anthropologists claim that the time has come to move away from caesurism, to make a fresh start, they risk replicating the structure of caesurism itself. Consider Pina-Cabral's forceful statement: 'My argument, to the contrary, is anti-caesurist …: it denies that there can ever be any decisive break, any paradigmatic shift, any radical theoretical caesura in the thinking of social scientists' (Pina-Cabral 2010: 167). It is hard to resist the thought that 'anti-caesurism' itself is a caesurist move. It gathers together the way anthropologists previously dealt with theory, ignoring the substance of what they actually felt was at stake in the particular breaks they proposed, and casts the move of making a break itself into irrelevance, proposing an alternative for a better epistemological future. Not unlike comparison – of which it is after all an instance – 'caesurism' has a way of encompassing its alternatives.

This neat reversal may seem a bit facile: one could conceptually speaking imagine a change in perspective that is not a caesura. But a less glib way to put the same point is to note that critiques of caesurism – and these are widespread in the discipline beyond the particular case invoked here – often leave us with an uncomfortable sense of uncharitableness. The critique of caesurism as a self-aggrandising procedure of theoretical empire-building may hit home in some cases, but it seems to occlude the after all enduring sense that our friends and colleagues who attempt to draw clear lines across epistemology (including, by the way, Pina-Cabral's own distinction between caesurism and anti-caesurism) are also engaged in a genuine attempt to order and make sense of key moments and alternatives in the discipline. In sum, anti-caesurism shares with caesurism an affect if not a structure: it opens itself up to the critique that it is yet another instance of the uncharitable desire not to consider the arguments of previous authors who felt that something radical was at stake in breaking with the past. Another fork in the road.

But a fork, as Yogi Berra reminds us, is also a utensil. One can pick things up with it. One way to break the paradox of (anti-)caesurist critiques of caesurism is to accept that tracing forking paths in the history of theory can be a useful tool for particular theoretical and practical ends – and not simply for the teaching of undergraduates, although there's nothing wrong with that. We could accept the ultimately fictional nature of these accounts of radical rupture, yet appreciate the work they can do in certain contexts. This has also been, historically, the most convincing response to critiques of binarism in anthropological accounts of cultures or ontologies (see below, Chapter 8): indefensible as statements of empirical fact, these are nevertheless useful tools for thinking. The solution, quite simply, is to treat caesurism itself as a heuristic.

The most systematic working out of this observation in relation to the forking paths of epistemology comes from Abbott's account of self-similarity in sociological theory in *Chaos of disciplines* (Abbott 2001) – a work which, as we shall see below, informs and underpins his later interest in heuristics. Abbott notes that some of the classic contrasts in the history of sociology, some of which we encountered in the previous chapter – positivism and interpretation, history and synchronic sociology, individualism and emergentism, freedom and constraint – have a deictic structure: they index differences contextually rather than in absolute terms. One is a positivist in relation to one's broadly interpretivist department, but might be seen as rather interpretivist in the context of a more hard-core positivist audience. As a result, these contrasts also produce fractal subdivisions: having categorised sociologists or their theories into positivist and interpretivist camps, one will soon find that that distinction replicates within each of its terms – amongst any group of interpretivists, some will be more 'positivist' and others more 'interpretivist'. The pattern replicates on every scale. It relies on 'the tricky logical device of making a distinction and then repeating it within itself' (Abbott 2001: 9).

Anthropologists will have no trouble recognising two familiar forms in Abbott's account. One is the segmentary lineage model of classic kinship theory (Evans-Pritchard 1940) – and Abbott acknowledges his debt to Evans-Pritchard explicitly. Another – and here the parallel seems to be coincidental as far as references in either case suggest – is the focus on fractal patterns in the work of Marilyn Strathern (2004). There is a difference in emphasis, however. Strathern notes, in the manner of an ethnographic observation, that fractal self-similarity – the fact that complexity remains invariant regardless of the scale at which a phenomenon is observed – is 'an organizational facility of Western pluralist cultural life' (Strathern 2004: xx; see also xxix), which might be contrasted to other non-Euroamerican epistemic devices. Abbott by contrast sees in self-organisation a basic property of cultural and social systems in general. We shall return to the relevance of this difference below.

Abbott's fractal vision is not merely synchronic, however (a matter of logical categories and sub-categories), but also diachronic, and it is in this guise, as an account of how theory changes, that it provides a close analogue to 'caesurism' as discussed above. Drawing on a series of close examinations of particular theoretical shifts and debates in the history of sociology, Abbott argues that fractal distinctions provide an engine for theoretical change. This can happen in various way, but a key mechanism he retains is that of 'fractal cycles' (Abbott 2001: 22). To summarise, Abbott's vision is one in which, with each generation, young mavericks and iconoclasts (re)discover a formerly abandoned alternative – the minor or abandoned branch of an enduring fractal distinction – and build upon it a new vantage point from which to critique their elders as they sit comfortably on the major branch. Thus an individualist innovation can be brought in to challenge a well-established emergentist paradigm. In time, these young mavericks grow to elderhood, and get comfortable on their now well-established side of the contrast, only to find that a new generation of thinkers will come to dethrone them with their own reinvention of an emergentist challenge.

Whereas fractal patterns are usually imagined as constantly proliferating, the distinctiveness of Abbott's fractal cycles is that they represent a pattern of constant extinctions and rebirths. With each generational reversal, one pole of the contrast, one line of conceptual descent, becomes sterile and another fertile. The victorious proponents of the fertile line find they have to occupy the territory held by their now sterile forebears. They thus need to remap the latter's concerns into their own. Individualists thus find they have to stretch their ideas to cover the paradigmatic cases which had been well explained by emergentism, for instance. This in turn introduces stresses within their paradigm, which will later provide the faultlines along which a new internal split is generated and exploited by a new generation of emergentist mavericks who come to overthrow the individualist status quo. In sum, in this vision, there are thus only ever two terms, perpetually recycling. And yet in another sense the terms are always new, generated from within.

There is a hint of world-weariness to Abbott's vision of a perpetual generational war of position in which everything changes in order for everything to stay the same (Lampedusa 2007). We are only one step away from a denunciation of caesurism. But the step is important. The drawing of caesuras is recognised here, not as a fault of historiography, but as an engine of the discipline. Abbott notes that the device of changing the signs of an old contrast is, in each case, generative. With each reversal, new problems and concepts are identified, new insightful case studies and demonstrations produced, and there is a profound and real sense in which the discipline moves forward.

The fractal cycle is at heart a profoundly traditional mechanism. Like any good ritual it unites opposites. On the one hand, it generates perpetual change. Old ideas are perpetually being thrown out. Intellectual autocracy is perpetually overthrown. On the other, it produces perpetual stability. The new ideas are always the old ideas under new labels. The new people are the old people in new roles ... [O]n the whole, the ritual is profoundly useful. We get to keep our best concepts forever and yet retain our belief in perpetual intellectual progress.

(Abbott 2001: 26–27)

There are some straightforward ways in which this view of recurrent binaries can be used to parse the story of anthropological comparatism presented in the previous chapter. The most obvious fit for our story would be the contrast between the use of comparison to generalise and the use of comparative techniques to focus on particular cases. The story might begin with Tylor and Durkheim highlighting the comparative purpose of generalisation, followed by Boas and Malinowski swinging in very different ways back towards the particular, followed by Radcliffe-Brown and Lévi-Strauss – again, in different ways – returning to grand comparative schemes, followed by interpretivist and postmodern returns to the particular, followed by the recent renewed calls for 'transparticular' (Howe and Boyer 2015) comparison. Another contrast which could fit this bill quite neatly is the contrast between comparisons which foreground difference and those which foreground similarity. In that view Tylor and Durkheim, with their emphasis on concomitant variation, foreground similarity, to which Boas responds by a foregrounding of difference which challenges the identification of common terms across contexts (Salmon 2013a); Malinowski and Radcliffe-Brown, in different ways and on different scales, foreground similarity once again; Lévi-Strauss and the structuralists, and in their own way, the interpretivists too, foreground difference. Note that these two accounts of fractal cycles map different trajectories and constitute different groupings throughout the history of comparatism: in one, Malinowski and Radcliffe-Brown end up on opposite sides, in another they are in the same camp. They can also be used to draw different lessons. Examining the fractal cycle of similarity and difference, one might draw the conclusion that we have been rhetorically foregrounding difference for quite some time now (in various ways, since the structuralists) and it might be time for another turn of the wheel. With slightly more massaging of terms, distinctions and concerns, one might see a similar set of 'fractal cycles' between 'interpretation' and 'positivism', between appeals to concreteness and appeals to abstraction, or as demonstrated by Webb Keane in a pithy overview of (mainly) US anthropology, between epistemologies of estrangement and epistemologies of intimacy (Keane 2005).

This multiplicity highlights an important point: Abbott doesn't of course suggest that any disciplinary history could be reduced to the operation of a single fractal cycle. Rather, he sees multiple fractal cycles cutting across each other in diverse ways, along with, of course, a host of other inter- and intra-disciplinary processes. One particularly interesting observation is his suggestion that one look out in particular for the mapping of multiple contrasts on to one another in what he terms a 'methodological manifold' (Abbott 2001: 28) – a concatenation of fractal distinctions which tend to be reversed together: thus the contrast between positivism and interpretation tends to be mapped on to a contrast between the emergent and the individual, and on to a contrast between quantification and narrative and so forth. Interesting things happen, Abbott notes, when one of these component contrasts is uncoupled from the others (when interpretivists seek to deploy quantification, for instance). In our case, one might say, for instance, that positivist visions of comparison are usually assumed to be engaged in the drawing up of abstract typological schemes, and foregrounding similarity, whereas visions which are interpretivist tend to focus on the specific and to foreground difference (Holy 1987). Multiple contrasts are stacked up in each case. Having mapped this general pattern, one can start to see that interesting things happen when the contrasts become unhooked from one other – as, for instance, in the structuralist combination of abstraction with a focus on difference, or in the neo-diffusionist reinvention of tracing which makes concepts into things.

With this observation, Abbott's scheme starts to yield not only descriptive but also heuristic dividends. Indeed, Abbott's later work on heuristics (2004) draws directly on his previous work on fractal distinctions, to show how classic contrasts in the history of the discipline can be redeployed as tools for generating new ideas. Take a problem which has usually been thought of in terms of one pole of such a classic contrast, Abbott advises, and swap the signs: you will soon find a new idea emerging. Caesurism can become not simply a device for ordering the history of anthropological comparatism, but also a device for generating new visions of comparison.

In sum, a key device of Abbott's fractal account of the history of theory is a reduction of the differences between each 'recurrence' in favour of highlighting the similarities. On a greater or smaller level of granularity, what one sees is 'always the same thing coming back'. To this I would like to counterpose a different invocation of fractal patterns. This is drawn from an analogy to the work of Marilyn Strathern – more specifically, from Alfred Gell's famous comment/reconstruction of Strathern's arguments about Melanesian relationality in *The gender of the gift* (Strathern 1988).

In what Gell playfully terms 'system M' – M for Marilyn or for Melanesia (Gell 1999: 34) – things in the world are objectifications of relations. Thus a person is an objectification of the relation between their two parents. And relations in turn can encompass other relations in a fractal pattern. In Gell's reconstruction, this means that a relation is encompassed within one term of another relation, or to use Strathern's terminology, that a relation is eclipsed by another relation.

What Gell has primarily in mind here is not the obvious fractal pattern of genealogy, in which relations on every scale are of the same kind – a person objectifies the relation between their two parents, each term of which in turn includes an analogous relation between a pair of grandparents, etc. This would bring us to something rather similar to Abbott's vision. Rather, Gell, via Strathern, is particularly interested in the ability of one relation to encompass, or more precisely to 'eclipse', a relation of an ostensibly different kind. For instance, when the labour relation between a husband and wife is objectified in the production of a pig, this relation in turn eclipses the reproductive relation between the two pigs, which might, in another view, have been seen to have 'produced' the pig. Since the wife is mainly involved in raising the pigs, Gell denotes this by including the pig–sow relation within the 'wife' term of the husband–wife relation. When the husband gives the pig to an exchange partner, this relation between donor and recipient in turn eclipses the relation between husband and wife – including that relationship in the husband/donor term of the new exchange relation. The thing in the world – be it a pig or a person – is thus an objectification of multiple nested relations. It is thus both a single unit and also potentially a decomposable fractal. For the term 'eclipsing' (Gell 1999: 81) in this discussion denotes the fact that one relation, when it is encompassed within a term of another relation, is in effect hidden or backgrounded – but that it can in certain contexts be revealed again. When this 'return of the repressed' happens, the objectification (person, pig, etc.) is revealed as a fractal, composite of multiple nested relations.

Without pursuing the discussion further into the intricacies of Gell's rendering of Strathern, the point I want to make here is that this fractal pattern, in which relations on different nested levels need not be of the same kind, is different from the pattern described by Abbott, and provides a neater fit for the account of successive caesuras given in the previous chapter. In Abbott's version of fractal conceptual debates, what is eclipsed with each generational 'turn' is, in effect, one term of the relation. Over and over, the same contrast – albeit, it is true, producing novelty along the way.

By contrast, an analogy to the Gell/Strathern schema would enable us to see comparison as a fractal composed of nested contrasts of *different* kinds.⁴ There is no movement 'back and forth' between the same two positions, but a succession of different, and in some senses incommensurable, alternatives, each of which eclipses another within one of its terms.⁵ The contrast between the comparative method and the historical method is eclipsed within the 'empiricist' term of the contrast between empiricism and structuralism; the latter contrast in turn is eclipsed within the first term of the positivist–interpretivist contrast; which in turn is eclipsed within the first term of a contrast between realisms of various stripes and postmodernism, etc. The intellectual sin of caesurism picked up by Pina-Cabral – the fact that it traduces the approaches which it encompasses under the 'old' pole of its old–new contrast, simplifies them and eclipses their differences – is thus given a theoretical formulation.

The objectification of all these nested contrasts is that key figure looming over anthropology, namely 'comparison'. It is both one and multiple. It appears at times as the objectification of a contrast between two terms ('There are two ways of comparing …'). At other times, as with fractal persons, the internal multiplicity of comparison can be revealed when previously eclipsed alternatives are brought back into view. For, in setting up a succession of alternatives, the caesurist vision also creates objects which are ripe for later reappropriation. We have thus seen how frequently, in recent times, previously eclipsed alternatives (structuralist abstraction, Boas's historical method) have been revived as the solution to new problems of comparison. The move is old: Radcliffe-Brown, defending the Comparative Method in 1951 – one year after Evans-Pritchard's devastating critique – was himself self-consciously recuperating a Tylorean technique which had been marked as evolutionist. This was an explicitly antiquarian move.

This model gives a coherent account of the paradoxes we have encountered through this part of the book: anthropological comparison is one thing – it is many things, there are only ever two ways of doing it – yet these alternatives keep changing. These alternatives are all present in the history of comparison, but they are not linked into an overarching hierarchy or logical arrangement in which all could be seen at the same time: only by eclipsing some alternatives can other possibilities come into view.

What caesurism simultaneously reveals and produces in the history of anthropological comparison, in other words, is the peculiar way in which anthropologists are simultaneously in the same business – the business of comparing – and yet divided by alternative visions of comparison which are alternatives *to* each other, but not alternatives *for* each other (Laidlaw 2014: 213). Beyond the differences we have picked out here between the Abbott and the Strathern/Gell model, this focus on *incommensurability within relations* is in a sense the profound truth of fractal devices, be they applied in the field of epistemology, or in anthropology's own comparative engagements with cultures or ontologies (Strathern 2004). A fractal vision replaces continua with breaks and subdivisions. What is already evacuated in Abbott's schema, for instance, is the idea of a 'continuum' between say interpretivist and positivist sociologists. There is no continuum, just a set of proliferating breaks:

We cannot assume that the dichotomy of narratives versus causality simply produces a linear scale from pure narratives to pure causality, because the second-level distinctions produce in this case groups that have moved past each other on the scales.

(Abbott 2001: 14)

Abbott exemplifies this principle in a brilliant demonstration of the way in which, in the 1970s, 'historical sociologists' and 'sociological historians', albeit seemingly animated by the same set of concerns, never met in the middle but in fact talked past each other (Abbott 2001: chapter 4).

## The Normativity of Caesurism

At first sight, a 'tool' still suggests a possible encompassment by the maker and user who determines its use. Yet our theories of culture already tell us that we perceive uses through the tools we have at our disposal.

(Strathern 2004: 40; see also 43–44)

Importantly, the vision of multiplicity entailed here is different from the vision of multiplicity evoked in our discussion of heuristics. Here, the anthropological comparative project is a whole made up of contrasts of which some have to be eclipsed in order for others to come into view. There is a profound *incompossibility* to different versions of comparison. In a heuristic view, by contrast, different comparative devices can be assembled and reassembled at will, in a joyful and relaxed tinkering mode, to see what works – as long as one keeps in mind a few basic principles of good design. The history of anthropological comparison becomes, not a maze of interlocking incompossible alternatives, but rather a large store of spare parts. Take a bit of this from structuralism, a bit of that from evolutionism, and one cog from the ontological turn, and see what you get. It might work or not – just keep tinkering!

There is much to like about the heuristic view and I will be deploying it myself in the second half of this book. But the caesurist alternative – and that is perhaps its key value – spotlights a number of things which the heuristic view itself tends to systematically ignore. A heuristic view has its inbuilt normativity, as we saw above – it is a normativity made of robustness, tolerant acceptance of failures as long as they are recognised, a distaste for brittle calls to change everything all at once and single-factor solutions to complex problems. One might think of this as the politics, or the ethics, of the heuristic view. But a caesurist view also has its own normativity, its own politics and ethics. These turn precisely on those things that the heuristic view tends to background or omit.

After all, the heuristic vision which thinks of the practices and procedures of comparison as 'tools', as mere means to ends (e.g. Goodenough 1970: 119), is itself a heuristic. This vision too has a footprint. It omits much. When a heuristic perspective is combined – as in Wimsatt's case – with evolutionary epistemology, it can come to seem as quite simply the truth of how the world works – conceptually, biologically and technically. Then, the omissions of that view become hard to keep in mind (Strathern 1988: 20).

What are these omissions? The key one is perhaps the entanglement of means and ends. The thought that one can posit tools in relation to and therefore distinct from purposes is a surprisingly powerful move when one thinks about it. It allows us to decontextualise and recontextualise techniques and varieties of comparison, leave behind problematic assumptions and aims we no longer share, and refashion old tools to suit new purposes. This is the key to the delightful adaptability of heuristics, which can fly, as I noted above, under the radar of grand philosophical distinctions.

But this assumes a picture of enquirers as rational and free individuals making fully informed decisions in view of explicitly held goals. This also comes with the sense of goals which can be stipulated ahead of the enquiry. To this seductive but partial image, the caesurist view adds the caveat that different aims are not always commensurate, are sometimes identified *post hoc*, and can often only be thought relationally. It reminds us that people think and work in relation with and opposition to others, and that particular bundles of heuristics and specific aims might actually come in packages which are not so easily 'decomposable'.

These considerations echo the old problem of cultural 'units' and their travelling 'parts'. Marilyn Strathern once forcefully contrasted the perspectives thrown up in political or academic debate and those conjured up by the image of intercultural dialogue.

Unlike the discourse created by different theoretical positions, taken up competitively in explicit relation between themselves, different histories and cultures are not necessarily formed with other histories and cultures in mind. 'Dialogue' is as much a contrivance as is the anthropologist's 'translation of cultures'. And a dialogue of cultures is a fancy. It certainly cannot be taken for granted that, simply because they are collected together, the voices will address in their different versions the same problem.

(Strathern 1988: 29)

Strathern's point – here as elsewhere – was to deepen our sense of cultural difference, by pointing to the fact that it cannot be imagined on the model of our own academic or political debates. The point is reversible: academic disputes emerge as less radical than the sorts of differences anthropologists have imagined as cultural. But the truth is somewhere in between. Some cultural differences are articulated around shared problems. Conversely, in some academic debates, opposing sides have forgotten so much about the other's position that they are no longer in any meaningful sense addressing the same problem.

For instance, I have above praised Nadel's carefully heuristic approach, and we could even pick out elements of Nadel's method and re-engineer them for present use. And yet, I would hazard that Nadel's aim of seeking to derive from comparative study a number of universal propositions of the form 'if A, then B' (Nadel 1951: 223) will not enthuse the majority of contemporary anthropologists. Even on a purely intellectual level, Nadel's enthusiasms and his hopes are not ours (Ingold 2008: 72–73) – and that's before we get to his politics (see below).

We tend to think of this as the effect of a shift away from positivist anthropology. But the history of caesuras briefly mapped above suggests that the move is general. Nadel's enthusiasms were just as alien to an earlier generation of structuralist-inspired critics for whom generalisation was indeed desirable, but could not be approached in this way. Tabulating and comparing social facts of this kind was mere 'butterfly collecting', not because it had been done carelessly, but because the imagined point and purpose of this work was seen then, as now, as misguided. But to the structuralists, the reasons were different. Generalisation had to start from abstraction. From a later purview, in which grand theory itself is what has been rejected, structuralism, too, begins to look like 'tabulated nonsense' (Leach, cited in Holy 1987: 3).[6] And what is left of the careful discussions of the power and limits of a Geertzian hermeneutics of culture once the nature/culture distinction itself has been identified as the source of all anthropological error? Each successive eclipse maps a point at which the aims of previous approaches – their imagined and hoped-for futures – were left behind.

By contrast, a heuristic view too easily assumes that 'we' are all in the same business. Of course, as we saw above, point 5 of Wimsatt's definition was that *heuristics are purpose-relative*. There is a space there for multiplicity. But the language of 'tools for jobs' is itself not anodyne. It already suggests a shared set of values, above and beyond particular ends and purposes: efficiency, pragmatism and accountability, for instance. But what is posited as shared can be even more specific. Much of what is attractive about Wimsatt's tone and style – his no-nonsense pragmatism in which epistemology is no more mysterious than fixing a car, his qualified optimism, his charitable approach to alternative positions – derives from a broader sense that we are all in the same business of getting a firmer grip on the world. I certainly have no quarrel with that characterisation, and many anthropologists would agree, in a general sort of way. But the devil is in the details. In turns out that the aim, for Wimsatt, of ensuring 'robust' knowledge, is to distinguish

the real from the illusory; the reliable from the unreliable; the objective from the subjective; the object of focus from artifacts of perspective; and in general, that which is regarded as ontologically and epistemologically trustworthy and valuable from that which is unreliable, ungeneralizable, worthless, and fleeting.

(Wimsatt 2007: 46)

At that point, many anthropologists would find they have to part ways with Wimsatt. Why for instance, should the ungeneralisable be unreliable, or the fleeting worthless?

In Abbott's less engineering-focused vision, heuristics are more explicitly detached from issues of objectivity, realism and generalisation – they are focused principally on the production of new ideas. The problem to which Abbott's invocation of heuristics is the solution, is the problem of how one might say something new, in the face of the overwhelming amount of everything that has already been said. But the value of invention and novelty is itself something which would need to be situated. The particular dynamic of invention standing out against a background of convention which is the taken-for-granted background to Abbott's invocation of heuristics, is a feature of a particular western epistemological imaginary (Wagner 1981). Either way, the no-nonsense language of 'tools for jobs' is in other words rooted in particular historical and cultural assumptions and equivalences.

The problem is not – let me be clear – that the invocation of heuristics itself 'comes from somewhere', conceptually or culturally speaking. Everything does. The problem is that the foregrounding of efficacy – getting a job done – can pre-empt a proper discussion of what the job ought to be, and what success looks like (Heywood 2018c).

Nadel is once again a case in point. His careful attention to foregrounding the merely heuristic nature of his structural-functionalism is remarkable and it actually defuses most of the conceptual criticisms classically articulated against that school of thought. But this view of structural abstraction as a mere tool is blind to the implicit assumptions about what job this tool is *supposed* to do. We have mentioned his epistemic horizons above. But there is another horizon here. As Faris has detailed, Nadel was unusually explicit about the 'right and duty of anthropologists to judge, criticise, and add constructively to social development and political planning of all kinds' (Nadel 1951: 155; Faris 1973: 155). Most immediately, for Nadel this involved advising with questions of colonial administration and 'indirect rule'. He himself had undertaken his fieldwork in the Sudan at the behest of the colonial administration, and then served in the British Military Administration in Eritrea during the war as secretary for colonial affairs. In this context, as Faris points out, a number of the conceptual tools Nadel crafted in aid of better comparison – most obviously the heuristic reduction of social structure to quantifiable measures of 'command' over people and resources (Nadel 1957b: 114–124) – were clearly marked by Nadel's sense of what 'the job' was (Faris 1973: 162–163; see also Pincheon 2000: 45). This was not mainly a failure of reflexivity. Faris – writing from a Marxist perspective – wryly notes, 'the unity of theory and practice in Nadel is remarkable—and had it served different interests, we might even call it enviable' (Faris 1973: 162). The point, in other words, goes beyond the specific and much discussed case of structural-functionalism and British colonialism (cf. Asad 1973a; Candea 2018b; Kuper 1973). It highlights a fundamental affordance of the heuristic view: however explicit one is about both one's tools and one's purposes, the thought that these might be essentially separable, that the tools – here, comparative heuristics – are merely intellectual abstractions which can then be 'applied', obfuscates the extent to which one's purposes (some explicit some implicit, even to oneself) enter into the crafting of one's tools, which in turn contribute to sustaining those purposes as self-evident.

Another way of putting this is to say that the heuristic vision, like the language of engineering and technicity more generally, has an inherently 'anti-political' streak built into it: it tends to bracket conflicts of interest (whether these be epistemological or political) and translate them into problems of good design. A heuristic approach is one that says – here, I've built this device, what you do with it is up to you!

The key benefits of the heuristic vision for thinking through the history of comparison – its ability to defuse the obstreperousness of academic debate and to see value in old solutions – can also become its key liability, if a discussion of heuristics is made to pre-empt a discussion of ends and purposes. As Heywood (2018c) suggests, this need not be the case. A conceptual separation of ends from means could be deployed precisely in order to highlight the former and bring them up for discussion. That would be the mark of a heuristic vision which has not forgotten that it is itself heuristic – that it has the power to bracket divergences of purpose, but not to erase or resolve them.

Keeping those points firmly in view is the essence of the normative message of caesurism. This is why, ultimately, we cannot do without caesurism, or reduce it merely to another tool for generating novelty. For what caesurism keeps in view – its deep truth, as it were – is precisely the divergence of purposes which is so easy to forget from a heuristic perspective. This divergence of purposes is what needs to be 'eclipsed' for heuristics to become visible. Conversely, the persistence of the same tools, ever reinvented, needs to be eclipsed for caesurism to come into view.

Absent the caesurist vision, the fact that methods and moves which were once obsolete can rise again, the same points can be made over and again and yet be new each time, or positions once seen as irreconcilably different can come to seem as mere versions of the same thing – all of this can just be chalked down to a merry-go-round of trendiness. Hard-headed engineers of the discipline can discount this as theoretical fluff and urge us all to get back to business. But they will miss the point that we do not agree on what the business is.

Thinking of approaches to comparison as paradigms gives a shorthand way of referring to the way bundles of problems, aims and solutions hang together in a meaningful way for those who deploy them. But thinking of them as caesuras shows that this coherence and purpose is relational also in a different direction. A caesurist history of anthropological comparison, however rough and ready, reminds us that positions are taken not in isolation, but rather in opposition to others. They map an 'us' and a 'them' committed not just to different topics but to alternative ways of imagining anthropology.

The bottom line is this. Some methods might be more exacting or efficient than others, but ultimately, all methods are impossible. That is the lesson of heuristics. The question is whether (and why) we consider it worthwhile to struggle with particular impossibilities, whether (and why) our failures in so doing still seem productive (cf. Strathern 2002). This is not a question which can be answered in a purely heuristic view.

Rather, the space for a thoughtful discussion of ends and purposes lies at the intersection of heuristics and caesurism. With heuristics, one can no longer ignore an opponent's or a predecessor's approach simply because one has shown it has particular blind-spots – everything does! The additional requirement becomes to ask whether these blind-spots matter for the purposes for which the heuristic was being deployed. Once these purposes have been foregrounded, there begins a different sort of argument, which bears on whether those purposes are misguided or acceptable, or even simply interesting. In sum, the inter-section between heuristics and caesurism forces us to make explicit the difference between two very different kinds of critique, which are often conjoined or conflated in disciplinary discussions. On the one hand, a limited critique which seeks to constructively find a better solution for the aims or problems outlined; on the other, a radical critique which sets out new problems. These two forms of critique are complementary. Disentangling them opens up another hopeful possibility, namely that interest might be an emergent property of that discussion itself – that one might learn to interest another in one's own aims.

## Conclusion: How Far Have We Got?

The ostensible aim of this first part of the book was to find a path through the sheer multiplicity of accounts and visions of comparison in anthropology. Rather than start off, as many have sought to do, by typologising comparisons, the procedure attempted here was to study the constitution of such typologies themselves. We examined the ways – in each case multiple – in which anthropologists have envisioned anthropological comparison as a singular method, as a pair of stark alternatives, or as a manifold. Out of this examination we picked out two recurrent forms – caesurism and heuristics – which, when paired, provide a new methodological device for approaching the history of anthropological comparison.

In the second part of the book, we shall move from the problem of mapping anthropological discussions of comparison to a set of proposals regarding comparative method itself. The discussion in this part of the book has provided us with two essential ingredients for that project. On the one hand, an account of a set of tools, techniques and comparative devices on various scales – a library, as it were, of heuristics to choose from. On the other hand, some normative prescriptions for what a good method might be, including some which limit the vision of knowledge production as merely a matter of picking and choosing heuristics. The task of the second half of the book is to assemble these into a semblance of form.

So while, on the face of it, this might look like a move from a (very long) 'literature review' to the 'argument', that isn't quite the dynamic. Much of the argument, in fact, has already happened. Indeed, this part of the book itself has been a sustained exercise in comparison, using as its material not ethnographic cases, but anthropological writings on comparison. Throughout these three chapters we have been deploying different comparative devices, to different effect, testing their limits and their entailments. We have drawn up diagrams and typologies, probed radical contrasts, categorised similarities, elicited structures, pointed to concomitant variations, traced transformations, distinguished and conflated concepts, relations and things. In the very process of drawing up an account of the multiple forms of anthropological comparatism, we have borrowed devices from here and there in that picture as it emerged.

One might think of this as a recursive instantiation of the heuristic vision articulated in this chapter. Insofar as it has worked (and that is not for me to say), the experiment of this half of the book has been a demonstration that comparison is alive and well, and that one can in effect pick and choose from the great panoply of anthropological tools and techniques, cutting across paradigms and distinctions, in order to build up an account that has an effect.

But that was only one half of the picture – the heuristic half. It now remains to articulate the other – caesurist – half. The task of the second half of the book is thus to draw together these various heuristic moves into a single account which, somehow, hangs together and can articulate a purpose. It is time to make a fresh start.

# Part II

## An Archetype

FOUR

# *Comparatio*

*Archetype, n.*
1. The original pattern or model from which copies are made; a prototype.
2. a. A coin of standard weight, by which others are adjusted.
   b. An assumed ideal pattern of the fundamental structure of each great division of organized beings, of which the various species are considered as modifications.
   c. A pervasive idea, image, or symbol that forms part of the collective unconscious.

(*Oxford English Dictionary*: archetype, n.)

## Why?

Let's begin by stating an end. Wouldn't it be nice if, when anthropologists discuss comparison, they had more of a shared sense of what they mean, of precisely where they agree and where they disagree? If you think the answer to that question is 'no', then you are unlikely to be convinced by what follows. But read on, you never know. Such a shared sense could be a prelude to collaboration, of course, but it could just as well be a prelude to a good old row or a clear parting of ways. It would simply mean that when we do part ways, we have some shared map of where the other is going,[1] and that when we hurl invectives at one another, these invectives might at least be in the same language.

The device adequate to such a purpose would not be a model, even less a set of precise prescriptions or a detailed blueprint for how comparison ought to be done. That way lies the vision – misguided to my mind, and in any case unrealisable – of disciplinary unification (cf. Hunt 2007). I am not for a moment suggesting that we need *a* comparative method which all anthropologists would share. As if one could turn back the clock on the progressive multiplication of method described in the first part of this book! Even if one were somehow able to impose this – and I fail to see by what means – the benefits would be marginal. The necessary narrowness of a single account of 'the comparative method' would defeat the purpose outlined above: while it might enforce collaboration of a narrowly conceived kind, it would no longer be in any serious sense a language for articulating differences. And anyway, such narrow stipulated comparative methods exist already – we have seen many instances of them, old and new, in the historical debates examined above, and others are everywhere in the methodological literature of the social sciences. The problem is not the lack of such clearly stipulated comparative methods – the problem is that there is no way to talk across them. Whether they envision the proper form of comparison as a version of quantitative generalisation, or as 'controlled equivocation' (Viveiros de Castro 2004), these methodological proposals are the analogue of state-imposed national languages. What I am envisaging instead is a *koine*.

To that end, rather than a model of the comparative method, what is required is an *archetype*. To the transcendental anatomists of the nineteenth century (cf. Chapter 2), an archetype was the fundamental structure or form of which empirical organisms and species were the variations. For some of them, the archetype was a Platonic idea, for others, it was the effect of geometrical laws. With Darwin, the archetype became an ancestor, the 'ancient progenitor' of a taxonomic class (Amundson 1998: 165). Lévi-Strauss revived a version of the archetype in his vision of 'elementary forms', that 'table of possible permutations', of which empirical particulars were in each case one possible instance. One finds the figure of an archetype also, albeit not so named, in Strathern's vision of a Melanesian 'aesthetic' (Strathern 1988: 340–341).

While I will draw rhetorically on aspects of these different visions, the kind of archetype I have in mind would be neither a Platonic ideal of comparison, nor a historical origin point (hypothetical or otherwise), nor a complete system grounded – somehow – in human cognitive universals. It would not 'explain' comparison either cognitively, historically, or theologically. It would simply describe a heuristic form that is definite enough to be recognisable amidst a broader panoply of intellectual strategies, yet broad and simple enough to accommodate the huge variety of comparative methods which anthropologists have historically been, and currently are, enthused about – from positivist typological generalisations, to neo-diffusionist immanentism; from structuralism to interpretivism; from the critical study of world systems to the ontological turn. Such an archetype would thus serve, amongst other things, as a measure of the limits of our own analytical devices: one could really tell when one had found *something else* – be it in an ethnographic encounter with the epistemologies of non-Euroamerican peoples, or in the realms of philosophical speculation.

I noted in the introduction that 'comparison' is at once so broad and so specific that it seems to elude any kind of classification. There is a built-in elusiveness to comparison. It might thus seem entirely illusory to try to find an archetype for it. But we have come a long way since then. My concern is no longer with 'comparison' in general, but with 'anthropological comparison' specifically – this is where the project differs from, even while it is informed by, more ambitious and far-reaching attempts to characterise comparison philosophically (e.g. Lloyd 2015).

This being said, we have not, nor do I believe we could, come to a specific *definition* of what anthropological comparison is, a neat criterion that would distinguish in the world what constitutes anthropological as opposed to other kinds of comparison. However, the three chapters of Part I have brought us closer to an approximate sense of that object. In the palimpsest of problems and distinctions, of borrowings, suggestions, critiques, misunderstandings and new departures charted in the first part, lies the raw material, the elements of a rough cartography of anthropological comparison. The archetype I am after would be adequate to *that* object, with its internal contradictions and trailing edges. Given how much the debates examined in the previous section overlap with those in other disciplines, an archetype adequate to them could not belong, properly speaking, to anthropologists alone. But it would capture something of the tone and flavour of that anthropological discussion.

Such an archetype would be, however, more than a typological tool – the most general account of comparison which is not yet something else, or the lowest common denominator between anthropological comparatisms. It would also be constructed in such a fashion that one might see how different versions and variations of comparison could be generated from its permutations – both versions which exist and versions – prototypes – which one might not yet have devised. Finally, such an archetype would also have some measure of normative force. Without any precise stipulation or micro-management, it would nevertheless embody not merely a description of actual practices, but some minimally shared sense of what constitutes a job well done. This second part of the book is devoted to outlining such an archetype.

Needless to say, this archetype is somewhere between an invention and a discovery. More than a hypothesis, it is a proposal. A *koine* cannot be decreed, but one can devise elements of it and hope others might pick them up. I will do my best to draw up an archetype which is broad enough to accommodate the gamut of anthropological comparatisms, and definite enough that it still leaves us saying something to one another across those differences. Despite my best efforts, the proposal may leave some feeling that the archetype is too broad and others feeling that it is too narrow. That's fine – my key aim, ultimately, is not that the particular version I am proposing be taken up, but to convince you that there is something worth attempting in the general project. If others take it up and tinker or transform that archetype, or even propose a radically different device through which a shared language for our conversation can be reimagined, then at least we will have started along the same path.

## Building an Archetype

The discussions of the first part suggest a few possible candidates for an archetype. The broadest, simplest attempt to characterise comparison as an elementary form is Condillac's definition, which we encountered in the introduction: 'comparison is only a double attention' (Condillac 1795: 1.7; Goyet 2014: 162). For our purposes as articulated above, however, this is too general to be of much use. Like anthropologists' frequent observation that comparison is 'a general cognitive feature' or an aspect of everyday life – these very general observations hardly give us the elements of a *koine*.

We encountered another candidate archetype in Evans-Pritchard's description of 'the experimental method' in Chapter 1. As I noted there, the substance of Evans-Pritchard's account may no longer be tenable, but in its form, that stepwise account of the process of anthropological knowledge-making contains all of the structural elements from which the anthropological comparative methods we encountered in Chapter 2 were built: an encounter with difference, the building of descriptive cases, abstraction, decontextualisation and recontextualisation, a procedure for matching old cases to new ones and generating problems. Anthropological comparatisms before and after can be reconstructed mainly by *removing* particular aspects of Evans-Pritchard's account, rearticulating what remains into new structural arrangements, and giving them distinctive substance. By that very account, however, we see that Evans-Pritchard's method, while close to an archetype, is too specific, too detailed, too particular in its arrangement. Too much is already entailed, particularly about the direction of travel of anthropological knowledge, which other comparatisms could not share. It is too close, in sum, to a specific stipulation. Our archetype would lie closer to Evans-Pritchard than to Condillac, but we will not find it in 'the experimental method' itself.

I will begin, instead, from a figure we briefly encountered in the introduction. This is a concrete archetype – something that might pass for an 'ancestor', in the Darwinian sense, of anthropological comparisons. It is the figure of *comparatio* as articulated by historian of rhetoric Francis Goyet (2014). *Comparatio* was a classic rhetorical device, familiar to the educated elites of Europe from Antiquity through to the modern age: a careful, sustained practice of holding two objects in attention at the same time, in order systematically to consider their similarities and differences. A canonical instance cited by Goyet is Cicero's *comparatio* between the jurist and the military leader, addressed in a letter to Murena, who is the former:

You pass wakeful nights that you may be able to reply to your clients; he that he and his army may arrive betimes at their destination. You are roused by cock-crow, he by the bugle's reveille. You draw up your legal pleas, he sets the battle in array. You are on the watch that your clients be not taken at a disadvantage, he that cities or camps be not so taken.

(Cicero, in Goyet 2014: 161)

*Comparatio* was a device suited to many ends. It was – and still is – deployed as an intellectual exercise, in the sense of a pedagogical training routine – the ancestor of our 'compare and contrast' essays. It could be deployed as an analytical method suited to classification and to inductive generalisation. It could be a mode of moral judgement, as for instance in the 'comparisons' which cap each of Plutarch's 'parallel lives', in which the actions of one Greek and one Roman historical figure, having first been considered separately, are examined side by side.[2] It could be a device for literary criticism, or for poetic invention.

Goyet introduces *comparatio* as part of a broader family of conceptual and rhetorical devices, which include the quick, intuitive assimilations of metaphor ('this is that'), and analogy ('this is like that') or the artistic practices of musical, visual or poetic counterpoint. To that list, one might add the endless chains of association built by parataxis (that, and that, and that, and that ...). All of these rhetorical and conceptual devices might be thought of as 'comparative' in Condillac's elementary sense: they all involve a double (or multiple) attention.

But *comparatio* is distinctive. Indeed, a key point of Goyet's genealogy to which I will return is that contemporary theorists too often conflate comparison and analogy. *Comparatio* is not mere analogy, in the sense of pinpointing similarities between different objects. As we shall see again in the next chapter, analogy is often imagined as one of a pair, its opposite being contrast, opposition, or in Lloyd's terms 'polarity' (1966; 2015: 3; see also Chapter 5). But the device of *comparatio* described by Goyet straddles that distinction. So much so, indeed, that – Goyet notes – French eighteenth-century rhetorical textbooks translated *comparatio* as *contraste*. Goyet's key point – which will be crucial to my own argument here and in the next chapter – is that the effects of *comparatio* rely not on analogy or on contrast alone, but on the articulation of the two. *Comparatio* consists in 'making a parallel between $x$ and $y$ in order to bring out resemblances and differences' (Goyet 2014: 162).

The second, and related, mark of the distinctiveness of *comparatio* is its pace or tempo. Partly as a consequence of considering both similarities and differences, *comparatio* differs from an analogy, or from a metaphor,[3] in that it is thorough and takes time: 'The result is not a little formula tossed off in passing, a figure of style, but a long, complete development' (Goyet 2014: 160). Thus Cicero's *comparatio* above, for instance, runs to many pages.

We find some clear instances of *comparatio* in anthropology. Liisa Malkki's classic ethnography *Purity and Exile* (1995) is articulated around a comparative study of the experience of Hutu refugees from

Burundi in two Tanzanian contexts – the refugee camp of Mishamo and the township of Kigoma. Malkki painstakingly attends both to these refugees' shared experiences of trauma and uprooting, and to the radically different articulations they give to these experiences in the two contexts. The refugees in Mishamo invested themselves in explicit identity-work, recounting narratives of exile through which they articulated themselves as first and foremost Hutu, and envisioned a hope for a collective return. These narratives countered the discursive erasure which comes with popular representations of refugees as rootless and just generically human. By contrast, the refugees in Kigoma sought as far as possible to elude categorisation, to operate under the radar of official nomenclatures and to fade into the everyday multiplicity of the township while keeping their options open as to possible futures. Malkki's argument is woven from a set of analogies and contrasts, which stand out against one another on different scales. On the one hand, analogies of historical experience are mapped against differences in location and context. On the other, different structural pressures (erasure on the one hand, categorisation on the other) are correlated with different attitudes to identity-work (self-essentialisation on the one hand, self-invisibilisation on the other) to suggest elements of the same dynamic. In both cases, refugees were partly reacting to and resisting a set of violent, discursive and structural impositions. This skein of analogies and contrasts provided a sophisticated intervention into contemporary debates about identity, memory, power and resistance. Crucially for my purposes – we shall see that this is a characteristic feature of *comparatio* – that intervention could not be boiled down to a single take-home point. Or rather, it could be parsed into a number of such points – that identity is situational, that refugees are not blank slates, that 'resistance' can take multiple forms, and so forth. But the *comparatio* as a device was more than the sum of those isolated conclusions.

Another instance – articulated around a very different vision of anthropology – comes from Bruno Latour's *The making of law* (2009). After an extended and painstakingly detailed tracing of practices, relations and debates in the French Conseil d'état, Latour suddenly steps back and articulates a *comparatio* between law, as figured in this case, and science as it emerges from his previous works on the subject (Latour 2009: 198–214). Again the key feature which makes this a *comparatio* is the intricate elicitation of interlocking similarities and differences. Both practices – law and science – are portrayed as modes of veridiction which operate immanently, producing aspects of the world, rather than merely commenting on it. The notion of the French high court as a factory of law directly recalls the vision of the scientific laboratory as a factory articulated in Latour and Woolgar's *Laboratory life* (1979). But the spaces and materials of law and science are different. Laboratories are broadly closed off from the public, but one can circulate freely within them; courts are a concatenation of open and closed spaces, some formally open to the public, others painstakingly secretive. Scientists operate by manipulating materials in a hands-on fashion, articulating discursive explanations around their experiments in an initially disjointed and piecemeal language of approximation; the materials handled by judges at the high court are exclusively texts and words, and their discussions are meticulously articulated in an arcane and well-oiled language. Law and science appeal to a number of shared notions, originally imported into the language of the latter from that of the former: laws, of course, but also judgement, witnessing, evidence, detachment and objectivity. But the dynamic of the practices these notions designate differ radically. Thus scientists are – Latour claims – expected to be passionately attached to their favourite theories and experimental devices, and to fight their corner relentlessly in the run-up to their public statement in a peer-reviewed paper. Once these are published, however, the authors are expected to stand back and let the scientific community be the judge. Judges by contrast are expected to be impartial in considering different possibilities and legal constructions in the process of judgement, taking up opposing positions on the same question at will – but cannot tolerate any questioning of a judgement once it is passed. And so, while both practices build realities, the realities they build have different dynamics: on the one hand, the provisional facts of science, on the other, the irreversible judgements of law.

Latour and Malkki operate on different scales. The kinds of phenomena they pick out are very different. The relations they imply are also: Malkki's account can be seen as implying causal entailments of fairly traditional kinds, whereas Latour is working from some rather more uncanny metaphysical postulates. And while the former is a *comparatio* worked out at book length, the latter is – depending on your perspective – a *comparatio* on the scale of only eight pages, or on the scale of an entire career. On the other hand, Latour's *comparatio* shares with Malkki's a particular kind of intricacy, in which analogies and contrasts build upon each other. It also shares a facility for making more than one point. One could of course reduce Latour's *comparatio* to its main stated conclusion, namely that applying the language of law to science is misguided, and that scientific experts ought never to be given the authority of closing a dispute, any more than judges should be given the authority to decide on nature. Alternatively one could see in it the lineaments of a broader unitary project, that of lining up different 'modes of existence' as analogues of each other. Indeed this passage marks the inaugural move of the much broader comparative project Latour later conducted under the title of *An enquiry into modes of existence* (2013). But neither of these reductions exhausts the potential of the *comparatio* itself. Its intricacy is its richness – one can always return to it to pick out a different strand or draw a different conclusion. In sum, in both cases, alongside the demonstration of a number of specific 'conclusions', *comparatio* operates as an aesthetic device which produces more than the sum of its parts. Goyet makes a similar point of the use of a version of *comparatio*, namely musical or poetic counterpoint:

The focus of attention is shifted from the parts to the whole. It is no longer a double attention, but, so to speak, a triple one. If intellectual contrast serves to examine each of the two elements, to illuminate each by the other, contrapuntal harmony seeks to merge them into a whole that simultaneously transcends and respects them. Then the whole is more than the sum of its parts, and the parts in turn are enhanced by the light that their comparison yields. Taken as a whole, the aesthetic dimension is the pleasure of *com-prehending* in the sense of holding the two contrapuntal lines together.

(Goyet 2014: 163)

## Conclusion: A Roadmap to Part II

I will argue in this second part of the book that *comparatio* as illustrated in the two examples above – actually three, since that double example ended with my own *comparatio*, albeit a relatively thin and impoverished one – can be articulated in more formal terms to serve as a building block for an archetype of anthropological comparison in all its vibrant variety.

To do so will mean addressing some immediate and obvious objections. Over and again in the history of anthropology, the vision of comparison as the tracing of similarities and differences between things has been the foil against which other, putatively more innovative or interesting visions have been articulated: comparison as reflexive translation, comparison as the study of transformations, comparison as serial analogy, comparison as controlled equivocation. This is not just a 'postmodern' move. As we saw above (Chapter 2), even the 'original', nineteenth-century method of concomitant variation was articulated as a systematic alternative to the mere comparison of similarities and differences. On the face of it, *comparatio* might thus seem to be a poor candidate indeed for an archetype. It seems to be just one particular version of comparison, and an old-fashioned, staid and limited one at that – the butt of every rebuttal in the history of comparatism.

Indeed, *comparatio* might seem to be the perfect foil for all of the accumulated objections against the comparative method which we have encountered in Part I of this book. We can return once more to the three broad families of problems identified in Chapter 1. The first objection bears on the economy of similarity and difference *comparatio* implies. Over and again, anthropologists have argued that comparison envisioned as a matching of similarities and differences always ends up privileging similarity over difference. The 'argument by analogy' (e.g. Bartha 2013; see Chapter 5), which builds on similarities in order to deduce further similarities, is the usual suspect here. It is against this that visions of comparison bearing essentially on difference have been articulated. This objection relates to what I called in Chapter 1 problems of purpose. The alternative between searching for identity and making space for diffe-rence – cast variously or simultaneously in epistemological, moral or political terms – is perhaps the starkest and most fundamental diffe-rence of purpose which traverses anthropology at the present moment. We shall address this alternative in Chapter 5.

The alternative between searching for identity and for alterity also relates straightforwardly to what in Chapter 1 I have called problems of 'mapping', the identification of differences and similarities between objects, predicates and relations. The same is true of the second objec-tion. Imagined as an argument by analogy, *comparatio* seems naively to assume objects out there in the world, with their inherent differences and similarities, ready to be compared. This vision of comparisons oper-ating in a world of discrete, stable objects has been identified over and again as a poor analogue for the relational entanglement and processual complexity of social and cultural life: surely, many have argued, what one ought to be comparing are not things at all but relations! We shall address this objection in Chapter 6.

The third objection relates to what in Chapter 1 I called problems of 'communication'. It concerns the place of the observer. *Comparatio* seems to take us back to classic formulations of comparative method which are all about the lining up of things in the world, be they objects or relations. This vision, as critics recurrently pointed out, eluded the epistemic-political question of the position from which this lining up operates, and the core point that anthropology turns on an intersubjective encounter with other people. We shall address this objection in chapters 7 and 8 below.

Of course, these three objections are interwoven – to many they might all seem like aspects of the same problem. But we will take the time to consider them and their implications separately, spooling out into specific discussions aspects of comparative practice which are often run together. At the risk of seeming at times artificial or overly 'slow', this analytical procedure will enable us to show how different versions of *comparatio* have emerged to deal with different aspects of these problems. Each of these versions of our initial archetypal figure can be thought of as a more precise heuristic form, good for some things and not for others. Increasingly as the chapters progress, we will begin to recombine these more specific versions back into one archetypal figure of anthropological comparison, more complex and specific than *comparatio*, but still derived from it and bearing some of its logical and normative entailments.

We have already encountered, in the first part of this book, the most important of these subdivisions of *comparatio*, namely, the distinction between lateral and frontal comparisons (Candea 2016a). Each of these describes a broad family of heuristics, which we will specify further. At the most general level, however, one can say that each can be seen as a form of *comparatio*, with this crucial difference: while lateral comparisons entail a consideration of cases lain side by side – a comparison of *this and that* – frontal comparisons entail a consideration of two cases, one of which includes the perspective doing the comparing – a comparison of *us and them*. Chapters 5 and 6 will explore different dimensions of lateral comparison, in the process subdividing this general form into more precise heuristic devices. Chapters 7 and 8 will do the same for frontal comparisons.

In other words, the chapters that follow outline the panoply of solutions to the problems of comparison which we methodically picked out in Chapter 1: chapters 5 and 6 focus on the problem of mapping, chapters 7 and 8 on the problem of communication. Lateral comparisons, in their many different varieties, engage substantively with questions of mapping but are constitutively blind to questions of communication. Frontal comparisons are directly concerned with problems of communication, but in the process tend to evade questions of mapping, in ways that can be both productive and problematic. Neither kind of device can stand alone: they are in practice combined in any anthropological argument. In their combination lies the promise of a distinctive kind of comparative anthropological rigour (Chapter 9), in which problems of mapping and communication are resolved in relation to one another. This second part, as a whole, outlines a solution also to the problem of purpose, in the ability of shared devices to serve multiple ends.

Before we begin, however, an objection of a different order ought perhaps to be addressed. Another feature which makes *comparatio* an ideal building block for an archetype of anthropological comparison is one which might on the face of it seem like a serious problem. This is the fact that *comparatio*, as a concrete historical practice, carries a trailing set of associations – I mean, it's even in *Latin* for goodness' sake! – to the activities and concerns of a cultivated European elite. But that is in fact entirely apposite, since the same is true, historically, of anthropological comparison. Devising some purely formal scheme derived a priori might give us the misleading sense that we are starting anew, or communing with the universal. By contrast, grounding our archetype of anthropological comparison in the historical practice of *comparatio* reminds us that anthropological comparison is not a view from nowhere, merely an abstract set of operations with no political, ethical or historical entailments. It reminds us that every time anthropologists compare, they draw on a bundle of practices with particular roots in gendered, racialised and classed histories. There have been, and there are, other visions of comparison, with other histories and other contemporary entailments, as anthropologists have shown (Viveiros de Castro 2004; Lloyd 1966, 2015; Humphrey 2016).

This doesn't mean that anthropological comparisons today necessarily carry the same political or ethical entailments as those of Tylor, Malinowski or Radcliffe-Brown, those of seventeenth-century European poets, or those of classical Greek or Roman rhetoricians. And it certainly doesn't imply that anthropological comparison today 'belongs' in some way to one or other cultural group, or that its history determines its potential futures. But recalling the roots of our abstract moves in a concrete history – genealogy, in the Foucauldian sense – acts as a control against the temptation to see anthropological comparison as nothing but a convenient heuristic. This transformation of the political into the technical is, as we saw (Chapter 3), the key omission of a heuristic view. Recalling the concrete practice of *comparatio* keeps this omission from turning into a forgetting. It keeps live the political and ethical questions which invoking a 'purely formal' archetype would easily allow to slip from view.

# FIVE

# Two Ends of Lateral Comparison: Identity and Alterity

If our faces were not similar, we could not distinguish man from beast; if they were not different we could not distinguish man from man.

(Montaigne 1965: 819)

## Introduction: Different Ends

Does the value of comparisons lie in identifying things, or in differentiating them? Answers to that question map a profound split in anthropological understandings of comparison, which speak directly to what I described in Chapter 1 as the problem of purpose.

This chapter focuses on the first of the three objections raised at the end of Chapter 4. On a cursory reading, *comparatio* – the move of putting things in parallel in order to elicit their similarities and differences – could be mistaken for one of its particular versions, namely that of an argument which 'cites accepted similarities between two systems to support the conclusion that some further similarity exists' (Bartha 2013: n.p.). This specific form is sometimes known as 'the argument by analogy' – not to be confused with the much broader category of analogical devices examined for instance by Lloyd (2015). *Comparatio* has indeed often been used in anthropology and beyond, in the form of an argument by analogy, in order to generalise from particulars. On the horizon of arguments by analogy, there often lies a commitment to reducing differences to similarities, and similarities to identity. In the guise of a search for human universals (cf. Murdock 1949) or for human nature (Bloch 2005; Goodenough 1970: 1), this has occasionally been proposed as the purpose of anthropological comparison – and indeed of the discipline – as a whole. Hunt, another proponent of this view, notes that this vision relies on identifying regularities in human behaviour, through the study of correlations, and more broadly, on identifying different things (particular objects and their properties) as instances of the same thing ('kinds' and 'dimensions' – Hunt 2007: x–xi, 15–17).

This aspiration has long been the focus of critique. In his account of what he termed the 'classical episteme', Michel Foucault (1970) argued that a whole family of comparative devices was born of the desire to reduce similarity to identity. Foucault locates this shift in the seventeenth-century critique of an earlier episteme of echoes and resemblances. By contrast to this free play of resemblance, the classical episteme decreed that

From now on, every resemblance must be subjected to proof by comparison, that is, it will not be accepted until its identity and the series of its differences have been discovered by means of measurement with a common unit, or, more radically, by its position in an order.

(Foucault 1970: 55)

With this panoply of techniques, comparison was pinned to a particular aim – the elicitation of identity – be it in the form of typology, or in the form of universal laws.

In *identity* we thus name the other of comparison. In the classical episteme, one cannot compare something to itself – although one can of course compare the same thing, form or relation at different times or in different states, just as one can compare different aspects, parts or modes of the same relation, form or thing. Between a thing and itself, however, there can be neither analogy nor contrast (although as we shall see in the next chapter, a consideration of 'intensity' challenges that view). Identity is the limit of comparison (Viveiros de Castro 2003). The family of moves identified by Foucault cast identity as not simply the limit, but also the *end* of comparison – both in the sense that that is what comparison aims at, and also as where any given comparison finishes, where it has succeeded and another comparison can begin. We can now finally give this term 'end', which we have been using throughout the book, a more technical meaning, combining the idea of a purpose and a limit.

It is against this vision of comparison as the elicitation of identity that much anthropological writing since at least the 1970s has been explicitly articulated. As Daniel M. Gross notes, Foucault's own vision of genealogy is usually understood in these terms, as a historical method which corresponds

to the acuity of a glance that distinguishes, separates, and disperses, that is capable of liberating divergence and marginal elements – the kind of dissociating view that is capable of decomposing itself, capable of shattering the unity of man's being through which it was thought that he could extend his sovereignty to the events of his past.

(Foucault 1984: 87; cf. Gross 2001: 58)

By contrast to the sensibility which seeks to reduce different things to instances of the same, one might describe this sensibility as *heterological* (Buchanan 1996; cf. Pefanis 1991). It sets itself as an end – a purpose and a limit – the opposite of identity: difference, or more radically alterity. In this vision, the end of comparisons, the mark of their success and the point at which they come to rest, is when they have elicited, noted or indeed *made* a difference.

To the heterologically minded, starting from *comparatio* to build an archetypal figure for anthropological comparison might seem to be thoroughly misguided. Does this not ground us in precisely the kind of generalising episteme from which so much anthropology has sought to separate itself? Indeed, to many of these critics, the very term 'comparison' itself is so entangled with the elicitation of sameness that it needs to be jettisoned in favour of something else –equivocation, for instance (Viveiros de Castro 2004).[1] This heterological challenge is particularly sharp for being recursive. Indeed such critics would presumably see the very move of trying to produce an archetype at all as precisely an instance of that kind of 'saming'.

This chapter's main response to this double objection is that not all *comparatio* takes the form of an argument by analogy in the sense of seeking to establish further similarities on the basis of existing ones. This should already be suggested by the variety of uses of *comparatio* briefly invoked in Chapter 4 above. True, *comparatio* can be used for purposes of classification or the search for general rules, but it can also be turned to the ends of poetry, music, invention, exhortation or critique. Throughout the rest of this book, I will show that the archetypal figure of *comparatio* can be expanded, twisted and torqued into various more specific devices – often very much at odds with the analogical argument. Indeed, I will go further and argue that, in one way or another, anthropologists who sought to move away from analogy typically did so through some reconfiguration of the basic figure of *comparatio*.

In relation to the heterological challenge specifically, it is crucial to remember that *comparatio* can be used to elicit differences, as well as similarities: it can be made to evoke alterity, and not only identity. *Comparatio* ought not to be reduced to the drawing out of similarities between putatively different things (Goyet 2014). The distinctiveness of *comparatio*, and its value as the starting point of an archetype of anthropological comparison, lies precisely in the way it conjoins analogies and contrasts. This is why *comparatio* is a shared technique which anthropologists (and others) can deploy to radically different ends.

But this chapter also levels a second response to critiques of comparison as analogy. This is simply that generalisations grounded in arguments by analogy are ineradicable in anthropology. Many of us have given up on the universal. But as Hunt (2007: 148–149) rightly notes, quoting Spiro (1966: 88), generalising and universalising are far from the same thing. Even if universalism were dead – as indeed it is in many quarters of anthropology – generalisation would still be ineradicable. On a small scale, mostly under the epistemological radar, we continue to make claims about states of affairs in the world which take the form of caveated micro-generalisations, drawn from analogies of particular cases. Ethnography is replete with such claims, even in works which would seek to do without the classic trappings of representationalist or realist epistemology. I raise this point in this chapter not as an empty paradox or as a snide comment destined to prick theoretical pretensions or drag conceptual revolutions back to earth. I raise it because it will open up on to one of the most interesting, thorny and productive questions relating to anthropological comparisons, namely the question of what makes comparisons rigorous. This is also, as we shall see in Chapter 9, the question of what makes anthropology into a discipline.

## The Argument by Analogy

The argument by analogy is perhaps the most instantly recognisable form of *comparatio* (see Gross 2001). Given how large this particular form of *comparatio* looms in discussions of comparison, it is important to identify and pin it down, in order to show that *comparatio* can in fact be so much more. It is against this form that most of the explicit innovations of anthropological comparison have been cast. And yet, as we shall see, this form itself persists and is perhaps ineradicable.

In reference to what I wrote in the previous chapter, to call arguments by analogy a form of *comparatio* is to say that they are more than mere instant, immediate, analogies made in passing. They have a particular tempo, and they rest on a combined consideration of similarities and differences. Bartha's extended exposition of the logic of such arguments (2013) will serve to unpack this particular intricacy (see also Tambiah 1973 for a classic anthropological account, which, like Bartha's, draws

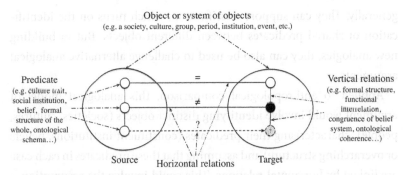

Figure 5.1 The argument by analogy (after Bartha 2013: n.p.)

on Hesse 1966). In a nutshell, an argument by analogy is an elaborate form of induction. Arguments by analogy identify two (or more) objects or systems of objects, with their respective predicates or properties. One of these – the source – is better known than the other – the target. Arguments by analogy seek to discover as yet unknown predicates of the target. In order to do so, they identify *horizontal relations* between the known predicates of these two (or more) objects. These can be relations of similarity (positive analogies) or difference (negative analogies). Building on these known analogies, further hypothetical analogies are used to identify as yet unknown predicates.

As Bartha notes, following Hesse (1966), the structure of arguments by analogy supposes a further set of relations between the predicates of each object, which he terms vertical relations (Figure 5.1). In order for analogical arguments to be more than mere guessing games, they must assume that the predicates of objects are linked to one another in some non-random fashion – that there is, for instance, some functional, structural or logical coherence between these different predicates of each object. For our purposes, vertical relations between predicates of the object could also be themselves seen as predicates of the object. Finally, analogical arguments of the kind outlined by Bartha can be used to a number of different ends. They can be a tool of generalisation – by arguing inductively that what is true in cases A, B and C is true generally. They can support classification, which turns on the identification of shared predicates between different objects. But in building new analogies, they can also be used to challenge alternative analogical arguments.

Applied to anthropological comparison, this analogical model of argument would involve identifying distinct objects (societies, cultures, people), characterising their predicates (constituent institutions, beliefs or overarching structure) and assuming that these predicates in each case are linked by horizontal relations. This could involve the assumption – or support the hypothesis – that institutions form a structure, or that concepts are coherently articulated to one another, or even more simply and basically, that there is some regularity to the way people behave, such that from the observation of a few instances, one might say something more general about typical behaviours.

We have seen in Chapter 2 the way in which, in the work for instance of Tylor, Durkheim or Radcliffe-Brown, the identification of some measure of identity between different things was the mark of a success, an advance, an improvement. This could take the form of discovering law-like regularities, of mapping more and more general problems (where generalisation means rising above particulars), or of discovering concomitant variations – 'proportionalities' – between different phenomena which suggested the same causes were at play. In that last guise of proportionality, one might say that structuralist comparisons, too, foregrounded analogy – even though they were radically opposed to the kind of generalisation courted by Radcliffe-Brown. Arguments by analogy were also central for those who aimed or aim at devising overarching 'etic' terminologies (Goodenough 1970; Hunt 2007) and identifying cross-cultural universals (Jankowiak et al. 2015). In some of these enterprises, arguments by analogy were or are combined with a quantitative vision – statistics becomes a method for framing and controlling analogical inductions.

## The Persistence of Caveated Generalisation

Most of these grand visions of analogical comparison have either disappeared or become marginal in contemporary social and cultural anthropology. So much so, indeed, that the need to steer clear, not merely of 'universals', but even of 'generalisation' itself has come in some quarters to sound like a truism. And yet this sense of consensus hides in plain sight the fact that anthropologists still generalise all the time. These are, it is true, *caveated* generalisations, of the form 'this is broadly the case, with important exceptions' (Wimsatt 2007: 33; cf. Candea 2017). One might take an instance from a book which is otherwise profoundly invested in the critique of the use of comparison to generalise:

In my view there is no escaping the fact that a continuing hierarchical mentality prevails in India that prevents care arrangements from being extended to the urban poor. We do not thereby return to a holistic view of an Indian caste system, as in Dumont's *Homo Hierarchicus*, because that would certainly be a wrong perspective on modern India. However, it does imply that turning our back on the significance of hierarchical values in Indian society by focusing on youth culture and media and other manifestations of an Indian cosmopolitanism does not make hierarchy go away.

(Van Der Veer 2016: 139; see also 79, 131)

This propensity to generalise only disappears from view if 'to generalise' is taken to entail a claim to absolute universality. On that account, caveated generalisations are not generalisations at all. But whatever they are, claims such as Van der Veer's above – about, say, what kind of mentality 'prevails' in India – and much smaller ones also – such as the claim that people in this or that fieldsite tended to do X or Y – are still inductive statements built out of analogies between particular cases. Analogies from particular cases are not, of course, the only alternative to absolute particularity. We have seen many others, and will encounter others still: structural formalism, conceptual invention, relational holisms of various kinds, are all different ways of saying things which are not particular yet not inductive generalisations. But in the main that is not what anthropologists are doing when they describe, in a pervasive broadly pretheoretical way, what is the case in the places they have worked.[2] Implicitly or explicitly such basic statements of fact are local generalisations which rely on the device of citing 'accepted similarities between two systems to support the conclusion that some further similarity exists' (Bartha 2013).

At a low level of abstraction, close to the descriptive ground of anthropological practice, caveated micro-generalisations are ineradicable. We saw this point in the discussion of Malinowski (Chapter 2): ethnographic description is woven through with micro- (and sometimes even meso-) generalisation. Of course, ethnographic description turns on the singular and the specific. Accounts are often articulated around descriptions of particular events, or words said by particular people at particular times. But these singular instances are woven into a tissue of commonplace micro-generalisations. The collation of particular observed events into an account of how this or that ritual or meeting tends to unfold; what the architecture is like in this part of town; what sorts of clothes people tend to wear; how they tend to pause or hesitate before this or that unwelcome intrusion; the collation of particular things said by particular people into claims about what 'many people I worked with' think or feel about this or that – these micro-generalisations are there in the very weave of ethnographic description. Sometimes they are, fleetingly, almost shyly or reticently mentioned in passing, at other times they form the substance of the account and are boldly foregrounded with the self-assured voice of the knowing participant observer. But they are ineradicable wherever there is description, and they systematically take the form of inductive, analogical micro-generalisations, from a set of observed or experienced instances to a caveated yet still – *however slightly* – more general claim.

It is a core claim of this book that such analogical micro-generalisations are not simply ineradicable, but indeed productive and constitutive of anthropology. We may lose sight of this claim in this and the next two chapters, which are structured around a consideration of moves away from analogical arguments of this type. But it will come back with a vengeance in chapters 8 and 9. For, indeed, this ineradicability of micro-generalisation poses a problem. To the unending irritation of self-definedly scientific or quantitative social scientists, on this banal micro-level, a more or less implicit appeal to quantitative generalisation persists, even in the most rigorously qualitative accounts. As Nadel perceptively noted, 'when we speak of the "presence" of an institution or form of grouping we speak implicitly of the prevalence of the respective modes of action; so that our qualitative variations always conceal quantitative ones' (Nadel 1951: 224). Readers and listeners of anthropological arguments are told over and again that most, many or some people think, say or do this or that. When, as is often the case, these claims are inserted into accounts whose explicit epistemological reflections seek to challenge the very grounds of quantitative inductive generalisation of this type – either because the account is interpretive, or because it proposes a Deleuzian challenge to the very notion of an extended world of things, or because it aims to critique the very canons of western knowledge in some other way – these moves tend to operate under the radar. There is rarely any sustained account of how these micro-generalisations are built, any sense of how they might be controlled. To scientifically minded observers, this is a classic case of having one's cake and eating it: of seeking to make claims without a corresponding form of rigour. That irritation is understandable, but it is not quite to the point: what it misses is the fact that the peculiar rigour these claims rest on is *collective* – a matter of collaboration within and beyond the discipline. We shall return to this question of rigour, which forms the core of Chapter 9.

## Alterity

The bundle of moves I have characterised above as 'heterological', by contrast, aims away from identity. Epistemologically, they follow the

Wittgensteinian dictum 'Don't take comparability, but rather incomparability, as a matter of course' (in Gross 2001: 58). Ontologically, they might agree with Gabriel Tarde that 'to exist is to differ' (2016: 50).

We can pause to consider a terminological problem. To say that some comparisons aim at 'difference' does not name the same sort of limit as 'identity'. Two merely different things can still be compared. Difference is, in that sense, the converse of similarity, not of identity. Philosophers, anthropologists and others have frequently sought to name a *real* converse to identity, one that would analogously limit comparison 'on the other side' – absolute difference, 'alterity', incommensurability, the Other. But as soon as they are articulated these become comparative terms. There is a self-defeating dynamic to the identification of a class of phenomena on the basis that they cannot be classed. As Lloyd (2015: 36) notes, 'even the ineffable may always be said to be ineffable'. As soon as one has named 'alterity', the identification of a more 'radical alterity' beckons. Perhaps that's fine: if the whole point of the operation is to aim away from identity, why try to articulate that aim in a symmetrical language? Why not have an asymmetrical, lopsided vision of comparison, in which there is a clear end-point on the one hand (identity – the radical other of comparison) and on the other side only an eternal flight forward – a Deleuzian *ligne de fuite* – into more and increasingly different difference?

However that may be, with Foucault, Levinas, Derrida and their postmodern cohorts, comparison forked radically: on the one hand a family of devices which aim at identity, on another a family of devices which aim away from it. There are many avatars of a heterological vision in contemporary discussions of comparison, a number of which we encountered in the first part of the book. Heterology hovers around in the form of a very general critique of generalisation on the grounds that reality is always more complex (Dan-Cohen 2017). It grounds a vision of 'holism' as the elicitation of cultural worlds whose parts do not correlate in a one-to-one fashion (Van der Veer 2016: 27). It is sharpened to a point in the radical and philosophically intricate convolutions of Dumontian comparatism (Iteanu and Moya 2015), Strathernian fractals (Strathern 2004) or visions of an ontological turn in which even simply 'to think is to differ' (Holbraad and Pedersen 2017: 296).

From a post-Foucauldian perspective, it also became possible to identify some older moves as analogues of the present concern with heterology. Thus Boasian anthropology could be recuperated as essentially *about* difference (Salmon 2013a). In his wake, one could come to see the lineaments of an anthropology aiming at difference in the work of interpretivism also (Handler 2009; Holy 1987). In structuralism too, albeit only if one bracketed the foundational importance of the unity of the human mind to the logic of structuralist arguments (Salmon 2013b). Weber's critique of the use of analogies for generalisation (Gad and Bruun Jensen 2016: 5–6) could be read as pointing in that direction, although there again, one would need to bracket his insistence that contrasts in turn would need to be causally explained. Some anthropologists' focus away from comparison and towards descriptions of particulars could itself be recuperated as potentially radical.

If those moves are old, what postmodernism named, however, was the effect of the explicit observation that the very search for generality was itself particular. With that recognition, for many anthropologists the magic charm of typologies, grand narratives and the search for laws was broken. The caveat that whatever one was doing was not 'naively' generalising became *de rigueur*. Amongst anthropologists concerned primarily with the problem of communication, as we saw in Part I of this book, translation as an attempt to establish intelligibility often came to be seen as problematically close to an imposition of the *Same* on to the *Other*.

That being said, comparisons aiming at identity did not die at midcentury. In the 1970s and '80s, anthropologists concerned with political economy sought to rise above the identification of particulars – dismissively seen as a 'billiard-ball' vision of cultures bumping into each other – in order to show profound structural linkages and historical entailments between worldwide phenomena (Mintz 1985; Wolf 1983). That inspiration persisted in the 1980s and '90s focus on discovering the workings of 'hegemony' and 'counter-hegemony' in the most diverse phenomena – the move which Sahlins acerbically mocked in *Waiting for Foucault* (Sahlins 2002). Some contemporary engagements with neo-liberalism (Ferguson and Gupta 2002; Muehlebach 2010) are built on a similar pattern: anthropology's core gain is seen as the identification of the same force, be it neo-liberalism or its avatars (financialisation, self-making, etc.) acting in different ways in different locales. Not unrelated, but built on a different conceptual pattern, was the rise of an anthropological concern with human suffering (Robbins 2013), or ordinary ethics (Das in Lambek et al. 2015). Grounded in a critique of anthropological exoticism, this seeks to recover and make visible the viscerally recognisable plight of distant others – immediately, experientially analogous to our own. In sum, powerful strands of contemporary anthropology are articulated around the discovery of identity as a moral and political, as well as epistemic, goal. In many quarters, the reason why identity is pursued has shifted dramatically – from an epistemological belief that the general is inherently more valuable than the particular (although see Graeber 2015: 6), to the moral and political commitment to critique which turns on uncovering the hidden pattern of structural inequality, the recurrent work of privilege, or the recognisable fact of human suffering, in the amorphous jumble of different situations.

This contrast between comparisons which aim at identity and comparisons which aim at 'alterity' names a profound, perhaps irreconcilable rift in anthropological visions of comparison.[3] Readers of the first part of this book will recognise in the above an instance of Abbott's fractal contrasts. Identity and 'alterity', difference and similarity, generalising and specifying, or, in critical mode, attacks on othering and attacks on saming, are perpetually linked in discussions of anthropological comparison, and when anthropologists see two paths forking before them, it is often in those terms. If you perceive the status quo to be articulated around similarity or generality, focus on difference; if you find anthropologists obsessed with alterity, rediscover shared problems. There can be no better proof of the fractal, deictic nature of that contrast than the fact that a number of positions – most obviously structuralism, but Chapter 3 above made the point of fractal visions too – can be seen as being essentially 'about' difference or essentially 'about' similarity.

In some of these breaks, what is at stake is an ontological question – which, of difference or similarity, actually lies at the heart of things (Stasch 2014: 635; Toren and de Pina-Cabral 2009: 13–14)? In others, comparison alone is envisioned as making difference and similarity (Holy 1987: 16), and the question is essentially one of moral or political choice – which, of saming or othering, should be our aim (cf. Lloyd 2015: 30–31)? In the former cases the alternative is grounded in a commitment to the Real; in the latter it is grounded in the commitment to the Good. And there are, here and there, conceptually acrobatic visions (recursivity, structuralism) which seem to be at least in part committed to a certain form of the Beautiful. Whatever its guiding principles, however, the parting of anthropological ways between analogical and heterological ends of comparison could not be more profound and radical.

## Compare and Contrast

On a methodological level, however, we find anthropologists (and indeed, possibly everyone else – cf. Lloyd 2015) recombining the same two basic devices – analogies and contrasts – to reach in these two different directions. In speaking of analogies and contrasts, we have already moved 'inwards' from the two extremities of identity, on the one hand, and ever-proliferating difference, on the other. These terms are slippery, of course. But let us heuristically fix them, for the purposes of the present discussion: let us say 'analogies' point out similarities between different things, relations or forms, while 'contrasts' point out differences between things, relations or forms which have first been set alongside each other for the purpose of comparison. This 'setting alongside' implies some form of commensurability. Often this commensurability is loosely typological, envisioning these two things which are being contrasted as instances of a class – if only in the sense that both are, for instance, 'things' or 'relations' or 'forms'. Sometimes, there is no such typological implication, but the simple fact of the contrast itself relates the things which are being opposed (Jackson 1987; Lloyd 2015: 30; Strathern 2004: 51). Analogies do not therefore imply perfect identity between the things, relations or forms compared (indeed they imply precisely the opposite[4]). Conversely, contrasts do not equate to a perfect or absolute difference, since they presuppose some prior commensurability. The difference between analogy and contrast, thus defined, is primarily one of emphasis and, as it were, of direction: the former points towards identity and the latter towards alterity – but each stays well clear of its respective horizon.

In the combination of analogies and contrasts lie the elementary moves of comparison. The thought that analogies and contrasts can be made to work together to different effect is very old indeed. As we discussed in the first part, one finds it developed in Aristotle's *Topics* (Aristotle 1997: esp. I.16 and I.17) – an outline of the formal properties of different logical arguments (Smith 1997: xxiv–xxvi). There we find both the figure of analogies within a genus, which can be used to suggest identical attributes, and of proportional analogies between genera (A is to B as C is to D – Gross 2001; Lloyd 2015: 79–83). Differences, too, differ depending on where they are found. As we saw above, with the thought that differences within genera are essentially differences of quantity, Aristotle names the basic move of the structuralist study of 'transformations'. In his search for the 'identical attributes' of disparate particulars, he names the generalising devices of Radcliffe-Brownian comparatism. By articulating such contrasts and analogies to each other in different ways, these devices can be used to identify particulars and their essences or alternatively to build both typologies and inductive generalisations. Mill's discussion of induction (see Chapter 2) provides a permutation on Aristotle's. Mill's methods of difference and agreement sharpen the alternative between seeing difference between otherwise similar cases, and seeing similarity between otherwise different cases, while his method of concomitant variation recalls Aristotle's use of proportional analogies.

We can draw one immediate conclusion from the above. Comparisons which aim at identity and generalisation (be it in the form of typology, proportionality or laws) are not 'made out of' identity alone – they rely on contrasts as well as analogies. This is fairly obvious, and broadly uncontested.

Less banal, and in some quarters perhaps even controversial, is the converse observation. Heterological devices are not simply 'made out of difference': they rely on analogies as well as contrasts, albeit differently reassembled. There are different ways of demonstrating this point, apposite for different flavours of heterological argument. To the various critics of generalisation for whom reality is always 'more complex', one can point out that the very same procedures of analogy and contrast deployed in the ardent search for generalisation are those which enable us to critique and challenge others' generalisations. This was an explicit point of Aristotle's topics, which are devices for critiquing as much as for constructing. And, as we saw in Chapter 2, J. S. Mill left anthropologists both with the aim of generalisation and with the best tools for challenging poorly grounded generalisations. Mill's methods of induction are also methods for ferreting out incorrect assumptions of identity. Indeed, Mill even prefigured anti-generalisers' best argument – social phenomena are just too complex and multi-causal to be treated like the phenomena of physics. Much of the time, when anthropologists use comparison to critique generalisation, they do so very much on Mill's own terms.

Furthermore, we saw above that descriptive micro-generalisation forms the basic substrate of ethnographic accounts, and thus persists below the radar of even the most heterological approaches. But analogies are not merely a substrate, a descriptive device which could be isolated from the work of heterological theory 'proper'. Analogies play a role at the very heart of the most sophisticated and systematic heterological arguments. Daniel Gross pointed this out in the case of Foucault himself. His above-quoted heterological principles notwithstanding, Foucault's work (early, middle and late) is rife with analogies – between types of 'order' in different *episteme* (Gross 2001: 62), between forms of 'investigation' in the sciences of the mind and the sciences of nature (Gross 2001: 64), or between forms of *ascesis* in ancient Greece and the modern world. Indeed, Gross notes perceptively that Foucault's description of the magical play of sympathies in *The order of things* 'purports to describe a figure unique to the Renaissance, but actually appears to be a displaced description of Foucault's own poststructuralist methodology' (Gross 2001: 76). This methodology repurposes, Gross argues, elements of both classical and Wittgensteinian visions of analogy. From the former it retains a notion of proportionality, from the latter, a vision of family resemblances which defy abstract categorical articulation. The specificity of Foucault's analogies lies in his systematic refusal to see a transcendent order behind analogies, seeing them instead as immanent traces to be situated and related to particular transformations in forms of power. Building on this description one might say that in Foucault's analogies, we thus find a conceptual middle-man between the diffusionist tracing of traits, and the postmodern neo-diffusionisms evoked in Part I.

In a different vein, Paolo Heywood has noted that the intensely heterological moves associated with the ontological turn in anthropology are themselves grounded in a postulated identity – the identity of concepts and things – and in an analogy – the recursive analogy between what the ethnography describes and the form of the arguments it brings to bear on that description (Heywood 2018a,

2018b). We shall return to this point in Chapter 7. But since we are thinking of recursivity, we might note that, in the very move in which heterological critics contrast their approach to that of earlier generalising comparatists, they are simultaneously identifying them as instances of the same thing – anthropological devices. This is the 'in a nutshell' form of *comparatio*. Recall Cicero: whereas you build abstractions from the similarities between particulars, he builds abstractions from a system of differences. Whereas you seek general law-like propositions, he seeks to trace transformations …[5] There is no escaping the interweaving of analogies and contrasts. *Comparatio*, with its interlocking analogies and contrasts, thus already – empirically, as it were – provides a common device through which we conduct our debates about comparison.

In sum, comparisons that point to difference and comparisons that point to similarity can be seen, on a greater level of granularity, as similarly built of analogies and contrasts, differently articulated. To say this is not, however, to say that they are all the same. This was the normative lesson of caesurism in Chapter 3 – take seriously claims to a radical break. The crucial difference between analogical and heterological varieties of *comparatio* lies in whether they take identity or incommensurability as their aim. That is the name of a radical parting of ways. The point of mapping that alternative as an alternative between varieties of the same archetypal form is not to reduce it once more to identity. By pointing to all that comparative moves necessarily share, the radically different ends to which they can be oriented become even clearer. One can more clearly pinpoint what makes, say, the ontological turn and quantitative generalisation incommensurable. It is not that the one is entirely made out of differences, and the other entirely made out of similarities, but rather that each articulates difference and similarity to different effect, in order to reach different aims (Howe 1987).

## Conclusion: *Comparatio* as Common Ground

The discussion above has built on a key theme of Goyet's genealogy of comparison, namely that contemporary theorists too often conflate comparison with mere analogy (this is like that), forgetting in the process that *comparatio* operates on both similarity and difference, and could just as accurately be rendered as contrast (this is not like that). Analogies and contrasts, however, are abbreviated forms of *comparatio* – they might be the 'bottom-line', the 'take-home point', the 'payload' of a specific *comparatio*. But insofar as it is a developed, detailed, involved procedure, rather than a pithy one-liner, a *comparatio* is necessarily more than the contrast or analogy to which it can be reduced.

Pushing Goyet's point, one might say that analogy and contrast are relations between things (or relations, or forms), whereas *comparatio* is a relation between analogies and contrasts. In another, more precise view, analogy and contrast are the limit cases of *comparatio*. Analogy is *comparatio* reduced to a statement of similarity – which retains an appeal to difference only in the sense that it bears on two distinct objects (one is not comparing something to itself). It points the way, however, towards a horizon[6] of identity. Contrast is *comparatio* reduced to a statement of difference – which retains an appeal to similarity only in the sense that, through its very operation, it demonstrates that two things can be embraced at once. It points the way, however, towards the horizon of 'differencing differences' (Tarde 2016).

Imagine mapping these various terms on a single figure (Figure 5.2). Analogy and contrast take us one step inwards from the extremes of identity and alterity, the ends at which comparison is extinguished. But individual analogies and contrasts are still thin comparisons. The figure of *comparatio* takes us a further step 'inwards' to the space between simple analogy and contrast – the space in which multiple analogies and contrasts are interwoven into a thick skein. *Comparatio*, as a relation between analogies and contrasts, sits in the middle, a form that can vary in either direction.

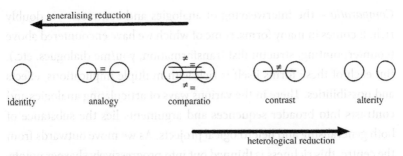

Figure 5.2 Identity and alterity

The reduction of *comparatio* to a search for analogies, and of analogies to a search for identity, marks the direction of travel from the particular to the general. Conversely, the reduction of *comparatio* to the articulation of contrasts, and of contrasts to the demonstration or creation of a more multiple world, marks the direction of travel of heterological comparatisms.

Readers of Chapter 3 will have recognised in the above account and Figure 5.2 a fractal pattern. One simple distinction (identity/difference) is recursively imbricated within itself. As we argued previously, a fractal vision enables us to retain an attention to commonality which does not erase radical divergences of purpose. Even if all comparatisms are in some sense 'made out of' differences and similarities, it matters very much indeed which way they point.

That fractal pattern also points to an important difference between the various options lined up alongside each other in Figure 5.2, and that is a difference in *recursive intricacy*, or in what one might think of as a kind of 'fractal thickness'. At the extremities, we have ideal aims or horizons, briefly if ever attained, and brittle to the touch – identity and 'alterity'. One step in, we have conclusions, punchlines, take-home points – analogies and contrasts – swift and memorable, but by themselves devoid of the power to convince. In the centre is where the action is, where the actual craft of anthropological comparison operates.

## Two Ends of Lateral Comparison

*Comparatio* – the interweaving of analogies and contrasts – is doubly rich. It comes in many forms, some of which we have encountered above (counterpointing, structuralist transformation, you/me dialogues, etc.). But each of these forms itself is rich with multiple implications, effects and possibilities. There in the various ways of articulating analogies and contrasts into broader sequences and arguments lies the substance of both generalising and heterological projects. As we move outwards from the centre, this richness is thinned out into progressively sharper points.

With this account of *comparatio* as the concatenation of analogies and contrasts, we have come some way towards articulating an archetypal form of anthropological comparison. By showing that the empirical variety of *comparatio*-devices can accommodate both anthropologists who aim at identity and those who aim at alterity, we have responded to the substance of the critique raised above: no, *comparatio* doesn't inherently aim at imposing identity. We have in the process also defused its recursive bite: neither does the present argument.

By mapping *comparatio* in relation to thickness and thinness of argument, we are also approaching one element of a normative common ground, a shared sense of a job well done that might cut across the generalising and the heterological alternatives. We are echoing, in fact, a point which anthropologists often make of ethnography, namely that good description ought to be 'thick' (Geertz 1974), ought to provide a richness which grounds the precise points it articulates, but also something more. This 'something more' can be imagined, in a generalising vein, as a richness of data to support further re-study and critical examination; it could be imagined, in a heterological vein, as a commitment to complexity which challenges any attempt at summation. But either way the thickness of description is a cross-cutting criterion, one on which anthropologists cursorily come to agree even where they definitively part ways in respect of broader aims. My argument is that this particular vision of ethnographic thickness is an instance of a broader kind of normativity, of which the thickness of *comparatio* is the name (on 'thick comparison', see Scheffer and Niewöhner 2010).

That thickness ensures that whichever way our comparisons point, there is always a 'remainder' (Strathern 2004). Thus, *comparatio*, even when it is designed to elicit an analogy or a generalisation, still retains a sense of its caveats: 'this is like that which you already know, but with the following differences' (Wimsatt 2007: 33). Conversely, even when designed to elicit a difference, *comparatio* produces a sense of what two cases nevertheless share, which further heterological efforts can seek to once again subdivide.

This argument is, as it were, the archetype of the argument of the book as a whole: as a discipline, we share our comparisons, even as our aims diverge. The remaining chapters will repeat and amplify this argument in different directions, and in the process thicken and specify the proposed archetype of comparison.

## Coda: A Note on Diagrams

Before I go any further, I should pause to consider the use of diagrams from this point onwards in the book. Up to this point, diagrams had been used fairly sparingly and in an ad hoc manner, to illustrate each time a particular point. From now on, they are going to come thick and fast and become something other than mere illustration. Figure 5.2 is the first in a series of diagrams which run alongside the argument developed in the rest of this book. They follow one particular constraint: they retain the same visual language, introducing new figures as new forms, concepts and distinctions are introduced, and tracking each main step of this argument, towards its conclusion. The crafting of an archetype of comparison will thus be done simultaneously in two media: in words and diagrams.

In deploying this technique I have in mind Gell's discussion of the power and limits of anthropological diagramming (Gell 1999: 31–32). As

Gell noted, anthropologists' enthusiasm for diagrams – so pronounced in the age of functionalism or structuralism – had waned by the late twentieth century, as the discipline turned its attention towards textual forms. Diagrams became suspect in some quarters for introducing a misleading sense of coherence and clarity, papering over the cracks in arguments through a sort of spurious visual authority. This objection is well taken, and it is certainly something to watch for: diagrams can lie in important ways, and I will try to make some of these explicit as I go along. But much the same can be said, of course, of words. The expression of an argument in words is partly a matter of formulation and conviction, and many cracks can be papered over in that medium too. At the same time, both words and diagrams require a specific kind of rigour – particularly when one seeks, in both media, to keep the terminology stable. The key point is that those kinds of rigour are different (see also Leach 1966: 17).

In sum, diagrams are deployed in the rest of this book not simply as illustration or to lend visual authority to the textual claims, but precisely because their capacities and their requirements differ from those of discursive arguments. Keeping an argument coherent and keeping a set of diagrams (or a notational system) coherent are two cross-cutting requirements, and the rigour of the one often teases out the omissions of the other. Thus more than once I have found that in trying to represent visually a move in the verbal argument, an incoherence or a gap was made visible; conversely, I have also found once or twice that a move suggested by a neat visual transformation of a previous diagram actually fell apart when I tried to put it into words. Words and pictures are heuristics with different footprints: each suggests possibilities which the other might miss, and each controls the other. This argument has been driven forward by both, and also in some measure controlled by both.

SIX

# Another Dimension of Lateral Comparison: Identity and Intensity

[O]ne of the most important tasks of a thinking being, and one of its greatest difficulties, is this: to give an account in words of the comparison not between a thing and another thing, but between a thing and itself.

(Garcia 2016b: 47)

Chicago happened slowly, like a migraine. First they were driving through countryside, then imperceptibly, the occasional town became a low suburban sprawl, and the sprawl became the city.

(Gaiman 2004: 82)

## Introduction: A Genealogy of Intensity

What do anthropological comparatists miss when they imagine a world made out of discrete, thing-like objects, whose parts or attributes are ripe and ready for comparison? At the end of Chapter 4, I noted that three counterpoints could be raised to the vision of *comparatio* as an archetype for anthropological comparison. We addressed the first – heterological – challenge in the previous chapter. The second strikes perhaps more deeply still, by challenging the very vision of a discrete world of things, objects or entities, upon which *comparatio* operates. This challenge opens up a second – often interwoven – path away from identity, besides the one which points at difference, namely the one that points towards intensity.

## Another Dimension of Lateral Comparison

The notion of intensity is often associated with the philosophy of Gilles Deleuze. Its relevance to questions of anthropological comparison may not seem immediately apparent, beyond one very specific and theoretically complex invocation by Martin Holbraad and Morten Pedersen (2009; cf. 2017) to which I return below. However, the relevance of the notion of intensity to questions of comparison goes well beyond this particular instance, and beyond even the broader circle of Deleuzian-influenced anthropology. In essence the problem to which the notion of intensity points is a very basic and recurrent one for anthropological comparison, and the Deleuzian invocation of intensity is the tip of a much larger iceberg. The broader questions raised by the notion of intensity concern the respective roles of objects and relations, states and processes.

This emerges clearly from the useful genealogy of the notion of intensity, presented in a recent exposition by philosopher Tristan Garcia (2016b). As Garcia notes, the basic problem of intensity is raised not by the comparison of two things, but by the attempt to compare a thing to itself: how do I make sense of the continuous variation through which this dawn gradually lightens to become day, or this headache gradually worsens to the point of being unbearable (Garcia 2016b: 45–46), or as in the Gaiman quote above, of the gradual move through suburban sprawl into a city? On a first reading this problem might seem to be cast in unnecessarily paradoxical terms: surely, one is not comparing a thing to itself, but two moments or states of the same thing? But on Garcia's account, such a reaction is itself characteristic of the particular (neo-) classical episteme which we encountered via Foucault above. It is a reaction which seeks to quantify intensity, to reduce it, in other words, to a vision of extension – a world of separate units or states.

The problem of comparing a thing 'to itself' was once cast in very different terms. It appeared in the (actually) classical philosophical vision of an *eidos* or ideal form through which a thing might be judged as a more or less adequate instance of itself: how much does this particular mountain instantiate mountain-ness? Again the temptation is to read this question through the neo-classical episteme's focus on classification: given an arbitrarily defined type of mountain, how does this one compare? But the *eidos* was something else: an internal feature of each being which could be discovered, rather than a standardised arbitrary measuring-rod. In the Aristotelian version of that question, what is not yet called the 'intensity' of a thing is the extent to which it actualises the particular quality of being itself. This precursor of intensity is a material 'force': Aristotle's *phusis*, or the Stoics' *pneuma*. While not quantifiable, it is prone to a particular kind of increase and decrease, intensification and remission, specific to each thing. In this form the varieties and permutations of intensity occupied medieval philosophers (Garcia 2016a: 51–55).

With the advent of Newtonian physics, Garcia argues, force was parsed out as an abstract and general property, a general term for intensity, absent any particular identity, leaving behind a world of extended things, without any intensity. The rift between intensity and identity was consecrated. In Garcia's account this rift animated two twin moves within modernity: on the one hand, the attempt to reduce and quantify this still mysterious 'force', reducing all that is real to extension – segmenting the flow of experience into objects and dimensions (cf. Hunt 2007: 12).[1] Intensity came to be seen as essentially subjective or perceptual. On the other hand, there is the attempt to recapture and foreground intensity through various poetic, scientific or philosophical devices. Garcia makes much of the way in which the advent of electricity, concomitant with the modern age, came to stand as a master metaphor for intensity, lending its concrete power and magic to this hoary philosophical notion. Intensity, like electrical current, came to be seen as a pure difference, a vital power, an energy which flows between two poles, and gives life to animate and inanimate things alike.

Intensity had come to mean simultaneously the variation of a quality, the measure of the comparison of a thing to itself, the measure of change, of becoming, a pure difference, that which could explain the sensibility of the living, desire, that which made a life livable, the value of everything which cannot be quantified or mapped onto extension – and an electric shock.

(Garcia 2016b: 66)

This new vision of intensity, Garcia argues, became a master-trope of a modernity, the ethics, aesthetics and politics of which came to take on some form of the injunction to be more fully oneself. Intensity is the master-word of consumer culture, but also that of anti-capitalist radical politics or of a modern art freed from the classical requirements of standards of beauty. Of course, to be ever more fully oneself is also to be always in movement, always transforming, never stable, and thus always other to oneself, in a perpetual move away from any stable identity. Philosophies of becoming such as that of Gilles Deleuze, or, we might add, theoretical movements in anthropology such as the ontological turn, share in this modern aesthetics, ethics and politics of permanent intensification, open-endedness and self-differentiation (Holbraad and Pedersen 2017).

In these various guises, Garcia tells us, the modern era has witnessed the rise of 'intense man'. Intense man, Garcia notes with a tinge of gentle irony, is dogged by the shadow of boredom, self-sameness – in a word, of identity.

Maybe because perception essentially grasps relations, intense man never perceives the thing itself, but that which distinguishes a thing from another, or that invisible articulation between two moments, two beings. The potential of a sensitive being can only be revealed through its contact with an other, and it is by passing from one relation to the next that the potential of its nature can be realized. It is true that intense man gets bored easily. He always wants to be an other.

(Garcia 2016b: 120)

Garcia is persuasive as a moralist of sorts, and his genealogy acts as a relativisation of the narratives of a great heterological march forward into ever-more differing difference. His own inspiration is in one sense anthropological. He asks us to imagine how this modern 'obsession' with intensity might be viewed from other traditions (Garcia 2016b: 24), and this enables him to contextualise what seems to wish to escape context: intensity itself.

## Varieties of Intensity in Anthropological Comparison

For my purposes here, what is most relevant is Garcia's tracing of this very general problematic of intensity through to its most extreme achievement in the work of Deleuze, in which it comes to reverse the very vision of extension. The Deleuzian watchword, 'we must interpret everything through intensities' (Garcia 2016a: 84), inverts the relation which, since Newton, has obtained between extension and intensity. Intensity had once been relegated to the inner subjectivity of the viewer of a world which was *really* made of extensive objects. For Deleuze, by contrast, the world itself is intensity – a world of relations, which is to say differences. The vision of an extended world of objects is our own perceptual effort to organise this world of proliferating relations into a set of terms, units, objects. The world of things is a mere secondary vision superimposed upon a real world of intense, differential relations.

In this contrast between terms and relations, we have reached the most obvious point of application of these philosophical discussions of intensity to anthropology. Over and again in the history of anthropological comparison, it has been claimed more or less radically that relations, rather than things, were where the action was. In the most radical versions of this view, the claim, as for Deleuze, has been that identities are only temporary and perspectival stabilisations of differential relations, or in other words, of intensities. Indeed, just as the claim that comparisons ought to focus on difference rather than similarity recurs with predictable regularity throughout the history of anthropology, the claim that comparisons ought to be about relations *rather than* units is just as recurrent. We have encountered a number of avatars of this concern with intensity in the first part of the book. Let me pick out two main varieties.

## *Eidos, Structure, and Concept-things*

A move from identity towards intensity could be achieved through a focus on structure – the recasting of things as systems of differences. We saw in Chapter 2 what anthropological evocations of structure owed to the transcendental formalist biology of the nineteenth century, which, reviving the old notion of *eidos*, had turned organisms into comparisons – each species a transformation of the archetype. We thus find the echo of the original vision of *eidos* as a form of which objects were more or less intense variations, in the Lévi-Straussian move from seeing empirical 'units' as concrete building blocks to seeing them as mere possible instantiations of a more fundamental structural form. It is in this particular sense that structuralism suggested, not a comparison of units, but a comparison of relations, and more profoundly, of transformations.[2]

The very different theoretical devices of interpretive anthropology were nevertheless also sustained by a vision of different cultures, each consisting of variations of a pattern (Benedict 2005; Geertz 1973c), each instance or element of which could be seen as a more or less intense version of the archetypal form of that culture itself. In a broader view, these distinct cultures might in turn be seen as variations upon a broader pattern (Benedict 1934), different books in the same library of human cultural variation. Building up a holistic picture out of the echoes produced by internal variations was also one of the core devices of Malinowski's monographic aesthetic and, as we saw in Chapter 2, this invocation of one example could in turn scale up to encompass humanity as a whole.

For all their important differences, what these structuralist, interpretive or Malinowskian comparative devices share is the Aristotelian insight, repurposed by structuralist biology, that difference within kinds is a matter not primarily of the substitution of parts, but of increase and decrease relative to an archetypal form or *eidos*.[3] And it is another, yet again different, echo of that eidetic vision that we encounter in Strathern's claim that

the apparently numerous social systems of Melanesia can be considered as versions of one another ... I do not mean that the differences are not real, but that they are, so to speak, the same difference ... Melanesian societies share a common aesthetic. Such reductionism will not please everyone. For it also underlines the failure of a comparative method whose persuasion rests in elucidating a repetition of instances. That arithmetic – based on the plurality of units – has disappeared. Here we have varieties of or versions of a 'single' instance.

(Strathern 1988: 340–341)

Armed with Garcia's genealogy, we are thus now in a better position to appreciate the import of one key explicit invocation of intensity in anthropological discussions of comparison, namely Holbraad and Pedersen's (2009, 2017) Deleuzian reading of Strathern. The authors invoke Deleuzian notions of intensity to gloss the contrast introduced by Strathern between what she terms 'plural' and 'post-plural' visions. Plural visions – including plural visions of anthropological comparison – operated upon an 'extended' world of objects in space and time, an objective world upon which any number of subjective perspectives can be taken. Strathern explores the rise of a 'post-plural' view – what others have called postmodernity – in a number of works, without referring to Deleuze or intensity (Strathern 1992, 2004). Such post-plural visions imagine themselves as being 'after nature' – the anchoring work of a single extended world of natural objects has fallen away. They are left instead with proliferating relations – differences – themselves made up of relations, in a fractal recursion. The conceptual echoes to the Deleuzian vision are indeed enticing.

What Strathern's work theorises and exemplifies in *Partial connections*, and Holbraad and Pedersen seek to recharacterise in Deleuzian terms, is what anthropological comparison itself might look like in this post-plural mode. In Holbraad and Pedersen's reading, such post-plural comparison takes the form of an 'intense abstraction', in which the classic device of abstracting up from particulars (recall Mill's definition in Chapter 2) is subverted. Rather, they claim, in Strathern's work ethnographic particulars are sharpened to a conceptual point, without ever being 'abstracted' into general comparative categories. The result is a kind of hybrid: 'abstentions' (Holbraad and Pedersen 2009: 379–380) – a new, third sort of entity, which is neither abstract concept nor concrete thing, but the mark of an overcoming of that distinction: a 'concept-thing', one might say, which the authors represent through the diagram of a cone laid on its side, with a thick ethnographic end and a sharp conceptual end. Such concept-things – which Holbraad and Pedersen then also use to characterise the peculiar productions of the ontological turn – overcome the classic tensions of a plural vision.

Some (e.g. Laidlaw 2017) have challenged Holbraad and Pedersen's reading of Strathern, and it is hard not to concur that this reading involves at least a shift in emphasis. Treated as a conceptual 'invention' in its own right, however, this notion of 'concept-things' is thought-provoking, which is surely the point. It evokes once again, transmogrified via Deleuze, the classical notion of *eidos*: the vision of things carrying within themselves a kind of standard by which one could compare them to themselves. Terms, objects, things, are already relations. But while in that classical – essentialist – vision each thing was a relation to (an ideal version of) itself, the concept-things which emerge, on this account, from anthropological comparisons are relations between ethnographic particulars (facts about 'them') and ('our') theoretical inventions. Another element is being invoked here, which will occupy us in the next two chapters, namely the question of reflexivity. We will therefore delay further explication of this notion of concept-things, and its particular power and limits, until Chapter 8.

## Genealogies, Traces and Processes

One must ask if the idea of comparison can deal with change at all.

(Yengoyan 2006a: 2)

To these eidetic and structural versions of the concern with intensity one can add the broad family of comparative devices which relate to questions of history, process and flow. Thus, Foucauldian genealogies were not simply, as discussed above, aiming to foreground difference: they were also a vision of intense transformations. Change, differentiation, were the stuff of history, while points of stabilisation – identities – are merely perspectival and temporary stopping-points. This is why Garcia's genealogy is so piquant: it is amongst other things a genealogy of genealogy. Garcia reminds us that, long before Foucauldian genealogy, intensity was already the key concept of a Darwinian view of life as perpetual transformation, which from the start, sat in an uneasy tension with the classificatory impetus of an earlier biological science. As soon as the view shifts from the comparison of two distinct objects to the problem of tracing the transformation of a thing into something else, or another version of itself, to questions of growth and flow, we are in the realms of intensity. The study of flows, '-scapes' and multi-sited or travelling phenomena partakes of this sensibility (Appadurai 1996; Marcus 1995; Petryna 2002).

In a less conceptually baroque sense, anthropologists' repeated calls to reintroduce history, process and change into a discipline perceived as occupied with static, stable objects partakes of this same modern genealogy of intensity (Yengoyan 2006b). A panoply of critical responses to 'structural functionalism' from the 1950s and '60s onwards all sought to reintroduce a study of process. The Manchester school's 'extended case analysis' (Burawoy 2009; Englund 2018; Van Velsen 1967), the transactionalist vision of structures as effects of individual actions, moves and purposes (Barth 1990; Leach 1964; Sneath 2018), the various reconfigurations of evolutionism (Sahlins and Service 1960) and Marxist world-systems theory (Mintz 1985; Wolf 1983) – all of these revisions of the nature and ends of comparison sought to upend an anthropological vision of 'billiard-ball' cultures though a comparison of *processes* (Moore 2005). The struggle between structuralist and historical anthropologists, or between cultural relativists and materialists (cf. Ortner 1984), could be cast in part as a struggle between two competing visions of intensity: the eidetic vision characterised above, set against the processual vision.

Earlier still, as we saw above (Chapter 2), Boasian diffusionism applied to culture the Darwinian vision of life as a perpetual difference from itself. But one might go further back: even the original identification of concomitant *variation* as the keystone of comparison in Tylor or Durkheim was already a partial move away from a simply pluralist world of objects and towards a vision of processes and transformation. The problem of intensity as process was built into our comparative devices from the start.

## Intensity and Identity: A Second Axis

In all of these cases, whether intensity is envisioned as process or as *eidos*, it stands in a tense relationship to identity. We saw in Chapter 5 that even the most heterological visions, when put into comparative practice, still invoke some form of similarity, and the most analogical forms of comparison still require there to be at least two different things being compared. Similarly, none of the visions above, however much they may foreground or aim towards *eidos*, process or flow, can quite do away with the invocation of objects, states, identities, periods, events or moments. These invocations of identity may be marked as secondary, residual, or even straightforwardly heuristic, fictional or as if. But they are still required for exposition to make sense. Conversely, however much they may have pointed towards stabilisation, objectification and identification, anthropology's comparative devices were from the start haunted by the ghost or worry of process and variation. Even Radcliffe-Brown, the usual suspect of 'solid-state anthropology', explicitly defined the discipline as the study of processes (Radcliffe-Brown 1952: 4).

In thinking of the contrast between identity and intensity, we can thus perform an analogous move to that performed above for the contrast between identity and alterity (cf. Figure 5.2 above). We can see, on the one hand, a fundamental distinction of aims and horizons in the alternative between comparisons which aim to stabilise identities, to frame and define units, and those which, by contrast, seek to focus attention on flows, intensities, differing differences or comparisons as pure relations. On the other hand, we can also see that these radically different horizons are in practice pursued through techniques which recombine identity and intensity in various ways (see Figure 6.1).

At the centre of this figure lies that particular kind of *comparatio* which seeks capture a *transformation*: the same thing changing such as to no longer be (quite) itself. In this middling version, the study

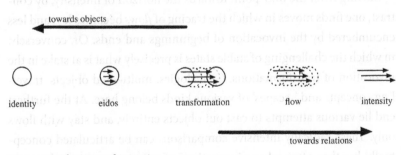

Figure 6.1 Identity and intensity

of transformation requires *both* relations *and* terms, states, stabilised 'objects' at the beginning and end of a process (Robbins 2004; Sahlins 1985). The two – terms and relations – relativise each other. Insofar as a transformation compares a thing to itself, it is an analogy; insofar as it shows a shift, it is a contrast. In that broad family of moves belong most historically informed anthropological visions, most attempts to study process which do not simply reduce it back to a succession of subsequent thing-like states. To proponents of a radical Deleuzian vision of absolute intensity, this middling vision of intensity as, quite simply, process may seem like anathema. But one might, conversely, say that their vision reminds us how radical a disturbance the banal notion of process has always, from the start, produced in a comparative view.

Moving away from that mid-point, towards the horizon of identity, we find techniques which seek to compare a thing to its *eidos* or ideal form – either in a classical sense, in the modern structuralist or interpretivist sense of finding in 'objects' mere instances of more profound forms and patterns, or in the ontological sense of self-comparing object-things. One finds an interestingly recursive appeal to *eidos* in certain versions of the anthropology of ethics, which appeal to *both* the Aristotelian vision of people as aiming towards self-intensification and the Geertzian vision of a collectivisation of such aims, such that one might speak of particular examples as instances of a shared ethos (Laidlaw 2014).

Moving from the mid-point towards the horizon of intensity, by contrast, one finds moves in which the tracing of *flows* becomes less and less encumbered by the invocation of beginnings and ends. Or, conversely, in which the challenging of stable states is precisely what is at stake in the invocation of transformations. Genealogies, multi-sited objects, travelling concepts and '-scapes' of various kinds belong here. At the furthest end lie various attempts to cast out objects entirely, and stay with flows only. These radically intensive comparisons can be articulated conceptually, but they often rely on invocations of states, moments and entities as productive or temporary fictions. 'Intense man' is – still, always – haunted by identity.

## Conclusion: The Plane of Lateral Comparison

In sum, objects and relations, like similarities and differences, form a fractal pair whose recombinations can be mapped alongside one another. In the figure of pure 'intensity' we find a third end – a purpose and limit – of comparison, alongside identity and alterity. Intensity is something else comparisons can aim at, and another point at which they are extinguished. Pure intensity, like pure identity or pure alterity, is beyond comparison.

We have thus drawn an analogy between the way comparison relates to identity and alterity (Figure 5.2) and the way comparison relates to identity and intensity (Figure 6.1). But what is the relation between these two arguments and between these two figures? Clearly in many concrete cases, points on Figure 5.2 correspond to points on Figure 6.1; thus Deleuzian-inspired comparatisms are heterological and also oriented towards intensity, concerned with relations rather than terms. Yet these two figures do not always correspond. Thus invocation of *eidos* can take a generalising or heterological form.

In keeping with my device, outlined at the end of Chapter 5, of building up a visual, diagrammatic argument alongside the textual one, let me suggest we plot these two figures against each other, to form two axes of a geometrical plane (Figure 6.2). The x-axis tracks the move from identity to intensity, or from a focus on things to a focus on relations; the y-axis leads from identity and alterity. For reasons which will become clearer in the next chapter, I will call this xy plane the plane of lateral comparison. We could simply for now take this as a reference to the way in which, on this plane, cases, objects and relations are laid side by side for the purposes of comparison. This is also in essence the plane on which questions and problems of mapping are asked and resolved.

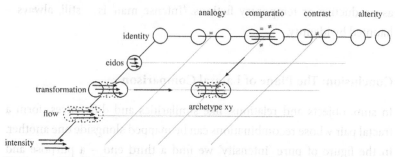

Figure 6.2 Identity, alterity, intensity: the plane of lateral comparison

Let us explore some of the conceptual possibilities opened by this visualisation of identity, alterity and intensity as the coordinates of a plane. Firstly, this highlights the above-mentioned observation that these two axes of variation are not straightforwardly the same. This analytical device forces us, therefore, to distinguish problematics which are often interwoven in practice. With this vision of a plane in mind, we can ask of any given comparison where it might sit in respect of both problematics, and imagine receiving different answers in each case.

The vision of a plane of lateral comparison allows us to imagine, at the metaphorical centre of that plane, a revised archetype of comparison: a form which lies at the intersection of two kinds of intricacy. *Comparatio*, as we saw in Chapter 5, is a relation between analogies and contrasts. It resists reduction to a single contrast or analogy, but retains a certain kind of slowness, a painstaking commitment to working through similarities and differences. A different source of intricacy emerges along the x-axis. One can gear a comparison towards foregrounding relations or objects, but there is a particular richness which comes from keeping both of those in view, at least for a time, and keeping live the sense in which each challenges and relativises the other. This is captured in the mid-point figure of 'transformation'.

*Comparatio* and transformation thus emerge as analogues of each other. Of any two things, one can ask in what respects they differ or are similar. But of any two things, one can also ask – and that is not the same question – in what respects they are related, in what respects they are transformations of each other, or even ultimately, in what respects they are moments or instances or heuristic stabilisations of the same process, the same relation. If we keep both of these intricacies in view at the same time, we can imagine the form of a second-order archetype of comparison at the intersection of these two sets of themselves intricate questions (Figure 6.2).

This archetype sits in the middle of the plane of lateral comparison, on which anthropological comparisons can multiply in two directions beyond the initial vision of an argument by analogy: towards an elicitation of difference, towards a dissolution of objects into relations. In doing so, anthropologists are still articulating the same basic ingredients – objects, predicates and relations – and recombining the same basic moves – contrast, analogy, stabilisation, destabilisation. But the effects are various. Anthropologists use comparison to generalise on various scales, yes, to demonstrate that two things were actually one thing, or that two situations were caught up in the same process; but they can recombine the same basic ingredients and moves to critique generalisations, or to show that a larger entity or a flow can be disaggregated into constituent states or parts, or relations.

Secondly, these different horizons recall the fundamental point that comparative devices can be deployed to radically different, even incommensurable ends. This was most obvious in relation to 'saming' and 'othering' in Chapter 5, but it emerges also in relation to the ends of stabilising and destabilising. Whether one wishes to foreground stable identities or transformational processes is an analytical decision, or a political or ethical requirement; either way it is in part a matter of purpose (see also Lloyd 2015: 30–31). It is important to add, however, that our purposes also encounter resistances. Anthropological comparisons do not take place in a vacuum: they are addressed to readers, within and beyond the discipline, including often the people most directly concerned by these descriptions. More broadly, the world too can resist our purposes. These questions will be addressed in Chapter 9, when we consider what makes anthropological comparisons rigorous.

All three bounding coordinates of this plane – pure static identity, pure relational flow, pure alterity – are comparison's 'ends' in the double sense we introduced earlier. They can be horizons for particular comparative moves, but they also mark comparison's methodological points of extinction. Anthropological comparisons in their vibrant variety happen in between, and their thickness (cf. Scheffer and Niewöhner 2010) increases the closer they lie to the mid-point designated by our archetype above (Figure 6.1).[4]

Having outlined, in the past two chapters, this plane of lateral comparisons – comparisons of *this and that* – we now turn to another family of comparative moves, the frontal comparisons which are concerned, not with comparing *this and that*, but with comparing *us and them*. In so doing we will need to take into account a third dimension of anthropological comparatism, that which concerns the position of the anthropologist him- or herself. Concomitantly, we will move from a plane of comparison to a vision of a three-dimensional space.

A small reminder before we proceed – diagrams can lie. The facility to imagine conceptual contrasts articulated together in dimensional space opens up various possibilities. It is important to note, however, that a crucial source of potential misunderstanding creeps in with this representation. Figure 5.2 and Figure 6.1 each represented fractal contrasts. While they could be seen as pointing in different directions, there was no assumption that these contrasts would form a continuous cline, from identity to difference, say, or from relations to entities. This point was made more generally of fractal contrasts (Chapter 3, above): they are made of a repetition of differences, not a sequence of continuities; mid-points might, as a result, move past each other.

Imagining a plane made of two dimensions, by contrast, seems to imply that continuous variation is possible along both axes, and that this difference might be quantified. I don't think this is the case of anthropological comparison. It would be futile to try to pinpoint, for any given comparison, the 'quantity' of difference or relationality that it includes, or to map its precise position on that plane. To put it otherwise, imagining knowledge mapped on to a graduated space suggests that it might be 'divided up into discrete units or entities' (Corsín Jiménez 2011: 142), erasing precisely the sense in which knowledge is analogical, simultaneously a matter of relations and of flows.

This is why, while I will work with these images, it is important to remember the sense in which this is a fiction. There is no graduated or continuous space (2D or 3D) within which one might 'measure' anthropological comparisons. The device is intended, rather, to convey – taking my lead from Alberto Corsín Jimenez (2011) – the value of introducing a sense of 'perpendicularity' into our conceptualisation of knowledge. Epistemic devices – here, modes of comparison – are not simply in agreement or in disagreement: they can also be – productively – perpendicular to one another.

# SEVEN

# Two Ends of Frontal Comparison: Identity, Alterity, Reflexivity

It is not [Melanesians] who need this book or who would need to write one like it. But if any should care to read it, I hope ... the use of 'we' to mean 'we Westerners' will not prove too much of an irritant ... [I]t is a pity that English does not have a dual, for then one could also use 'we' in the sense of 'we two,' an inclusion that would not obliterate separateness. Indeed, the work can be read both as an apology and an apologia for a language and a culture that does not make that particular possibility of central concern to the way it imagines itself.

(Strathern 1988: xv)

## Introduction: 'Us and Them' not 'This and That'

What are anthropologists doing when they compare, not simply two contexts – cultures, societies, what have you – but two contexts, one of which is described as being in some sense 'our own', the context of the anthropologist and their intended readers? This question is the subject of this and the next chapter. The possibility of such comparisons starts from a challenge. To a number of critics, comparison as we have considered it so far in this part of the book, namely comparison as the holding in view of two objects, forms or relations, seems a particularly reductive device for a discipline which is all about an encounter with people and their worlds. Anthropological comparisons cannot simply be comparison of 'this and that'. It doesn't matter per se whether the emphasis here is on the objects – *this* and *that* – or on the relations – this *and* that. Over and again, anthropologists have argued that classic comparative schemes eluded what was in fact the key question of the discipline, namely the relation between observer and observed, self and other – not 'this and that', but 'us and them'. To anthropologists animated by such concerns, the intricate archetype of comparison at which we arrived at the end of the previous chapter is still missing one crucial ingredient because it eludes the question of *who* is 'making a parallel' or articulating a contrast, and with what commensurating devices. The objection is simultaneously epistemological and political.

This objection foregrounds the contrast between the lateral comparison of cases or relations laid side by side – the kinds of comparison which happen on the plane identified at the end of the previous chapter, and the frontal encounter between 'observer' and 'observed' often scaled up to an encounter between 'our' and 'their' cultures or 'worlds'. That contrast between frontal and lateral comparison maps an alternative that can be as radical as the one between generalisation and heterology, or between objects and relations. If comparison is double attention, this names three, not two, entities: the two which are held in the double attention and a third doing the holding.

The argument of this chapter is that, while this objection is well taken, it can be addressed not by imagining a radical alternative to *comparatio* but by multiplying the figure of *comparatio* itself. For what proponents of a frontal comparison are calling for can be articulated as a particular form of *comparatio* – one which is outlined from within one of its terms. Recall Cicero again – 'whereas you ..., he ...' – and change the pronouns: 'Whereas we ..., they ...' That is, in essence, the form of a frontal comparison.

Like the vision of an alternative between generalising and heterology, to which it is often linked, the vision of an alternative between lateral and frontal comparisons has a long history in anthropology. The clearest instance comes from Evans-Pritchard's contrast between 'translation' and 'comparison' (Chapter 1). But a similar contrast was drawn by Ruth Benedict (2005) when she noted that anthropologists have a double skill-set: on the one hand, they can draw from the comparative anthropological literature in order to compare cultures more or less closely related to the one they focus on; on the other, they are well versed in thinking of the latter by contrast to their own culture. Lewis (1955) makes a distinction between comparisons which set out to test hypotheses drawn from literature on non-western societies, and comparisons which set out to test hypotheses drawn from western societies. Handler (2009: 628) and Holy (1987), in different ways, both argue that whereas positivists sought to line up cases in order to generalise, interpretivists pursue a comparison which puts their own cultural categories at stake. Lambek (1991) contrasts second-person and third-person comparison. Dumont (1986: 5), hailing from a very different epistemic perspective, nevertheless draws a similar contrast between the 'radical' comparative move, which includes the observer's perspective, and the empiricist collation of differences and similarities between cases or monographs. Viveiros de Castro (2004) contrasts the 'translative comparisons', in which the anthropologist's own categories are at stake, with the mere lining up of different spatial or temporal instances of the same sociocultural form. Michael Herzfeld (2001) sets out a distinction between comparison and reflexivity which echoes the above but presents them as complementary moves. Gingrich and Fox (2002b) contrast 'weak' comparisons – the ubiquitous cultural translations of the unfamiliar which ground all anthropological enterprise – with the 'strong' comparisons which lay out an explicit comparative inventory across different historical or spatial instances.

Once we lay out these various contrasts alongside each other, we see that they are only partly overlapping. In some cases the focus is on the respective conceptual or political effect of these two moves; in others the focus is on their particular way of playing on sameness and difference; in others still, the difference turns on a tension between first-person

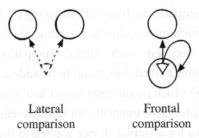

Lateral        Frontal<br>
comparison    comparison

Figure 7.1 Lateral and frontal comparison

fieldwork and subsequent analysis, or between objectivism and inter-pretation. None of these secondary distinctions maps on to every one of the pairs invoked above. But the core distinction which emerges in every single one of these contrasts bears on the position of the anthro-pologist. *In frontal comparison, the anthropologist's own perspective is (or is included in) one of the terms of the comparison. In lateral comparison, the anthropologist's own perspective is outside the frame – or indeed, it is the frame* (Figure 7.1).

Viewed through the perspective of this distinction, it should now become clearer why we termed the xy plane of Figure 6.2 the plane of lateral comparison. Comparative devices on this plane are concerned with the laying side by side of objects and relations, differences and similarities, with the making and dissolution of cases. Some of these comparisons seek to identify things, to reduce them down towards that state of stable and known identity. Others point away from identity, in two different directions. Along one axis, they seek to differentiate things, rather than identify them; along another axis, they seek to unravel things into processes. Possibilities along these two axes can be recombined in various ways. Nevertheless, all of these comparative moves, how-ever divergent their ends, share one feature: they are concerned with the world, things and relations in themselves – *this* and *that*, or this *and* that. On this plane – the plane of lateral comparison – objects and relations stand alone. This is, to borrow Lambek's useful scheme, a plane of 'third-person comparisons' (1991: 48), implying a privileged, detached observer – or, to put it more radically, implying no observer at all.

The contrast between such lateral comparisons and frontal comparisons requires a third dimension to be added, along an axis (let us call it the z-axis) which points away from identity in a different direction: not towards alterity, or intensity, but towards reflexivity (Figure 7.2; cf. Abbott 2004: 29 for a similar device applied to the related question of forms of explanation). 'Identity' as we have encountered it so far is that philosophical vanishing point, namely the vision of a single, fully mapped thing in itself. The converse to this entirely observer-free position would be a purely or fully reflexive position – an entirely self-sufficient 'first-person' perspective from which the object is absent. This

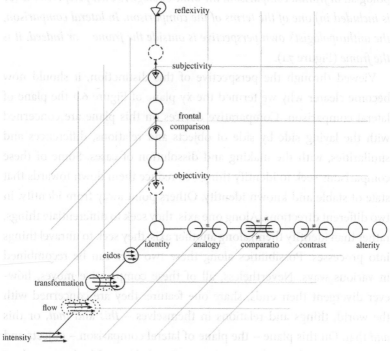

Figure 7.2  A space of comparison

is the vanishing point Lambek has in mind when he points out that a first-person perspective 'may be reflexive, but ... has no Other against which to keep such reflection honest' (Lambek 1991: 48).

In the practice of real existing anthropological comparatisms, an entirely absent observer is as rare as an entirely and utterly self-regarding one. Like pure alterity, pure intensity or, for that matter, pure identity, the vision of pure or full reflexivity maps an *end* of comparison – something one might aim towards, but which, if reached, would extinguish the very possibility of comparison.

Near the base of this z-axis lies the figure of objectivity – the basic realisation that an objective observer is required as the perspectival point of any rigorous lateral comparison. This is, as it were, the first step away from simply considering things in themselves. Just as we noted above that analogies are not identities, objectivity is not the object itself. It is already a relation – a relation between an object and an objective observer (Daston and Galison 2007). Its interest and focus is, however, primarily on the former, as suggested by the dashed lines in Figure 7.2. The converse of objectivity – let's call it subjectivity, but keeping in mind this is just my own temporary definition of a fuzzy term – could thus be mapped one step 'inwards' from the horizon of pure reflexivity as described above. It is not yet the point at which all objects are dissolved and the observer is left contemplating only her or his own naked self-instantiation, but rather, one step earlier – a form of subject–object (or I–Thou) relation in which the object (or the other) still features, but in a rather ghostly way, while attention is focused primarily on the observer and their perspective.

Frontal comparison sits at the mid-point of these two positions: it sees both the observer and the observed, the self and the other, the subject and the object, in simultaneous focus. In frontal comparison an observer situates and objectifies her or his own position in relation to the subject/objects she or he simultaneously keeps in view. Note that simultaneity of focus is not to be confused with a symmetry of perspective: it is a systematic and crucial feature of frontal comparison, examined further in the next chapter, that it places the object ('them') in front, and the source of the perspective ('us') behind.

Frontal comparison thus recalls the third form in Lambek's typology of comparisons, namely 'second-person' comparison which 'entails the interplay of our language with that of the Other' (Lambek 1991). It is notable, however, that the quote actually invokes the first-person plural (*our* language'). An alternation between the first- and the third-person plural (we and they) is far more characteristic in practice of frontal comparison than the second person.

Indeed, while fieldwork often takes a second-person, You-and-I dialogical form, written ethnographies rarely do so. Anthropological texts may be born of actual dialogues, but they are seldom themselves dialogues in a more than metaphorical sense, despite critiques and proposals of the 1980s (Crapanzano 1986; cf. Laidlaw 2018). Outside their acknowledgements, anthropologists seldom write 'you'; they often write 'they'. That much is common to all forms of comparison. What distinguishes frontal comparison from the usual third-person invocations (them, and them and them) is not the presence of the second person, then, nor the absence of a third-person perspective, but rather the introduction of the first-person plural. The key device of frontal comparison is that of contextualising one's own perspective – it is the device which moves from I to 'we'. The power and the limits of frontal comparison turn on the crucial, elusive, and sometimes treacherous form of that first-person plural.

As we shall see again in the next chapter, anthropologists' way of saying 'we' has been under recurrent scrutiny (Pina-Cabral 1992: 6; 2006; Chua and Mathur 2018). As Chua and Mathur have noted '[t]his "we" is both intellectual and structural, modelled on the figure of an individual, ambivalent Western scholar constantly pushing against his "own" society, and shored up by various structural mechanisms and inequalities that striate the contemporary academic world system' (Chua and Mathur 2018: 4). The present chapter and the next (see also Candea 2016a) echoes these authors' interest in the genealogy of this figure, although here as elsewhere in the book, my main focus is on the conceptual structures of this articulation.

From that perspective, a key theme will be the elusiveness of the 'we', the fact that its invocation in frontal comparison rests on an uncertainty of reference. As noted by Boas (1896: 903) and Strathern (1988: xv), the first-person plural, in English, has a peculiar grammatical feature which suggests broader cultural proclivities and puzzles: it can contextually refer either to the collective made up of the self and the person spoken of (its 'dual' mode), or, more commonly, to the collective made up of the self and the person addressed. Frontal comparison in anthropology plays on this ambiguity of the first-person plural. It relies centrally on the invocation of a 'we' made up of the anthropologist and their imagined readership – often problematically assumed to be 'western' or 'Euroamerican'. This is an exclusive 'we' which pits 'us' against a 'them' who are being written about. At the same time frontal comparison often implicitly or explicitly invokes a dual 'we' – the 'we' made up of the anthropologist and their subjects. This dual 'we' is the echo or trace of a dialogical, second-person encounter, of which a frontal comparison is necessarily a one-sided write-up (cf. Crapanzano 1986).

One can also think of this troubling yet productive elusiveness of the 'we' in scalar terms. As Garcia notes,

The particularity of the first person plural, by contrast to the first person singular, is that it allows a permanent variation of amplitude, since it can just as well designate 'you and I' as the totality of everything that lives, and even beyond.

(Garcia 2016a: 1)

## Two Ends of Frontal Comparison

These variations of amplitude are key to the power of frontal comparison. They allow anthropologists to leverage a dialogical fieldwork experience into a contrast between distinct cultures or ontologies – 'My fieldwork experience demonstrates that whereas we do this, they do that' – without ever needing to specify precisely what the shape of these broader entities is. This oscillation between clear-cut contrasts and elusive broader entities is the subject of the next chapter.

But the same scalar device enables frontal comparisons to act as tools for generalisation and analogy. The 'we' they evoke can be imagined expansively as a human one. It is on this interplay between analogy and heterology that the present chapter focuses, by asking about the purposes of frontal comparison. Why aim towards reflexivity at all? The question is particularly relevant in the wake of the excoriation of the supposed 'navel-gazing' of the 1980s' crisis of representation. One classic answer has been to link reflexivity to alterity. The critique of lateral comparison in the name of frontal comparison is frequently associated with a heterological critique of identity – so frequently in fact that the two moves might seem to be indistinguishable: a recognition of anthropology as a frontal encounter is simultaneously a recognition of the *otherness* of the other. And yet I will argue in this chapter that this is not always the case. As often as not, frontal comparisons have been deployed in anthropology to highlight analogies, and not simply contrasts, between the self and the other (see Lloyd 2015: 30–31). We have become so used to thinking of frontal comparisons as a way to elicit difference, that it bears reminding how often such comparisons between 'us' and 'them' have played the opposite role: that of establishing an analogical bridge. Indeed, once that analogical version of frontal comparison has been identified, we will find its persistence in the most unlikely of places – the very core of some of the most avowedly heterological programmes. In other words, this chapter focuses on the plane formed by the intersection of the z- and y-axes – the plane whose coordinates are identity, alterity and reflexivity.

## Tylor's Ejections

Let us return to one of the earliest explicit comments on comparative method in anthropology first introduced above (Chapter 2). In E. B. Tylor's account, comparative method began with the tabulation of enormous amounts of ethnographic materials, imagined as collections of 'customs' belonging to different 'peoples', in order to discover higher than expected 'adhesions' between seemingly unrelated customs. If seemingly unrelated customs co-occurred a significant number of times, this suggested for Tylor a common causation. Accounts of Tylor's method often tend to stop there (e.g. Handler 2009). From these correlations between customs amongst different peoples across the world, Tylor is said to have sought to deduce evidence of the universal workings of the human mind and the orderly progress of history. Tylor stands as a textbook case of universalising, typological lateral comparatism.

But this popular account of Tylor's method, although broadly speaking correct, skims over an important intermediate step. Tylor did not jump directly from correlations of customs to general conclusions about function or historical sequence. Rather, he applied a three-step comparative method. The first step was the lateral one described above, of identifying 'adhesions' between customs which suggested common causes. The next step, however, was speculative explanation of these common causes, to be tested (third step) by further comparison.

The first and third steps, with their quantitative aesthetics, their tables and adhesions, speaks of a thoroughly lateral project. There lie cases, neatly tabulated. The speculative explanation, however, is inherently frontal. It turns – somewhat surprisingly for those who recall Tylor as a grand old positivist (e.g. Handler 2009) – on a speculative meeting of minds between the anthropologist and the people they are writing about. In this way, Tylor's grand project of reconstructing the course of human history intersects with a more modest and familiar anthropological project, that of making sense of seemingly strange customs.

Tylor introduces the customs he uses as key examples – mother-in-law avoidance, the levirate or fictive kinship – by noting their strangeness, in the dismissive and patronising tone so profoundly jarring to our contemporary ears. For instance,

The point I chose was a quaint and somewhat comic custom as to the barbaric etiquette between husbands and their wives' relatives, and vice versa: they may not look at one another much less speak, and they even avoid mentioning one another's names.

(Tylor 1889: 246)

Here begins the three-step procedure. The first step is to seek correlations to other customs. Having noted that his tables reveal a higher than expected 'adhesion' between the custom of post-marital residence in the wife's parents' household and the custom of parent-in-law avoidance, Tylor continues (second step):

Hereupon, it has to be enquired whether the facts suggest a reason for this connexion. Such a reason readily presents itself, inasmuch as the ceremony of not speaking to and pretending not to see some well-known person close by, is familiar enough to ourselves in the social rite which we call 'cutting'. This, indeed, with us implies aversion, and the implication comes out even more strongly in objection to utter the name ('we never mention her,' as the song has it). It is different, however, in the barbaric custom we are considering, for here the husband is nonetheless on friendly terms with his wife's people because they may not take any notice of one another. In fact, the explanation of this ceremonial cutting may be simpler and more direct than in civilised Europe. As the husband has intruded himself among a family which is not his own, and into a house where he has no right, it seems not difficult to understand their marking the difference between him and themselves by treating him formally as a stranger. So like is the working of the human mind in all stages of civilisation that our own language conveys in a familiar idiom the same train of thought … we have only to say that they do not recognise him and we have condensed the whole proceeding into a single word.

(Tylor 1889: 247–248; cf. Candea 2018b)

In the grand scheme of things, then, Tylor is indeed seeking to establish the universal workings of the human mind. But in so doing, he relies not only upon lateral correlations of customs across peoples, but also upon speculative frontal encounters between 'them' and 'us'. Within this articulation of frontal and lateral comparison, the role of frontal comparison is clear. Its end is to build an epistemic bridge, and to establish a similarity despite, beyond or across difference. What started off as a 'quaint and somewhat comic custom' becomes recognisable as an analogue of proprieties familiar to his readership.

Here we have, from the very start of the articulation of an anthropological comparative method, the double dynamic of frontal and lateral comparison. Each plays a different role. Lateral comparison studiously and steadfastly lays out cases in order to pick out statistical adhesions. A speculative frontal encounter between 'their' world and 'ours' is the yeast which makes this heavy bread of lateral comparison rise.

To characterise the logic of that frontal analogy, I will borrow a term from nineteenth-century biologist and metaphysician George Romanes, namely 'ejection' (Romanes 1895; cf. Thompson 1994). Romanes is (in)famous in ethological circles for his defence of anthropomorphic interpretations of animal behaviour (Romanes 1883); less known is the fact that he derived his views from a metaphysical variety of panpsychism. In other words, Romanes was thoroughly representative of the nineteenth-century moment which, according to John Durham Peters (2001), marked the birth of the contemporary version of the 'problem of communication'. It is neither Romanes's thoughts about animals nor his metaphysics which need arrest us here, however, but the specific answer he gave to the problem of communication, namely his theory of 'ejection'. Alongside objects (known from the outside) and subjects (known to themselves by introspection), Romanes coined the term 'ejects' to refer to the inferred subjectivity of beings other than the subject. Subjects, he argued, cannot access ejects (that is to say, each other) as they can access themselves, namely through introspection, and yet they have a sense that other beings are more than mere objects. Ejective knowledge provides a third way of knowing – neither subjective nor objective, but analogical. Analogies between my observed behaviour and that of the other-as-object are explained by analogies between my subjective perspective and the hypothetically analogous perspective of the other-as-eject. For instance, I know by introspection that when I exhibit the objective behaviour of screaming and writhing I am usually experiencing a subjective state of being in pain. If I then observe another being, human or indeed animal, screaming and writhing, I can deduce by analogy that they are also in pain. The logic of ejection thus follows the classic formula of proportional analogy:

Myself as Object **is to** Myself as Subject **as** the Other as Object **is to** the Other as Eject

Ejection thus provides a bridge out of solipsism, an analogical, hypothetical access to the other which stops short of telepathy (cf. Peters 2001). It also provides a levelling of sorts: from the initial asymmetrical confrontation between a subject and an object, ejection produces a symmetrical encounter between two entities which are simultaneously objects and subjects. Tylor's ejections seek to bridge a gap, not between species or individuals, but between varieties of human experience. 'Barbaric, quaint or comic customs' are made accessible through much the same analogical procedure. Firstly, these customs are shown to exhibit objective patterns (in-law avoidance correlates with post-marital residence); then these objective patterns are shown to be analogous to objective patterns in 'our own' behaviour, whose logic is immediately obvious to us. By analogy this makes the logic of those initially unfamiliar patterns of behaviour easy to understand also. Readers may recall that, as we argued in Chapter 2, Tylor's lateral comparisons between different peoples in his sample are focused on concomitant variations – another version of proportional analogy. One might say then that Tylor's method relies on a combination of lateral and frontal proportional analogies.

Whereas Romanes's ejection starts from his own individual experience, Tylor's ejections begin with a form of collective rather than individual introspection. The 'subject' here is collective: a 'we' formed of Tylor and his readership who are presumed to share a set of familiar reference points. But ejection is a dynamic procedure which seeks, precisely, to bridge an initial opposition. For Romanes, the possibility of ejective analogy spoke to an ethological hypothesis about the mindedness of higher animals (indeed beyond that, to a metaphysical hypothesis about the mindedness of all matter). Tylor's ejections don't require such far-reaching metaphysical postulates, but they do support his broader argument about the psychic unity of humankind. Ejection thus draws the 'other' closer through a kind of telepathy (Peters 2001): it suggests a direct connection between 'our' perspective (on in-laws, for instance) and 'theirs'. Ejection takes Tylor from a 'we' 'expressing the self and the person addressed' to a 'we' 'expressing the self and the person spoken of' (Boas 1896: 903). In that widening of the 'we' from the exclusive to the dual lies the key device of anthropology's collective ejections, its frontal analogies. Yet this quasi-telepathy comes, from the start, with caveats. Tylor is well aware that this frontal comparison is an 'as if'. He clearly marks this speculative move out from his lateral algebra (Tylor 1889: 248).

The possibility of accessing the other's perspective remains carefully circumscribed as a working hypothesis. Ejection builds bridges 'outwards' between 'us' and 'them', but these thin speculative bridges need to be buttressed by lateral proof. Ejection makes the strange (speculatively) familiar.

## The Persistence of Ejection: Interpretivism and Methodological Equation

Ejective frontal comparison of this kind – understanding 'them' by analogy to 'us' – has often been criticised, on the grounds of how difficult it is to distinguish from mere projection. Indeed, to some critics as we shall see below, any analogical attempt to understand others is *ex hypothesi* an imposition. And yet, ejection remains an enduring anthropological heuristic, surprisingly resistant to major shifts in epistemological direction and theoretical school. We find ejective frontal comparison, for instance, when Malinowski analogises Kula valuables to British crown jewels (Malinowski 1922: 91; see also 94–95). As noted above, this was an implicit response to the problem of 'communication' raised by Boas when he invoked the heterogeneity of psychological causes lying behind the same phenomenon (Boas 1896; cf. Chapter 2).

Analogising Balinese cockfights to Shakespearian theatre (Geertz 1973a) involves much the same device. More broadly, some recourse to ejection is intrinsic to any kind of anthropological argument which seeks to portray what Runciman (1983) called 'tertiary understanding', namely the sense of 'what it is like' to experience some given reality which is initially assumed not to be familiar to readers. Through the medium of writing at least, there is no other way for anthropologists to go about conveying such understanding except through some form of ejective frontal comparison, which analogises a putatively unfamiliar experience to one putatively familiar to the readership.[1]

But a consideration of interpretivism highlights a more profound and equally persistent use of ejective frontal comparison. This turns not on identifying analogies of particular perspectives or contents, but rather on a deeper analogy between the observer's method and the outlook or method of the observed. The best-known version of this argument has been articulated precisely by proponents of interpretive or hermeneutic approaches to social science. The argument goes like this: anthropology (or sociology) can be interpretive because it is a science of humans, who are themselves self-interpreting animals. We can thus understand them insofar as understanding is what they themselves do (Taylor 1985; Weber 1978).

This argument thus rests on an ejective move of a particular kind: a basic analogy between what every one of us knows through introspection that we can do (interpret, understand) and what every outward sign suggests other humans can also do – including their pretty conclusive ability to enter into conversation with us. This is no longer simply, as in Tylor's case, an analogy concerning a particular state of affairs (say, the way one relates to in-laws). Rather this is a form of *methodological ejection*: the method (interpretive social science) is justified insofar as it is analogous to the everyday practice of the object-who-is-also-a-subject (humans as interpretive animals). As Runciman puts it, on this view 'the study of self-conscious human behaviour is itself self-conscious human behaviour' (Runciman 1983: 2). Our method is of a piece with (or at least analogous to) the object (or rather, eject) it seeks to know. This type of methodological ejection is not yet an account of any particular case, or set of similarities and differences. But it founds the possibility of understanding the other as, analogously to us, a subject with motivations, intentions and perspective. Just as with Tylor, however, this ejection is justified by a purported identity: the essential likeness of 'the working of the human mind' (interpretivists no longer felt the need to add 'in all stages of civilisation').

Through this methodological ejection, proponents of interpretivism (from Weber through to Geertz) have always tried to separate themselves out from objectivist attempts to study humans 'from the outside'. And yet identifying ejection as a form shows that this caesurist distinction between interpretivism and positivism is only partial. Firstly, a careful reading shows that the most objectivist or positivist approaches in anthropology at least tend to involve some interpretive moment (as we have seen in the case of Tylor).

Secondly, and more profoundly, the figure of methodological ejection – the analogy drawn between the method of the observer and the method of the observed – is present also in forms of explanation which are not in any other sense interpretive. I will give some examples. The functionalist Nadel, after discussing at length the method of concomitant variation (see Chapter 2), makes the point that identifying concomitant variations is in fact what people themselves do in everyday social interaction (Nadel 1951: 242). Ward Goodenough, a proponent of a grand universalist comparative project seeking to create a general etic language in which all emic forms might be unified, grounds it in the fact that people *themselves* are for ever seeking to give themselves rules. And since, furthermore, people actively aim their behaviour towards functional purposes, 'The fundamentally functional orientation of anthropological science is appropriate to its subject matter and to its practitioner alike' (Goodenough 1970: 122).

As for structuralism, the point has been made many times, as we saw in Chapter 2 that it relies on the assumption of analogical operations in the minds of subject and analyst (Geertz 1967; Leach 1974; Salmon 2013b). I will just take one, nicely complex example. Needham's article distinguishing between polythetic and monothetic forms of classification ends with a consideration of the fact that each of these methods of categorising is also a method that people themselves deploy. In other words, Needham invokes a double methodological ejection. On the one hand, comparative schemas based on formal logical categories are valid because 'our analysis may be guided by the same logical constraints as must have been effective in producing the systems that we study' (Needham 1975: 365–366). On the other hand, the critique of anthropologists' polythetic confusions itself builds a bridge since 'men in any tradition' are also *ex hypothesi* analogously confused:

Now the outcome of analyses of this kind should not be seen as merely a local or technical rectification of European academic argument, but as pointing to a general hazard of language which presumably afflicts men in any tradition when they classify their fellows and their nature. 'In seeking to translate alien concepts ... we have to appreciate that the foreign words in question are themselves words that may be in the same state as our own,' so that the speakers of another language, constrained through it by their own collective representations, 'must be assumed to be the victims of just such linguistic defects, traps, and diversions as are we ourselves when we formulate our own thoughts' (Needham 1972: 233). Thus the realisation of the confusions brought about in social anthropology by stock classificatory terms may serve to prepare our understanding in coming to terms with alien concepts which, in a fashion that is similarly unrecognised by those whose modes of thought we want to comprehend, are also polythetic.'

(Needham 1975: 367)

In sum, methodological ejection is not simply the province of interpretivism. In each of the cases above, 'our' method is justified on the basis of an analogy to the method of the subjects under study. The move is frontal: it claims that what 'we' do in explaining 'them' is fundamentally analogous to what 'they' themselves do in understanding or explaining everything else, or quite simply in operating in the world. Methodological ejection is a kind of methodological telepathy: it puts us and the other in a direct mental communication.

## Ejection and Satire

Of course, analogies between the other and the self, however constituted, have a counterpart: by making the strange familiar, they also introduce the possibility of making the familiar strange. The counterpart of ejection, its shadow, as it were, is the kind of device which Geertz has characterised as 'satire': 'portraying the alien as the familiar with the signs changed' (Geertz 1988: 107). Satire, Geertz notes, is a well-established literary form – consider, for instance, Swift's *Gulliver's travels*. The effect of satire, Geertz notes, is to unsettle and estrange the familiar. Satire turns on

[t]he juxtaposition of the all-too-familiar and the wildly exotic in such a way that they change places … [T]he culturally at hand is made odd and arbitrary, the culturally distant, logical and straightforward. Our own forms of life become the customs of a strange people: those in some far-off land, real or imagined, become expectable behaviour given the circumstances. There confounds Here. The not-us (or Not-U.S.) unnerves the Us.

(Geertz 1988: 106)

Geertz is commenting on the work of Ruth Benedict, to which I will return below, but the comments apply equally to Tylor. Indeed, 'satire' is already implied or entailed by the procedure of ejection. We have seen that the logic of ejection produces a levelling of an initially asymmetrical confrontation between an intimate subject (known from the inside) and an inscrutable object (known from the outside). Through ejection, the object is revealed – or hypothesised – as possessing an interiority analogous to our own. But, in the process, ejection also requires us to see ourselves as objects. This self-objectification is necessarily a form of estrangement (see also Keane 2005).

Picture the scene. As Tylor gave his learned address on comparative method to an audience of scholars and members of the Royal Anthropological Institute, he briefly allowed to flicker into view a familiar everyday world outside that room, a world of comic songs, in-laws and polite rudeness which his audience would all recognise. This invocation served to familiarise the alien world of 'barbaric' marriage customs. It simultaneously sought to establish, and used as a methodological presupposition, 'the likeness of human minds in all stages of civilisation'. Yet this familiarisation of the object relied also on an objectification of the familiar. The ability to see the banal proprieties of 'everyday life' in the same terms in which one sees the strange customs of 'barbarians' is already implied here. One can imagine the polite titters amongst Tylor's learned audience as he evoked 'the *social rite* which we call "cutting"' (Tylor 1889: 248, emphasis added). The familiar is objectified and, in the process, estranged.

The double move of 'making the familiar strange and making the strange familiar', the twinned moves of ejection and satire, emerge as the atom of frontal comparison in its various forms. That frontal comparative form – making the strange familiar and the familiar strange – is itself intensely familiar, of course. But we estrange it somewhat by tracing it all the way back to that lateral arch-generaliser, Tylor. Satire and ejection – even here – are thus revealed as correlates of each other. Yet they have inverse epistemological implications. In ejection, 'our' background is a resource for understanding. With satire, by contrast, comes the possibility that our point of view was mistaken. As Geertz writes of Benedict, the picture wasn't wrong but we were holding it upside down (Geertz 1988: 121). Thus, by the end of Tylor's demonstration, the reader is supposed to realise that thinking of customs such as in-law avoidance as quaint or comic was an error. They are only so if seen from 'our' perspective. They make sense, however, if we see them from what would later be called 'the native's point of view'. In Tylor, however, this 'other' point of view is still in effect ours – it is the universal human point of view – transposed to another set of constraints.

## Equivocation and Recursivity: Ejection Inside-Out

To say this is to recall vividly the fact that the canonical pair 'making the strange familiar and the familiar strange' can be put to radically different uses. While one might find that double device instantiated in Tylor's ejections as much as in, say, Benedict's contrasts between Japan and the USA, or even in more recent frontal contrasts between variously 'India',

## Two Ends of Frontal Comparison

Melanesia, Amazonia and the West (Dumont 1966; Strathern 1988; Viveiros de Castro 1998), it is important to remember that the key aim of Tylor's comparisons, its horizon, remained generality and the universal. A universal, furthermore, which was profoundly hierarchised, with 'primitives' incorporated into a broader human 'we' only by imperfect analogy to the exclusive 'we' of the civilised. It was at that price that the strange could be made familiar (Handler 2009: 628). In this example, the satirical device of 'making the familiar strange' is something of an after-thought in the articulation of that generalising and hierarchical scheme.[2] In other cases, estrangement and its critical potential – 'satire' – are in the foreground. This is what Geertz argues of Benedict: in his account of her work, the ejective move of 'making the strange familiar' is actu-ally a residual effect of a primarily satirical aim to challenge American self-understandings.

Others have gone further. Eduardo Viveiros de Castro, in one of the most radically heterological visions of frontal comparison (Viveiros de Castro 2004), sought to split that atom of anthropological argu-ment: retain the effect of making the familiar strange while, somehow, making the strange even stranger. It is important to note that Viveiros de Castro's proposed method of 'controlled equivocation' starts from a radically different understanding of the core problem that frontal com-parison is designed to solve. In frontal comparison conceived on an ejective mode, differences are taken as the root of the problem of com-munication: how can we understand the other despite the differences between us? Analogy here is the answer. It is the starting-point and ground for the reframing of those differences. The other is understood when she or he has been mapped as a version of us, with some – minor or major – differences. The inherent limit of this procedure is that it cannot easily be distinguished from projection.

Viveiros De Castro's controlled equivocation begins with *that* problem. If there is a problem to which the method of 'controlled equivocation' is addressed, it is not the failure of communication, but rather the failure to recognise that such a failure has occurred. If anything, equivocation revels in the failure of communication, just as Peters writes of Levinas:

The failure of communication ... invites us to find ways to discover others besides knowing. Communication breakdown is thus a salutary check on the hubris of the Ego. Communication, if taken as the reduplication of the self (or its thoughts) in the other, deserves to crash, for such an understanding is in essence a pogrom against the distinctness of human beings.

(Peters 2001: 21)

The problem here is the over-eager understanding of the other by analogy to the self, and the politically and epistemologically unacceptable 'saming' that ensues when important differences are elided. That type of mistranslation is an uncontrolled equivocation. By contrast, equivocation revels in recognising and maximising the difference of the other.

The example given by Viveiros de Castro (2004: 16–21) is that of the term *txai*, a kinship term which the Cashinawa deploy to rhetorically index their friendship and openness to strangers and outsiders – much as in a number of European languages one might speak of a stranger as a 'brother'. *Txai* has thus on occasion been translated as 'brother'. This is, however, an equivocation. *Txai*'s kinship equivalent is not the brother, but the brother-in-law. In this equivocation hides, Viveiros de Castro argues, a profound ontological difference. Our use of 'brother' as a rhetorical term for closeness between strangers points to deep assumptions that relations are at heart about similarity, and that biological relatedness is the archetype of such similarity. To treat all humans as 'brothers' is thus to extend to humanity the archetypal relation, namely one grounded in biological similarity.

By contrast, the use of brother-in-law as the term to index this ideal form of relation points to an ontology in which relations are conceptualised as being inherently about difference. Imagine a world in which one might index one's love of humanity by saying that all humans are brothers-in-law. Would that not be a world organised on very different principles indeed to our own? This would be an ontology in which the archetypal relation is not one of genetic or biological closeness, but rather one of difference – the sort of difference which might enable one man to become another's brother-in-law. That difference cannot be computed in terms of biological or natural closeness (except in the negative sense that brothers-in-law are not biologically related); rather it is a difference in perspective on the same relationship: brothers-in-law are defined by the fact that the woman who is a wife to the one is a sister to the other.

Crucially the point of this demonstration is not simply to arrive at a better translation – to replace the equivocation that *txai* means brother with the correct translation that *txai* means brother-in-law. The point is to keep the equivocation live by forcing the reader to confront the alterity of a conceptual world in which one might imagine that 'all men are brothers-in-law'. The other is not simply reduced to a version of the same, with differences ('they mean the same as us, they're just using a different word'). Rather the point is to keep the difference live – to sharpen it and hold it in view, by eliciting the possibility of a radical alternative to our very way of understanding the links between relations, nature, perspective, kinship and humanity.

Note the cleverness of Viveiros de Castro's *txai* example: the example itself can be deployed as an instance of the method he is proposing. This is the 'recursive' twist. With the benefit of Viveiros de Castro's demonstration, we can see that ejective frontal comparisons (such as Tylor's) are entirely congruous with a world in which relations are imagined as in essence about similarity. Ejection, which feels it has understood the other when it has located our similarity despite our differences, is the epistemology which fits with an ontological landscape in which all men are brothers. The deep justification of ejection, in its various forms, is always some reference to the likeness of human minds, the – ultimately natural – *unity of humankind*. Ejection is thus 'our' frontal comparison.

What then would be 'their' frontal comparison, appropriate to an ontology in which all men are brothers-in-law? Well, precisely, 'controlled equivocation' itself: a mode of frontal comparison in which it is the differences in our perspectives, not the sameness, which make our relationship possible.

This kind of recursivity, which involves mapping our own analytics on those of our informants, is an increasingly popular and explicit move (e.g. Candea 2010a; Gad and Bruun Jensen 2016; Holbraad 2012; Miyazaki 2004; Strathern 1988). Recursivity can be seen as a form of methodological ejection read backwards. As we saw above, methodological ejection tends to outline a technique and then justify it on the basis of a generalisation about its predominance amongst humans, and therefore amongst our human subjects too: we can interpret because they interpret, we can produce structural abstractions because they do, we can identify functional correlations because they do too. Methodological ejection is usually an after-the-fact justification for the perceived effectiveness of a method. Why does this work? It is because they, after all, are doing this too. Recursivity instead starts from a postulate about the failure of previous methods. Martin Holbraad gives a clear account of failure as a starting-point: it is the moment at which something our informants say seems to be nonsense (Holbraad 2012). Instead of devising a better analogical extension of our own conceptual devices, such that 'they' can be seen to make sense on 'our' terms, recursivity seeks to 'distort' our own analytical devices and ontological frameworks, until these can be made to accommodate what initially seemed like nonsense. The result is not an explanation of the other by analogy with the self, but a multiplication of our own conceptual world to include a new possibility – a possibility which is drawn recursively from the shape of a different conceptual world. That new possibility, derived recursively from the conceptual devices of our informants, cannot be neatly added to the list of existing Euroamerican concepts, since it in turn makes a nonsense of that pre-existing arrangement.

Where ejection begins with an introspection and uses it as a frame for understanding others, these moves require an 'extrospection' (Holbraad and Pedersen 2009: 389): seeing ourselves from the other's point of view. Methodological ejection finds instances of our conceptual devices everywhere, and thus licenses anthropological research programmes to repeat the same moves over and again. Recursivity is an ever-repeated procedure, which (in principle, but see Candea 2016b; Holbraad 2016) creates a different conceptual disturbance each time, introducing a teeming multiplicity within our conceptual world by devising concepts in the shape of others' devices.[3]

And yet this radical frontal heterology, too, is grounded in a fundamental frontal analogy (Heywood 2018a, see also 2018b). The basic analogy which underpins this move is that of people(s) facing problems, people(s) making sense of their worlds. Like 'us', 'they' have their explanations, their ontologies, their problems, concerns and concepts. Like 'us', 'they' make sense on their own terms. *These* analogies are not in any sense extrospective – they follow the usual pattern of collective introspection, projected outwards. These implicit arguments rely on getting the readership to recognise in the other a propensity which the readership shares with the author. The analogical claim that 'they', like 'us', *make sense* on their own terms is a preliminary step to arguing that their sense-making directly challenges ours, or that it can, in a recursive mode, become our method.

## Conclusion: Identity, Alterity, Reflexivity

In sum, this chapter has argued that frontal comparison is not necessarily associated with heterology. It comes in a variety of forms – ejection, methodological ejection, satire, equivocation, recursivity – which turn on different recombinations of analogies and contrasts between 'us' and 'them'. In fact, it exhibits the same structure in terms of its potential relations to similarity and difference, alterity and identity that we

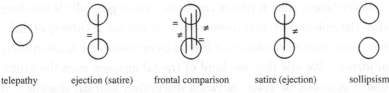

telepathy     ejection (satire)     frontal comparison     satire (ejection)     sollipsism

Figure 7.3 Frontal comparison between solipsism and telepathy

described for *comparatio* in general in the previous chapter. In this respect frontal comparison is a special case of *comparatio*. If we bracket for a moment the complexity of including the observer into the 'us' term of the comparison, we could thus reiterate here the diagram at the end of Chapter 4, while changing the terms (Figure 7.3).

Thus, as with *comparatio* more generally, we find frontal comparison saddled in pursuit of two radically opposed aims. One path leads us from the exclusive 'we' (the speaker and those addressed) to the inclusive 'we' (the speaker and those spoken about). It proceeds by a frontal analogy – the kind of move I have described above as 'ejection' – extending the familiar out to embrace the unfamiliar and to postulate a broader common, perhaps universal humanity. Its horizon is a kind of telepathy. The other path starts from the premise that extending that exclusive 'we' outwards – the 'we' that binds the anthropologist to their audience – will necessarily end up distorting the other, or incorporating them in a hierarchised and oppressive manner, as subordinate to 'our' concerns. Frontal devices imagined in that heterological vein focus instead on subdividing that initial 'we' – producing more difference within through the devices of satire, defamiliarisation and the invention of new ethnographic concepts – rather than extending analogies without. The animating spirit of frontal comparison in this heterological mode is perfectly captured in Strathern's quote at the head of this chapter: it is 'both an apology and an apologia for' our own conceptual universe, with its inability to extend outward to real 'alterity'. Its horizon is a kind of (collective) solipsism.

Nevertheless, what is true of *comparatio* more generally is true here also. Heterological frontal comparisons are not made entirely of difference any more than analogical frontal comparisons are made entirely of identity. We saw that any kind of frontal analogy, even the evolutionist ejections of Tylor, carries a disruptive, satirical shadow – it necessarily makes the familiar strange in making the strange familiar. Conversely, we have seen also that even the most radically heterological visions retain, through the appeal to recursivity, the shadow of an analogical or ejective move. This is mapped backwards, as it were (from 'their' devices back to 'ours'), but it establishes a proportionality all the same.

We are now in a position to repeat the operation undertaken at the end of Chapter 6, and combine our z- and y-axes into a plane defined by the three coordinates of identity, alterity and reflexivity (Figure 7.4). At the centre of that plane lies a second archetypal recombination. This second archetype lies at the intersection of *comparatio* – the intricate relation between analogies and contrasts – and frontal comparison – a comparison undertaken from within one of its terms.

If one sought an empirical instance of this very abstract figure, one might turn for example to James Laidlaw's account of the purpose of an anthropology of ethics. Anthropological accounts of radically unfamiliar ethical and moral universes have of course been a staple of the discipline. In Laidlaw's view, however, the key to the potential of an anthropology of ethics is its ability to envisage frontal comparisons as yielding an account, not of alternatives *to* us, but as alternatives *for* us. In this guise, the anthropology of ethics might be more than mere defamiliarisation, satire or projection: it might be a form of pedagogy in which we learn from others (Laidlaw 2014: 213–224; see also Detienne 2008: 39; Lloyd 2015: 30–31).

This example is particularly valuable in that it reminds us that while we have been describing purposes of comparison as aiming towards some kind of extreme or vanishing point (identity, alterity, intensity or

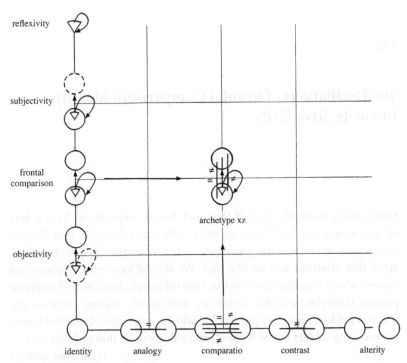

Figure 7.4 Identity, alterity, reflexivity

reflexivity), those are not the only directions in which anthropological comparisons can point. There is a purposefulness, too, in staying in the middle. This observation is in a sense the key message of this book. I will return to it in Chapter 9 and the conclusion.

# EIGHT

# The Oscillations of Frontal Comparison: Identity, Intensity, Reflexivity

Some might ironically suggest that such binary oppositions have a sort of nineteenth-century flavor, or state with Mary Douglas that 'binary distinctions are an analytic procedure, but their usefulness does not guarantee that existence divides like that. We should look with suspicion on anyone who claims that there are two kinds of people, two kinds of reality or process' (Douglas 1978, 161). To this we shall quietly respond that there are two ways of looking at any piece of knowledge, a superficial one that leaves the knowing subject out of account, and a deeper one that includes him.

(Dumont 1986: 5)

But who am 'I,' and what is 'my' world, such that 'Bedouin culture' is 'in' it?

(Keane 2005: 77)

To the depths of the unknown, to find something new!

(Baudelaire, "The voyage")

## Introduction: Intense Critiques, Intense Responses

How could some anthropologists ever imagine a world starkly divided into 'us' and 'them'? How could they continue to invoke such a vision now, after the thorough and relentless deconstruction of orientalist binaries and billiard-ball visions of culture? These questions bring us to a consideration of the intersection between reflexivity and intensity.

We saw in the previous chapter that frontal comparisons could be deployed in order to evoke similarities, and not only differences between 'us' and 'them'. But this is only a partial response, as if the only problems that comparisons (frontal or lateral) had to consider were those of similarities and differences between objects (or subjects). As we saw in Chapter 6, the question of intensity comes in amidst this extended vision of a world of things to ask about the place of flows, continua, processes and transformations.

When frontal comparison has come under challenge in anthropology, it has often been from this perspective: surely, critics have charged, the vision of a binary between 'us' and 'them' is untenable once we admit that there are no starkly delineated cultures, societies or civilisations in the first place? In a world viewed as an entanglement of flows and global processes, frontal comparison seems like a strangely archaic vision, quaint at best, colonial at worst.

The most obvious difficulty, which has dogged frontal comparison to this day, is its double reference to an epistemological relationship (observer and observed, subject and object) and a contrast between two purported cultural or civilisational units (the Modern and the Primitive, the West and the Rest; cf. Holbraad and Pedersen 2009: 389). The vision of 'the West' as a natural context for anthropological practice, of the 'rest' as an object of knowledge, can be seen as echoing earlier evolutionist schemas, the worst excesses of western exceptionalism and a colonial global order of knowledge. Douglas's discomfort with the binarism inherent in frontal encounters between 'us' and 'them' – quoted above – is thus widely shared in anthropology. The use of 'paired, dialectically generated essentializations' (Carrier 1992) between particular people and 'the West', which so often comes with frontal comparisons, has long been the focus of vehement critique.[1]

What better way to introduce these critiques than through an unstinting review by one anthropologist who, despite everything, persists in his commitment to what he elsewhere called 'the art of translation in a continuous world' (Ingold 1993):

> In closing this introduction I should insert a note about my own use of the concepts of 'the Western' and 'the modern'. These concepts have been the source of no end of trouble for anthropologists, and I am no exception. Every time I find myself using them, I bite my lip with frustration, and wish that I could avoid it. The objections to the concepts are well known: that in most anthropological accounts, they serve as a largely implicit foil against which to contrast a 'native point of view'; that much of the philosophical ammunition for the critique of so-called Western or modern thought comes straight out of the Western tradition itself (thus we find such figures as the young Karl Marx, Martin Heidegger and Maurice Merleau-Ponty enlisted in the enterprise of showing how the understandings of North American Indians, New Guinea Highlanders or Australian Aborigines differ from those of 'Euro-Americans'); that once we get to know people well – even the inhabitants of nominally Western countries – not one of them turns out to be a full-blooded Westerner, or even to be particularly modern in their approach to life; and that the Western tradition of thought, closely examined, is as richly various, multivocal, historically changeable and contest-riven as any other.
>
> (Ingold 2000: 6–7)

To these mainly epistemological concerns are added more explicitly political ones. It is often felt that '[t]he false "us and them" dichotomy is no more than a bad caricature of [the] hierarchical, power-laden and partially intersecting double contexts of analysis and publication' (Gingrich and Fox 2002b: 20). The thought that one might imagine anthropology as addressing a singular and implicitly or explicitly Western 'we' (Chua and Mathur 2018; Pina-Cabral 2006) is no less troublesome than the much critiqued 'essentialisation' of the other. To these critics, such radical frontal encounters are redolent of colonial visions of anthropology as the science of 'primitive peoples'.

Proponents of a frontally driven anthropology over the past three decades have responded to such critiques by arguing in various ways that a confusion had been made by both their forebears and their critics between a properly frontal comparison (a transformational or critical challenge to our own point of view) and a merely lateral comparison between two supposed cultures or ontologies. One could retain the benefits of frontal defamiliarisation and self-critique, they felt, while jettisoning the problematic lateral vision of bounded cultures, contexts or ontologies as actual things in the world. In support of this argument, proponents of frontal comparison have pointed, in different languages and with different implications, to the partly fictional nature of the us–them distinctions they and others invoked: these ought to be read as a form of serious satire (Geertz 1988), or as critical, strategic moves within a broader political context (Asad 2009b; Chakrabarty 2007), or as conceptual positions internal to an anthropological account (Strathern 1988), or as a particular kind of 'invention' (Holbraad and Pedersen 2017; Wagner 1981).

If the critiques of frontal comparison were cast in the language of intensity – identifying 'us' and 'them' is impossible in a world of flows and transformations – at the heart of these responses lies another kind of appeal to intensity. These responses, too, put relations first and challenge entities. In one way or another, these responses cast the binarism of frontal comparison as relational in the sense that there is an 'us' only insofar as there is a 'them', and conversely. The vision of there being two terms is merely the effect of a relation. There is no point objecting (cf. Strathern 2011: 98) in the language of mapping – these anthropologists claim – that no such entities exist, for the us/them binary they deploy is not a description of the world, it is a fiction, a device for doing something. Frontal comparisons are thus reclaimed as intense in the sense also that they are transformations, emergences, activities: ways of changing things and/or concepts, rather than merely describing them (Holbraad and Pedersen 2017, cf. Garcia 2016b).

Yet, as we shall see below, no proponent of frontal comparison fully or consistently seeks to withdraw into fiction or performative invention.

## The Oscillations of Frontal Comparison

All continue to claim, albeit sometimes only in passing, to touch base in some way with 'the real world'. Indeed it must be so, in fact, for the device of frontal comparison to work at all. The result is an oscillation (Laidlaw and Heywood 2013), in many recent visions of frontal comparison, between mutually incompossible positions. While some have sought to find a way out of such oscillation, I will argue that it is built into the device of frontal comparison from the start. It is not only inescapable, but indeed productive, as long as it is taken to entail, and concretely instantiates, the combination of two different types of rigour.

## An Unstable Compound

Given imperfect observations of a thing-we-know-not-what, using experimental apparatus with biases-we-may-not-understand, we can achieve both a better understanding of the object (it must be, after all, that one thing whose properties can produce these divergent results in these detectors) and of the experimental apparatus (which are, after all, these pieces that can be affected thus divergently by one thing).

(Wimsatt 2007: 58)

Heuristics, Wimsatt suggests, are descended from other heuristics (Wimsatt 2007: 346). Whatever one makes of the evolutionary epistemology underlying that statement, the vision is a useful heuristic for thinking about the relationship between different conceptual operations in the history of anthropological comparison. Thus, 'frontal comparison' can be envisioned as a mutated form of lateral comparison. To the basic form of lateral comparison – identifying cases and the differences, similarities and relations between them – it adds a new mutation: the inclusion of the observer into one of the terms.

On this view, the problem of combining the binary us/them of frontal comparison with an intense vision of transformation and flow is not new at all. Indeed, frontal comparisons appeared in anthropology as a kind of 'supplement' to an intense vision of social life as constant trans-formation – that of evolutionism. Thus, casual readers of Louis Dumont may be surprised to find that he explicitly traces the roots of his radical frontal comparative method to Marcel Mauss (Dumont 1986: 5). What could the Maussian lining up of cases in a quasi-evolutionary sequence have in common with Dumont's frontal contrasts? The connection will seem less outlandish once we note that in Mauss, as in Durkheim's com-parative series, 'our own (Western) society' was always an implicit final term, imagined to be an extreme form of the phenomenon under study (Durkheim 1915; Jenkins 2010; Mauss 1970). One can trace that point backwards to other evolutionisms too, which were all, in some sense or other, an attempt to reconstruct a series whose end-point was the pos-ition occupied by the analyst himself. Dumont claims that the crucial transformation occurs in Mauss's (mostly implicit) recognition that the West is not just another case, but rather opens on to a double view.

As well as being the final point in the series, this is also the one *from which* the entire series was articulated. Dumont admits (1986: 3) that Mauss, in claiming that 'they believe this', doesn't explicitly say 'in rela-tion to us who believe that' – but he reconstructs this as an implicit clause based on what Mauss says elsewhere about the exceptional nature of 'our' modern ideas. On Dumont's account, the transformation of lat-eral evolutionary comparisons into frontal ones could thus be visualised as in Figure 8.1 below.

By showing how frontal comparisons derived from lateral evolu-tionist ones, this reconstruction shows both where some of the problems identified above stem from, and also what is lost in the process of this 'frontalisation'. Thus, critics of frontal comparison such as Carrier argue that it was precisely the loss of the evolutionist 'connective tissue' in Mauss's brilliant arguments about the gift which allowed them to degen-erate into an essentialist binary (Carrier 1992) contrast between 'gift economies' and 'commodity economies'.

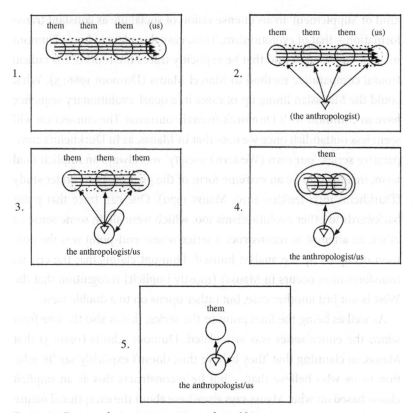

Figure 8.1 From evolutionist intensities to frontal binaries

Dumont's own point in evoking Mauss, however, is to show that frontal comparison involves a particular kind of double vision. In the Maussian view as imagined by Dumont – which, as we shall see below, is in effect (also) Dumont's view – 'modern' society appears twice: once as case amongst cases (lateral comparison) and again as a perspective from which cases are viewed (reflexivity).

Each of these views relies on a different kind of intensity. The first – evolutionist, or simply historical – vision evokes intensity as process: modern society is seen as a point along a continuum of objective variation. It is just another society in the world, and also the end-point of a transformation that relates it to all the others. It is both a thing and a moment in a flow. The second vision – modernity as 'our' perspective – evokes a different kind of intensity: the intensity of a singular relational contrast between the knowing subject and the known object. Note that the fact that the 'object' might be one or more other subjects – a point that was so important in our discussion of ejection above – doesn't change this. This is a purely relational contrast, an intensity which cannot conceive of a decomposition into multiple states, continua, traces or gradients – only into a vision of two 'units', themselves defined strictly as an effect of their relation to one another: there is a subject because there is an object, and vice versa.

Both visions are relational, in other words, but not in the same sense. Recall Gell's distinction between external and internal relations. A processual world of historical flows, evolution and diffusion is a world of external relations, 'relations between objects which are theoretically independent of one another' (Gell 1999: 33). Precisely because they are theoretically independent of one another, it is a matter of contingent empirical fact what the boundaries of such objects are, where they flow into one another or, on the contrary, stand as partly or wholly separate units. The societies evolutionists thought of as modern were envisioned as having inherited aspects of earlier societies and therefore being partly continuous with societies envisioned as more primitive; in other respects they were distinct. Any evocation of objects in such an interconnected world of external relations is limited to the approximations of polythetic categorisations and rules of thumb (Needham 1975; see above, Chapter 2). By contrast, the subject–object relation has the character of an internal relation in Gell's sense: it forms a logical pair, two terms which are defined strictly by opposition to one another and entirely exhausted by that relation.[2]

Frontal comparison is the compound of these two kinds of relations (Figure 8.2). On the one hand, we have a stark distinction between a

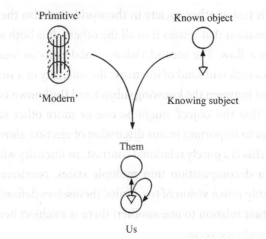

Figure 8.2 Mauss's compound

lone subject confronting the objective world including other subjects.[3] On the other hand, we have the sense of broader civilisational entities (however interwoven, partially connected or polythetic they might be). The latter can be evoked to suggest context for the former. There is no need to specify every particular of these broader units, or even to claim that they are entirely distinct. All that is needed is the suggestion that the initial subject–object – or subject–subject – relation is more than individual. It is no longer simply the anthropologist, but the 'modern' or 'western' (or whatever) anthropologist, one of 'us', at any rate – whoever that might be – who says that 'they think that'. Conversely, this perspectival effect relativises the invocation of civilisational entities: it is after all only in relation to a postulated 'us' that one can claim there is a 'them' who think this.

Dumont is, of course, clear that he wishes to recover from Mauss the perspectival distinction between us and them, not the evolutionary distinction between modern and primitive. Mauss's evolutionism, on this account, is the unwelcome remainder of his brilliant discovery of the frontal us–them contrast, which relativises the anthropologist's perspective (Dumont 1986: 4). We shall see below that separating the wheat from the chaff in this way is not so simple – but let's park that thought for now.

In sum, frontal comparison was born as a compound of two very different kinds of relational – intensive – visions: a lateral reference to an external world of interwoven civilisational forms, and a reflexive distinction between the knower and the known.[4] The former is a lateral comparison which acts as the empirical reference point of the resulting frontal contrast between 'them' and 'us'. The latter is something else: a move beyond the plane of lateral comparison and into a particular form of reflexivity. The former scales the latter up to broader significance (it is not just the individual anthropologist, but 'us' who think this), while the latter relativises the former ('they' only think this in relation to 'us'). The former provides a sense of empirical grounding (a lateral invocation of interrelated things, partly similar and partly different), while the latter provides a sense of radical disjuncture (there may not be 'two kinds of people' but there certainly are 'two kinds of ways of conceiving knowledge'). As Annelise Riles writes of a different context, in such a double view, 'it is in seeing the form of each in turn that both become real' (Riles 2000: 27).

Nevertheless, like oil and water, these two visions can be combined but their differences remain. Anthropology's frontal comparison was born as an unstable compound, and its history is the history of the successive ways in which these two elements have been stabilised, separated and recombined.

## Frontal Comparison Stabilised: The West, Anthropology and the Rest

He then lives his experiences over again critically and interpretively in the conceptual categories and values of his own culture and in terms of the general body of knowledge of his discipline ... Then, the society is not only culturally intelligible, as it is, at the level of consciousness and action, for one of its members or for a foreigner who has learnt its mores and participates in its life, but also becomes sociologically intelligible ... The social anthropologist discovers in a native society what no native can explain to him and what no layman, however conversant with the culture, can perceive – its basic structure.

(Evans-Pritchard 1950: 121–122)

A classic way of stabilising frontal comparison was to distinguish, within a reference to the 'we', between a cultural collective (we moderns/westerners) and a disciplinary one (we anthropologists). The anthropologist thus found she or he had two places to stand – she or he was both a surprised westerner, registering frontal challenges, and a masterful analyst, remapping these challenges into stable lateral comparisons.

This move was enabled by a more basic feature of frontal comparison, namely its distinctive asymmetry. The appearance of symmetry between the two 'units' which are brought together in frontal comparison – the image of two 'cultures' or 'ontologies' facing up to each other – hides in plain sight the fact that the 'us' position, by definition, never needs as much elaboration as the 'them' position. As we saw above, this 'us' was initially the broadly self-evident end-point of a series of cases. Envisioned as a lateral comparison between two cultures or civilisations, a frontal comparison is thus a relatively incomplete and stunted one, since, by definition, an 'us' position is assumed to be shared, and thus can be briefly and sketchily drawn. By opposition to the ethnographic object, which is often imagined as a 'far shore', a portion of a wide-open uncharted territory out there (Viveiros de Castro 2011), let me call this 'us' position the *hinterland*. The hinterland is the space behind the ethnographer, the commonplace conceptual shores from which she or he sailed out in the first place. It is the (partly) shared ground from which the anthropologist and his or her intended audience draw their intellectual tools, assumptions and perspectives.

In drawing frontal comparisons, anthropologists may need to focus their audience's attention on particular aspects of their 'shared' hinterland (western attitudes to objective knowledge, individual personhood or common assumptions about animals, say), they might even draw on a few classic references or choice illustrative quotes to underpin these generalisations, but they do not usually need to elaborate on or ground these descriptions very much more than that.[5] It is sufficient for the device to pick out some elements which the readership will feel they recognise as familiar, without further elaboration of precisely how deep this *hinterland* is or how internally divided. For the *purpose* of the frontal, as we saw in the previous chapter, is not actually to detail or describe the hinterland, but rather to critique it and/or to build bridges to an elsewhere. If anything, the difficulties with characterising the hinterland are usually assumed to relate to over-familiarity.[6]

Having identified the hinterland, we can also see that, in practice, frontal comparisons came to envision this hinterland as constitutively double. In the very act of articulating a 'we', anthropologists simultaneously name a collective and separate themselves from it. For characterising the 'we' of modern or western society was also the mark of anthropologists' professional expertise – their disciplinary 'we'.

The move is old – recall Tylor. Tylor's ejection, as described in the previous chapter, operates across a difference – which it helps to construct – between a 'they' ('primitive peoples') and 'we' (civilised Victorians). Both terms of that contrast have a peculiar scalar elusiveness. Thus, I noted above that one dynamic of his account – that of generalising, ejective, frontal comparison – lies in expanding that 'we' outward towards a universal human 'we'. The 'other' of frontal comparison thus has a peculiarly scale-free character: it can be a specific group of people, a collective 'non-western other', or yet another instance of a broader human 'we'. Conversely, the satirical shadow of that ejective move – the ability to make the familiar strange – subdivides the initial 'we' inwards.

## The Oscillations of Frontal Comparison

The event – a lecture on comparative method at the Royal Anthropological Institute – was also a key moment in the disciplining of anthropology. As its title suggested, the explicit purpose of the lecture was not simply to demonstrate the psychic unity of humankind, but also to demonstrate the integrity of anthropology as a scientific discipline. At the very moment he invokes the everyday as a shared background, Tylor is simultaneously setting it off from a smaller shared space: that of the anthropologist and their audience, for whom this hinterland has become visible as hinterland. The ability for self-objectification simultaneously dramatises the 'scientific' distance which the men in that room allowed themselves from the surrounding taken-for-granted everyday (compare Hecht 2003; White 2005). In Tylor's vision, the ability to objectify oneself is not universally shared, either by a human 'we', or even by a modern, Victorian, 'civilised' 'we'. That ability belongs to a smaller – and also implicitly gendered and classed (cf. Chua and Mathur 2018) – scientific or disciplinary 'we'.

Tylor's lecture thus celebrates this double vision, this double 'we' of anthropologists as those professionals of comparison who make the familiar strange and the strange familiar, who both address and speak of 'the West' (Figure 8.3). In the economy of Tylor's argument, the 'we' is thus a figure which scales up or down: from the individual theorist and their community of practice, to Victorian 'moderns', to humanity as a whole. Each of these inclusions, save the last, is also an exclusion. Together they outline both a commonality and a hierarchy of difference. We find once again the double vision identified by Dumont in Mauss: a radical distinction comes into view alongside a vision of a progressive, intensive scale of difference.

In Tylor's case, the duality of the hinterland sets up a scalar dynamic which enables him to move from his own encounter with materials, to a lecture room in London, and all the way up to the collective 'we' of humankind. But the double hinterland is just as much in evidence in frontal comparisons which aim at difference, rather than identity. Ruth Benedict's book *The chrysanthemum and the sword* (2005) is often

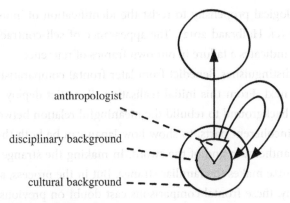

anthropologist

disciplinary background

cultural background

Figure 8.3 The double hinterland

remembered negatively, for its purportedly uncritical essentialisation of cultural difference. Yet that work was articulated around a sustained reflection on the effects and limits of western understandings of cultural difference. Indeed, the aim of *The chrysanthemum and the sword* was explicitly to challenge and reconfigure these understandings. Benedict begins by noting that our 'lay' western vision of cultural difference is often superficial and limited in that we fail to realise the depth of misunderstanding and the radical divergences of purpose between different cultures. Anthropologists, Benedict notes, are well placed to ameliorate this, partly because of their great store of examples which allow them to triangulate any given case. More profoundly, they have the disciplinary knack of allowing otherness to challenge their own taken-for-granted self-perceptions.

Thus, Benedict begins by noting that other western commentators on Japan have frequently described Japan and the Japanese in terms of mutually inconsistent characteristics: deferential yet outrageous, individualistic yet authority-bound, sentimental yet violent ... The crux of Benedict's approach is to argue that this seeming strangeness in the object reveals in fact a failure in the observer's perspective, as Geertz (1988) noted. Benedict's move reveals the antiquity of the basic anthropological propensity to resist the identification of 'nonsense' in the other (cf. Holbraad 2012). The appearance of self-contradiction in the other indicates a failure in our own frames of reference.

What distinguishes Benedict from later frontal comparatists is what she does next. From this initial realisation, Benedict deploys her disciplinary background to rebuild the meaningful relation between these seeming incoherent parts, to show how Japan can be both the land of the chrysanthemum and of the sword. In making the strange familiar, this of course makes the familiar strange. But in the process, and more profoundly, these frontal comparisons cast doubt on previous western attempts to understand others. The role of the anthropologist – past master in the reflexive art of being 'conscious of the eyes through which one looks' (Benedict 2005: 22) – is crucial, and this brings us back to the duality of the hinterland.

For Benedict, as for Evans-Pritchard or Tylor, the partial disjuncture between those two subsets of the hinterland – the disciplinary 'we' of anthropology and the broader 'we' of the West – is what authorised the anthropologist's particular in-between position. Their disciplinary hinterland allowed the anthropologist to stand slightly outside their cultural hinterland. They had their culture, yes, but also their training and the accumulated wisdom of their discipline, which enabled them to see what ordinary laypeople couldn't (Evans-Pritchard 1950: 122).

The duality of the hinterland is echoed in the duality of the anthropologist her- or himself as a particular kind of western professional. As a confrontation between cultures, frontal comparison works as a transformational 'culture shock' (Pina-Cabral 1992). As a confrontation between anthropological knowledge and a new object, it works as a form of 'hypothesis testing'. Both 'the conceptual categories and values of [our] own culture' and 'the general body of knowledge of the discipline' (Evans-Pritchard 1950: 121) are put to the test of an independent reality. For Benedict, our cultural assumptions fail the test, but our disciplinary knowledge passes with flying colours: the notions of cultural difference and cultural integration, key elements of the general body of knowledge of the discipline, find their confirmation in this new case.

The double hinterland – and the double perspective of the anthropologist – thus stabilises the device of frontal comparison. The anthropologist learns to juggle the surprise of the westerner with the mastery of the disciplinary practitioner. Benedict's frontal comparisons, like Tylor's or Evans-Pritchard's, can thus deploy the classic revelatory pattern of 'scientific thinking' (Bachelard 1934): training in a discipline allowed one to learn to see the world again by divesting oneself of common notions and the primary experience shared by ordinary people. The anthropologist rested on their disciplinary authority, the weight of their accumulated concepts and comparative knowledge, to leverage a position that was at odds with that of their readership imagined as a western public.

As a westerner, Benedict sees through the same eyes as her imagined readership. Her position is in this sense frontal: she is one of 'us' looking at 'them'. As an anthropologist, she sees that cultural background as background, and 'us' – or rather, now, 'the West' – as a case in the same way that Japan is a case. In that sense her perspective is lateral. In sum, the trick of being 'conscious of the eyes through which one looks' (Benedict 2005: 22) is, in effect, that these eyes are doubled. Once again, a vision of radical binaries coexists with a vision of transformations, processes, relations. The anthropologist finds she has two places to stand.

Stabilised in this way, frontal comparison becomes a mighty tool of anthropological authority. The anthropologist is both immanent and transcendent, both culturally situated and the judge of natural position from which all cultures are contextualised. The self-critical potential of frontal comparison is aimed at the anthropologist's 'culture', but not at the anthropologist's discipline. It is precisely the disciplinary hinterland which ensures that the anthropologist has an edge which no 'layperson' can emulate.

## After Culture: Frontal Comparison Destabilised

Stated like this, it is clear why frontal comparison came under such a sustained attack in the 1970s and '80s. The crisis of representation eroded the possibility of marking out the empirical referent of the hinterland – the West – as a coherent cultural unit (Carrier 1992; Pina-Cabral 2006). It simultaneously brought home to anthropology the broader critique of the superior 'scientific' ability of experts to break with common notions. Anthropological knowledge seemed after all just as culture-bound as the hinterland it sought to gather a perspective upon, and the accounts of 'others' it conjured up were 'creatures of anthropological imagination' (Appadurai 1988b: 30) – fictions at best (Clifford and Marcus 1986), and at worst self-interested projections of 'our' concerns (Asad 1973b; Fabian 1983; Said 2003). Most profoundly, perhaps, the crisis of representation laid bare the political economy that underpinned the story about 'us' anthropologists enlightening 'us' westerners about 'them'. In that increasingly untenable aesthetic, anthropology's 'subjects and its audience were not only separable but morally disconnected, that the first were to be described but not addressed, the second informed but not implicated' (Geertz 1988: 132).

To that antiquated vision were counterposed two main critiques: firstly, that anthropologists wrote also for the people they worked with – 'they read what we write' (Brettell 1993) – and thus had to consider the effects of their writing beyond a 'home' audience; secondly, that not all anthropologists were western. The figure of 'native anthropologists' came to prominence in the 1980s and its entailments seemed to trouble the classic vision of frontal comparison. While that figure itself soon came under critique for retaining essential reference to cultural wholes, the more complex vision of 'halfie' and multiply located anthropologists (Abu-Lughod 1991; Narayan 1993) durably challenged the equation between a disciplinary hinterland and a cultural hinterland, and the direction of travel of anthropology's revelatory possibilities came under question.

These critiques all turned in different ways on the challenge brought to radical binaries by the vision of a world of power-laden flows, processes, unstable identities and intensive relations. One consistent response to these challenges was to argue for quite simply jettisoning frontal comparison altogether. This could be done by substituting the encounter between 'us and them' with an anthropology made of traces, connectivities and transformations. The identification of systems and entailments through our own analytical devices was fine, if the purpose was the critique of political economic arrangements, for instance. Alternatively, even defamiliarisation could be distributed: it could happen anywhere.

But as we saw earlier, that intensive world was the world in which frontal comparison was born in the first place. Little wonder, then, that it found ways to adapt. One radical variety of frontal comparison was retained in the scaling back of the 'us' to its smallest possible form, namely 'the self of the ethnographer' (Herzfeld 2001: 263). This was the core move of the postmodern musings on authorial devices, and the associated visions of a 'dialogical' ethnography. Crapanzano's critique of Geertz stands as a canonical instance of this type of move. What Crapanzano particularly targets are the devices whereby Geertz moves up in generality from his own encounter with particular Balinese people and practices, to construct a collective encounter between us and them, of which he is the all-seeing mediator. In the postmodern vision of ethnography after culture, the figure of a frontal encounter with alterity remained, but without the claim that that encounter could be scaled back up, on our side, to either a disciplinary 'we' or a cultural 'we': this was anthropology 'out of context' (Strathern 1987c). As Strathern points out, the reduction of scaling was not quite so clear on the 'them' side. While the vision of postmodern ethnography as a dialogical inclusion of other voices figured a certain kind of symmetry between us and them, the fact that this dialogue remained orchestrated by the ethnographer meant that postmodern ethnography ended up staging an encounter between the multifarious complexity of a single ethnographer (self-conscious, self-doubting, riven, etc.) and the multifarious complexity of a collective 'them'. Complexity aside, this reflected the classic arithmetic of a 'people–person report' (Handler 2009).

An alternative way to destabilise frontal comparison was to jettison the cultural us, but not the disciplinary us. A particularly clear instance of this argument can be found in Pina-Cabral's piece 'Against translation' (1992). The author's problem, initially, is the conundrum of 'anthropology at home'. Given the avowedly central role of 'culture shock' in anthropological subject formation and knowledge production (Pina-Cabral 2006: 9–10), is anthropology at home impossible? More searchingly, must one disaggregate degrees of difference in order to decide whether anthropologists are more or less 'at home' in particular contexts, and thus more or less likely to be able to become 'proper anthropologists' and produce good anthropological knowledge? The solution, for Pina-Cabral, lies in abandoning the antiquated notion of anthropology as translation:

Essentially, I am arguing that the metaphor of translation to describe ethnographic work has exhausted its usefulness. The ethnographer's principal task is not to make a particular foreign culture understandable to 'us'. Anthropologists must abandon this use of the first person plural, which implies that they all share the same culture, this is not only untrue, but is also irrelevant ... There is no sense in which it can be said that, in the fieldwork situation, two cultures are being confronted.

(Pina-Cabral 1992: 6)

For Pina-Cabral, fieldwork involves not a meeting of cultures, but an anthropological practitioner confronting experiences in the field to a disciplinary background consisting of 'the accumulated experience of his colleagues' (Pina-Cabral 1992: 8). The problem of anthropology at home – indeed, more broadly, the problem of frontal comparison after the demise of cultural holism – is thus resolved by eliminating the figure of the cultural hinterland altogether. For

If he is to be an ethnographer at all, our model doctoral student is trying as hard as he can to match what he observes in Portugal against the accumulated knowledge of his discipline and not against the worldview of the social group with which he most fully associates himself.

(Pina-Cabral 1992: 6)

Pina-Cabral retains, as it were, the final move of Evans-Pritchard's method – the stepwise comparison of new cases to a corpus of previous cases – but jettisons the initial move of translation. Pina-Cabral's solution thus allows us to glimpse a limited case of frontal comparison: one in which the cultural hinterland is entirely absent. In this scenario, no cultural 'us' needs to be articulated, while the disciplinary hinterland provides an all-purpose defamiliarisation – a vantage point applicable anywhere.

In this vision, the rhetorical figure of an encounter between the 'naive westerner' and the 'cultural other' falls away, and the conceptual possibility of generating culture shock is folded into the accumulated wisdom of the discipline. Anthropology retains the power to make strange any given ethnographic object, even the most familiar: 'Once the accumulated experience of "difference" becomes instituted in the body of anthropological knowledge, it then becomes possible for an anthropologist working in his own society to approach it as "different"' (Pina-Cabral 1992: 7). Frontal comparison for Benedict or Evans-Pritchard combined culture shock with hypothesis testing. Here, only the latter is retained: an existing body of anthropological work is confronted with a new case.

Beyond its specific articulation by Pina-Cabral, this was a widespread and particularly apposite strategy for a world perceived as heavily interconnected, a world in which cutting up cultural reality at the joints has become an impossible proposition. Setting up radical cultural difference as the prerequisite to anthropological work seemed impractical. Luckily, however much one might 'connect away' stark cultural difference, the difference between previous anthropological literature and the world encountered in fieldwork remained a solid anchoring point. In this radically thinned-out guise, frontal comparison lived on.

These moves paid one particular price, however: they jettisoned frontal comparison's ability to *contextualise* anthropology's own conceptual devices. While these solutions addressed the untenable nature of substantive us–them distinctions like those of Benedict, Tylor or Evans-Pritchard, by themselves they have little to say to the charge that anthropology itself might be a culture-bound project, or at least one with a distinctly western genealogy that still matters. In different ways, both the postmodern model and Pina-Cabral's left the anthropologist in the position of being the ultimate 'estranger', but him- or herself culturally decontextualised.

A final variation avoided this pitfall with brio. Michael Herzfeld's *Anthropology through the looking glass*, like Pina-Cabral's discussion, starts from the problem of anthropology at home, but takes it in a different direction. The device here is a sustained comparison between the discipline itself and a country – Greece – which is often figured, albeit ambivalently, as the very core of 'the West' and thus part of anthropology's 'hinterland', the source and context of some of its key analytical devices (Herzfeld 2001: 264). A similar dynamic animated important strands of the anthropology of nationalism and ethnic identity in the 1980s and '90s. Practices of national self-definition were brought into the same ethnographic frame as anthropology's own methodological nationalism – its commitment to a belief in units, cultures and the like. Both were thereby made strange, without ever needing to appeal to the anthropologist's own 'cultural' hinterland (e.g. McDonald 1989). Some of these variations in the figure of frontal comparison after the demise of culture can be visualised as in Figure 8.4.

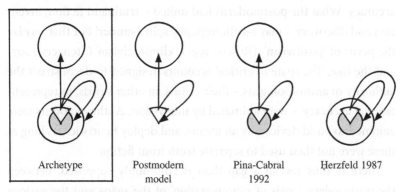

| Archetype | Postmodern model | Pina-Cabral 1992 | Herzfeld 1987 |

Figure 8.4 Frontal comparison after culture

## Not-Quite-Fictions: Frontal Comparison Refounded

An alternative bundle of strategies turns on the key move of invoking the us/them contrast framed in cultural or quasi-civilisational terms while simultaneously disavowing it: keeping it as a productive fiction, or rather, as we shall see, not-quite-fiction. The family of moves I am thinking of here are those which sought to retain the critical and conceptual potential of frontal comparison without remaining tied down to the vision of radically different cultures and civilisations: to save the baby of frontal reflexivity and throw away the bathwater of lateral essentialism.

Perhaps the key factor in these refoundations of frontal comparisons since the 1980s was a slightly relaxed attitude to representational realism. This was a direct offshoot of the postmodern claim that anthropological accounts ought to be seen as 'true fictions' (Clifford 1986: 6) – that they ought to be judged, in other words, not in terms of their representational accuracy, but rather as constructions, apparatuses, devices – in a word heuristics – for doing something. Once attention is moved away from the representational distinction between truth and fiction, the question that remains is what our devices, our 'true fictions', do. That observation originally entailed a critical caveat: the one illegitimate use of such heuristics was that which consisted in claiming, precisely, representational accuracy. What the postmoderns had united – truth and fiction, invention and discovery – may no ethnography split asunder! For that way lay the perils of 'positivism' (Roscoe 1995), 'eliminativism' (Stengers 2007) and the like. The spate of critical accounts designed to deconstruct the authority of anthropologists – their claims, in other words, to representational accuracy – were animated by that vision. Anthropologists were enjoined to build devices, by all means, and deploy heuristics, as long as these were not then used to separate truth from fiction.

There is thus less of a gap than is commonly supposed, between the postmodern 'crisis of representation' of the 1980s and the various instances of 'non-representational theory' (inspired variously by Deleuze, Latour or others) which followed. Non-representational theory is often proposed as a break with postmodern 'nihilism' – it seems to offer instead a 'New Real'. But the two are in essence the negative and positive articulations of the same move – a move that shifts the focus away from the problem of representing reality to the question of producing it – a shift articulated in a variety of languages (from ideology to discourse, from constative to performative, from truth to heuristics, from claiming to doing).

The move from a concern with representational accuracy to a concern with productive devices became the key mode in which past frontal comparisons could be recovered. One could now reread past authors and separate the transformative, critical or thought-provoking potential of frontal comparisons, from the question of the truth-value of their empirical claims about a world divided into distinct cultures. Clifford Geertz's rereading of Benedict's work gives us the archetype of this move.

## Full Frontal Fictions

Things don't have to be true to be interesting. That is in essence the message of Clifford Geertz's rereading of Benedict's frontal comparisons as a form of 'serious satire'. Indeed the point of Geertz's analogy between

Benedict and fictional satirists such as Swift wasn't simply that frontal contrasts are critical. The implicit lesson of this reading is that this critical potential is only loosely related to the facticity of the account. The point is underlined by Geertz's frequent assertion or implication that the empirical content of Benedict's work is somehow beside the point. Benedict, like Swift, 'hardly went anywhere' (Geertz 1988: 128); 'there is virtually nothing, folktales aside, of which she is the primary recorder' (Geertz 1988: 112). Geertz brushes aside Benedict's extensive and detailed invocations of historical and literary evidence as reliance on 'wildly assorted materials from wildly assorted sources' (Geertz 1988: 120). Geertz relentlessly reduces Benedict's work to its rhetorics:

> The empirical validity of these various assertions ... aside (and some of them do sound more like reports from a society supposed than from one surveyed), the unrelenting piling up of them, the one hardly despatched before the next appears, is what gives Benedict's argument its extraordinary energy. She persuades, to the degree that she does persuade ... by the sheer force of iteration.
>
> (Geertz 1988: 120)

These points could be read as an unfair and intemperate critique. On a close reading, Benedict's work is no more or less empirically grounded than many more recent ethnographies. But, reading charitably, one might say that Geertz's aim is less to discredit Benedict and more to save her from the rising wave of commentary which had her pegged as an essentialist and orientalist author. Once attention is deflected, in essence, from Benedict's substantive portrayal of the Japanese, what remains is the critical effect of this portrayal on American self-perception. Benedict can thus be recuperated as, in this respect, way ahead of her time. Her work is 'a deconstruction *avant la lettre* of occidental clarities' (Geertz 1988: 121).

It is notable that what gets evacuated in Geertz's reading of Benedict, alongside factuality, is precisely the work of lateral comparison. Geertz's focus on Benedict's 'relentless ... us/them rhetoric' brackets her constant invocation of lateral comparisons. Some, like her comparisons between Japan and China or Melanesia, point to analogies and continua of variation: features of Japanese culture emerge as intensifications or transformations of features of other societies in the region. These are 'comparisons of the near', to return to the mid-century contrast evoked above (Chapter 2). Others, such as those between Japanese and German authoritarianisms, or Japanese and French centralised school systems, are comparisons of the far – but Germany and France are emphatically not 'Us/U.S', at least not to begin with. Then, as Germany and France's similarities with Japan become the grounds for articulating their respective differences, this in turn enables Benedict to build up a broader picture of a division between East and West in which the very real differences between Germany, France and the USA are in turn absorbed. One finds here – again – the alternation between considering a cline of empirical differences and similarities, and envisioning a stark conceptual difference (compare Strathern 1988: 342–343).[7]

Reading Geertz without reading Benedict herself might leave one with the impression that the only comparisons drawn in the book are on a Japan–USA axis, and that they only bear on a fanciful conceptual inversion. Benedict's frontal comparisons can be recuperated as *avant la lettre* deconstruction, as long as one brackets their empirical reference to lateral comparison. For her lateral comparisons, by contrast, only make sense with a view to specifying boundaries, controlling extensions and making real claims about things in the world. Frontal comparison carries the seed of cultural critique. To lateral comparison falls the less exalted task (at least, it seems, in Geertz's view) of empirical specification. But without the resort to lateral comparison, the authoritative dynamic of the double hinterland also falls away. Geertz's Benedict is no longer an authoritative cultural comparatist, whose ability to challenge our assumptions is grounded in the panoptic observation of cases laid side by side. She becomes a trickster who imagines an unsettling alternative – it barely matters which.

I am not sure whether Benedict herself would have approved of this attempt to save her politics by sacrificing her data. But whatever one makes of it, Geertz's reading of Benedict has the benefit of dramatising an important point about the structure of frontal comparison: its ability to unsettle, challenge or deconstruct occidental clarities, its role as serious satire or cultural critique, is only loosely related to the question of its empirical validity. We have seen the reason for this: the stark us/them contrasts of frontal comparison were never quite a simple assertion of fact. They didn't derive from a complete mapping of two mutually exclusive cultures (as if such a thing were possible). Rather these us/them binaries were an unstable compound of a set of empirical claims about a partially interconnected world, and a radical logical distinction between subject and object. The us/them contrast, from the start, was a composite device, a double vision, which didn't quite mean what it said.

What Geertz's account suggests, in sum, is that if one is only interested in the self-critical potential of frontal comparison – and that is, as we shall see, an important if – then the account of the other upon which it rests just needs to be surprising or challenging. It doesn't need to be true. The fictional frontal encounters of Gulliver's travels, or Thomas More's Utopia, science fiction as deployed by Donna Haraway, or Miner's famous 'Nacirema' (American read backwards – Miner 1956), all produce unsettling effects in much the same way as the ethnographically grounded frontal comparisons of anthropologists. One might say the same, for instance, of Anna Tsing's attempt to project herself into the point of view of a mushroom spore (Tsing 2014). The evidently fictional nature of the device doesn't detract from the fact that it allows 'us' the glimpse of an alternative: what if our bodies grew into one another in a rhizomic way? What would 'kinship' feel like then? In sum, Geertz's account suggests that the facticity of frontal comparisons matters for different reasons and in different ways to its power of cultural critique. One can be right without being interesting. One can be interesting without being right.

## *The Wheat and the Chaff*

Comrades – capitalism is teetering on the edge of a precipice. We must go further!

*Romanian joke from the Communist period*

Geertz's account of Benedict gives us the archetype of a series of rereadings of past authors by later proponents of frontal comparison. These turned on a historical recuperation of the frontal comparisons of previous authors as promising but as yet incomplete prefigurations of a fully frontal, non-culturalist anthropology.

We have already encountered another instance in Dumont's rereading of Mauss: Dumont sought to save Mauss's invention of an epistemological us/them contrast, while leaving behind his unfortunate lingering evolutionism. This is also the message of a more recent rereading of Dumont himself by Van der Veer (2014; cf. 2016). Van der Veer credits Dumont's work for what he terms its holism – the way in which it deploys ethnography as a way 'to bracket Western assumptions' (Van der Veer 2014: 3). He charges, however, that Dumont retained, alongside his holism, an unfortunate tendency to 'wholism' – a reification of India and the West as 'artificial unities across time and space' (Van der Veer 2014: 7). Holbraad and Pedersen make a similar observation of two thinkers whom they nevertheless claim as sources of inspiration for their version of the ontological turn: David Schneider and Roy Wagner (Holbraad and Pedersen 2017: 69–109). Both thinkers, the authors claim, articulated powerful and sophisticated reflexive devices for challenging the very foundations of anthropological explanations. However, Schneider – and perhaps, albeit more tentatively, Wagner, too – is read as ultimately reinstating an effectively culturalist view which threatens to undermine the radical potential of his frontal devices.

These various rereadings of earlier authors all share a structure: they identify, in earlier frontal comparisons, an oscillation between two positions: on the one hand, a radical reflexivity which provides a challenge to 'our' conceptions, on the other an abiding culturalism which is untenable. Putting things in this way naturally suggests a solution: one needs to separate the wheat of frontal critique and reflexivity from the chaff of lateral claims about cultural differences in the world. The remainder of realist culturalism in these older accounts is taken as evidence that their reflexive insight has not been taken quite far enough. A more intense reflexivity is required. On the horizon lies a vision of a kind of fully frontal operation which no longer relies on particular quasi-civilisational objects such as 'Amazonia' or 'the West': 'the empirical material that occasions such reconceptualizations can be drawn from anywhere, anytime and by anyone' (Holbraad and Pedersen 2017: 7).[8]

It is important, however, not to overshoot. For the vision of a frontal comparison that entirely lifts off from the plane of lateral comparisons – a frontal comparison which could apply literally anywhere, that is to say, one for which actual differences between empirical contexts is entirely irrelevant – is equally untenable, as these authors themselves acknowledge. The risk of overshooting derives from a possible misreading of the way the frontal device was originally set up. Indeed – to reprise my account at the beginning of this chapter – the empirical lateral referent of frontal comparison was never a full essentialist mapping of two mutually exclusive cultures. No one – and certainly not those original evolutionists, for whom society was process – ever did this, for it is patently impossible. Rather, frontal comparison was born as a composition of two different relational visions: on the one hand, an encounter between partly interwoven cultures or civilisations, on the other, a fundamental contrast between two mutually entailed positions: the subject and the object (which could be another subject). It is the latter, not the former, which provides the sense of a radical encounter. The former provides a sense of empirical grounding: the subject is not simply a free-floating individual, but a person situated in a world of flowing and partly interconnected, partly separate contexts, a world mapped by anthropologists' lateral comparisons. The combination of these two moves gives broader relevance to the subject–object encounter, scaling it up from an encounter between 'me' and 'the world' to an encounter between 'us' and 'them'. But this encounter derives – respectively – its sense of empirical grounding and its sense of contrastive sharpness from two different sources. Frontal comparison, in sum, requires 'us' and 'them' to be seen twice: once as partly entangled contexts in the world, and again as two – definitionally separate – perspectives, one of which is seen from the inside and the other from the outside.

Imagining that one could do frontal comparison without reference to those putatively 'artificial unities across time and space' (Van der Veer 2014: 7) masks the fact that a claim to some kind of unity (and difference) across time and space is required to get frontal comparisons off the ground. Such lateral claims were always and remain today constitutive of frontal comparatisms. Claims made on the plane of lateral comparison about partly distinct contexts in the world were never the source of frontal comparison's binary sharpness. And neither are they just the chaff of frontal comparison, something which can simply be separated and left behind. Cut them away entirely, and the device falls apart.

In sum, however much they might seek to recuperate frontal comparison as fictional or heuristic, anthropologists always find some need to account for its continued grounding in the plane of lateral comparisons, the plane of claims about entities, relations, similarities and differences in the world. This becomes clear as soon as we move to a consideration of how anthropologists reclaimed frontal comparison in their own work, rather than identifying its incomplete potential in the work of others. For it is one thing to redescribe other authors as insightful yet (still) incoherent, and another to explicitly account for one's own frontal comparisons. In so doing, claims are made for the sense in which one's own productive fictions are still grounded in 'the real world' – both on the 'us' side and on the 'them' side. With those claims comes, yet again, oscillation.

## Grounding the 'Us'

Some of the most radical criticism coming out of the West today is the result of an interested desire to conserve the subject of the West, or the West as Subject.

(Spivak 1988: 271)

The claim to the existence of a hinterland – the fact that the anthropologist's experience can be contextualised as part of a broader 'us' – is essentially a matter of convincing the readership that they too share in the perspective which the author is depicting as 'our own'. The 'us' is in effect an intersubjective achievement between author and reader. The single most effective way of doing so is to ground one's claim in the very activity which the anthropologist and the reader are currently engaged in, namely the doing and reading of anthropology.

We find the clearest archetypal instance of this move in Tim Ingold's response to the various problems with the notion of 'the West' which he himself so clearly laid out in the passage I quoted above. Having shown all of the reasons why the West and modernity are unsatisfactory categories, he continues:

For those of us who call themselves academics and intellectuals, however, there is a good reason why we cannot escape 'the West', or avoid the anxieties of modernity. It is that our very activity, in thinking and writing, is underpinned by a belief in the absolute worth of disciplined, rational enquiry. In this book, it is to this belief that the terms 'Western' and 'modern' refer. And however much we may object to the dichotomies to which it gives rise, between humanity and nature, intelligence and instinct, the mental and the material, and so on, the art of critical disputation on these matters is precisely what 'the West' is all about. For when all is said and done, there can be nothing more 'Western', or more 'modern', than to write an academic book such as this.

(Ingold 2000: 6–7)

This move isolates the disciplinary component of the hinterland (here in the broadest sense of 'academic'), and turns it into the foundation for invoking a wider cultural or ontological background. Of course, grounding one's perspective in this way is not sufficient to establish the limits of such a perspective. There are, one might fairly object, a number of non-western ways of writing academic books or engaging in critical disputation (Lloyd 2015). Grounding the 'us' is only one half of the recuperation of frontal comparison, as we shall see below. But first let us examine a number of other ways in which the 'us' has been grounded.

A related move is that operated by postcolonial criticism, in which the analytical tools of anthropology and more broadly western academia (cultural translation, historicism, the individual subject, freedom and agency, modernity and tradition) are contextualised and revealed as western constructs. One might say that, here, it is the disciplinary hinterland and its ability to stand above and outside context which is jettisoned, or at least collapsed into cultural hinterland. This move addresses the blind-spot in arguments which jettison us/them contrasts altogether, namely the western origin of anthropological knowledge. It represents a direct reversal of Pina-Cabral's solution above. It retains the reference to a cultural hinterland and uses it to challenge – at least initially – the analytical distance of the anthropologist. By itself, however, this move would require a reinstatement of the sort of holistic units (cultures and civilisations) whose persuasive force the crisis of representation had so severely dented.[9] One must somehow invoke such units while simultaneously disavowing their existence.

'Strategic essentialism' (Spivak 1988) is the canonical name for that oscillation. Insofar as it refers to the West and its cultural products and concepts, strategic essentialism can play once again on the duality of the hinterland. The hinterland to which a new object is confronted comes to refer to a politically dominant view or conceptual position, one assumed to be broadly shared in the author's background, but one to which the author him- or herself is inimical by definition: Western 'liberal' understandings of freedom, say, or 'Eurocentric notions of modernity'. More profoundly, since these invocations of the West and its values, concepts or characteristics are themselves relational, implying a non-western alternative, it is the whole figure of an us/them contrast which emerges as a feature of 'our' hinterland – one of our background assumptions.

These concepts, regions and binary assumptions can be put to use through a characteristic move of disavowal-recuperation. This move turns on the empirical claim that such notions (the West and the Rest, the liberal individual, modernity, etc.), although not shared by the author, are indeed believed by many and as a result have concrete effects in the world, effects to which the work would provide a critical counterpoint. The clearest and most explicit version which comes to mind is from an anthropologically minded historian. This is how Dipesh Chakrabarty explains his continued reference to 'Europe' and 'India' in *Provincialising Europe*:

'Europe' and 'India' are treated here as hyperreal terms in that they refer to certain figures of imagination whose geographical referents remain somewhat indeterminate ... Liberal-minded scholars would immediately protest that any idea of a homogeneous, uncontested 'Europe' dissolves under analysis. True, but just as the phenomenon of Orientalism does not disappear simply because some of us have now attained a critical awareness of it, similarly, a certain version of 'Europe,' reified and celebrated in the phenomenal world of everyday relationships of power as the scene of the birth of the modern, continues to dominate the discourse of history. Analysis does not make it go away.

(Chakrabarty 2007: 27–28)

Note that this brings us back, in a roundabout way, to the author's ability to stand above and take a perspective on widely shared misconceptions amongst his readership. Both of the entities invoked – India and Europe – take on a ghostly quality as 'hyperreal' objects. As to the dynamic of the move, however, Chakrabarty retains just as much of an edge on unsuspecting Eurocentric readers of any nation as Benedict had on any Japan-denigrating Americans. These readers no longer need to be imagined as 'western' in any substantive cultural sense – they just need to have still been taken in by the belief in the existence of such a place. It is the conventional discourse of history which is inherently 'western', irrespective of who practises it.

Grounding the evidence of the existence of a western perspective in the activity of anthropology itself is also a core device of the work of authors such as Wagner, Strathern or Viveiros de Castro. This move is deployed in different ways and to different effects (for a thorough comparison, see Holbraad and Pedersen 2017). One example will suffice.

Like Ruth Benedict in *The chrysanthemum and the sword*, Marilyn Strathern in *The gender of the gift* also begins by pointing to previous western misunderstandings and mischaracterisations of a non-western 'other'. Crucially, however, whereas Benedict attributed these errors of perspective to historians, political scientists and American laypeople, and proposed the superior virtues of anthropological comparison as a way forward, the primary target of Strathern's critique is anthropologists themselves and their comparative imaginaries which, she argues, have signally failed in Melanesia (Strathern 1988: 3). What for Benedict had been a solution – the arsenal of anthropological analytics such as culture, society, functional integration, distinct domains of cultural practice and so forth – becomes, for Strathern, part of the problem. Attempts to simply step outside one's own cultural perspective to access a different reality through the technical terminology of anthropology fail, Strathern argues, because this technical terminology is still, after all, an outcrop of our own language (1988: 4). Concepts of individual, society, kinship and gender deployed analytically by anthropologists are inextricably western notions. Even the device of opposing Melanesia and the West is a device internal to western anthropological discourse, just as the image of a society based on a gift economy is a dream internal to the logic of a society suffused by commodity relations.

The proposed solution to this dilemma is therefore to stay within our own language, and to use one of these conceptual devices (the 'us/them' contrast) to try to bend out of shape some of the others. What would it mean, for instance, to describe ethnographic material from Melanesia without recourse to our most basic anthropological concepts, such as those of society or individuals? To imagine a form of life in which these concepts 'did not apply'? Strathern states, explicitly, that this account of a society without society is a device, not a statement of empirical fact.

> Their ideas must be made to appear through the shapes we give to our ideas. Exploiting the semantics of negation (the X or Y have 'no society') is to pursue the mirror image possibility of suggesting that one type of social life is the inverse of another. This is the fiction of the us/them divide. The intention is not an ontological statement to the effect that there exists a type of social life based on premises in an inverse relation to our own. Rather it is to utilize the language that belongs to our own in order to create a contrast internal to it.
>
> (Strathern 1988: 16)

What *is* entailed, however, is that there is a perspective from which all these fictions are being produced. These terms, categories, analyses and distinctions, Strathern reminds us, are 'ours'. Of course, the 'us' is a deictic: 'we' only think of ourselves as 'western' insofar as we imagine ourselves by contrast to others such as 'Melanesians'. But the very move which relativises and caveats the frontal contrast between Melanesia and the West – this is only 'our' account of that difference, after all – simultaneously grounds the reality of the 'us'. For this is, after all, 'our' account.

This is the precise inversion of Pina-Cabral's radical decontextualisation of anthropology, as distinct from any particular cultural background. Here, the very existence of anthropology (instantiated in the fact of the book or article that you are reading) is an instance of the existence of the West. Conversely, 'the West' is any place where anthropological concepts are at home, whether this is a village in England in the 1970s, or a university in Papua New Guinea in the 1980s (Strathern 1987a).[10]

If this were all, one could indeed imagine a fully frontal, and fully fictional, comparison. This would be a comparison reduced, as it were, to 'our' reflexivity. An anthropologist's own fictions, distorting and transforming the conceptual categories of the discipline into ever more recursive reconfigurations – insofar as they manage to engage a readership – would in and of themselves provide evidence of the existence of 'the West' and simultaneously be the engine of 'the West's' perpetual self-transformation. This work could indeed be occasioned by material from absolutely anywhere – including from 'our own' imaginations. And anyone willing to engage in this self-transformative project would, *de facto*, be a part of the 'us'.

But clearly, this is not all. Self-instantiation – this scaling up from the perspective of the anthropologist, to the discipline, to the West – can only get us half-way to a frontal comparison. After all, Tylor's example in the previous chapter shows that we could easily keep scaling up, until 'we' maps not just the West, but the whole of humanity. The simple fact that Ingold is writing an academic book and you or I are reading it may well be an instance of the substantial existence of 'western categories'. But by itself, it cannot tell us that these categories are not universally human. This argument needs to be complemented by some sense of an encounter, some account of a moment in which these western categories fail. And that is where fiction no longer cuts it.

### Beyond the 'Us'

The model of a reflexive, intensive and perpetual (western) self-experimentation exists, of course. That is what much of contemporary continental philosophy and a significant amount of fiction, particularly – actual – satire, is. The distinctiveness of anthropology, even when it shares those aims, is its claim to producing conceptual transformation through an encounter with something other than itself. Otherwise it would make no difference if, for instance, in seeking to challenge anthropological knowledge practices, one relied on a theoretical appeal to Foucault or Deleuze, or alternatively on an ethnographic invocation of a Melanesian aesthetic in which similarity is taken for granted and value inheres in the making of distinctions (Strathern 2004: 80–81). It would not matter, in other words, if the source of our thought experiments and our self-critiques lay ultimately inside or outside 'ourselves'.

Yet most anthropologists – including those committed to fundamentally frontal approaches – claim that it matters very much indeed, and much ink has been spilled on this problem. Are frontal comparisons truly bringing back 'home' to our conceptual world a contrast forged through fieldwork and defamiliarisation? Or was this forging a forgery? Were the new concepts invented through frontal comparison ultimately only versions of the old ones we started from? In seeking to encounter the other, are we only ever reproducing the same tired stereotypes, fighting the same internal battles, and never in fact truly encountering 'the great outdoors' (Viveiros de Castro 2011)? Satire, by itself, is not necessarily transformative, as a number of political commentators have pointed out. Certain kinds of satire are 'not normally intended to convert one's opponents, but to gratify and fortify one's friends' (James Sutherland, quoted in Coe 2013). Satire can also be repetitive.

While frontal comparatists are occasionally pricked into shrugging away such objections as naively realist, elsewhere they do find the need to claim that, yes, the differences they devise do originate in the world and not in their own minds. As Toren and Pina-Cabral point out, 'there is no possible description of what actually occurs in the ethnographic encounter that does not presume some form of realism' (Toren and Pina-Cabral 2009: 12–13). Yet the form and implications of such realism are rarely made explicit in accounts which are otherwise anti-representationalist. And thus, frontal comparisons, even after the crisis of representation, cannot afford to be just fictions. They cannot rely solely on first-person discourse, however self-critical, because, as Lambek puts it, '[f]irst person discourse may be reflexive, but it has no Other against which to keep such reflection honest' (1991: 48). Which is profoundly why the fundamental oscillation of frontal comparison, its double vision of two kinds of intensity, cannot in fact be eliminated. An intense, internal subject–object relation can be recovered as a productive fiction. An external relation between empirical similarities and differences in the world cannot – it belongs to the plane of lateral comparison. Frontal comparison remains pinned to two mutually incompossible visions, and thus it oscillates.

Recall Dumont's claim that one ought to retain Mauss's epistemic insight ('they think this in relation to us who think that') while jettisoning Mauss's lingering evolutionism. This might seem to be precisely what Dumont himself managed to do, at least on Iteanu and Moya's (2015) account. They note that while Dumont is remembered for his static contrast between Indian hierarchy and western egalitarianism in *Homo hierarchicus*, this ought not to be read as an essentialist claim but as a relational one. Dumont's contrast was as much a reflexive, critical observation about the methodological individualism of much western social science, as an observation about the Indian caste system: 'they think this, in relation to us who think that'. As a result Dumont's holism was to be read as a critical technique, simultaneously and recursively subverting that methodological individualism.

Furthermore, Iteanu and Moya note that, as in Strathern's *Gender of the Gift*, Dumont's 'us' and 'them' is a deictic distinction, not an essentialist one. For *Homo hierarchicus* was only the initial move in Dumont's work. Taken as a whole, the sequence of Dumont's works operated a progressive relativisation of his initial distinction. With every successive work (Dumont 1966, 1977, 1991), Dumont refined and partially challenged a previous characterisation.

As with Strathern, the dynamic is fractal: the opposition between India (Them/Hierarchical) and Modernity (Us/Egalitarian), which is at the heart of *Homo hierarchicus* (Dumont 1966) and *Homo aequalis I* (Dumont 1977), is replicated, within one of these terms, by the contrast drawn between Germany (Them/Hierarchical) and France (Us/Egalitarian) in *Homo aequalis II* (Dumont 1991). Here, whereas Germany has managed to integrate individualism within a broadly holistic frame, France has subordinated holism to individualism. Then, in the final chapter of that book, the hierarchical opposition is replicated within France itself. While French ideology as a whole is characterised as individualist, the holist element is encompassed as the right wing (Them/Hierarchical), encompassed by the left wing (Us/Egalitarian). In sum, unlike Van der Veer, Iteanu and Moya read Dumont, not as a lingering 'wholist', but as a strictly methodological, relational thinker, one who moves ever further away from identity in an *intensely* open-ended way:

Dumont's comparative method only produces provisional results. Repeated reconsiderations sharpen the image fashioned, but never reach a stabilized position, let alone perfection. Each result is nothing but the starting point of a further step that refines, reformulates, and displaces the difference between the two comparative poles that one decided to contrast.

(Iteanu and Moya 2015: 10)

And yet reading Dumont's binaries as strictly heuristic requires some erasures. For instance, in a striking comment on Herder (Dumont 1991: 23–24), Dumont argues that the latter's notion of culture is rooted in the deep past of German holism. It is this ultimately pre-modern inheritance, lost by the methodological individualisms of other disciplines, which gives anthropology its distinctive edge in dealing with non-modern realities elsewhere. This is perhaps why, whereas Dumont excoriates methodological individualism as 'our own' analytical strategy, there is no sense in his work, as there is in Strathern's, that the holistic reference point itself might be a particularly modern analytical strategy. Dumont seems – at that point in his argument at least – to suggest that the methodology of anthropological holism comes with the stamp of substantial truth from a pre-modern world – a world still surviving in India, and in encompassed form, in Europe as well.

In sum, Dumont's key move is to retain a double referent – heuristic and substantive – in his discussions of holism. Holism is, on the one hand, a real phenomenon in the world, manifested in various ways in various places (encompassing in India, encompassed in French politics, enshrined in the anthropological notion of culture, etc.). It is also, on the other hand, a methodological tool, born of a heuristic contrast with methodological individualism. The genealogy of culture through Herder provides a subterranean passage point between these two positions. Alongside the reading in which Indian hierarchy produced a distortion in Dumont's method, leading him to abandon 'our categories', there emerges a second reading in which the Indian material only comforted Dumont's anthropological perspective (in which cultural holism has a long and distinguished heritage), because both harked back to the same non-modern assumption.

This is another way of saying that Dumont is a historical thinker, a thinker of real, slow, partial changes and transformations (see also Dumont 1985), which he carefully and empirically traces in book after detailed book. His binarisms and contrasts rise above these material traces, partly grounded in them and partly articulating their own structural logic. They do not so much trump the complexity of the historical narratives, as articulate clear-cut differences in a different medium. To those who dislike these moments of grand clear binarism, Dumont pre-emptively retorts that it is not 'as if we had to remain perpetually hunched over our work without ever looking up towards the horizon' (Dumont 1977: 7).

What history achieves for Dumont, the irreducibility of ethnographic encounter and a sustained commitment to lateral comparisons achieve for *The gender of the gift*.[11] I will return to the latter in a moment. As for the former, consider the following observation:

In comparing 'our' categories to 'their' categories, one is, of course comparing two versions of our categories, the latter being derived from what we take to be salient or relevant to them, even as the ideas gained from what we take to be their categories come from '*our*' encounters. To extract certain distinct ideas out of the encounter is not to judge the people as distinct, nor necessarily entail a comparison of whole societies.

(Strathern 1988: 349, emphasis added)

The use of the word 'our' at the end of the first sentence is worth pondering on – in the context of Strathern's point elsewhere about the way 'we' in English is so rarely used as a dual (recall the quote at the beginning of Chapter 7). The second 'our' in the sentence could be read, in line with the first 'our', as 'expressing the self and the person addressed' (Boas 1896: 903). This would characterise the encounter itself as a solipsism: any encounter between 'us' and 'them' is only ever our version of that encounter, just as they may have their version. Alternatively, 'our encounter' could precisely be read as a rare intrusion of a 'dual' we, 'expressing the self and the person spoken of' (Boas 1896: 903), into a book that otherwise eschews it. 'Our' encounter would thus be for once a shared moment between anthropologist and interlocutors. At that moment, difference appears not simply as a fiction internal to the account, but as an external impetus for the elaboration of the fictional internal differences which constitute the account. This external impetus need not take the form of a contrast between whole societies or even distinct people.

There is thus an oscillation too in Dumont's and in Strathern's accounts. One can simultaneously glimpse a messy, entangled yet empirical encounter or history in which people are in some ways similar and in others different, in which some things are shared and not others, in which no 'whole societies' are visible. This is a vision built out of lateral comparisons on the xy plane. These scholars then draw out of this encounter or history a key conceptual difference which is then deployed as an 'as if' contrast between 'us' and 'them' in order to challenge and

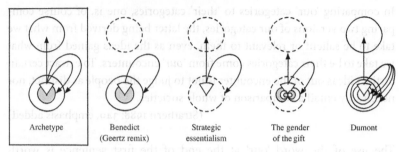

| Archetype | Benedict (Geertz remix) | Strategic essentialism | The gender of the gift | Dumont |

Figure 8.5 Fictions and not-quite-fictions

divide the intellectual baggage with which the analyst him- or herself had initially approached the encounter, or read the history. In return, this challenge to the analyst's intellectual baggage suggests a broader mapping of an 'us'. It might even produce a glimpse of what was going on, on the other side of that encounter, or in another vision of that history. In sum, one might imagine the range of fictions and not-quite-fictions through which frontal comparison was refounded after the crisis of representation, as in Figure 8.5.

## Oscillation and Rigour

The mode of the 'as if' is the only way to overcome the principle of non-contradiction without madness.

(Thomas 2011: 154)

I initially borrowed the notion of oscillation from a critique levelled by James Laidlaw and Paolo Heywood (Laidlaw 2012; Laidlaw and Heywood 2013) at an instance of the ontological turn (Pedersen 2011). The authors argue that proponents of the turn oscillate between a claim that is empirically grounded but unsurprising (to the effect that there are different worldviews), and a claim that is surprising but empirically untenable (there are different worlds). One can certainly find echoes of this oscillation in the most recent restatement of the turn by Holbraad and Pedersen (2017). How can it be simultaneously the case – a critic might ask – that 'The ontological turn is not concerned with what the "really real" nature of the world is' (Holbraad and Pedersen 2017: x), and yet that it is thoroughly grounded in the ethnographic record and is merely a device for better description – indeed, that these descriptions themselves ought to be judged by the canons of conventional representationalism (Holbraad and Pedersen 2017: 193)?

Proponents of radical frontal comparison have responded to such observations through a set of arguments which are well illustrated by the notion of Strathernian comparisons as concept-things ('abstentions') which we introduced in Chapter 6 above. With this paradoxical notion, Holbraad and Pedersen (2009, 2017) seek to resolve what I have described above as an oscillation between frontal and lateral comparisons by resorting to a philosophical paradox. Figured as cones with a sharp conceptual end and a thick ethnographic end, abstentions are themselves intense, differential relations between 'our' concerns and the ethnographic record. Neither ethnography nor theory, "our" concerns' or 'their world', comes first or grounds the other. Rather, as in the Deleuzian view, to identify such entities (us and them, concepts and things) can only be a post hoc separation of what was, first, an intense relation. Iteanu and Moya invoke a similarly paradoxical solution to characterise the nature of Dumont's contrasts between values such as hierarchy and equality:

Dumont's values are neither objective nor subjective facts, but only differences that appear through comparison. Consequently, it is futile to attempt to specify whether they are descriptive notions or artifacts (i.e., the products of a comparative experiment). They overcome the distinction between symbolic and real, representation and reality, action and thought, facts and values.

(Iteanu and Moya 2015: 118–119)

Such responses to the problem of oscillation can themselves be read in two ways. On the one hand, they can be read as calling for a caesurist break away from the distinction between things and concepts – away, in other words, from representationalism. On this view, oscillation is resolved through a further intensification. The gap between ethnography and theory is collapsed and frontal comparison can be recast outwith the representational distinction between fact and fiction. On this reading the old question of which – of ethnographic facts or conceptual fictions – has in the end 'made a difference' is quite simply misguided. As Heywood has noted, refusing the representational distinction between concepts and things produces a ready-made response to both realist critiques (since these things described are also concepts) and conceptual ones (since these concepts are after all already things in the world) (Heywood 2018a).

But one could also read the figure of comparisons as concept-things in a different way. Not as a way to resolve oscillation into a third, stable position, but as a way to embrace the oscillation and make it explicit – to retain *both* representational *and* non-representational techniques and use them in tandem (Holbraad 2012; Holbraad and Pedersen 2017: 193). This reading dovetails with the account I have been building here (see also Candea 2016b, 2016a). On the view articulated in this chapter, anthropological comparisons, imagined as a composite of frontal and lateral moves, are perpetually oscillating between two techniques. That oscillation is ineradicable, but nothing much would be gained by claiming that this oscillation is also somehow the mark of a third, conceptually coherent position. Strathern herself suggests something along those lines in a passing comment on her own method:

Thus one can manipulate received usages of terms such as 'persons' and 'things' or 'subjects' and 'objects'. And thus one can contrive an analysis which, to follow Tyler's musings about discourse as trope, in being '[n]either fully coherent within itself nor given specious consistency through referential correspondence with a world external to itself, … announces brief coherences and enacts momentary "as if" correspondences relative to our purposes, interests, and interpretative abilities.'

(Strathern 1988: 19, quoting Tyler 1984: 329)

There is no shame in oscillation, any more than there is in using two different tools – or indeed two hands, or two eyes – to a common end. No problem there, as long as one is clearly aware of the respective limits and entailments of each tool. An oscillation between representationalist ethnography and non-representational theory, *which combines the particular rigour appropriate to each endeavour*, is not to be sniffed at. That is where the crafting of new paradoxical hybrids – such as 'abstentions' or Iteanu and Moya's 'values' – can become a problem. I have no quarrel with these hybrids if they are read as requiring a double methodological rigour, a commitment to *both* conventional representational truth *and* conceptual invention, as the work of the above authors themselves in practice demonstrates. But the risk is that such formulations might lead inattentive readers to assume that *neither* kind of rigour is required – that one can get away with both a loose attitude to empirical facts (since after all this is not about garden variety realism) and a plentiful reliance on paradox and convenient self-contradiction (since after all alterity allows us to challenge the canons of conceptual argument).

Oscillation can become a tool for a double rigour, or alternatively it can become a way to evade any kind of critique. It matters thoroughly which. But this in turn raises a different issue, which is what sort of rigour is required for each of these different kinds of operation?[12] This question will occupy us in the final chapter. Firstly, let us draw out of this discussion of oscillation the archetype of anthropological comparison towards which the past four chapters have been building.

## The Frontal and the Lateral: A Constitutive Oscillation

In sum, identifying an oscillation in proposals for an ontological turn, as in the work of Dumont, Strathern or Mauss, does not necessarily lead one to claim that such oscillation must be transcended. Rather, these examples highlight the irreducibility of oscillation in *any* kind of frontal comparison. Frontal comparison cannot be sustained by fiction alone, or even by the peculiar moves of self-instantiation through which one can ground the hinterland. Some further claim about substantive difference in the world is required in order to enable frontal comparison to scale up an individual encounter between the subject and the object to a collective encounter between an 'us' and a 'them'. Crucially, this claim doesn't need to take the form of a fully delineated account of two entirely separate and self-contained entities. What is needed is simply a claim that key empirical differences exist between otherwise interrelated contexts. To that ingredient of empirical difference the subject–object contrast adds a sense of irreducibility and sharpness. Combining these two contrasts gives the sense that if they were – by impossibility – to be fully described, each of these contexts would hang together enough to ground a perspective. That neat frontal contrast which relativises one's own position is what one sees with one eye, while the other sees a lateral mapping in which 'we' and 'they' are very much interwoven and at times indistinguishable. That double vision gives us the figure of a third archetype, at the mid-point of the third plane delimited by the axes x and z (Figure 8.6).

Frontal comparisons' oscillation between two kinds of intensity can also be envisioned as, more broadly, an oscillation between the plane of lateral comparison, with its play of differences, similarities, entities and relations, and the three-dimensional space above, in which mapping and communication, empirical detail and productive fictions, caveated generalisations and conceptual flights of fancy are entangled and recombined in multiple ways.

We have shown this in the case of Dumont and his reliance on detailed historical tracing. But one might say the same for Strathern. Even more crucial in grounding Strathern's frontal comparisons than the figure of the ethnographic encounter is her sustained deployment of lateral comparisons drawn from an extensive review of the ethnographic record on Melanesia. No amount of frontal comparison, of 'self and other' binarism, can replace or render irrelevant this work of

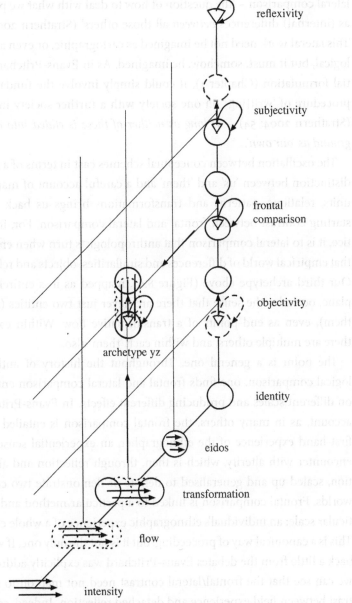

Figure 8.6  Identity, intensity, reflexivity

lateral comparison – 'the question of how to deal with what we perceive as (internal) differences *between* all those others' (Strathern 2004: 48). This lateral work need not be imagined as cartographic, or even as topological, but it must, somehow, be imagined. As in Evans-Pritchard's initial formulation (Chapter 1), it could simply involve the fundamental procedure of 'writ[ing] on one society with a further society in mind' (Strathern 2004: 54) – *as long as neither of these is elided into a background as 'our own'.*

The oscillation between conceptual schemes cast in terms of a radical distinction between 'us' and 'them' and a careful account of mappings, units, relations, patterns and transformations brings us back to our starting contrast between frontal and lateral comparison. For, in practice, it is to lateral comparison that anthropologists turn when engaging that empirical world of differences and similarities, objects and relations. Our third archetype above (Figure 8.6), mapped as it is entirely on a plane, occludes the sense that there are never just two entities (us and them), even as end-points of a transformative flow. Within each 'us' there are multiple others, and within each 'them' also.

The point is a general one. Throughout the history of anthropological comparison, one finds frontal and lateral comparison entwined on different scales and producing different effects. In Evans-Pritchard's account, as in many others, the frontal comparison is entailed in the first-hand experience of the ethnographer, an experiential sense of an encounter with alterity, which is then, through reflection and abstraction, scaled up and generalised to denote or demonstrate two cultural worlds. Frontal comparison is linked to a particular method and a particular scale: an individual's ethnographic experience of a whole culture. This is a canonical way of proceeding, but it is not the only one. If we step back a little from the debates Evans-Pritchard was explicitly addressing, we can see that the frontal/lateral contrast need not map on to a contrast between field experience and detached reflection. Indeed, some of the most canonically frontal instances of anthropological work, such as

*The chrysanthemum and the sword*, were not based on fieldwork at all. The sense of 'culture shock' can be evoked just as effectively through invocations of the literature.

This point in turn leads us to a reconsideration of scale. In Evans-Pritchard's view, frontal comparison constitutes single cases while lateral comparison builds on these cases to broader effect. One might envision Evans-Pritchard's account of comparison as the lateral comparison of the results of a succession of frontal comparisons, by different anthropologists operating from a shared disciplinary background.

But our discussion of Malinowski – in Chapter 2 – showed that the frontal move which lies at the beginning of that vision is itself the result of prior lateral comparative moves of two kinds. One is the elicitation of analogies across different domains of the same cultural or social whole – the tried and tested way of producing a sense of cultural holism, from Malinowski to interpretivism. Another is the fundamental descriptive device of micro-generalisation based on a comparison of distinct experiences, instances of the same ritual or saying, individual attitudes of different interlocutors, and so forth. In sum, what is, on one scale, an encounter between us and them is, on another scale, the effect of a thick weave of lateral comparisons of various kinds. This is after all the lesson of anthropology's commitment to *extended* fieldwork, which in this respect echoes the requirement for a detailed examination of literary or historical sources. A frontal encounter happens in time. It is grounded in descriptions of an empirical situation which are themselves micro-generalisations. The lateral thus precedes the frontal.

At the intersection of these two visions lies a fractal pattern. Look down: on a smaller scale again, each of those moments of fieldwork or each encounter with a particular document might be considered a frontal encounter. Beyond that scale of granularity lies the vanishing point of individual cognitive processes: it is irrelevant for our purposes to ask which comes first, experience as encounter or experience as double attention (Godfrey-Smith 2017). Now look up: if each mono-graphic vision of a society is, implicitly or explicitly, a frontal contrast – a 'people–person report' – built up from lateral comparisons, these in turn can be laterally compared to build up broader frontal contrasts. The procedure of building frontal comparisons from lateral ones is much the same in cases where the other is not a single culture or society, but rather a broader collective elicited from a review of the literature – or from the lining up of chapters in an edited volume, as in the case of the function-alist classics *African political systems* (Fortes and Evans-Pritchard 1940) or *African systems of kinship and marriage* (Radcliffe-Brown 1950). And thus frontal comparisons can easily take a regional form. 'Amazonian', 'African' or 'Melanesian' societies are made to stand against 'western' or 'Euroamerican' ones. These comparisons can operate in a mereographic generalising mode as in the Radcliffe-Brownian, typological collections above – which, beyond their specific regional conclusions, point also to a frontal challenge to 'our' conceptions of statehood or the family, as their respective prefaces make clear. Or they can operate through the discovery of an archetypal pattern in a system of differences, as in the abstractions of Lévi-Strauss, or in a different sense in those of Dumont or Strathern. If we abstract the profound difference in the ways of doing both frontal and lateral comparison in each case, we find a similar structure. Looking down from these broader visions, we find them to be grounded in the lateral comparison of monographic accounts, just as each monographic account – itself an implicit or explicit frontal comparison – builds on a lateral comparison of frontally encountered moments, instances and experiences. Looking up from these collections of monographic accounts, we find a frontal contrast between some element of 'our' familiar, hinter-land logic (scientific thought; naturalism) and alternatives which require anthropological elucidation (animism–totemism–analogism – Descola 2005b; the savage mind – Lévi-Strauss 1966).

This fractal vision of lateral comparisons scaffolding frontal comparisons which in turn scaffold lateral comparisons, and so forth, maps the common ground from which two radically opposed aims can be articulated. In one, the frontal is the basic procedure and the lateral is the valued outcome – 'translation is in the service of comparison' (Evans-Pritchard 1950; Radcliffe-Brown 1951); in the other, the dynamic is reversed – 'comparison is in the service of translation' (Asad 1986; Malinowski 1922; Viveiros de Castro 2004). Once again, the horizons envisaged are radically opposed, but they are rooted in the same methodological common ground.

We have thus described, for the third time, an intricate fractal interweaving of two forms. Let me briefly recall the first two. The first, central to the figure of *comparatio*, is a relation between analogies and contrasts. The second is the relation between objects and relations – the sense in which 'this *and* that' relativises '*this* and *that*'. The third, which now comes into view, is the relation between this and that and them and us. In the oscillation between the frontal questions of communication (we and they) and the lateral questions of mapping (this and that) lies the third form of intricacy which comes to complete our archetype.

## Conclusion: The Archetype of Comparison

It is now time, finally, to recompose what we have been decomposing. In this and the previous three chapters, we have sought to consider separately, then recombined, three contrasts which are often interwoven in anthropological discussions of comparison – contrasts between, respectively, comparisons aiming at identity or alterity, at identity or intensity, at identity or reflexivity. These three contrasts are not the same, but they do often come to form what Abbott terms a 'methodological manifold' (Abbott 2001). Anthropologists often move away from analogical generalising comparisons in a direction which is simultaneously heterological, reflexive and intense. In our vision of a three-dimensional space, comparative visions close in inspiration to the ontological turn, for instance, might be mapped at the symmetrical opposite of the argument by analogy, as a vision of comparison which aims at the maximum of alterity, intensity and reflexivity, where the former aims at reducing all three to a minimum. But once we have imagined such a three-dimensional space, a host of different recombinations can now be envisaged, starting from different positions along these three axes. The sense that there are only ever two ways of doing comparison, which paralysed us in Chapter 2, is finally exorcised.

When introducing the vision of a three-dimensional space in Chapter 6, I noted, however, the important sense in which it was misleading. The conceptual possibilities of anthropological comparison are not quantifiable – one cannot measure the 'amount' of identity, difference, reflexivity or intensity in any given comparative device. This is perhaps most obvious along the 'axis' of intensity, upon which are lined up radically different figures (*eidos*, transformation and flow) which cannot themselves be imagined as a graduated cline. But the same is true of the other three axes. In each case, what we find are fractal recursions of a basic contrast (identity/alterity, identity/intensity, identity/reflexivity).

The vision of a three-dimensional space is thus a fiction, but it is a facility for imagining how one might build an archetype out of a series of contrasts. At the mid-point of each 'axis' lies the thickest, most recursive intrication, and that is where I have in each case envisioned an archetypal form: *comparatio* along the first axis, transformation along the second, frontal comparison along the third. In turn, in the middle of each 'plane' we find the recursive intrication of two respective archetypes (Figure 8.7). And in the middle of our space, we find the intrication of those three intrications – what one might think of as the archetype of comparison (Figure 8.8). The vision of a three-dimensional space is just a scaffolding for that construction, a scaffolding which we can now discard.

So we are left with an intricate drawing (Figure 8.8) – so what? Even though, in appreciation of the considerable effort, both conceptual and visual, which it has taken me to produce it, I am tempted to have it

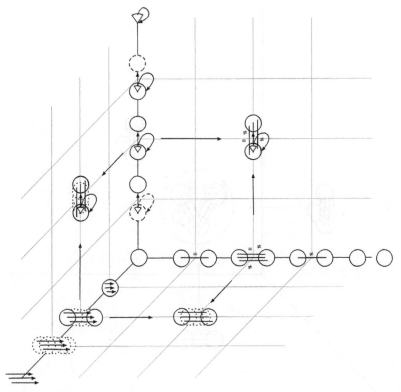

Figure 8.7 Three archetypes

tattooed somewhere on my person, it is clear that this gnomic drawing in itself is meaningless outwith the process of its production. By itself, it will not tell you anything about anthropological comparison, except perhaps to suggest that it is complex. Considered as the outcome of a process, however, this visual archetype condenses a particular argument, which began – if you recall the first pages of this second part of the book – with a search for a common language in which anthropologists might come to articulate their disputes and debates about comparison.

This argument, in a nutshell, is that anthropologists use comparison in pursuit of often incommensurable ends: to generalise from

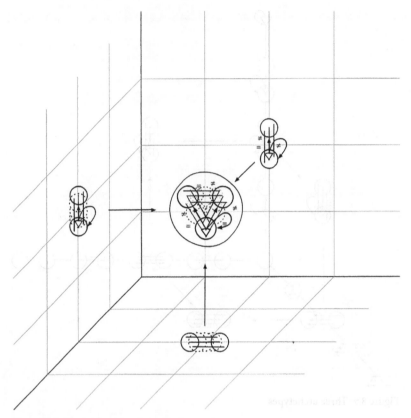

Figure 8.8 The archetype of comparison

particulars, to challenge generalisations, to unpick purported entities into flows and processes, or to identify shared ideals or concrete forms behind disparate processes, to suggest that some features of intersubjective encounter are widely shared, or to challenge their own analytical or cultural presuppositions. We have mapped some of these ends along three axes moving towards or away from identity. But as we saw at the end of Chapter 6, some purposes aim not towards identity or away from it, but in another direction altogether – for instance, towards the pedagogical transformation which occurs when an alternative *to* our ethical universe becomes an ethical alternative *for* our ethical universe (Laidlaw 2014; Lloyd 2015). Perhaps, just as a three-dimensional space can afford an infinity of vectorial directions, the discipline of anthropology can afford an infinity of possible purposes. Some of these purposes might be married or articulated to one another provisionally or durably. Others will be radically incommensurable. But there is little prospect of reducing these different ends to a single aim or point of anthropological comparison.

On the other hand, these different ends are all pursued through techniques of comparison which are built out of the same basic building blocks: analogies and contrasts, relations and intensities, objects and subjects. Combined and recombined, these form intricate heuristic arrangements adequate to the variety of purposes outlined above. The various archetypes elicited in the previous chapters map some of the basic forms of recombination of these different elements. These heuristic arrangements, like all heuristic arrangements, come with their distinctive facilities and their distinctive footprints. We have seen in particular how frontal comparisons gain the ability to elude questions of mapping, but only at the price of a certain kind of fiction, which means that they need in practice to be paired to lateral comparisons which have complementary entailments and limits.

Put in words, the archetype of anthropological comparison outlined visually above (Figure 8.8) could be described as *a consideration of similarities and differences, continuities and breaks, between three or more entities, at least one of which includes the perspective from which the comparison is taking place.* There is an echo here of Evans-Pritchard's model, from which this exploration initially set off. One way of thinking about this book's argument, indeed, is as a deconstruction and reconstruction of that first discussion of comparison – a re-engineering (cf. Wimsatt 2007) of Evans-Pritchard's outline of the impossible method, to fit a different moment in the discipline's history, a moment which requires the acknowledgement of a broader set of purposes and a different cast of characters.

## The Oscillations of Frontal Comparison

Even thus broadened, however, this archetype is not intended as a model of comparison as a whole, in the sense of encompassing all the possible combinations and recombinations imaginable. It simply suggests a vision of how comparative projects that are profoundly different can be put together out of elements that are basically the same. In so doing, the idea of an archetype suggests a way in which our disciplinary discussions of comparison might be reimagined as something other than a perpetual cycle of dismissal and overcoming, without ever being reduced to a simple vision of tinkering together towards a shared end. Neither the perpetual revolution of caesurism, nor the anti-political technicism of heuristics (Chapter 3), need be given the upper hand. Rather, we could imagine a shared language about where, how and to what effect we choose to walk together or part ways.

Nor is the archetype a complete *model for* comparison, in the sense of an ideal or perfect or somehow superior set of instructions for how one might go about doing it. And yet there is, nevertheless, a normative force to the argument of this book. This normativity is the subject of the next and final chapter, which turns on the problem of rigour.

NINE

# Rigour

An adequate philosophy of science should have normative force ... Mere descriptions of scientific practice, no matter how general or sensitive to detail, will not do. Without normative force, studies of methodology, however interesting, would translate as a catalogue of fortuitous and mysterious particular accidents, with no method at all.

(Wimsatt 2007: 24)

## Introduction: The Rigour of Comparisons

Over the course of the past four chapters, we have articulated a vision of an archetype of anthropological comparison, and in the process picked out some elements of a shared language in which anthropologists argue about comparison. We might now seem to have reached the initial aims set out in Chapter 4. Yet we also opened one particular can of worms by raising the question of rigour. We pointed to an ineradicable oscillation between frontal and lateral comparison – between an account of 'this and that' on the xy plane, and the crafting of conceptual contrasts or bridges between 'us and them' along the z axis. Ideally, we suggested, this oscillation will involve both the rigour specific to lateral comparisons and the rigour particular to frontal comparisons. But how might one characterise each of those kinds of rigour? Are they compatible, or mutually exclusive? And what, more generally, does the rigour of comparison consist in?

## Rigour

The problem of rigour – often cast in terms of how comparisons might be 'controlled' – is a recurrent theme in anthropological discussions. It opens directly on to questions of methodological normativity: it implies that there are better and worse comparisons, and not simply different ones. To talk of rigour is to suggest that when it comes to anthropological comparison, there is something like a 'job well done'.

Taking up this normative question might seem to mess up our attempt to articulate a space for discussion in which the radically different aims and visions of the discipline might meet. For surely, along with these radically different aims, come radically different understandings of rigour, of what counts as good method? Consider, for instance, the different invocations of the value of 'control' in Fred Eggan's 'controlled comparison' (1954) and Viveiros de Castro's 'controlled equivocation' (2004). For the former, control means sticking to comparisons in reasonably bounded local areas, such that one may generalise accurately, while avoiding flights of theoretical fancy. For the latter, control requires a radical flight of theoretical fancy to avoid the reasonable assumption that one has got the point of any given indigenous concept.

The point is well taken. To different aims correspond different comparative devices – to different devices, different kinds of rigour. The type of rigour required of frontal comparisons, I will argue, is primarily individual: it is a matter of a direct confrontation between an anthropologist and their own experience. As we saw in the previous chapter, anthropological comparison imagined as fully frontal could in principle take the form of pure thought-experiment. The rigour of lateral comparisons, by contrast, is primarily collective: it leans on previous lateral comparisons, and is open to challenge by cross-cutting collectives of expertise both within and beyond the discipline. And since I have argued that in anthropology (as opposed to fiction or philosophy, for instance) no frontal comparison can entirely stand on its own, entirely do away with lateral comparisons, this entails that anthropological comparatisms, however radically frontal their horizons, remain anchored in a collective anthropological – and also broader – sense of a job well done.

This is the core argument of the present chapter. As we shall see in the conclusion, however, the initially stark distinction between frontal and lateral, individual and collective, kinds of rigour is a device for introducing a broader picture of multiply anchored robustness. Once that picture is in place, we can let the binary device fade away.

## The Rigour of the Anthropologist

[T]he ontological turn takes the method of (self)experimentation to its necessary endpoint … self-experimentation, that is to say, all the way down.

(Holbraad and Pedersen 2017: 24)

We saw in the previous chapter that frontal comparison can occasionally play fast and loose with questions of mapping. The device of opposing 'them' and 'us' as two mutually constituted perspectival positions, the way in which both of those terms can extend on various scales – these two features combine to give frontal comparison a certain freedom from needing to specify precisely what entities it is talking about. If we consider it as a heuristic, we can see that the two classic charges against frontal comparison, namely the way it overgeneralises and fixes the other and its tendency to take the same old internal scapegoats as characteristic of the self, are nothing more than the inherent risk this procedure carries in anthropology, its characteristic 'footprint'. This is why the critic who counters that there is more complexity within the hinterland, or that a depiction of the 'other' is overly general, or that, in many respects, 'they' and 'we' are very much alike – that critic will tend to come across as uninteresting, nitpicking, as missing the point, the spirit of the practice. Frontal comparison was never required to be particularly rigorous in relation to mapping, for that is not where its interests lie. As Strathern writes, somewhat peremptorily, '"the Balkans" is rather like "Melanesia" or "Amazonia" insofar as it is an epistemic field for countless accounts of it ... There is no point in objecting that these are wild generalisations or in raising specific points in contradiction, since both moves are encompassed in the overall term' (Strathern 2011: 98).

This is not to say, however, that frontal comparisons need not be rigorous. Frontal comparisons require the anthropologist to be ethnographically sensitive, to be able to detect the effects of their own assumptions, to map the contours of a challenging utterance or transformative moment and be always ready to adjust their insights and 'see the eyes they are looking through'. They also need to be able to scale up these specific moments of conceptual disjuncture into broader logical or formal contrasts, picking out something which a readership will recognise as fundamental. The rigour required of frontal comparison thus calls forth a vision of individual self-awareness, creativity and logic. In sum, the specific rigour required of frontal comparison has always been, primarily, of an individual kind. Frontal comparison, by itself, is an individual experimental procedure, a 'personal equation' (Kuklick 2011): the account of a transformation operated by an anthropologist's experience of otherness, upon that anthropologist's consciousness of the familiar.

One can imagine an immediate retort which is that the rigour of frontal comparison is – or ought to be – not individual but dialogical (Lambek 1991). That was one of the key points articulated by 1980s critics of the 'exoticising' or 'orientalist' frontal comparisons of yore. It is, in a different genre, the radical requirement laid out by Isabelle Stengers when she notes that

no comparison is legitimate if the parties compared cannot each present his own version of what the comparison is about; and each must be able to resist the imposition of irrelevant criteria ... [C]omparison must not be unilateral, and, especially, must not be conducted in the language of just one of the parties.

(Stengers 2011: 56)

However, this radical requirement opens up on to an aporia. For where, concretely, should this dialogue take place? Where are these 'versions' to be presented? How can we know if the 'other party' has truly been allowed to resist?

Proponents of dialogism might thus find in some of the varieties of frontal comparison examined in the past two chapters a problematic denial of dialogue. Even when these moves are designed to put 'our own' categories to the test, it is rare to find informants' explicit reactions to the abstractions produced by anthropologists held up as evidence of the success of the account. As I argued in Chapter 7, the pronominal form of frontal comparison is not the second person, but rather the first-person plural. At this point, critics might start to suspect that the 'other' gets to object here merely as an object, not as a subject: once again, these critics might claim, (mostly northern and western) anthropologists seem to be building fictions on (mostly southern and non-western) others' backs without giving them a proper say!

And yet, conversely, experiments with dialogical writing since the 1980s have made clear that no amount of staging informants' voices within the ethnography can destabilise the authority of the anthropologist. Radically frontal comparatists might argue that to invite 'others' to have a say can all too often mean doing so in the terms set by 'our' language. The encounter between the anthropological expert, who has devised concepts to explain 'the other', and the 'informant', invited into the text to comment as the subject of those categories, is a peculiarly inegalitarian *mise-en-scène*. It is precisely against such theatrical 'dialogue' that the ontological turn and its predecessors have turned inwards, towards a challenge to anthropology's own sources of authority, its own settled explanatory devices. The hope is that this self-multiplication might produce a negative space in which others can come to articulate themselves *in their own terms*, rather than by commenting on 'our' anthropology's vision of them.[1]

This retort won't necessarily assuage the concerns of critics – they may point out that there is a bitter irony in the fact that 'turning inwards' has itself become an intensely authoritative move. But the upshot is that both sides are envisaging the problem in surprisingly analogous terms. Alone, the self-experimental rigour of the anthropologist is not enough. It always threatens to collapse into a form of one-sided monologue (cf. Lambek 1991). The aporia produced by Stengers's stringent requirement is one of the sharpest restatements of what in Chapter 1 I have called the problem of communication.

The key to unlocking this aporia is to remember that frontal comparisons never stand alone. Their escape from monological self-instantiation is due to the fact that their feet are still, despite everything, planted firmly in lateral comparison. At this point, however, we run into other problems. For in characterising the specific rigour required of lateral comparison, rigour in terms of the identification of objects and relations, we come straight back to the fundamental critiques articulated in Chapter 1. Rigour would seem to require something along the lines of correctly identifying objects and their predicates, properly distinguishing the respective role and reality of entities and relations, accurately mapping differences and similarities, or quite simply ensuring the accuracy of the 'reportage' (Runciman 1983) that people in this place tend to do or feel or say this or that. No form of anthropological comparison to date has managed to do without these sorts of basic descriptive claims, which inevitably take the form of caveated micro-generalisations. But their epistemic logic and their conditions of felicity tend to remain implicit. And we have hardly addressed Stengers's concerns, either.

This second problem is less paralysing, however, as soon as we realise that, unlike the rigour required of frontal comparison, the rigour required of lateral comparison is essentially collective. We will simply need to rethink our cast of characters. So far, we have written with one main protagonist in mind: the anthropologist. Chapters 7 and 8 introduced two further sets of characters: the people written about and the people written for. We saw how, over the course of the late twentieth century, it became clear that these two collectives could not be kept separate, ethically, politically or as a simple matter of fact. But their merging left us with an even starker opposition between the definitionally solitary anthropologist and everyone else. There is a conceptual affinity between this heroic vision and the devices of frontal comparison, since these turn on the scaling up of relations initially forged from the perspective of the I of the anthropologist, to various kinds of 'we'. Lateral comparisons, by contrast, entangle anthropologists in different sorts of collectivity: both the internal collectivities of the discipline, and other overlapping collectivities of expertise. Attending to these is a useful counterpoint to the excessive foregrounding of the normative figure of the anthropologist as heroic epistemic individual (see Chua and Mathur 2018: 3–4). It is in that latter guise that we might find a less aporetic place for taking seriously the sort of concerns raised by Stengers. As Gad and Bruun Jensen perceptively note, the worries raised by Stengers's demanding requirement begin 'to dissipate with the realisation that comparisons are at once omnipresent and multiple, immanent and cross-cutting, both among our informants and ourselves' (Gad and Bruun Jensen 2016: 15). In and of itself, the acknowledgement of the multiplicity of comparison both within and beyond anthropology has a soothing effect. But we can do more with this observation than dissipate worries, for in it, I will argue, lies the key to unlocking both the problem of communication and the problem of mapping. Doing so, however, will require an account of how the multiplicity of comparison can produce not just freedom, but also rigour.

## The Rigour of the Discipline

The dialogical or individual rigour outlined above is of course also a disciplinary matter. Indeed, if there is something like an *explicit* account of rigour in anthropology today, some criterion which most anthropologists would get behind either willingly, or if pressed, this probably turns on the need for an ethico-politico-epistemic concern with the relation between observer and observed – with the primarily individual or dialogical ethics and epistemics examined in the previous section, and the broader structural conditions of inequality which frame them. This kind of rigour is explicitly set out and collectively enforced in ethics codes and disciplinary associations.

As I noted in Chapter 2, however, the question of what makes lateral comparisons rigorous – so prominent for mid-twentieth-century anthropologists – seems to have rather fallen off the explicit agenda. Anthropologists do not share explicit criteria of what constitutes rigorous lateral comparison, nor do they seem at present particularly invested in seeking them. And yet, we evaluate each other's lateral comparisons all the time. What I have in mind here are not the kinds of 'evaluation' which consist in radical dismissive critiques of another's ends and purposes (Positivist! Deleuzian! Marxist!). As Fisher and Werner wisely wrote some time ago, 'any brand of anthropology can be shown to be woefully deficient if the objectives of one program of explanation are substituted for those of another explanatory program' (Fisher and Werner 1978: 194). Rather, I am thinking of the banal, everyday sense in which we cursorily judge each other's efforts – our assessment of the quality and richness of each other's 'reportage' (Runciman 1983), of the logic and coherence of each other's arguments, of the depth of each other's engagement with relevant literature, and so forth. That judgement happens daily in the practice of the discipline – in the seminars, edited volumes, conferences, peer-review, teaching and corridor conversations – in which anthropologists of radically different theoretical persuasions, who live and think in pursuit of often incommensurable goals, nevertheless work together. As Descola (2005a) puts it,

In their everyday practice, by contrast with their normative claims, anthropologists thus resort to very diverse methods and paradigms, the results of which are nevertheless commonly ratified as belonging to the discipline by the professional community that sustains its existence.

This is another version of the argument made so far, according to which, while our aims might be radically divergent, even incommensurable, our methods still form a common ground. There is still a sense in which anthropologists whose aims are radically different can agree that some comparisons are better crafted than others. That shared sense is the mark of the fact that we still have or 'are' a discipline, and it is one of the ways in which the shape and limits of that discipline are made visible. At the point at which one no longer feels able to *evaluate* another's method, one has reached a limit, a disciplinary boundary. My argument is that this limit, in anthropology at least, comes long after one has ceased to be able to relate to a colleague's aims.

This may seem a rose-tinted vision of the discipline. Many of us will, at some point or other, have encountered the avatars of the opposite – the incompetent and self-interested reviewer, the disengaged or overly interventionist journal editor, the cultish and uncomprehending seminar audience, the overly directive doctoral supervisor, or the departmental discussion of teaching which is entirely focused on formal indicators rather than substantive content. Of course anthropology is not just one happy family. But the very possibility of articulating such negative stereotypes makes my point. Recognisable negative stereotypes are one of the signs of a shared ethical conversation (Keane 2011). In the broadly shareable sense that these are all failings of a particular sort, we find the intimation of a vision of what a discipline *ought* to feel like. For these are not just failures of individual moral or intellectual character; they form a class insofar as they are failures of disciplinarity, moments when what ought to hold us together despite our differences is seen to be lacking.

The point applies also to the more profound critique that the disciplinary spaces I have invoked above are systemically skewed, for instance by the dominance of privileged actors in elite Euroamerican institutions (e.g. Chua and Mathur 2018). Implicit in these charges is a vision (again, assumed to be broadly shared) of what the discipline ought *not* to be like (intellectually blinkered, Eurocentric, internally hierarchised between 'theorists' and others, obsessed with novelty, etc.). Here again, specific critiques addressed by anthropologists to anthropology open up on to and help to constitute at least partly shared normative horizons.

To return to our specific topic, it would nevertheless be misleading to describe the sense of a lateral job well done as 'shared'. The reason it cannot be articulated as a single principle or as a checklist is that it is instantiated in practice in the sort of robustness which arises from the very subdivision of anthropologists into different national traditions, research programmes, thematic and regional specialisms.

This is a very different vision of what constitutes the rigour of a discipline from that imagined, for instance, by Hunt, namely a matter of 'established institutions which virtually freeze and bring under rational control ... semantic drift' (Hunt 2007: 57). Rather, as Abbott (2001) has suggested of academic disciplines more broadly, anthropology as a practice, a discipline, exists in the tension of its internal differences.

Anthropology is subdivided, not only into groups pursuing incommensurable ends and visions (heterology, generalisation, stabilisation, destabilisation ...), but also into groups constituted around the knowledge of particular areas and themes. Anthropology lives through the actual institutional spaces in which these differences are forged, sustained and exhibited – in seminars, in departments, in peer-reviewed journals, in book reviews, in conferences, edited volumes, and the like. It is in those spaces that questions of mapping are engaged collectively. Certainly, this doesn't equate to a progressive, rational stabilisation, a cumulative elimination of semantic drift. It remains an open-ended process in which terms, examples and concerns are trafficked within and between subdisciplinary collectives whose boundaries and areas of expertise are slowly reshaped in the process. At any given point in time, however, the set-up ensures that a given anthropological comparison will have to be subjected to multiple challenges and tests, from different directions. That complex and shifting intersection of forms of expertise constitutes the immanent normativity of anthropological practice – the rigour of the discipline.

Amongst the many such cross-cutting vectors of difference – including national traditions, conceptual schools, political imaginaries – I would like to focus on one: the subdivision of the discipline into collectives of expertise constituted around particular areas and themes. At its core lies the classic anthropological device which one might call the 'place–concept binary'. As Annelin Eriksen (forthcoming) notes, anthropologists usually go *somewhere*, to study *something*. This is a two-pronged affair: concepts (whether as categories, traits, themes or topics) play the role of cutting across places. Places, by contrast, cut through these conceptual moves, grounding, multiplying and specifying them (Candea 2007: 180, 182). One classic way of deploying this contrast is to identify the same concepts in different places – cross-cousin marriage, for instance, emerging here and there (Lévi-Strauss 1969). Another, now just as classic, is to imagine 'other' places breaking down 'our' concepts – as when we find that 'society' or 'nature' has no purchase on Mount Hagen (Strathern 1980, 1988). These map on to ideal-typical versions of the lateral and the frontal comparative heuristics, respectively. But these two moves do not by any means exhaust the potential of the place–concept binary. Anthropologists have also imagined concepts travelling through places, changing as they go (Howe and Boyer 2015), or places acting as arbitrary, partial or equivocal locations for rethinking conceptual entities and their interactions (Candea 2007; Cook et al. 2009; see also Gluckman 1958; Heywood 2015; Van Velsen 1967).

What remains fairly stable, however, despite these various intellectual acrobatics, is the fact that the place–concept binary organises (at least) two audiences for any anthropological argument, (at least) two communities of practice to which any writing can potentially be addressed. In very schematic terms these could be thought of as regionalist and thematic audiences. (For a detailed account of how these interlock in one case, see Candea 2016a.) However much anthropologists may rile against these – politically, conceptually and morally loaded – distinctions, they continue, for now, to organise our teaching, our institutional structures of recognition and reward, and most of all, our publication. Who hasn't had the experience of wondering whether to send a particular article to a 'generalist' or to a 'regional' journal? Most of us write with both of these imagined audiences in mind, albeit not equally in any given piece. The place–concept binary is rooted in the organisation of our disciplinary communities of practice (cf. Abbott 2004).

Of course, the regionalism of anthropological thinking has often been an object of disciplinary self-critique. Taken as fixed locations for particular theories – hierarchy in India, lineage in Africa, dividuals in Melanesia – regions have often been described as stultifying (Appadurai 1988a, 1988b; Fardon 1990). But as Englund and Yarrow note, if regions imagined as self-evident contexts in the world can be stultifying, regionalism deployed as a conscious device has specific potential.

Ethnographically, this leads us to consider logics and practices that spatially co-exist without relating. Theoretically, this regional framing points to the reflexive decomposition, differentiation, and recomposition of concepts, even as particular analysts disagree as to what might be important – or even the case – about any given place. Anthropologists need to allow places to put limits on their ethnographic and theoretical artifacts even as they recognize their own role in the construction of both.

(Englund and Yarrow 2013: 145)

The articulation of overlapping regional, theoretical and thematic collectives within anthropology – with each individual anthropologist multiply situated in one or more of each – provides both a set of cross-cutting forms of rigour and a set of fire-breaks or releases. Thus, on the one hand, any given comparison will be judged by a cross-cutting set of experts with different challenging standards. Specialists of the region will ask whether the ethnography sounds roughly reliable; specialists of particular themes will hold the author to account for engaging or not with the relevant literature. These comparisons will also be buffeted, more or less productively, by readers and listeners with diverse theoretical bees in their bonnets: some will push for more rigorous definitions, others for more reflexivity, others for a greater sensitivity to the way seeming objects are actually emptied out into flows, others still for an awareness of recurrent patterns of inequality or suffering.

The relation works both ways. If these communities of practice within anthropology strengthen and thicken our comparisons, it is precisely through our lateral comparisons that they are constituted and reconstituted. The subdivision of anthropology into multiple bodies of regional and thematic expertise is not a fixed, stable ground, a preliminary to the proper work of comparison. As Englund and Yarrow note, 'our sense of a world comprised of distinct regions is an artifact of comparison' (Englund and Yarrow 2013: 136). The same is true of the constantly shifting division of anthropology into collectives of regional (and thematic) specialists. That dispensation, too, is also an artefact of (lateral) comparison.

This subdivision is both a tool for control and a tool for extension, both a check and a release. On the one hand, the rigour of anthropological comparison is the resulting effect of these multiple cross-cutting challenges and critiques – often internalised and borne in mind by any single anthropologist as she or he compares and writes, even before anyone else has actually seen or heard the result. On the other hand, these cross-cutting communities of practice allow for the bracketing of some problems, which can be left to others. Not every term can be defined, not every concept worked out in any given account. References can do that work for us, and the empirical robustness of ethnographic accounts from other regions can be bracketed and its judgement left to others. The bottom line is this: we encounter the problems and potentials of lateral comparison, not alone, but as a (multiply and productively subdivided) collective.

The vision might – once again – seem naive. Isn't this a vision of anthropology as it was, perhaps twenty, thirty or more years ago, before the conjoined pressures of enforced interdisciplinarity, university administration dissolving and reorganising departments, audits and research assessment exercises and the like? Certainly, these developments work directly against the kind of disciplinary rigour I am outlining here, as Yarrow (forthcoming) has argued. By privileging that which is, in each discipline, the most general and immediately 'translatable', relevant and accessible to those with no specialist background, these various techniques of commensuration represent a frontal attack on specifically disciplinary expertise. They place value in brittle and sharp claims to theoretical innovation, 'world-leading' research, the 'radical' and the 'transformative'. What is devalued is precisely the painstaking work of ethnographic description, regionally focused scholarship, slow argument, difficult knowledge, and so forth, in which the distinctively disciplinary rigour of anthropology is grounded.

I agree, in other words, that the vision of disciplinary rigour I am describing here is a vision under threat. The above pressures have been exerted more or less drastically in different national and institutional contexts. To some readers these will seem like rumblings of future trouble; to others, they will occupy the foreground, and the vision of anthropology evoked here will already seem to be a thing of the past. To present this vision as a thing of the present is the mark of a hope, a rhetorical strategy and a political commitment. But it is also a recognition that the waters of disciplinarity run deep. As Abbott noted (2001: 122), the notion of 'interdisciplinarity' has been shadowing that of disciplinarity since as early as the 1920s. These challenges have been with us for some time. The micro-structure of disciplinary robustness is still deeply grounded in our everyday activities and assumptions, even though it will certainly not hurt to be more explicit in valuing it. This is one of the key purposes of this book.

## The Rigour of the World

The resistances created within anthropology map a particular kind of rigour, and a particular kind of solidity. Problems of mapping are, from the start, collective ones, and our cross-cutting specialisms and concerns contribute to keeping us on our toes. But anthropologists do not, however, just talk amongst themselves – even though they are sometimes accused of doing precisely that. Rather, they are thrown into a world already replete with categories, objects, relations, differences and similarities. Even a cursory glance at the actual history of anthropology's development as a discipline dissipates the vision of an epistemically self-sufficient academic community. Anthropological knowledge has always been in and of the world, crafted in particular places and through particular tensions and politics; more pointedly, its authority, including as regional knowledge, has always been grounded in collaboration and tension with occasionally invisible 'informants' and 'field assistants', as studies such as Schumaker's *Africanizing anthropology* (2001) make clear. And this was true long before anthropologists came to worry explicitly about the public reach of their concepts and categories in the world (Grillo 2003; Munasinghe 2008).

All of this is well known. But one interesting correlate of this point is that, properly considered, it makes one of the key difficulties of lateral comparison fall away. Indeed, it is hard to imagine how lateral comparison would ever get off the ground if it required, as a preliminary, a full definition of all the objects and predicates upon which comparison would bear, either by the individual anthropologist or by the discipline as a whole (cf. Spiro 1966: 91). Luckily for us, just as no single anthropological argument needs to be the final word, no single comparison needs to be the first word either. We are entering into a conversation which extends well beyond the discipline and was begun long ago. We may reconfigure or reject some of its terms, or introduce new ones, but we do not need to craft everything anew.

To illustrate this point, consider the various categories and comparative terms invoked in a single anthropological argument – chosen here for its typicality in this respect, rather than for any other reason: Mayanthi Fernando's (2010) article on French secularism and veiling debates. Fernando extends to France a particular kind of frontal comparison initially crafted by Talal Asad (2003) and developed by Saba Mahmood (2005). These are comparisons between the core conceptual, moral, or indeed 'ontological' (Fadil and Fernando 2015) principles of secular modernity and those of (reformist) Islam, imagined as 'traditions' in the sense of Macintyre (cf. Laidlaw 2014; MacIntyre 2013). As with the ontological turn, these arguments have faced the critique that their stark frontal contrasts minimise the difference both within Islamic everyday life (e.g. Marsden 2005; Schielke 2009) and within modern secular visions of freedom (Laidlaw 2014). And the response has been, similarly, to point to the formal and critical nature of these contrasts, while strenuously denying a vision of substantive 'billiard-ball' entities. The figure of an oscillation captures the difficulties and the potential of this position, even though the precise form of the oscillation is not the same as in the work of, say, Dumont or Strathern.

Carrying some of these arguments to the French context, Fernando examines tensions between French secularist understandings of freedom and the aspirations of some Muslim citizens, whose sense that veiling involves a complex mutual entailment of freedom and obligation cannot be articulated publicly without raising fears of religious extremism. I will not retrace the details of Fernando's fascinating argument here. Rather, I am interested in the kinds of entities her account summons up. Aside from the frontal constitution of a secularism–Islam contrast which operates at a high level of conceptual abstraction and systematisation, Fernando also invokes 'units' of different types. One is the unit constituted by her actual informants, rather than pious French Muslims in general, whom she characterises in the following way:

As in the rest of the Middle East and North Africa, the Islamic revival in France encompasses a broad swathe of doctrinal trends, ethical, religious, and political sensibilities, and ritual and hermeneutical practices. Moreover, in France, this diversity is complicated by generational divergences. I therefore do not ascribe the particular religious subjectivity under discussion to all participants in the Islamic revival (and certainly not to all Muslims in France). Most of my interlocutors for this article were 'second generation,' that is, the children of immigrants from the Maghreb and, to a lesser extent, sub-Saharan Africa; a few were converts (or 'reverts'). All of them had been born or grown up in France in the blue-collar suburbs (*banlieues*) of Paris, Rennes, Nantes, and Lyon. In addition, though their parents were or had been part of a proletarian workforce, most of my interlocutors had or were studying for post-secondary-school degrees, often in communications, accounting, or social work. The practices and sensibilities I describe here, then, are particularly salient to those I call 'Muslim citizens,' that is, women and men committed to practicing Islam as French citizens and to practicing French citizenship as Muslims, women and men who often identify as *citoyens français de confession musulmane* (French citizens of Muslim faith) and who comprise a demographically and politically significant aspect of the revival.

(Fernando 2010: 20)

What I am interested in here is the way in which Fernando's account takes up pre-existing entities of different kinds, originating from within anthropology, from other disciplines, and from the world beyond academia. Some, like the frontal contrast between Islam and secularism, have been articulated by a particular conceptual school within anthropology. She shores these up, with some minor modifications. Others, like the terms of class, occupation, age and so forth, are common sociological building blocks, from which she crafts a new bespoke object – 'those I will call "Muslim citizens"'. Some, like 'Islamist fundamentalism' as depicted in French popular discourses, are treated as incorrect and illusory categorisations which a more careful examination will allow her to unpick. Others still, like 'French popular discourses', Europe, religion, family or television, are objects out there in the world which are brought in to play the stabilising role they do in many such accounts – although in other accounts, of course, they can each come under scrutiny and find themselves unpicked.

This observation allows me to extend the point made in the previous section. Anthropologists do not simply shape and dispute their 'objects of comparison' amongst themselves. All of these operations upon objects and predicates are done, not only under the watchful eyes of disciplinary colleagues, but also and increasingly, through the watchful eyes of readers beyond the discipline: sociologists, historians, and – first and foremost – those once known as 'informants', who are increasingly being recognised as experts, collaborators and critics – para-ethnographers in their own right (Holmes and Marcus 2005; Howe and Boyer 2015). Increasingly, anthropologists are being figured as operators who take up concepts in the world, modify them and put them back. Moving beyond Evans-Pritchard's vision of a set of anthropologists sharing a set of problems and terms, a disciplinary and a cultural background, this increasingly intricate set of conversations in and beyond the discipline can give rise to a multiplicity of visions of collaboration and critique, as perspectives are shared across, from and in tension with multiple disciplinary and cultural hinterlands. Again, as in the disciplinary case, this cross-cutting expertise is both a constraint (comparisons need to withstand multiple tests) and a facility: we don't start from scratch, or need to create a world anew for the purpose of each argument. Rather, we work with what we are given, and redescribe it incrementally.

In sum, anthropological comparisons need to pass the robustness test, not only of differently situated colleagues within the discipline, but also of colleagues in other disciplines and of people directly invested in the subject of the account. Thus reframed as one constraint amongst many, Stengers's question of whether the 'parties' to the comparison have been allowed to object can be taken seriously, without becoming paralysing.

For many of us, the fact that our ethnographic interlocutors feel that what we write about them makes sense will constitute a fundamental criterion, even where this is in tension with the view of colleagues or other experts. And yet, there may be settings – most obviously, but not only, when one is 'studying up' – in which providing an account that is convincing to colleagues but may seem arcane, irrelevant or even downright critical to 'informants' may well be a mark of rigour. More profoundly, Stengers's stern admonishments write past the fact that there are often many 'parties' in any single ethnographic setting, whose senses of what the 'relevant criteria' are may well be profoundly at odds. This multiplication of the problem is, in its own way, the path towards a solution (Gad and Bruun Jensen 2016: 15).

This entanglement of anthropologists with the world at large has been much discussed in connection with advocacy, engagement, critique and collaboration. But writing in science studies suggests that we might cast our net more widely even than this. In considering the ways in which the world can inflect, control and resist anthropologists' comparisons, we might recall that the world isn't just made of people – interlocutors, informants, collaborators, experts or critics. Things too, objects, processes, relations, can enable, scaffold or resist our comparisons. In the revisions of the criteria for good science, proposed by authors such as Stengers or Latour, for instance, 'objects' are any thing which is allowed to object. Scientific 'objectivity', on this view,

does not attribute to the subject the right to know an object, but to the object the power (to be constructed) to put the subject to the test. This is thus the abstract definition of the singular rarity of the modern scientific practices I will propose: if it is no longer a question of vanquishing the power of fiction, it is always a question of putting it to the test, of subjecting the reasons we invent to a third party capable of putting them at risk. In other words, it is always a question of inventing practices that will render our opinions vulnerable in relation to something that is irreducible to another opinion.

(Stengers 2000: 139)

Stengers herself, in her ambitious overview of the sciences, has – somewhat narrowly to my mind – allotted to anthropology the role of studying human collectives. In this view anthropology might indeed collapse into mere diplomacy (Stengers 2011; cf. Latour 2013) – a matter of negotiations with human representatives of particular groups about the way these groups are to be represented. But anthropologists know this is rarely the case, in any straightforward sense: within any people there are other people (Candea 2011), and anthropology as the representation of homogeneous human groups has long ago ceased to be the main vision of what the discipline is about. As often as not, anthropologists, like sociologists or historians, compare not people, even less 'peoples', but a range of other entities: patterns, processes, styles, techniques, concepts, objects. Finding ways to give this broader set of entities the power to put our representations to the test – the power to object – is thus not merely a matter of identifying the appropriate human authority figure who can speak for them. The productive thickness of comparison, as Scheffer and Niewöhner point out, is in part an effect of 'the process of letting the world help to build and relate objects of comparison to each other and to the researchers' (Scheffer and Niewöhner 2010: 5).

## Conclusion

This chapter began with the challenge of identifying the distinctive types of rigour which attach, respectively, to frontal and lateral comparisons. We could summarise its argument by saying that, while frontal comparisons require a particular kind of individual rigour, lateral comparisons draw their rigour from the way they are embedded in broader cross-cutting communities of practice and interest. The division and lumping of lateral comparison, the identification of objects, predicates and relations, takes place from a third-party perspective, which is crucially a collective one: the collective perspective of anthropologists talking to each other both within and beyond their areas of specialism. And of course, this procedure simultaneously makes, unmakes and remakes the geographic and thematic 'specialisms' to which these anthropologists belong. Lateral comparisons necessarily come with the caveat of an only temporary stabilisation – they invite more lateral challenge.

In sum, the problems of mapping are never encountered *alone*. If one imagines lateral comparison as a matter of an anthropologist, on their own, first identifying all the relevant objects and predicates, and then proceeding to compare them, then it would be impossible. But this is not the situation. Rather anthropologists are thrown into a world of categories, terms, units and processes – some circulating within the confines of the discipline, some already at work in the wider world – and they muddle through with what they are given. Lateral comparisons unmake some objects, modify others, seek to identify some new ones. Two problems introduced in Chapter 1 as each insuperable on its own – the problem of mapping and the problem of purpose – thus emerge here as solutions to one another.

Nor is the discipline itself tasked with doing this alone. Our comparisons are buffeted by the requirements and challenges of different anthropologists, yes, but also beyond that, of academics from other disciplines, and beyond that of different people, including those anthropologists work with, and beyond that still, of a world of things that object. Like the internal resistances of anthropology, these external resistances put our comparisons to the test, and in the process, strengthen them. This is important, for even a 'community of critics' (Strathern 2006) such as that constituted by a discipline cannot be relied upon blindly[2]– an overly cosy disciplinarity can breed false robustness. The further tests of our comparisons as they travel (or not) beyond the discipline add a salutary corrective, even though they can never substitute, as in managerial visions of 'interdisciplinarity', for the rigour of the discipline.

Having reached this point, we can now acknowledge that an initial contrast was overdrawn. Imagining the respective rigour of lateral and frontal comparison in terms of a stark binary between two immiscible practices was of course a rhetorical facility. Little would be lost if we thought of this particular distinction as a matter of degree (Quine 1951: 43). For, after all, anthropologists also control and extend each other's conceptual inventions. As Abbott puts it, '[w]henever it comes, the ability of others to restate your idea clearly is the watershed' (Abbott 2004: 225, and more generally 221–226). Conversely we often give each other a pass on matters of empirical description (since after all each one of us has 'their' field) – or to put the point otherwise, we tend to implicitly expect each other to exercise an individual commitment to representational rigour and sincerity even when we are not being cross-checked. The stark initial distinction between individual and collective forms of rigour was thus a device for introducing a broader vision – that of different cross-cutting tests of robustness. Having got to that point, we can let go of the binary crutch. What is left is the sense of comparisons being strengthened, tested and extended from a range of different directions, by the objections we encounter, in the world, in our colleagues and in ourselves.

This vision in turn entails a broader, normative observation about what makes a good comparison. This observation, which is in effect the conclusion of the book, belongs there.

∾

# Conclusion

Far from being directed by certain criteria, it is comparison which will produce the criterion, the formative idea. The solidity of my work rests entirely on this point. I have no idea, comparison provides it.

(Dumont 1991: 8)

It is a well-founded historical generalization, that the last thing to be discovered in any science is what the science is really about.

(Whitehead 1958: 167)

## Good Comparisons are Comparisons that Object

This book's discussion has mainly been descriptive, rather than normative. I have tried to work from the rich material provided by anthropologists' discussions of comparison, to detect in this entangled discussion the lineaments of some archetypal moves. Even in discussing normativity in the previous chapter, I have been in an important sense descriptive, arguing that anthropologists' practice is already implicitly normative, that our discipline already contains a sense of what makes some comparisons better than others, a sense which is increasingly being worked out, not just in relation to other anthropologists, but in confrontation with the cross-cutting requirements of a wider world.

This being said, my argument so far has actually carried a normative undertow, which it is finally time to consider explicitly. This has

347

consisted in an appeal to the benefits of thickness and intricacy. In the context of anthropological discussions, it is easy to invoke 'thickness' as a good (Geertz 1973c; Scheffer and Niewöhner 2010). To call an epistemic device 'thick' is to set it alongside motherhood and apple pie. But there are different kinds of thickness. One kind of 'thickening', for instance, explicitly outlined by Aristotle, turns on introducing intermediary premises between a premise and a conclusion, thereby lengthening a chain of deductions (Aristotle 1994: 35; cf. Byrne 1997: 118–121). This thickening can be a way of making things explicit in a scientific argument or, on the contrary, it can be a way of dissimulating one's ultimate purpose from a contradictor whom one wishes to trap in their logical aporias (Aristotle 1997: 154–155). Another, very different kind of thickness is evoked by the metaphor of a many-stranded rope, a rope which still holds even when one or more of its strands break. This is the classic vision of inductive 'robustness' (Wimsatt 2007) and of an epistemology of family resemblances (Wittgenstein 1973). The Geertzian thickness of description (Geertz 1973c) is something else again: a matter of layering interpretations upon one another to evoke and hopefully reproduce the concomitant richness of human meaningful experience.[1]

So let us pause to pick out the specific sense in which thickness features as a good for comparison in the present argument – and the limits of that evaluation. We first encountered this theme in relation to the key building block of our archetype, namely *comparatio* (in Chapter 4). The peculiar tempo of *comparatio*, its willingness to take time, to keep in view both analogies and contrasts, was amplified, chapter by chapter, as we added the willingness to keep in view both relations and entities, and later, both frontal encounters and lateral mappings. The final archetype we arrived at, at the end of the last chapter, is defined by the intricacy of our three basic contrasts – similarity and difference, things and relations, objects and subjects. By contrast to this intricacy and thickness of the archetype, I have described as a process of 'reduction' the crafting of thinner comparisons, those which are sharpened to the point of an analogy or a contrast, for instance, as they move towards a particular political or epistemic horizon (identity, alterity, intensity or subjectivity). As it reaches those horizons themselves, comparison peters out: these are, as we saw, 'ends' of comparison in the sense of both purposes and extinctions. In sum, comparison happens in the middle of the three-dimensional space, and the closer it is to that middle – in one very particular sense, which remains to be made explicit – the better.

The language of intensity (see Chapter 5) will serve us to articulate this sense. Insofar as we are speaking of comparing actual comparisons to an archetype, we might say that the closer a comparison sits to the middle of our three-dimensional space (Figure 7.2), the thicker it is, the more a comparison becomes an instance of itself. The thicker a comparison, the more intensely *comparative* it is. The better it is, then, not in general, or even as a tool for knowledge in general, but at one particular thing, which is at being an anthropological comparison.

To some, this proclivity for middling solutions, away from extremes, will seem tiresome, if not pusillanimous. Surely, the horizon is where it's at, whether this horizon is radical alterity, perpetual intensification, the vertigo of solipsism, or some combination of the three – or, to the contrary, if it involves the accurate objective mapping of identities which provides a cumulative grasp on more and more facts about the world. Surely, whatever our purposes, we should be working to sharpen our comparisons to a point, not to keep them thick and pointlessly intricate?

I agree that dwelling in intricacy for its own sake is tedious. It recalls the knee-jerk invocation of 'complexity' to block any attempt at reduction (Dan-Cohen 2017). That is precisely why I am invoking intricacy here not as an all-purpose good, but just as a good *for comparisons*. It may well be good practice for any particular *argument* to be intensely comparative for a while and then be increasingly reductive until it reaches a particular point. I am proposing not that we dwell in intensely thick comparison for ever, but rather that we first construct intricate comparisons, that we commit to spooling out the potential of the initial contrast or analogy which caught our eye, and then, having done so, struggle against these thick comparisons, sharpen them back down to a point to reach our aims.

This might seem like a counter-intuitive procedure. Why not simply get to the point? What it speaks to is the sense that to be animated by a purpose, to set a course for a particular horizon, is not the same as just imagining one has reached it. In that latter belief lies the risk of dwelling in platitudes and truisms. There is a classic Romanian anecdote in which an old hermit returns to his village after fifty years spent in a cave, entirely devoted to pondering upon the meaning of life. He calls the villagers, announces that he has found the answer. Eagerly, the villagers gather around as the old man, pointing to the fountain in the village square, slowly and profoundly declares that 'life is like a fountain'. After a moment of silence during which many villagers nod pensively, one young boy steps forward and says, dismissively: 'No it's not!' The hermit, pondering for a moment replies, 'Fair enough.' Shrugging their shoulders, the villagers scatter.

By themselves, our horizons have little power to either convince or illuminate. After all, we can already see them from here. Certainly, from some perspective or other everything can be said to be alterity, or intensity, or identity, or subjectivity. So what? Of course, life is in some sense like a fountain, and also not. To take a classic recent instance, non-dualism in its various forms has been an ever-repeated rallying call for many anthropologists over the past thirty years: do away with a dualism (be it nature and culture, representation and reality, objects and relations, objects and subjects, etc.) and you will finally reach ... what? Mostly, a specific reconsideration of a particular case, and a general proposition that, in some vague sense, everything is everything. The former result is often interesting and shareable, the latter less so; sadly, the attention is often focused on the latter.

The flight to the horizon is often paired with a vague feeling that there has been too much constraint, too much method, too much in the way of gazing at 'our own devices'. As Miyazaki perceptively noted, a particular 'aesthetic of emergence' has taken hold in many quarters in anthropology since the 1980s, in which anthropological knowledge is envisaged as part of the emergent complexity and indeterminacy of the world (Miyazaki 2004: 130–140). This anthropological aesthetic values analyses which are provisional and indeterminate, in order to match the perceived provisionality and indeterminacy of the world itself. The result is a focus on documenting complex shifting relations, envisioning the mutual constitution of all things, and refusing to enter into clear attributions of causality or agency (Miyazaki 2004: 136). The effect of this aesthetic, Miyazaki fears, is the loss of a certain kind of hope in knowledge. Where anthropologists once put their hope in their own knowledge production, whose devices they permanently sought to revise, rethink and perfect in order to keep track of a changing world, the aesthetic of emergence lets the world do the work, as it were. It falls to the world itself to drag our knowledge forward through its own ever-changing nature (Miyazaki 2004: 139). All we have to do in the meantime, it seems, is refrain from saying anything too specific. Life is like a fountain.

Miyazaki's diagnosis points to the unravelling of the disciplinary move imagined by Evans-Pritchard (Chapter 1). Evans-Pritchard had envisioned anthropologists as able to move away from a naive empiricism, as long as they could agree to study problems, not peoples or cultural traits. This involved interposing a *discipline* – a set of shared problems, units and categories – between the endeavours of individual scholars and the pull of the world. The coordination of anthropology would be a matter for the epistemic decisions of a professional human collective, not simply the effect of studying the same world. And yet we saw how his own caesurism undercut that vision at the very moment at which he articulated it. The vision of anthropology as a discipline in full agreement on its shared problems, categories and ends was already a mirage as soon as it was articulated.

## Conclusion

The present account takes this point on board and yet its inspiration remains at odds with the aesthetic of emergence. This is an argument for seeing value in the heaping on of dualisms, intricately recombined with one another into multiform comparative devices; value in the explicit consideration of method, and in the self-limitations which such consideration entails. And it sees value, most of all, in the aim of saying something specific about comparative particulars, beyond quick and programmatic analogies and contrasts. It envisions as the archetypal comparisons those whose 'result is not a little formula tossed off in passing, a figure of style, but a long, complete development' (Goyet 2014: 160).

This normative valuation of intricacy echoes Wimsatt's principle of 'robustness'. Robust combinations of heuristics come at the same questions from different angles; they are interwoven in such a way that some can fail without sabotaging the entire enterprise. As we saw in Chapter 3, however, robustness as articulated by philosophers of science such as Wimsatt is implicitly wedded to one particular aim: the pursuit of the real, the objective and the generalisable. The kind of robustness envisaged here, by contrast, could be deployed in pursuit of a broader range of aims. Indeed it would come in part from the way in which anthropologists, aiming in radically different directions (towards generalisation or critique, objective identifications or increasing self-doubt), work alongside one another and hold each other to account, not only for their divergent aims, but also for their moves in a shared space of method. Comparisons which stand the test of these multiple cross-cutting critiques will be robust.

Of course, as I argued in the previous chapter, the world too is full of purposes, and much of what we do as anthropologists will be to follow and trace and wait for these to guide us, be it through the voices of expert informant para-ethnographers, or through the evidence of unfolding things and relations. But we also have our own devices, those we build at our own pace and under our own steam – whether these be the near and the far, methodological ejection, pedagogy or any of the other devices encountered in these pages. The strength of these devices lies to a great extent in their ability to interfere with our initial hunches and desires. This is why we ought to build comparisons which have their own resistance, independent of our ends. Comparisons which are intricate enough to object, to slow us down, to throw up all sorts of entanglements and complications even as we crave for a neat reduction. Whether we are trying to demonstrate the same process at work in those different things, or the inanity of this generalisation, or the limits of that taken-for-granted assumption, a slow, thick, intricate comparison will get us there, but it will also point out that this process actually plays out in two different ways, that there was a grain of truth to this generalisation, that the assumption actually did some useful work.

In other words – and that is the key to their value not just in themselves, but for us – good comparisons tend to give us more than what we aimed for. Whatever your ends might be, craft comparisons which are robust and intricate enough to *object* to them – that is the key normative injunction which this book has argued for and which, in the texture of its own comparative devices, it has sought to exemplify.

## Coda: Views from the Fence

Still, all the while, like warp and woof, mechanism and teleology are interwoven together, and we must not cleave to the one nor despise the other.

(Thompson 1961: 5)

This book was intended in part as a rebalancing act. One can read in it a gentle critique of tendencies to rush to extremes. If the gentleness were scrubbed away and one wished to make the point sharp, it might sound something like this: too much focus on the heady conceptual excitement of frontal comparison has sometimes made us lose sight of the fundamental value of the lateral, and too much caesurism has

## Conclusion

interfered with our ability to attend to our shared heuristics. I have developed those points in a more critical form elsewhere (Candea 2016b, 2016a). One might connect these points to the more despondent vision of the state of anthropology alluded to in the previous chapter, as a discipline under threat, one whose distinctive ways of making good knowledge are being undermined by external commensurating forces. Clearly, in that bleaker vision, those internal tendencies of the discipline are part of the problem rather than the solution (cf. Yarrow forthcoming).

But I have avoided that tone here, because I do not wish to suggest that what anthropological comparison requires is (once again) a swing away from one direction into another direction, another fractal reversal of our priorities, a new bearing. For there is no salvation in the lateral without the frontal, in heuristics without caesuras, or in means without end (Agamben 2000). Anthropological comparison doesn't need to be set on a new course. What is needed, rather, is a revaluation of the things we already do well – our mechanisms, to reprise Thompson's distinction – and an acknowledgement of the multiplicity of courses we already pursue – our teleologies. Some may see this as sitting on the fence. To this I would answer that, from that position, surprisingly radical possibilities can be glimpsed.

# Notes

## Preface: What We Know in our Elbows

1 For some thoughts on what is and is not implied by my use of that 'we', please see the final section of the introduction.
2 The reference here is of course to Wagner (1981) and, more obliquely, to Holbraad and Pedersen (2017).
3 Short sections from the original 2016 paper, in translation and with various revisions, are repurposed in Chapters 1, 3 and 7 of the present book. A full and slightly revised translation of the original paper has been published as Candea (2018d).

## Introduction

1 See, for instance, Burawoy (2009), Choy (2011), Descola (2005b), Detienne (2008), Gingrich and Fox (2002a), Handler (2009), Herzfeld (2001), Holbraad and Pedersen (2017), Iteanu and Moya (2015), Jensen et al. (2011), McLean (2013), Moore (2005), Scheffer and Niewöhner (2010), Strathern (2004), Van der Veer (2016), Viveiros de Castro (2004), and Yengoyan (2006b). For a more systematic characterisation of the contemporary renewal of interest in comparison, see Chapter 2, fork 6.
2 Comparison is 'a generic aspect of human thought' (Lewis 1955: 259), or 'an essential element of human life and cognition' (Gingrich and Fox 2002b: 20), 'implicit in any method of deriving understanding through explanation' (Peel 1987: 89); 'there is nothing the human mind is more prone to than to draw comparisons' (Detienne 2008: ix). Surprising as it might seem, one can even go further, since 'All animal life makes constant comparisons of the environment' (Hunt 2007: ix). Lloyd (2015) is a book-length argument for the universality of comparison (for humans at least).
3 Writing only of the period 1950–1954, Lewis found he had to discuss twenty-eight separate works which sought to explicitly theorise anthropological comparison (Lewis 1955: 262–263).

4 Concepts, including those of other anthropologists and my own coinage, will be coming thick and fast. While there is no glossary, readers will find all of the key terms in the index.

5 For a different invocation of the notion of 'lateral comparison', see Gad (2012) and Gad and Bruun Jensen (2016). Indeed, what Gad and Bruun-Jensen term 'lateral comparison' is in fact precisely what I would term 'frontal comparison'. My own invocation of the lateral is closer in spirit to Howe and Boyer's notion of 'lateral theory' (Howe and Boyer 2015; see also Ingold 1993).

6 For a close parallel, see Knorr-Cetina (1999: 267–268).

# 1 The Impossible Method

1 A focus on continua instead of classification 'achieves relational precision at the expense of taxonomic precision' (Wagner 1977: 385–386; cf. Strathern 2004: xiv).

2 See for instance Chakrabarty (2007); Franklin and McKinnon (2001); Schneider (1984).

# 2 The Garden of Forking Paths

1 indeed, even Lewis's own attempt to multiply comparisons ultimately resolves into a broad opposition between comparisons of the 'near' and the 'far' (see below).

2 For partly similar devices used to a different effect, see Strathern (2004: xxiv), and also Abbott (2004, chapter 6).

3 A thorough answer to the question of whether and in what sense anthropological knowledge can be said to be inductive is beyond the scope of this book. Certainly, if we take induction to cover all non-deductive inference (Lipton 2004: 5), then it will play a major role in anthropological as in all other forms of knowledge. Since I have invoked Mill, I will just note in passing – as a placeholder for future exploration – that I for one find Lipton's version of induction as inference to the best explanation (Lipton 2004: 5), also known as 'abduction' (cf. Gell 1998: 15), to be a more convincing account of the actual structure of most anthropological inductions than Mill's model of causal inference. Yet Mill's methods of induction capture some fundamental structural features of the use of comparison in anthropology.

4 There is a deeper history here. For at the heart of the method of concomitant variation lay the canonical formula of 'proportional analogy', from Aristotle's topics: 'the formulae being "A:B = C:D" (e.g. as knowledge stands to the object of knowledge, so is sensation related to the object of sensation), and "As A is in B, so is C in D" (e.g. as sight is in the eye, so is reason in the soul, and as is a calm in the sea, so is windlessness in the air)' (Aristotle 1997: 1.16; cf. Gross 2001). One

central use of proportional analogy in Aristotle, to which we shall return, was in his biology, where it served to grasp similarities – in particular similarities of function – across genera (Lloyd 2015: 79–83).

5 Tyler's article forms the historical starting point of a number of recent discussions of anthropological comparatism (Handler 2009; Strathern 2004: 49).

6 One might think here of Tylor: 'during many years I have been collecting the evidence found among between three and four hundred people' (Tylor 1889: 245–246). That being said, Tylor himself was already well aware of the need to keep a critical eye on the varying quality of people–person reports (see for instance Tylor 1871: 219 on Tongan numerals).

7 As Nadel points out, however, Durkheim hardly followed his own pronouncements about quantity. If one term in the series (say 'condensation') could be imagined as quantifiable, albeit never in fact quantified, the other (such as forms of religion, or personhood) could be described as changing in qualitative terms only (Nadel 1951: 223).

8 Or indeed for the same scholars at different points in their careers, as Eggan shows for Ruth Benedict (Eggan 1954: 750).

9 For another account which links Boas to Foucauldian genealogy, see Bunzl (2004).

10 We shall see below that a number of historians of biology have parsed the story slightly differently (Amundson 1998).

11 Note, however – and we shall appreciate the importance of this distinction below – what are envisaged here are primarily typologies of traits, institutions and relations, not typologies of whole societies.

12 To get a clear sense of all that separates this typological use of distant and regional comparison, from the method of concomitant variation, one might turn for instance to an argument which self-consciously combines both methods: see Nadel (1952).

13 Gell's distinction echoes the Humean division between 'relations of ideas' and 'matters of fact' (Hume 1993: 15) and the related philosophical contrast between intension and extension (see also Holbraad and Pedersen 2017: 188; Quine 1951).

14 Albeit not all – Amundson noted that a number of Edinburgh-trained biologists were structuralists.

15 The French functionalist Cuvier being one stand-out exception.

16 Thompson, who was a classicist as well as a biologist, drew explicitly on the Aristotelian principle that variation within kinds is merely a matter of increase and decrease (Thompson 1961: 273; for a discussion of uses of analogy in Aristotle's biology, see Lloyd 2015: 79–83).

17 Compare, for instance: 'In an organism, great or small, it is not merely the nature of *motions* of the living substance which we must interpret in terms of force (according to kinetics), but also the *conformation* of the organism itself, whose permanence or equilibrium is explained by the interaction or balance of forces, as described in statics' (Thompson 1961: 11).

18 Although see Lambek (1991: 50n17) for a perceptive comment on the fundamental 'frontality' of Lévi-Strauss
19 I am grateful to the series editors for pointing this out.
20 '[W]e can only understand the Other if we understand ourselves – and perhaps
   vice versa. All anthropology worthy of the name is at least comparative in this
   reflexive sense, but surely it can be much more, truly polyphonic as we bring
   more and more voices into the conversation' (Lambek 1991: 48).
21 For others, it is precisely a certain kind of political commitment – a commitment
   to the elucidation of suffering as a human universal – which has got in the way
   of a comparative view; the antidote is an anthropology of ethics which avoids
   the Scylla of radical otherness and the Charybdis of a singular vision of the good
   (Robbins 2013).

## 3  Caesurism and Heuristics

1 See also Navaro-Yashin (2009) on 'ruination'. Historians (who, some might
  think, should know better) are not immune from the same concerns
  (Anderson 2016).
2 Indeed, in Wimsatt's evolutionary epistemology, habits themselves, like other
  evolutionary adaptations, are heuristics.
3 The recent restatement of the ontological turn as an essentially 'heuristic' move
  makes this point explicit, although there has been some question as to whether
  this is a clarification of the previous position or a reinvention (Laidlaw 2017).
4 Note that I am here myself deploying the heuristic identified above, that of
  foregrounding difference where previously one had pointed to similarity.
5 This is why Strathern, unlike Abbott, sharply distinguishes fractals from segmentary systems. The only constant in her vision of a fractal model, the only
  repetition, as it were, is a repetition of the fact of difference itself (Strathern
  2004: xxii).
6 And of course, to anthropologists, the identification of something as 'nonsense'
  should ring alarm bells (Holbraad 2012).

## 4  *Comparatio*

1 To borrow a metaphor from Abbott (2001: 29–32).
2 More precisely, Plutarch's comparisons are tools for the discovery of the way to
  lead a good life, a question which interweaves what one might retrospectively
  think of as moral and factual questions. For instance: 'Since one of them [Nicias]
  was wholly given to divination, and the other [Crassus] wholly neglected it, and
  both alike perished, it is hard to draw a safe conclusion from the premises; but

failure from caution, going hand in hand with ancient and prevalent opinion, is more reasonable than lawlessness and obstinacy' (Plutarch 1989: 437).

3 I do not have space here to enter into the complex and fascinating discussions around the distinction between analogy and metaphor which have animated western philosophy and rhetorics since Aristotle (see Goyet 2014; Lloyd 2015).

## 5 Two Ends of Lateral Comparison: Identity and Alterity

1 In this, English speakers have the support of common usage. After all, to compare, as defined in the OED, is first 'To speak of or represent as similar; to liken', and only secondly 'To mark or point out the similarities and differences of (two or more things)' (comparison, n. n.d.; cf. Handler 2009: 627). The association between comparison and analogy – the sense that comparison, even where it does consider differences, is fundamentally *about* similarity – is deeply rooted in both everyday language and contemporary theory.

2 Or indeed in the literatures they have read: claims about what such and such a school, author or even book 'says' are also generalisations based on extrapolating from a number of instances (cf. Mol 2002a: 6).

3 This is a rift the radical nature of which is often underestimated by those who seek to recombine, for instance, elements of perspectivism (a 'differencing' programme if ever there was), with elements of a scientistic argument about the natural properties of living things, of language or of both (which ultimately points at the finding of identities); see, for instance, Kohn (2007).

4 'Comparability is achieved by constructing concepts of the same *kind* of thing, not identical things' (Hunt 2007: 15).

5 Indeed, for those who like their recursivity *really* recursive, one might point to Marilyn Strathern's arguments about different kinds of difference (adumbrated in Chapter 3). Against difference conceived in a continuous mode, as a scale of decreasing similarity, her own work has over and again articulated a vision of difference conceived in a fractal mode – difference as division, or cutting. But in the very move in which even differences are shown to be different from each other, they are also shown to be two instances of the same thing – difference.

6 My invocation of horizons here and in the remainder of this book echoes in some respects Lambek's (1991: 48) elaboration of that notion as deployed by Gadamer.

## 6 Another Dimension of Lateral Comparison: Identity and Intensity

1 'Scientific observation is analytical in that the flow of experience is divided into segments ... [S]ome of these segments are objects, like planets, apples and

oranges, and chemical elements, and sometimes these objects are placed in tax-onomies ... Some of the segments are dimensions of things, such as length, mass, atomic weight, and color, which are usually presented as variables' (Hunt 2007: 12).

2 '[T]he effect of the structural method is to decompose the basic unit of anthro-pology – a culture – into two groups of transformations: one composed of the virtualities it excludes, which are realised in other more or less distant cultures; the other composed of its own internal variations' (Salmon 2013b: 283, my translation).

3 'Again, it is essential that our structure vary in its entirety, or at least that "inde-pendent variants" should be relatively few ... Such independent variants as these Aristotle himself clearly recognised: "It happens further that some have parts which others have not; for instance, some [birds] have spurs and others do not, some have crests, or combs, and others not; but as a general rule most parts and those that go to make up the bulk of the body are either identical to one another, or differ from one another in the way of contrast and of excess and defect. For the more and the less may be represented as "excess" or "defect"' (Thompson 1961: 1035, citing Aristotle).

4 If we cast our mind back to the scalar dynamic introduced in our original dis-cussion of the argument by analogy, we can add an additional intricacy to this archetypal figure, since all of these questions of mapping can be asked of objects and their predicates or relations and their constituent relations.

## 7 Two Ends of Frontal Comparison: Identity, Alterity, Reflexivity

1 Whether ejection is involved in the anthropologist's initially gaining such ter-tiary understanding is a different matter, and one pertaining to metaphysics or psychology, rather than to my subject here. At this interpersonal level, many have contested the initial premise of the ejective argument, namely the partial opacity of minds to each other which would require understanding by analogy in the first place. If minds are in fact interactively emergent phe-nomena, rather than separate interiorities whose distance must be bridged, as a number of philosophers and social scientists have suggested, then the whole problem of communication falls away. The simple everyday practice of intersubjectivity does away with any need for the clunky device of ejective analogy. Be that as it may, intersubjectivity does not carry through written texts in the same way. However tertiary understanding has been gained in fieldwork, in the written text, anthropologists still frequently stage and convey this understanding to a readership which does not share their intersubjective experiences. In this process, more often than not, they rely on ejective frontal comparisons, analogising between what X means to us and what Y means to them.

2 Although elsewhere in Tylor's work, such as in reconsiderations of the religious sentiments of his contemporaries, the move could be quite profoundly challenging.

3 As Heywood has noted (2018b), this puts Viveiros de Castro in a logical self-contradiction, since the moment at which 'equivocation' becomes a method for anthropology – such as in Viveiros de Castro's own example – it has ceased to be other to the ontology it applies to.

# 8 The Oscillations of Frontal Comparison: Identity, Intensity, Reflexivity

1 See, for instance, amongst many others, Fabian (1983), Pina-Cabral (2006) and Said (2003).

2 Note that Gell's distinction is not philosophically unproblematic – his 'internal relations' echo the figure of 'analytical truth' famously deconstructed by Quine (1951). Whether or not there can be such things as analytical truths in language is not my concern here, however. Here, as elsewhere in this book, my aim is to try to characterise the sorts of assumptions which arise from anthropologists' use of different kinds of comparative moves. Gell's distinction provides a useful way of doing so.

3 As Herzfeld notes, 'At one level, the fundamental ground of comparison is almost always the self of the ethnographer' (Herzfeld 2001: 263).

4 Beyond its immediate source in Dumont, this account of frontal comparison builds on – while diverging in a number of particulars from – a number of influential accounts, including Holbraad and Pedersen (2017), Ingold (1993), Salmond (2013, 2014) and Strathern (2011).

5 As Geertz has noted in relation to Benedict's work, the technique is one of 'negative-space writing' (Geertz 1988: 113): the 'us' as a lateral case is everywhere implied, occasionally invoked, but never described at any length.

6 'As for the general principles of our shared cosmology, the problem is not a lack of information which we must fill, as I have done in the case of animism or totemism, but rather an over-abundant knowledge which must be purified in order to recover its main traits' (Descola 2005b: 244, my translation).

7 This frontal/lateral dynamic is prefigured in the carefully lateral *Patterns of culture* (Benedict 1934; cf. Handler 2009).

8 In one sense, this formulation rejoins Pina-Cabral's vision above: this would be a world in which anthropologists no longer need to appeal to separate cultural contexts in order to do their work. Anthropological exposition becomes an encounter not between fixed cultures or ontologies, but between anthropology itself and the world. In another sense, of course, the vision is the opposite of Pina-Cabral's. The latter jettisoned the appeal to 'culture shock' and retained the vision of hypothesis-testing – each new case can be

added to the repertoire of the discipline. The vision of a fully heuristic onto-logical turn, by contrast, jettisons or at least backgrounds that cumulative case-work, in order to focus on culture shock – what they nicely call 'aha! moments' (Holbraad and Pedersen 2017: 1) – reconfigured as perpetual, ever-intensifying, self-experimentation.

9 We have seen a special case in which this circle can be neatly squared by establishing a direct comparison between anthropology's conceptual hinterland and its cultural hinterland, in Herzfeld's *Anthropology through the looking glass* (Herzfeld 1987). Indeed the inspiration and politics of that move were 'post-colonial' too in the sense that Herzfeld was concerned with Greece's political and conceptual subordination at the hands of western/northern Europe.

10 I am simplifying a complex argument in more ways than one. But one bit of complexity deserves to be reinstated. *The gender of the gift* deploys diffe-rence inwards, as well as outwards, exploiting the deictic properties of the us/them divide in many directions at once. Anthropology does not simply stand for the West, any more than Strathern's own perspective stands for anthropology. Rather, the 'us' is produced by a process of division, both externally (the West is simply the correlate of a possible Melanesia), and internally. For, in actually characterising the content of a western per-spective, Strathern is careful to characterise it not primarily through overarching unities, but again, through subdivisions. Thus, the account of 'our' language in *The gender of the gift* is actually an account of profound divisions between feminism and anthropology, and – in turn – within each term of that contrast. If there is a unity which arises from this account, it is, on each scale, a unity of ways of differing. Anthropologists disagree with each other in ways which, from the purview of feminism, seem similar, and vice versa. In turn, one can imagine a commonality between these two different ways of doing difference, if one counterposes it to a fictional other produced at the intersection of anthropological and feminist discourse. We find here the root of the fractal imagery which occupies Strathern's *Partial connections* (2004).

11 Although there is also a diffusionist, historical aspect to Strathern's vision (see, for instance, 1988: 46, 342).

12 While Holbraad and Pedersen (2017) refer approvingly to material, ethnography and detail, and sometimes suggest that representational accuracy could even be left as the judge, there is no sustained account of what makes a description better than another description, aside from its internally non-contradictory nature. But non-contradiction is a standard for judging concepts and internal relations, not things and external relations – things are often contradictory. The question of what distinctive rigour is required for lateral and frontal com-parison respectively remains open.

## 9 Rigour

1 For a related point, see Spivak's evaluation of the respective merits of Derridean and Deleuzian approaches in relation to feminism: 'in the context of the problematic I have addressed, I find [Derrida's] morphology much more painstaking and useful than Foucault's and Deleuze's immediate, substantive involvement with more "political" issues – the latter's invitation to "become woman" – which can make their influence more dangerous for the US academic as enthusiastic radical. Derrida marks radical critique with the danger of appropriating the other by assimilation' (Spivak 1988: 306).

2 I am grateful to Marilyn Strathern for this observation.

## Conclusion

1 Scheffer and Niewöhner (2010) never define quite what they mean by thick comparison, except by analogy to Geertzian thick description. For them, however, it seems to imply something else again, namely a particular commitment to allowing the subjects to object.

# References

Abbott, A. 2001. *Chaos of disciplines*. University of Chicago Press.

2004. *Methods of discovery: heuristics for the social sciences*. New York: W. W. Norton and Company.

Abu-Lughod, L. 1990. Can there be a feminist ethnography? *Women and Performance: A Journal of Feminist Theory* 5, 7–27.

1991. Writing against culture. In *Recapturing anthropology*, ed. R. C. Fox, 137–162. Santa Fe, NM: School of American Research Press.

Agamben, G. 2000. *Means without end: notes on politics*. Minneapolis: University of Minnesota Press.

Amundson, R. 1998. Typology reconsidered: two doctrines on the history of evolutionary biology. *Biology and Philosophy* 13, 153–177.

Anderson, A. 2001. *The powers of distance: cosmopolitanism and the cultivation of detachment*. Princeton University Press.

Anderson, B. 2016. Frameworks of comparison. *London Review of Books*, 21 January, 15–18.

Appadurai, A. 1988a. Introduction: place and voice in anthropological theory. *Cultural Anthropology* 3, 16–20.

1988b. Putting hierarchy in its place. *Cultural Anthropology* 3, 36–49.

1996. *Modernity at large: cultural dimensions of globalization*. Minneapolis: University of Minnesota Press.

Aristotle 1994. *Posterior analytics* (trans. J. Barnes). 2nd edition. Oxford: Clarendon Press.

1997. *Topics: books I and VIII* (trans. R. Smith). 1st edition. Oxford University Press.

Asad, T. 1973a. *Anthropology and the colonial encounter*. New York: Humanity Books.

(ed.) 1973b. Two European images of non-European rule. In *Anthropology and the colonial encounter*, ed. T. Asad, 103–118. New York: Humanity Books.

1986. The concept of cultural translation in British social anthropology. In *Writing culture: the poetics and politics of ethnography*, ed. J. Clifford. Berkeley: University of California Press.

# References

2003. *Formations of the secular: Christianity, Islam, modernity.* Stanford University Press.

2009a. The idea of an anthropology of Islam. *Qui Parle* 17, 1–30.

2009b. *Is critique secular? Blasphemy, injury, and free speech.* Berkeley: Townsend Center for the Humanities, distributed by University of California Press.

Astuti, R. (ed.) 2007. *Questions of anthropology.* Oxford: Berg.

Austin, J. L. 1975. *How to do things with words.* Cambridge, MA: Harvard University Press.

Bachelard, G. 1934. *Le nouvel esprit scientifique.* Paris: Librairie Félix Alcan.

Barad, K. M. 2007. *Meeting the universe halfway: quantum physics and the entanglement of matter and meaning.* Durham, NC: Duke University Press.

Barth, F. 1990. The guru and the conjurer: transactions in knowledge and the shaping of culture in southeast Asia and Melanesia. *Man* n.s. 25, 640–653.

Bartha, P. 2013. Analogy and analogical reasoning. In *The Stanford encyclopedia of philosophy*, ed. E. N. Zalta (Fall 2013 edition).

Bashkow, I. 2004. A neo-Boasian conception of cultural boundaries. *American Anthropologist* 106, 443–458.

Bashkow, I., M. Bunzl, R. Handler, A. Orta and D. Rosenblatt 2004. Introduction. *American Anthropologist* 106, 433–434.

Bateson, G. 1967. Review of *Person, time, and conduct in Bali: an essay in cultural analysis*, by Clifford Geertz. *American Anthropologist* 69, 765–766.

1972. *Steps to an ecology of mind: collected essays in anthropology, psychiatry, evolution, and epistemology.* San Francisco: Chandler.

Bayly, S. 2018. Anthropology and history. In *Schools and styles of anthropological theory*, ed. M. Candea. London: Routledge.

Beckner, M. 1959. *The biological way of thought.* New York: Columbia University Press.

Benedict, R. 1934. *Patterns of culture.* Boston: Houghton Mifflin Harcourt.

2005. *The chrysanthemum and the sword: patterns of Japanese culture.* Boston: Houghton Mifflin.

Bloch, M. 2005. Where did anthropology go? Or the need for 'human nature'. In *Essays on cultural transmission*, ed. M. Bloch, 1–20. Oxford: Berg.

Bloch, M. and D. Sperber 2002. Kinship and evolved psychological dispositions: the mother's brother controversy reconsidered. *Current Anthropology* 43, 723–748.

Boas, F. 1896. The limitations of the comparative method of anthropology. *Science*, 901–908.

1938 [1911]. *The mind of primitive man.* New York: Macmillan.

Boon, J. 2009. *Other tribes, other scribes: symbolic anthropology in the comparative study of cultures, histories, religions and texts.* Cambridge University Press.

Borges, J. L. 2000. *Collected fictions.* Harmondsworth: Penguin.

## References

Brettell, C. B. 1993. *When they read what we write: the politics of ethnography*. Westport, CT: Bergin and Garvey.

Brightman, R. 1995. Forget culture: replacement, transcendence, relexification. *Cultural Anthropology* 10, 509–546.

Buchanan, I. 1996. What is heterology? *New Blackfriars* 77, 483–493.

Bunzl, M. 2004. Boas, Foucault, and the 'native anthropologist': notes toward a neo-Boasian anthropology. *American Anthropologist* 106, 435–442.

Burawoy, M. 2009. *The extended case method: four countries, four decades, four great transformations, and one theoretical tradition*. Berkeley: University of California Press.

Byrne, P. H. 1997. *Analysis and science in Aristotle: new essays on auto/biography*. Albany, NY: SUNY Press.

Candea, M. 2007. Arbitrary locations: in defence of the bounded field-site. *Journal of the Royal Anthropological Institute* 13, 167–184.

2010a. *Corsican fragments: difference, knowledge and fieldwork*. Bloomington: Indiana University Press.

2010b. 'I fell in love with Carlos the meerkat': engagement and detachment in human–animal relations. *American Ethnologist* 37, 241–258.

2011. Endo/exo. *Common Knowledge* 17, 146–150.

2012. Different species, one theory: reflections on anthropomorphism and anthropological comparison. *Cambridge Anthropology* 30, 118–135.

2013a. The fieldsite as device. *Journal of Cultural Economy* 6, 241–258.

2013b. Suspending belief: epoche in animal behavior science. *American Anthropologist* 115, 423–436.

2016a. De deux modalités de la comparaison en anthropologie sociale. *L'Homme* 218, 183–218.

2016b. We have never been pluralist: on lateral and frontal comparisons in the ontological turn. In *Comparative metaphysics: ontology after anthropology*, ed. P. Charbonnier, G. Salmon and P. Skafish. London: Rowman and Littlefield.

2017. This is (not) like that. *HAU: Journal of Ethnographic Theory* 7, 517–521.

2018a. Paradoxical pedagogies: reassembling individual (animal) subjects. In *Recovering the human subject*, ed. M. Holbraad, J. Laidlaw and B. Bodenhorn. Cambridge University Press.

2018b. Severed roots: evolutionism, diffusionism and (structural-)functionalism. In *Schools and styles of anthropological theory*, ed. M. Candea. London: Routledge.

2018c. The two faces of character: moral tales of animal behaviour. *Social Anthropology* 26, 361–375.

2018d. Going full frontal: Two modalities of comparison in social anthropology. In *Regimes of comparatism: Frameworks of comparison in history, religion and Anthropology*, ed. R. Gagné, S. Goldhill and G. Lloyd. Sl: Brill.

Carrier, J. G. 1992. Occidentalism: the world turned upside-down. *American Ethnologist* 19, 195–212.

# References

Chakrabarty, D. 2007. *Provincializing Europe: postcolonial thought and historical difference*. Princeton University Press.

Choy, T. K. 2011. *Ecologies of comparison: an ethnography of endangerment in Hong Kong*. Durham, NC: Duke University Press.

Chua, L. and N. Mathur 2018. Introduction: who are we? In *Who are 'we'? Reimagining alterity and affinity in anthropology*, ed. L. Chua and N. Mathur, 1–34. New York: Berghahn.

Clifford, J. 1986. Introduction: partial truths. In *Writing culture: the poetics and politics of ethnography*, ed. J. Clifford and G. Marcus, 1–26. Berkeley: University of California Press.

Clifford, J. and G. Marcus (eds.) 1986. *Writing culture: the poetics and politics of ethnography*. Berkeley: University of California Press.

Coe, J. 2013. Sinking giggling into the sea. *London Review of Books*, 18 July, 30–31.

Condillac, Étienne Bonnot de. 1795. *La logique, ou, Les premiers développement de l'art de penser*. Paris: F. Dufart.

Cook, J., J. Laidlaw and J. Mair 2009. What if there is no elephant? Towards a conception of an unsited field. *Multi-sited ethnography: theory, praxis and locality in contemporary research*, ed. M.-A. Falzon, 47–72. Abingdon: Routledge.

Corsín Jiménez, A. 2011. Daribi kinship at perpendicular angles: a trompe l'oeil anthropology. *HAU: Journal of Ethnographic Theory* 1, 141–157.

Crapanzano, V. 1986. Hermes' dilemma: the masking of subversion in ethnographic description. In *Writing culture: the poetics and politics of ethnography*, ed. J. Clifford and G. Marcus. Berkeley: University of California Press.

Dan-Cohen, T. 2017. Epistemic artefacts: on the uses of complexity in anthropology. *Journal of the Royal Anthropological Institute* 23, 285–301.

Daston, L. and P. Galison 2007. *Objectivity*. New York: Zone Books.

Deleuze, G. and F. Guattari 1994. *What is philosophy?* (trans. G. Birchill and H. Tomlinson). London: Verso.

Descola, P. 2005a. On anthropological knowledge. *Social Anthropology* 13, 65–73.

——— 2005b. *Par delà nature et culture*. Paris: Gallimard.

Despret, V. 1996. *Naissance d'une théorie éthologique: la danse du cratérope écaillé*. Collection les empêcheurs de penser en rond. Le Plessis-Robinson, France: Synthélabo.

Detienne, M. 2008. *Comparing the incomparable* (trans. J. Lloyd). Stanford University Press.

Douglas, M. D. (ed.) 1966. *Purity and danger: an analysis of the concepts of pollution and taboo*. London: Routledge and Kegan Paul.

——— 1970. Smothering the differences: Mary Douglas in a savage mind about Lévi-Strauss. *The Listener*.

——— 1978. Judgments on James Frazer. *Daedalus* 107, 151–164.

Dumont, L. 1966. *Homo hierarchicus: le système des castes et ses implications*. Paris: Gallimard.

1977. *Homo aequalis: Tome I, Genèse et épanouissement de l'idéologie économique.* Paris: Gallimard.

1985. A modified view of our origins: the Christian beginnings of modern individualism. In *The category of the person: anthropology, philosophy, history,* ed. M. Carrithers, S. Collins and S. Lukes, 257–281. Cambridge University Press.

1986. *Essays on individualism: modern ideology in anthropological perspective.* University of Chicago Press.

1991. *Homo aequalis: l'idéologie allemande: France–Allemagne et retour.* Paris: Gallimard.

Durkheim, E. 1915. *The elementary forms of the religious life* (trans. J. W. Swain). London: George Allen and Unwin.

1964. *The rules of sociological method.* New York: Free Press.

Eggan, F. 1954. Social anthropology and the method of controlled comparison. *American Anthropologist* 56, 743–763.

Engels, F. 1972. *The origin of the family, private property, and the state.* New York: Pathfinder Press.

Englund, H. 2018. From the extended-case method to multi-sited ethnography (and back). In *Schools and styles of anthropological theory,* ed. M. Candea. London: Routledge.

Englund, H. and T. Yarrow 2013. The place of theory: rights, networks, and ethnographic comparison. *Social Analysis* 57, 132–149.

Eriksen, A. forthcoming. *Going to Pentecost.* Oxford: Berghahn.

Evans-Pritchard, E. E. 1940. *The Nuer: a description of the modes of livelihood and political institutions of a Nilotic people.* Oxford University Press.

1950. Social anthropology: past and present; the Marett Lecture, 1950. *Man* 50, 118–124.

1951. *Social anthropology.* London: Cohen and West.

Fabian, J. 1983. *Time and the other: how anthropology makes its object.* New York: Columbia University Press.

Fadil, N. and M. Fernando 2015. Rediscovering the 'everyday' Muslim: notes on an anthropological divide. *HAU: Journal of Ethnographic Theory* 5, 59–88.

Falzon, M.-A. (ed.) 2009. *Multi-sited ethnography: theory, praxis and locality in contemporary research.* Aldershot: Ashgate.

Fardon, R. 1990. *Localizing strategies: regional traditions of ethnographic writing.* Smithsonian series in ethnographic inquiry. Washington: Smithsonian Institution Press.

Faris, J. 1973. Pax Britannica and the Sudan: S.F. Nadel. In *Anthropology and the colonial encounter,* ed. T. Asad, 153–170. New York: Humanity Books.

Ferguson, J. and A. Gupta 2002. Spatializing states: towards an ethnography of neoliberal governmentality. *American Ethnologist* 29, 981–1002.

Fernando, M. L. 2010. Reconfiguring freedom: Muslim piety and the limits of secular law and public discourse in France. *American Ethnologist* 37, 19–35.

# References

Fisher, L. E. and O. Werner 1978. Explaining explanation: tension in American anthropology. *Journal of Anthropological Research* 34, 194–218.

Fortes, M. 1953. The structure of unilineal descent groups. *American Anthropologist* 55, 17–41.

Fortes, M. and E. E. Evans-Pritchard (eds.) 1940. *African political systems*. Oxford University Press.

Foucault, M. 1970. *The order of things: an archaeology of human sciences*. London: Tavistock Press.

1979. *Discipline and punish: the birth of the prison*. Harmondsworth: Penguin.

1984. Nietzsche, genealogy, history. In *The Foucault reader*, 76–100. New York: Pantheon.

Franklin, S. and S. McKinnon 2001. *Relative values: reconfiguring kinship studies*. Durham, NC: Duke University Press.

Gad, C. 2012. What we talk about when we talk about sailor culture: understanding Danish fisheries inspection through a cult movie. *Culture Unbound: Journal of Current Cultural Research* 4, 367–392.

Gad, C. and C. Bruun Jensen 2016. Lateral comparisons. In *Practising comparison: logics, relations, collaborations*, ed. J. Deville, M. Guggenheim and Z. Hrdlickova. Manchester: Mattering Press.

Gaiman, N. 2004. *American gods: The author's preferred text*. London: Headline.

Garcia, T. 2016a. *Nous*. Paris: Grasset.

2016b. *La vie intense: une obsession moderne*. Paris: Editions Autrement.

Geertz, C. 1963. *Old societies and new states: the quest for modernity in Asia and Africa*. New York: Free Press.

1967. The cerebral savage. *Encounter* 28, 25–32.

1971. *Islam observed: religious development in Morocco and Indonesia*. University of Chicago Press.

1973a. Deep play: notes on the Balinese cockfight. In *The interpretation of culture: selected essays*, ed. C. Geertz. New York: Basic Books.

1973b. *The interpretation of cultures: selected essays*. New York: Basic Books.

1973c. Thick description: towards an interpretive theory of culture. In *The interpretation of culture: selected essays*, ed. C. Geertz. New York: Basic Books.

1974. 'From the native's point of view': on the nature of anthropological understanding. *Bulletin of the American Academy of Arts and Sciences* 28, 26–45.

1988. *Works and lives: the anthropologist as author*. Stanford University Press.

1998. The world in pieces: culture and politics at the end of the century. *Focaal: Tijdschrift voor Antropologie* 32, 91–117.

Gell, A. 1998. *Art and agency: an anthropological theory*. Oxford University Press.

1999. *The art of anthropology*. Oxford: Berg.

Gellner, E. 1983. *Muslim society*. Cambridge University Press.

1987. *Relativism and the social sciences*. Cambridge University Press.

# References

Gingrich, A. and R. G. Fox 2002a. *Anthropology, by comparison.* London: Routledge.

2002b. Introduction. In *Anthropology, by comparison,* ed. R. G. Fox and A. Gingrich. London: Routledge.

Gluckman, M. 1958. *Analysis of a social situation in modern Zululand.* Manchester University Press.

Godelier, M. 1980. The emergence and development of Marxist anthropology in France. In *Soviet and western anthropology,* ed. E. Gellner. London: Duckworth.

Godfrey-Smith, P. 2003. *Theory and reality: an introduction to the philosophy of science.* New edition. University of Chicago Press.

2017. *Other minds: the octopus, the sea, and the deep origins of consciousness.* 1st edition. New York: Farrar, Straus and Giroux.

Goodenough, W. H. 1970. *Description and comparison in cultural anthropology.* The Lewis Henry Morgan lectures, 1968. Chicago: Aldine.

Goody, J. 1995. *The expansive moment: the rise of social anthropology in Britain and Africa, 1918–1970.* Cambridge University Press.

Gould, S. J. 2002. *The structure of evolutionary theory.* Cambridge, MA: Belknap Press of Harvard University Press.

Goyet, F. 2014. Comparison. In *Dictionary of untranslatables: a philosophical lexicon,* ed. B. Cassin, E. Apter, J. Lezra and M. Wood, 159–164. Princeton University Press.

Graeber, D. 2015. Radical alterity is just another way of saying 'reality': a reply to Eduardo Viveiros de Castro. *HAU: Journal of Ethnographic Theory* 5, 1–41.

Grillo, R. D. 2003. Cultural essentialism and cultural anxiety. *Anthropological Theory* 3, 157–173.

Gross, D. M. 2001. Foucault's analogies, or how to be a historian of the present without being a presentist. *Clio* 31, 57.

Handler, R. 2009. The uses of incommensurability in anthropology. *New Literary History* 40, 627–647.

Haraway, D. J. 1989. *Primate visions: gender, race and nature in the world of modern science.* London: Routledge.

2016. *Staying with the trouble: making kin in the Chthulucene.* Durham, NC: Duke University Press.

Harding, S. 1991. Representing fundamentalism: the problem of the repugnant cultural other. *Social Research* 58, 373–393.

Harding, S. 2005. Negotiating with the positivist legacy: new social justice movements and a standpoint politics of method. In *The politics of method in the human sciences: positivism and its epistemological others,* ed. G. Steinmetz, 346–365. Durham, NC: Duke University Press.

Hastrup, K. 2002. Anthropology's comparative consciousness. *Anthropology, by Comparison* 27.

Hecht, J. M. 2003. *The end of the soul: scientific modernity, atheism and anthropology in France.* New York: Columbia University Press.

# References

Helmreich, S. 2009. *Alien ocean: anthropological voyages in microbial seas.* Berkeley: University of California Press.

Henare, A., M. Holbraad and S. Wastell (eds.) 2007. *Thinking through things: theorising artifacts ethnographically.* Cambridge University Press.

Herzfeld, M. 1987. *Anthropology through the looking-glass: critical ethnography in the margins of Europe.* Cambridge University Press.

——— 2001. Performing comparisons: ethnography, globetrotting, and the spaces of social knowledge. *Journal of Anthropological Research* 57, 259–276.

Hesse, M. B. 1966. *Models and analogies in science,* vol. XXXVI. University of Notre Dame Press.

Heywood, P. 2015. Equivocal locations: being 'red' in 'Red Bologna'. *Journal of the Royal Anthropological Institute* 21, 855–871.

——— 2018a. *After difference: queer activism in Italy and anthropological theory.* London: Berghahn.

——— 2018b. Making difference: queer activism and anthropological theory. *Current Anthropology* 59.

——— 2018c. The ontological turn: school or style? In *Schools and styles of anthropological theory,* ed. M. Candea. London: Routledge.

History and Development of the HRAF Collections 2013. Human Relations Area Files – Cultural information for education and research, available online: http://hraf.yale.edu/about/history-and-development/, accessed 22 February 2018.

Højer, L. and A. Bandak 2015. Introduction: the power of example. *Journal of the Royal Anthropological Institute* 21, 1–17.

Holbraad, M. 2012. *Truth in motion: the recursive anthropology of Cuban divination.* University of Chicago Press.

——— 2016. The contingency of concepts: transcendental deduction and ethnographic expression in anthropological thinking. In *Comparative metaphysics: ontology after anthropology,* ed. P. Charbonnier, G. Salmon and P. Skafish. London: Rowman and Littlefield.

Holbraad, M. and M. A. Pedersen 2009. Planet M: the intense abstraction of Marilyn Strathern. *Anthropological Theory* 9, 371–394.

Holbraad, M. and M. A. Pedersen 2017. *The ontological turn: an anthropological exposition.* Cambridge University Press.

Holbraad, M., M. A. Pedersen and E. Viveiros de Castro 2014. The politics of ontology: anthropological positions. *Cultural Anthropology Online,* available online: http://culanth.org/fieldsights/462-the-politics-of-ontology-anthropological-positions, accessed 11 July 2018.

Holmes, D. R. 2013. *Economy of words: communicative imperatives in central banks.* University of Chicago Press.

——— 2016. Fascism 2. *Anthropology Today* 32, 1–3.

Holmes, D. R. and G. E. Marcus 2005. Cultures of expertise and the management of globalization: towards the re-functioning of ethnography. In *Global assemblages: technology, politics and ethics as anthropological problems*, ed. A. Ong. Oxford: Blackwell.

Holy, L. 1987. Description, generalization and comparison: two paradigms. In *Comparative anthropology*, ed. L. Holy. Oxford: Blackwell.

Howe, C. and D. Boyer 2015. Portable analytics and lateral theory. In *Theory can be more than it used to be: learning anthropology's method in a time of transition*, eds. D. Boyer, J. D. Faubion and G. E. Marcus. Ithaca: Cornell University Press.

Howe, L. 1987. Caste in Bali and India: levels of comparison. In *Comparative anthropology*, ed. L. Holy. Oxford: Blackwell.

Hume, D. 1993. *An enquiry concerning human understanding; [with] A letter from a gentleman to his friend in Edinburgh; [and] An abstract of a treatise of human nature*. Indianapolis: Hackett Publishing.

Humphrey, C. 2016. Placing self amid others: a Mongolian technique of comparison. *L'Homme. Revue française d'anthropologie* 151–181.

2018. Marxism and neo-Marxism. In *Schools and styles of anthropological theory*, ed. M. Candea. London: Routledge.

Hunt, R. C. 2007. *Beyond relativism: comparability in cultural anthropology*. Lanham: AltaMira Press.

Ingold, T. 1993. The art of translation in a continuous world. In *Beyond boundaries: understanding, translation and anthropological discourse*, ed. G. Palsson, 210–230. Oxford: Berg.

2000. *The perception of the environment: essays on livelihood, dwelling and skill*. London: Routledge.

2008. Anthropology is not ethnography. *Proceedings of the British Academy* 154, 69–92.

Irvine, R. D. G. 2018. Cognitive anthropology as epistemological critique. In *Schools and styles of anthropological theory*, ed. M. Candea, 134–147. London: Routledge.

Iteanu, A. and I. Moya 2015. Mister D.: radical comparison, values, and ethnographic theory. *HAU: Journal of Ethnographic Theory* 5, 113–136.

Jackson, M. 1987. On ethnographic truth. *Canberra Anthropology* 10, 1–31.

Jankowiak, W. R., S. L. Volsche and J. R. Garcia 2015. Is the romantic-sexual kiss a near human universal? *American Anthropologist* 117, 535–539.

Jean-Klein, I. and A. Riles 2005. Introducing discipline: anthropology and human rights administrations. *PoLAR* 28, 173–202.

Jenkins, T. 2010. One or three: issues of comparison. In *The social after Gabriel Tarde*, ed. M. Candea, 103–110. London: Routledge.

Jensen, C. B., B. Herrnstein Smith, G. E. R. Lloyd et al. 2011. Comparative relativism: symposium on an impossibility. *Common Knowledge* 17, 1–165.

Johnson, J. 2018. Feminist anthropology and the question of gender. In *Schools and styles of anthropological theory*, ed. M. Candea. London: Routledge.

# References

Keane, W. 2005. Estrangement, intimacy, and the objects of anthropology. In *The politics of method in the human sciences: positivism and its epistemological others*, ed. G. Steinmetz, 59–88. Durham, NC: Duke University Press.

2011. Indexing voice: a morality tale. *Journal of Linguistic Anthropology* 21, 166–178.

Knorr-Cetina, K. 1999. *Epistemic cultures: how the sciences make knowledge.* Cambridge, MA: Harvard University Press.

Kohn, E. 2007. How dogs dream: Amazonian natures and the politics of trans-species engagement. *American Ethnologist* 34, 3–24.

Kuklick, H. 1991. *The savage within: the social history of British anthropology, 1885–1945.* Cambridge University Press.

2011. Personal equations: reflections on the history of fieldwork, with special reference to sociocultural anthropology. *Isis* 102, 1–33.

Kuper, A. 1973. *Anthropologists and anthropology: the British School, 1922–1972.* London: Allen Lane.

1999. *Culture: the anthropologists' account.* Cambridge, MA: Harvard University Press.

2002. Comparison and contextualisation: reflections on South Africa. In *Anthropology, by comparison*, ed. A. Gingrich and R. G. Fox, 143–166. London: Routledge.

2005. *The reinvention of primitive society: transformations of a myth.* London: Routledge.

Laidlaw, J. 2012. Ontologically challenged. *Anthropology of This Century* 4, available online: http://aotcpress.com/articles/ontologically-challenged/, accessed 11 July 2018.

2014. *The subject of virtue: an anthropology of ethics and freedom.* Cambridge University Press.

2017. Review: The ontological turn. *Social Anthropology* 25, 396–402.

2018. Interpretive cultural anthropology: Geertz and his 'writing-culture' critics. In *Schools and styles of anthropological theory*, ed. M. Candea. London: Routledge.

Laidlaw, J. and P. Heywood 2013. One more turn and you're there. *Anthropology of This Century* 7, available online: http://aotcpress.com/articles/turn/, accessed 11 July 2018.

Lambek, M. 1991. Tryin' to make it real, but compared to what? *Culture* 11, 43–51.

Lambek, M., V. Das, D. Fassin and W. Keane 2015. *Four lectures on ethics: anthropological perspectives.* Chicago: Hau.

Lampedusa, G. T. D. 2007. *The leopard.* Revised edition. London: Vintage.

Latour, B. 2004. How to talk about the body? The normative dimension of science studies. *Body and Society* 10, 205.

2005. *Reassembling the social: an introduction to Actor–Network-Theory.* Oxford University Press.

2009. *The making of law: an ethnography of the Conseil d'etat.* Revised edition. Cambridge, UK: Polity Press.

2012. *Enquête sur les modes d'existence: une anthropologie des modernes*. Paris: La Découverte.

2013. *An inquiry into modes of existence: an anthropology of the moderns*. Cambridge, MA: Harvard University Press.

Latour, B. and S. Woolgar 1979. *Laboratory life: the social construction of scientific facts*. London: Sage.

Lazar, S. 2012. Disjunctive comparison: citizenship and trade unionism in Bolivia and Argentina. *Journal of the Royal Anthropological Institute* 18, 349–368.

Leach, E. R. 1964. *Political systems of highland Burma*. London: G. Bell and Sons.

1966. *Rethinking anthropology*. London: Athlone Press.

1974. *Claude Lévi-Strauss*. New York: Viking Press.

Leibniz, G. W. 2012. *Philosophical papers and letters: a selection*. Dordrecht: Springer.

L'Estoile, B. de 2005. 'Une petite armée de travailleurs auxiliaires'. La division du travail et ses enjeux dans l'ethnologie française de l'entre-deux-guerres. *Les Cahiers du Centre de Recherches Historiques*, 36, available online: http://ccrh. revues.org/3037.

Lévi-Strauss, C. 1958. *Anthropologie structurale*. Paris: Plon.

1963. *Totemism*. Boston: Beacon Press.

1966. *The savage mind*. University of Chicago Press.

1969. *The elementary structures of kinship*. Boston: Beacon Press.

Lewis, O. 1955. Comparisons in cultural anthropology. *Yearbook of Anthropology* 259–292.

Lezaun, J. 2010. Eloquence and incommensurability: an investigation into the grammar of irreconcilable differences. *Social Studies of Science* 40, 349–375.

Lipton, P. 2004. *Inference to the best explanation*. 2nd edition. London: Routledge.

Lloyd, G. E. R. 1966. *Polarity and analogy*. Cambridge University Press.

Lloyd, G. E. R. 2015. *Analogical investigations*. Cambridge University Press.

Lynteris, C. 2017. Zoonotic diagrams: mastering and unsettling human–animal relations. *Journal of the Royal Anthropological Institute* 23, 463–485.

McDonald, M. E. 1989. *We are not French*. Cambridge University Press.

MacIntyre, A. 2013. *Whose justice? Which rationality?* 2nd edition. London: Bloomsbury.

McLean, S. 2013. All the difference in the world: liminality, montage, and the reinvention of comparative anthropology. In *Transcultural montage*, ed. C. Suhr and R. Willerslev. New York: Berghahn.

Mahmood, S. 2005. *Politics of piety: the Islamic revival and the feminist subject*. Princeton University Press.

Malinowski, B. 1922. *The argonauts of the western Pacific: an account of native enterprise and adventure in the archipelagoes of Melanesian New Guinea*. London: Routledge and Kegan Paul.

# References

Malkki, L. H. 1995. *Purity and exile: violence, memory and national cosmology among Hutu refugees in Tanzania.* University of Chicago Press.

Marcus, G. E. 1995. Ethnography in/of the world system: the emergence of multi-sited ethnography. *Annual Review of Anthropology* 24, 95–117.

Marsden, M. 2005. *Living Islam: Muslim religious experience in Pakistan's North-West Frontier.* Cambridge University Press.

Martins, H. 1974. Time and theory in sociology. In *Approaches to sociology,* ed. J. Rex. London: Routledge and Kegan Paul.

Marx, K. 1973. *Grundrisse.* Harmondsworth: Penguin.

Maurer, B. 2005. *Mutual life, limited: Islamic banking, alternative currencies, lateral reason.* Princeton University Press.

Mauss, M. 1970. *The gift: form and functions of exchange in archaic societies.* London: Routledge.

Mayr, E. 1959. Darwin and the evolutionary theory in biology. In *Evolution and anthropology: a centennial appraisal,* ed. B. J. Meggers, 1–10. Washington, DC: Anthropological Society of Washington.

Messina, J. and D. Rutherford 2009. Leibniz on compossibility. *Philosophy Compass* 4, 962–977.

Mill, J. S. 1856. *A system of logic, ratiocinative and inductive, being a connected view of the principles, and the methods of scientific investigation,* vol. II. London: J. W. Parker.

Miner, H. 1956. Body ritual among the Nacirema. *American Anthropologist* 503–507.

Mintz, S. W. 1985. *Sweetness and power: the place of sugar in modern history.* New York: Viking Penguin.

Miyazaki, H. 2004. *The method of hope: anthropology, philosophy, and Fijian knowledge.* Stanford University Press.

Mohanty, C. T. 1984. Under western eyes: feminist scholarship and colonial discourses. *Boundary* 2 12/13, 333–358.

Mol, A. 2002a. *The body multiple: ontology in medical practice.* London: Duke University Press.

——— 2002b. Cutting surgeons, walking patients: some complexities involved in comparing. In *Complexities: social studies of knowledge practices,* ed. J. Law, 218–257. Durham, NC: Duke University Press.

Montaigne, M. de 1965. *Complete essays.* Stanford University Press.

Moore, S. F. 2005. Comparisons: possible and impossible. *Annual Review of Anthropology* 34, 1–11.

Muehlebach, A. K. 2010. *The moral neoliberal: welfare and citizenship in Italy.* University of Chicago Press.

Munasinghe, V. 2008. Rescuing theory from the nation. In *Knowing how to know: fieldwork and the ethnographic present,* ed. N. Halstead, E. Hirsch and J. Okely. New York: Berghahn.

Murdock , G. P. 1949. *Social structure.* New York: Macmillan.

Murdock, G. P., C. S. Ford and A. E. Hudson 1950. *Outline of cultural materials*, 3rd revised edition. New Haven: Yale University Press.

Nadel, S. F. 1951. *The foundations of social anthropology*. London: Cohen and West.

1952. Witchcraft in four African societies: an essay in comparison. *American Anthropologist* 54, 18–29.

1957a. Malinowski on magic and religion. In *Man and culture*, ed. R. Firth. London: Routledge and Kegan Paul.

1957b. *The theory of social structure*. London: Cohen and West.

Nader, L. 2017. Anthropology of law, fear, and the war on terror. *Anthropology Today* 33, 26–28.

Narayan, K. 1993. How native is a 'native' anthropologist? *American Anthropologist* new series 95, 671–686.

Naroll, R. 1970. What have we learned from cross-cultural surveys? *American Anthropologist* 72, 1227–1288.

Navaro-Yashin, Y. 2009. Affective spaces, melancholic objects: ruination and the production of anthropological knowledge. *Journal of the Royal Anthropological Institute* 15, 1–18.

Needham, R. 1972. *Belief, language, and experience*. Oxford: Blackwell.

1975. Polythetic classification: convergence and consequences. *Man* 10, 349–369.

Nzegwu, N. U. 2006. *Family matters: feminist concepts in African philosophy of culture*. Albany, NY: SUNY Press.

Ong, A. 1988. Colonialism and modernity: feminist re-presentations of women in non-western societies. *Inscriptions* 3, 79–93.

Orta, A. 2004. The promise of particularism and the theology of culture: limits and lessons of 'neo-Boasianism'. *American Anthropologist* 106, 473–487.

Ortner, S. B. 1984. Theory in anthropology since the sixties. *Comparative Studies in Society and History* 26, 126–166.

1995. Resistance and the problem of ethnographic refusal. *Comparative Studies in Society and History* 37, 173–193.

Pedersen, M. A. 2011. *Not quite shamans: spirit worlds and political lives in northern Mongolia*. Ithaca: Cornell University Press.

Peel, J. D. Y. 1987. History, culture and the comparative method: a West African puzzle. In *Comparative anthropology*, ed. L. Holy. Oxford: Blackwell.

Pefanis, J. 1991. *Heterology and the postmodern: Bataille, Baudrillard and Lyotard*. Durham, NC: Duke University Press.

Perrin, R. G. 1976. Herbert Spencer's four theories of social evolution. *American Journal of Sociology* 81, 1339–1359.

Peters, J. D. 2001. *Speaking into the air: a history of the idea of communication*. New edition. University of Chicago Press.

Petryna, A. 2002. *Life exposed: biological citizens after Chernobyl*. Princeton University Press.

# References

Pina-Cabral, J. de 1992. Against translation: the role of the researcher in the production of ethnographic knowledge. In *Europe Observed*, ed. J. de Pina-Cabral. London: Macmillan.

2006. Anthropology challenged: notes for a debate. *Journal of the Royal Anthropological Institute* 12, 663–673.

2009. The all-or-nothing syndrome and the human condition. *Social Analysis* 53, 163–176.

2010. The door in the middle: six conditions for anthropology. In *Culture wars: context, models and anthropologists' accounts*, ed. D. James, E. M. Plaice and C. Toren, 152–169. EASA series 12. New York: Berghahn.

Pincheon, B. S. 2000. An ethnography of silences: race, (homo)sexualities, and a discourse of Africa. *African Studies Review* 43, 39.

Plutarch 1989. *Lives*, vol. III. Cambridge, MA: Loeb.

Poincaré, H. 1914. *Science and method* (trans. F. Maitland, with a preface by B. Russell). London: Thomas Nelson and Sons.

Povinelli, E. A. 2001. Radical worlds: the anthropology of incommensurability and inconceivability. *Annual Review of Anthropology* 319–334.

Quine, W. V. 1951. Main trends in recent philosophy: two dogmas of empiricism. *The Philosophical Review* 60, 20.

Rabinow, P. 2011. *The accompaniment: assembling the contemporary*. University of Chicago Press.

2012. *Designing human practices: an experiment with synthetic biology*. University of Chicago Press.

Radcliffe-Brown, A. R. 1940. On social structure. *Journal of the Royal Anthropological Institute of Great Britain and Ireland* 70, 1–12.

(ed.) 1950. *African systems of kinship and marriage*. Oxford University Press.

1951. The comparative method in social anthropology. *Journal of the Anthropological Institute of Great Britain and Ireland* 81, 15–22.

1952. *Structure and function in primitive society*. London: Cohen and West.

Riles, A. 2000. *The network inside out*. Ann Arbor: University of Michigan Press.

2011. *Collateral knowledge: legal reasoning in the global financial markets*. University of Chicago Press.

Robbins, J. 2004. *Becoming sinners: Christianity and moral torment in a Papua New Guinea society*. Berkeley: University of California Press.

2007. Continuity thinking and the problem of Christian culture: belief, time, and the anthropology of Christianity. *Current Anthropology* 48, 5–38.

2013. Beyond the suffering subject: toward an anthropology of the good. *Journal of the Royal Anthropological Institute* 19, 447–462.

Romanes, G. J. 1883. *Animal intelligence*. New York: D. Appleton and Company.

1895. *Mind and motion and monism*. New York: Longmans, Green, and Co.

Rorty, R. 1983. Postmodernist bourgeois liberalism. *Journal of Philosophy* 80, 583–589.

Roscoe, P. B. 1995. The perils of 'positivism' in cultural anthropology. *American Anthropologist* new series, 97, 492–504.

Roth, G. 1978. Introduction. In Max Weber, *Economy and society: an outline of interpretive sociology*, ed. G. Roth and C. Wittich. Berkeley: University of California Press.

Runciman, W. G. 1983. *A treatise on social theory, vol. 1: The methodology of social theory*. Cambridge University Press.

Sahlins, M. 1963. Poor man, rich man, big-man, chief: political types in Melanesia and Polynesia. *Comparative Studies in Society and History* 5, 285–303.

1985. *Islands of history*. London: Tavistock.

2002. *Waiting for Foucault, still*. Chicago: Prickly Paradigm Press.

Sahlins, M. and E. R. Service (eds.) 1960. *Evolution and culture*. Ann Arbor: University of Michigan Press.

Sahlins, M. D. 1976. *The use and abuse of biology: an anthropological critique of sociobiology*. Ann Arbor: University of Michigan Press.

Said, E. W. 2003. *Orientalism*. London: Routledge and Kegan Paul.

Salmon, G. 2013a. Forme et variante: Franz Boas dans l'histoire du comparatisme. In *Franz Boas: le travail du regard*, ed. M. Espagne and I. Kalinowski., 191–220. Paris: Armand Colin.

2013b. *Les structures de l'esprit: Lévi-Strauss et les mythes*. Paris: Presses universitaires de France.

Salmon, G. and P. Charbonnier 2014. The two ontological pluralisms of French anthropology. *Journal of the Royal Anthropological Institute* 20, 567–573.

Salmond, A. 1982. Theoretical landscapes: on cross-cultural conceptions of knowledge. In *Semantic anthropology*, ed. D. Parkin, 65–88. London: Academic Press.

Salmond, A. J. M. 2013. Transforming translations (part 1): 'The owner of these bones'. *HAU: Journal of Ethnographic Theory* 3, 1–32.

2014. Transforming translations (part 2): Addressing ontological alterity. *HAU: Journal of Ethnographic Theory* 4, 155–187.

Schapera, I. and M. B. Singer 1953. Wenner-Gren Foundation Supper Conference: comparative method in social anthropology. *American Anthropologist* 55.

Scheffer, D. T. and J. Niewöhner 2010. *Thick comparison: reviving the ethnographic aspiration*. Leiden: Brill.

Schielke, S. 2009. Being good in Ramadan: ambivalence, fragmentation, and the moral self in the lives of young Egyptians. *Journal of the Royal Anthropological Institute* 15, S24–S40.

Schneider, D. M. 1984. *A critique of the study of kinship*. Ann Arbor: University of Michigan Press.

Schumaker, L. 2001. *Africanizing anthropology: fieldwork, networks, and the making of cultural knowledge in central Africa*. Durham, NC: Duke University Press.

# References

Segerstråle, U. C. O. 2000. *Defenders of the truth: the battle for science in the sociobiology debate and beyond.* Oxford University Press.

Smith, R. 1997. Introduction. In *Aristotle Topics Books I and VIII*, xi–xxxv. Oxford University Press.

Sneath, D. 2018. From transactionalism to practice theory. In *Schools and styles of anthropological theory*, ed. M. Candea. London: Routledge.

Sober, E. 2000. *Philosophy of biology.* Boulder, CO: Westview Press.

Sokal, R. R. and P. H. A. Sneath 1963. *Principles of numerical taxonomy.* San Francisco: W. H. Freeman.

Spencer, H. 1896. *The study of sociology.* New York: Appleton.

    1899. *Social statics: abridged and revised: together with The man versus the state.* New York: Appleton.

Spiro, M. E. 1966. Religion: problems of definition and explanation. In *Anthropological approaches to the study of religion*, ed. M. Banton, 85–126. London: Routledge.

Spivak, G. C. 1988. Can the subaltern speak? In *Marxism and the interpretation of culture*, ed. C. Nelson and L. Grossberg, 271–313. Chicago: University of Illinois Press.

Stasch, R. 2014. Linguistic anthropology and sociocultural anthropology. In *The Cambridge handbook of linguistic anthropology*, 626–643. Cambridge University Press.

Stengers, I. 2000. *The invention of modern science.* Minneapolis: University of Minnesota Press.

    2007. Diderot's egg: divorcing materialism from eliminativism. *Radical Philosophy* 144, 7.

    2009. Thinking with Deleuze and Whitehead: a double test. In *Deleuze, Whitehead, Bergson: rhizomatic connections*, 28–44. London: Palgrave Macmillan.

    2011. *Cosmopolitics, vol. II.* Minneapolis: University of Minnesota Press.

Stocking, G. W. 1989. The basic assumptions of Boasian anthropology. In *A Franz Boas reader: the shaping of American anthropology, 1883–1911*, ed. G. W. Stocking, 1–20. University of Chicago Press.

    1991a. *Colonial situations: essays on the contextualization of ethnographic knowledge.* Madison: University of Wisconsin Press.

    1991b. *Victorian anthropology.* New York: The Free Press.

    1998. *After Tylor: British social anthropology, 1888–1951.* London: Athlone.

Stoler, A. L. 1989. Rethinking colonial categories: European communities and the boundaries of rule. *Comparative Studies in Society and History* 31, 134–161.

    2001. Tense and tender ties: the politics of comparison in North American history and (post) colonial studies. *Journal of American History* 88, 829–865.

Strathern, M. 1980. No nature, no culture: the Hagen case. In *Nature, culture and gender*, ed. C. MacCormack and M. Strathern, 174–222. Cambridge University Press.

1981. Culture in a netbag: the manufacture of a subdiscipline in anthropology. *Man*, new series 16, 665–688.

1987a. An awkward relationship: the case of feminism and anthropology. *Signs: Journal of Women, Culture and Society* 12, 276–292.

1987b. The limits of auto-anthropology. In *Anthropology at home*, ed. A. Jackson. London: Tavistock.

1987c. Out of context: the persuasive fictions of anthropology [and comments and reply]. *Current Anthropology* 28, 251–281.

1988. *The gender of the gift: problems with women and problems with society in Melanesia*. Berkeley: University of California Press.

1992. *After nature: English kinship in the late twentieth century*. Cambridge University Press.

2002. Foreword: not giving the game away. In *Anthropology, by comparison*, ed. A. Gingrich, xii–xvii. London: Routledge.

2004. *Partial connections*. Savage, MD: Rowman and Littlefield.

2006. A community of critics? Thoughts on new knowledge. *Journal of the Royal Anthropological Institute* 12, 191–209.

2011. Binary license. *Common Knowledge* 17, 87–103.

Swanson, G. 1971. Frameworks for comparative research: structural anthropology and the theory of action. In *Comparative methods in sociology: essays on trends and applications*, ed. I. Vallier and D. E. Apter, 141–202. Berkeley: University of California Press.

Tambiah, S. 1973. Form and meaning of magical acts: a point of view. In *Modes of thought: essays on thinking in Western and non-Western societies*, ed. Robin Horton and Ruth Finnegan. London: Faber & Faber.

Tarde, G. 2016. Monadology and sociology. In *The social after Gabriel Tarde: debates and assessments*, ed. M. Candea, 31–65. 2nd edition. London: Routledge.

Taylor, C. 1985. The person. In *The category of the person: anthropology, philosophy, history*, ed. M. Carrithers, S. Collins and S. Lukes, 257–281. Cambridge University Press.

Thomas, Y. 2011. *Les opérations du droit*. Paris: Seuil.

Thompson, D. W. 1961. *On growth and form*. Cambridge University Press.

Thompson, N. S. 1994. The many perils of ejective anthropomorphism. *Behavior and Philosophy* 22, 59–70.

Thornton, R. J. 1988. The rhetoric of ethnographic holism. *Cultural Anthropology* 3, 285–303.

Toren, C. and J. de Pina-Cabral 2009. Introduction: what is happening to epistemology? *Social Analysis* 53, 1.

Tsing, A. L. 2014. Strathern beyond the human: testimony of a spore. *Theory, Culture and Society* 31, 221–241.

Tyler, S. 1984. The poetic turn in postmodern anthropology: the poetry of Paul Friedrich. *American Anthropologist* 86, 328–336.

# References

Tylor, E. B. 1871. *Primitive culture: researches into the development of mythology, philosophy, religion, art, and custom, vol. 1.* London: John Murray.

1889. On a method of investigating the development of institutions; applied to laws of marriage and descent. *Journal of the Anthropological Institute of Great Britain and Ireland*, 18.

Van der Veer, P. 2013. *The modern spirit of Asia: the spiritual and the secular in China and India.* Princeton University Press.

‹ 2014. The value of comparison. *HAU: Journal of Ethnographic Theory*, Morgan Lectures Initiative, 1–14.

2016. *The value of comparison.* Durham, NC: Duke University Press.

Van Velsen, J. 1967. The extended-case method and situational analysis. In *The craft of social anthropology*, ed. A. L. Epstein, 129–149. London: Tavistock.

Viveiros de Castro, E. 1998. Cosmological deixis and Amerindian perspectivism. *Journal of the Royal Anthropological Institute* 4, 469–488.

2003. And. *Manchester Papers in Social Anthropology* 7. University of Manchester.

2004. Perspectival anthropology and the method of controlled equivocation. *Tipití (Journal of the Society for the Anthropology of Lowland South America)* 2, 3–22.

2011. Zeno and the art of anthropology: of lies, beliefs, paradoxes, and other truths. *Common Knowledge* 17, 128–145.

Wagner, R. 1977. Scientific and indigenous Papuan conceptualizations of the innate: a semiotic critique of the ecological perspective. In *Subsistence and survival*, ed. T. O. Bayliss-Smith and R. Feachem, 385–410. London: Academic Press.

1981. *The invention of culture.* University of Chicago Press.

Walford, A. 2015. Double standards: examples and exceptions in scientific metrological practices in Brazil. *Journal of the Royal Anthropological Institute* 21, 64–77.

Weber, M. 1924. *Gesammelte Aufsätze zur Sozial- und Wirtschaftsgeschichte.* Tübingen: Mohr.

1978. *Economy and society: an outline of interpretive sociology.* Berkeley: University of California Press.

White, P. S. 2005. The experimental animal in Victorian Britain. In *Thinking with animals: new perspectives on anthropomorphism*, ed. L. Daston, 59–81. New York: Columbia University Press.

Whitehead, A. N. 1958. *An introduction to mathematics.* Oxford University Press.

Willerslev, R. 2011. Frazer strikes back from the armchair: a new search for the animist soul. *Journal of the Royal Anthropological Institute* 17, 504–526.

Williams, B. A. O. 2005. *In the beginning was the deed: realism and moralism in political argument.* Princeton University Press.

Wimsatt, W. C. 2007. *Re-engineering philosophy for limited beings: piecewise approximations to reality.* Cambridge, MA: Harvard University Press.

# References

Wittgenstein, L. 1973. *Philosophical investigations* (trans. G. E. M. Anscombe). Oxford: Wiley-Blackwell.

Wolf, E. 1983. *Europe and the people without history*. Berkeley: University of California Press.

Yarrow, T. forthcoming. *The space between: life and work in an architectural practice*. Ithaca: Cornell University Press.

Yengoyan, A. A. (ed.) 2006a. Introduction: on the issue of comparison. In *Modes of comparison: theory and practice*, ed. A. A. Yengoyan, 1–27. Ann Arbor: University of Michigan Press.

2006b. *Modes of comparison: theory and practice*. Ann Arbor: University of Michigan Press.

# Index

# Index

biology, 3, 5, 9–12, 18–25, 62, 99,
102–103, 109–117, 233, 357n10,
357n14, *see also* analogy, organic;
evolution; functionalism;
structuralism
  as anthropology's Other, 18–25
  Aristotelian, 57, 357n16, 357n4
Boas, Franz, 124–130
  critiques of the comparative method,
44, 52, 72–96, 152
  postmodern returns to, *see*
diffusionism: neo-
  on pronouns, 249, 255, 309
  Dominic, 140, 168, 335, 356n5
Bruun Jensen, Casper, 141–142, 213, 331,
343, 356n5

caesurism, 15, 23, 55, 146–147, 219
  as a heuristic, 163–174
  and heuristics are complementary,
181–183
  as an intellectual error, 149–152, 351
  politics of, 174–181
Carrier, James, 271, 275
cause
  causal explanation, 85–86, 120–124,
173, 213, 252
  plurality of causes, 59–61, 71–78,
82–83, 87, 97, 98, 102, 130, 256
Chakrabarty, Dipesh, 7, 300–302
classification, *see* typology
cognitive anthropology, 135
collaboration
  amongst anthropologists, 47–51, 96,
187–191, 211, 319–324, 331–339
  with 'informants', 142, 211, 339–346
colonialism, 6, 7, 52, 94, 178, 271, 272
communication (problems of), 108,
*passim* in Chapters 7, 8, *see also*
interpretivism
  in Boas, 73–75
  defined, 33–34, 40–47
  solution to, 200, 331

*comparatio*
  as an archetype of anthropological
comparison, 193–201, 202–207,
219–223, 225, 235, 238–239, 243,
266–269, 319, 320, 348
  as a rhetorical exercise, 5, 192–193
*Comparative Studies in Society and
History* (journal), 125, 135
complexity
  as an end-point, 222, 288, 349–351
  of social phenomena, 8, 35–40, 59–71,
87, 88, 91, 98, 153, 198, 212, 217, 327
  of society as a mathematical variable,
109–110, 115
concomitant variation, 58, 63–64,
197, 217, 356n4, *see also* analogy,
proportional
  and functionalism, 63–71, 81, 88, 115,
153–154, 208, 234, 255, 258, 357n12
  and Galton's problem, 72–75
  and structuralism, 115, 153–154, 208
Condillac, Etienne Bonnot de, 4, 191, 193
context, 34–47, 77, 79, 95, 98, 105, 121,
130, 133, 156, 168, 175, 191, 229
  decontextualisation of anthropology,
287–290, 303
  in frontal comparison, 242, 248, 271,
278, 297–298, *see also* holism
contrast, *see* analogy
controlled comparison, *see* regional vs
distant comparison
Corsín Jiménez, Alberto, 241
crisis of representation, 33–52, 132–133,
270–274, 286–313
  as a nihilistic earlier stage, 1,
133–144, 250
  prefigured by Boas, 72–75
Cross-Cultural Survey, *see* Human
Relations Area Files
culture, *see* Boas, Franz; context;
diffusionism; holism; interpretivism;
mapping, problems of
culture shock, 284, 288, 289, 317, 361n9

# Index

# Index

# Index